PEREGRINE BOOKS

D. H. LAWRENCE: NOVELIST

Dr Frank Raymond Leavis, a University Reader in
English from 1959 to 1962, was a Fellow of Downing
College, Cambridge, from 1937 until 1962, and an
Honorary Fellow for the following two years. Born at
Cambridge in 1905, he was educated at the Perse School
and Emmanuel College, where he read History and
English. While engaged in University teaching he helped
to start the well-known quarterly review *Scrutiny*, which
he edited from 1932 until 1953, when it ceased publica-
tion. (Complete sets of the journal fetch as much as £100,
and the whole has been reprinted in twenty volumes by
the Cambridge University Press.) Among his publications
are *Mass Civilization and Minority Culture* (1930), *New
Bearings in English Poetry* (1932), *For Continuity* (1933),
Revaluation (1936), *The Great Tradition: George Eliot,
James and Conrad* (1948), *The Common Pursuit* (1952), *Two
Cultures?* (1962), *Anna Karenina and Other Essays* (1967)
Lectures in America (1969) and *English Literature in Our
Time and the University* (1969). Dr Leavis, who was
Visiting Professor at the University of York in 1965, is
an Hon. Litt.D. of that university and of the University
of Leeds. He is married and has two sons and a daughter.

D·H·LAWRENCE : NOVELIST

F. R. LEAVIS

PENGUIN BOOKS

IN ASSOCIATION WITH
CHATTO & WINDUS

Penguin Books Ltd, Harmondsworth, Middlesex, England
Penguin Books Australia Ltd, Ringwood, Victoria, Australia

First published by Chatto & Windus 1955
Published in Peregrine Books 1964
Reprinted 1968, 1970
Copyright © F. R. Leavis, 1955

Made and printed in Great Britain by Hazell Watson & Viney Ltd,
Aylesbury, Bucks. Set in Monotype Bembo

FOR

RALPH,

KATE,

AND

LAWRENCE ROBIN

Sometimes I think that Lawrence was the last green shoot on the tree of English civilization. Anyhow, whether English civilization is dead or not, and I hope it isn't, Lawrence is the last shoot of it that has grown ahead and pierced the air.

When I think that nobody wanted Lawrence's amazing genius, how he was jeered at, suppressed, turned into nothing, patronized at best, the stupidity of our civilization comes home to me. How necessary he was! How badly needed! Now that he is dead and his great love for his fellow-men is no longer there in the flesh, people sentimentalize over him.... Critics indeed! Had they been able to *take* instead of criticizing, how much richer their own lives might have been!

FRIEDA LAWRENCE, *Not I, But The Wind*

Had Lawrence been sent to a public school and taken honours at a university he would not have been a jot the less ignorant; had he become a don at Cambridge his ignorance might have had frightful consequences for himself and for the world, 'rotten and rotting others'.

T. S. ELIOT

reviewing *Son of Woman* (*The Criterion*, July 1931)

And I am English, and my Englishness is my very vision.

D. H. LAWRENCE

in a letter (21 October 1915)

CONTENTS

ACKNOWLEDGEMENTS

Acknowledgement is made to Mrs Frieda Lawrence and
Messrs William Heinemann Ltd for permission to print
the extracts from the works of D. H. Lawrence
included in this book.

For permission to use the substance of Chapter 2,
'Lawrence and Class', I am indebted to the Editor of the
Sewanee Review. The substance of Chapters 3, 4, 5, and 6
appeared in *Scrutiny* between Spring 1950 and
October 1953.

F. R. L.

INTRODUCTION

THIS book carries on from *The Great Tradition*. If work on it has had a different feel from work on the earlier book, that is because of the nearness – in more than one sense – of Lawrence. Though it is now a quarter of a century since he died, not only is he our last great writer; he is still the great writer of our own phase of civilization. The questions and stresses that preoccupied him have still the most urgent relevance for us today. The way things have developed since his death has had no tendency to make his diagnostic insight the less important to us, or the positive enlivening and enlightenment – the education – he brings the less necessary.

I myself, in this book, am dealing with a writer who has been for me a major contemporary fact. I read him first before the war of 1914. I read a tale by him (not one of the good ones, but it made an impression on me) in Ford Madox Hueffer's *English Review*, to which I subscribed at school. I didn't remember – if I ever noticed – the name of the author. But I found the tale when, in 1919, having for the first time the opportunity to begin exploring contemporary literature, I took down *The Prussian Officer* from the 'First Class' shelves of the Cambridge Union; and I registered that the author I had read six or seven years before was D. H. Lawrence. From then on I read him pretty steadily; I turned up the pre-war books, and read the new ones very much as they came out (I remember reading Middleton Murry's reviews of *Aaron's Rod* and *Women in Love* in the *Nation and Athenaeum*).

By the time of Lawrence's death, then, I felt (however mistakenly) that I was qualified to attempt a critical essay on his work. I committed, in fact, what, on looking back, I see – what I very soon saw – to have been the quixotic folly (I don't regret it) of publishing an essay on Lawrence in the *Cambridge Review*, that very institutional journal which is owned and, one hears, watched over, by an innominate committee of dons. The essay was expanded into a longer critique that appeared as a pamphlet later in 1930 (and was reprinted, later still, in *For Continuity*). I took immense pains over that piece of work, going through and through all that was accessible of Lawrence, but when I look at it now I cannot judge that my sense of being critically qualified was well-grounded. And yet when I ask where I could have found the hint for a better understanding of (say) *Women in Love*, the answer is, 'Nowhere'. There was, so far as I know, nothing more enlightened or enlightening critically than Middleton Murry's review of the book (it can be found reprinted in *Reminiscences of D. H. Lawrence*). And my essay was at any rate a serious tribute to a great writer by someone wholly convinced of his greatness, and convinced that he demanded much further study – that he would repay endless frequentation as Joyce would not. (Those two, it seems to me, were pre-eminently the testing, the crucial authors: if you took Joyce for a major creative writer, then, like Mr Eliot, you had no use for Lawrence, and if you judged Lawrence a great writer, then you could hardly take a sustained interest in Joyce.)

I recall the climate of that time – the time of Lawrence's death – when I recall the letter written by E. M. Forster to the *Nation and Athenaeum*, and the pleasure and relief with which I read it. It seemed to me (and still seems) the perfectly judged obituary salute, things being as they were. Two established writers distinguished themselves by the honourable parts they played in relation to Lawrence. Aldous Huxley's name stands on the title-page of the *Letters*, and his services to Lawrence during the last days are common knowledge. But E. M. Forster's generous championship is less well known. The force of my 'generous' is made plain by the phrasing of his letter:[1]

Now he is dead, and the low-brows whom he scandalized have united with the high-brows whom he bored to ignore his greatness. This cannot be helped: no one who alienates both Mrs Grundy and Aspasia can hope for a good obituary Press. All that we can do ... is to say straight out that he was the greatest imaginative novelist of our generation.

I quote this, the essential part of the letter, because, in my sense of the honour due to E. M. Forster, I want to put on record these sentences

1. *Nation and Athenaeum*, 29 March 1930.

which will, I think, be classical; and because, as I have indicated, they suggest very eloquently what was the prevailing attitude to Lawrence among the *élite* when the obituary occasion presented itself. No one will suppose that, on such an occasion, Mr Forster assumed lightly that note of indignant rebuke: my testimony that there was ample cause for it hardly adds anything. And those who look up the *Nation and Athenaeum* of that time will find that a retort to Forster's letter appeared the following week from T. S. Eliot. Eliot remarked, with an implausibility that would be comic if the whole exhibition were not so lamentable, that he was the 'last person to wish to disparage the genius of D. H. Lawrence', but (and the sour primness on such an occasion, and with such an intention, still shocks, a quarter of a century after Lawrence's death)

the virtue of speaking out is somewhat diminished if what one speaks is not sense. And unless we know exactly what Mr Forster means by *greatest, imaginative* and *novelist*, I submit that this judgement is meaningless.[1]

Clive Bell followed up in a similar spirit; he, too, ostensibly to castigate Forster's crudities of expression – crudities that must make his letter offensive to a person of intellectual refinement. Lawrence, it may be added, got (unlike Bridges and Harold Monro) no obituary notice in The *Criterion*, which, however, published within the year an essay called 'The Perversity of D. H. Lawrence'. And Eliot himself wrote (The *Criterion*, vol x, no. xli) a review of Murry's *inqualifiable* (I cannot find an English word I may use) *Son of Woman*[2] in which, hailing it as a 'brilliant book' and 'a definitive work of critical biography, or biographical criticism', he pronounced: 'The victim and the sacrificial knife are perfectly adapted to each other.' It is a memorable formulation – one of those neat and confident strokes (both 'placed', and Law-

1. Mr Forster rejoined: 'Mr T. S. Eliot duly entangles me in his web. He asks what exactly I mean by "greatest", "imaginative" and "novelist", and I cannot say. Worse still, I cannot even say what "exactly" means – only that there are occasions when I would rather feel like a fly than a spider, and that the death of D. H. Lawrence is one of them.'

2. No one should read *Son of Woman* without checking it against Catherine Carswell's admirable and indispensable *The Savage Pilgrimage: a Narrative of D. H. Lawrence* (Chatto & Windus, 1932).

rence placed with Murry) into which Mr Eliot's impulses have so often betrayed him.

What I am brought to at this point is my own involvement in the history – it is proper that I should mention it if only to make it plain that I do not pretend to have been *au-dessus de la mêlée*. In fact, I had better say that, looking back, I can only see that involvement as a matter of my having been engaged in a long battle to win recognition for Lawrence, and to kill the currency of the grosser misconceptions and prejudices. *Scrutiny* started in 1932, and over the next twenty years I took, in its pages, the opportunities and challenges that offered. A number of the major challenges or provocations came from T. S. Eliot: there is then a history behind my references in this book to his attitude towards Lawrence. Two of the things that I wrote, 'The Wild, Untutored Phoenix' (dealing with the charge that Lawrence was un-educated, and lacked 'social training') and 'Mr Eliot, Wyndham Lewis, and Lawrence', are to be found reprinted in *The Common Pursuit*. A third will be found at the end of the present book.

I have to confess that the misconceptions and prejudices appear to have remained in almost unimpeded circulation to the present day. When (as has happened a good deal) one's tips have been taken up, something has generally gone wrong with them; they have been stultified in the application. Thus, twenty-five years ago, I threw out a hint on the affinities between Lawrence and Blake: Aldous Huxley, in his Introduction to the *Letters*, mentioned my note approvingly. What I find in the recent guide to Lawrence issued with all the authority of the British Council is this: 'Lawrence's two ancestors are Blake and Whit-man.' But I have never (need I say?) suggested – who could? – that Blake was an 'ancestor' of Lawrence, and to bracket Blake with Whit-man is to defeat my whole intention. When I mentioned Blake, I was thinking of the vital intelligence, unthwarted by emotional disorders and divisions in the psyche, that makes him (as I have suggested in an analysis of Swift's irony) the antithesis of Swift. As for Whitman, with his expansive 'Camerado!', his large democratic embrace, his 'ache' of 'amorous love', and his enthusiasm for merging,[1] it would be difficult

1. What Santayana says of Dickens in contrast to Whitman might have been said of Lawrence: 'The spirit of Dickens would be better able to do justice to America than was

to think of a writer more radically unlike Lawrence (whose treatment of him in *Studies in Classic American Literature* should alone have been enough to warn anyone off the assimilation).

I deal with some of the grosser and absurder falsities about Lawrence in the following pages. There is one that I will mention here: the view that he lacks a sense of humour (it is closely related to the view, equally absurd, that he is characteristically 'angry'). It is advanced as indisputable fact by Eliot in *After Strange Gods*,[1] and as such it seems to be generally current. One might well despair of killing an absurdity that, being as plainly refuted by Lawrence's work as this is, has yet persisted so long. What do those who are committed to it see in (say) *Things, Two Blue Birds, Jimmy and the Desperate Woman, Mother and Daughter, St Mawr*? Whatever they may suppose themselves to have done, they have certainly not read them. For the plain fact is that Lawrence is one of the great masters of comedy. This truth is illustrated with at least as many distinct shades of comedy in the half-dozen tales I have mentioned; tales evoking many different kinds of smile and laughter, though never the cruel, the malicious or the complacent. And the play of humour and wit is not confined to the tales. It is the natural expression of Lawrence's supremely intelligent vitality – the vitality that comes out so often in a characteristic high-spirited amusement, and has its essential part in the delicacy and vividness of his observation of people. But a world that finds the quintessence of wit in Congreve and Wilde will perhaps continue to find Lawrence humourless.

As for anger, no sensitive and highly vital man was ever less given to it, if we are to judge by his humour, irony, and the tone of his writing in general. His characteristic poise in circumstances that might have

---

that of Walt Whitman; because America, although it may seem nothing but a noisy nebula to the impressionist, is not a nebula but a concourse of very distinct individual bodies, natural and social, each with its definite interests and story. Walt Whitman had a sort of transcendental philosophy which swallowed the universe whole, supposing there was a universal spirit in things identical with the spirit that observed them; but Dickens was innocent of any such clap-trap, and remained a true spirit in his own person' (*Soliloquies in England*, pp. 63–4).

That is, Lawrence, like Dickens, was a *novelist*.

1. See *After Strange Gods*, p. 58. And see footnote to p. 23 below.

seemed to make indignant anger inevitable is exemplified in the matter of the slander brought against him by Norman Douglas. When Norman Douglas's essay making 'insinuations – to put it mildly – regarding my introduction to Maurice Magnus's *Memoirs of the Foreign Legion*' was reprinted in *Experiments*, Lawrence ('One becomes weary of being slandered') wrote a letter to the *New Statesman*, which had reviewed Douglas's book. The letter will be found in *Phoenix* (page 806), followed by a further comment from Lawrence. I mention the affair because the allegation has recently come up again – produced, indeed, as if it were a matter of known fact – that Douglas 'showed up Lawrence'. It must be said, then, that (apart from the inherent probabilities, given the two men) no one who had bothered to consider the evidence could question Lawrence's account (it ends – the sentence gives the tone: 'As for Mr Douglas, he must gather himself haloes where he may'). But the author of *South Wind*, uncreative, dilettante, an approved 'character', dealing as an artist in the known and the cheap, offering as wisdom the stale cynicism of the 'man of the world' (leisured upper-class), is a pre-ordained rallying-centre for the literary world[1] – even when it rallies in a Socialist weekly. Inevitably it backs Douglas against Lawrence, in the face of the probabilities and the evidence.[2]

Lawrence's genius has very striking manifestations outside his novels and tales; but it is to these that I have confined myself (except in so far as I have touched on other things – notably *Psychoanalysis and the Unconscious* and *À Propos of Lady Chatterley's Lover* – incidentally to discussing the fiction). It is very relevant to the insistence on supreme intelligence as being the mark of his genius to note that he was a very remarkable literary critic – by far the best critic of his day. I shall deal with him as such elsewhere. But what seems to me to be clearly of most importance is to win recognition for the nature of his achievement as a novelist, and the attempt to do that is what I concentrate on in the present book.

In pursuing that end I have confined myself resolutely to the essen-

1. See p. 310 below: 'Being an Artist'.
2. The private letters written by Lawrence in 1925 about 'Douglas's pamphlet on me and Magnus' should be looked up: that to Curtis Brown (*Letters*, p. 631), and that to H. W. Mathews (*Letters*, p. 633).

tial. I want the stress to fall unambiguously on *The Rainbow*, *Women in Love*, and the tales. As I explain in my opening chapter, I judged that my essential purpose would not be materially advanced by a close examination of the early novels, *The White Peacock*, *Sons and Lovers*, and *The Trespasser*. And I have not discussed *The Boy in the Bush*, the Australian novel by M. L. Skinner that Lawrence revised. I deal with the lesser novels from *The Lost Girl* to *Lady Chatterley's Lover* in the opening chapter, and in dealing with them concede to adverse criticism of Lawrence as an artist what I think has to be conceded. I am then free to make and enforce my claims for those works on which Lawrence's position as a great novelist is firmly based. If I had thought it good policy to take more space I should have spent my additional pages on other tales. For I am far from suggesting that those which I have, at less or greater length, dealt with are all that I admire, or should have liked to deal with. I thought that my actual choice was such as to make the particular examination of others not strictly necessary.

My aim, I repeat, is to win clear recognition for the nature of Lawrence's greatness. Any great creative writer who has not had his due is a power for life wasted. But the insight, the wisdom, the revived and re-educated feeling for health, that Lawrence brings are what, as our civilization goes, we desperately need. It is the work and the art that I have insisted on. But it is impossible to study the work and the art without forming a vivid sense of the man, and touching on the facts of his history. It will, I hope, be possible to say that, in spite of the hostility of an increasingly powerful literary world (powerful in the control of reputations) his greatness did at last compel recognition. That would itself be an encouraging fact. And (if I may quote from myself what provides the note I should like to close on here), when I think of the career that started in the ugly mining village in the spoilt Midlands, amidst all those apparent disadvantages, it seems to me that, even in these days, it should give us faith in the creative human spirit and its power to ensue fulness of life.

1

MANY other books will be written about D. H. Lawrence. Some of them will aim at a comprehensiveness that doesn't belong to my own purpose. And if voluminous 'authoritative' treatment was needed for, say, Hopkins and Yeats, then the authority on Lawrence certainly will not be able to confine himself to a single volume, even a large one. Whatever may be the point of such works, the treatment that Lawrence stands in need of now is different. The very largeness and complexity of the subject he represents makes it necessary to define, clearly and challengingly, where the centre lies. *What*, above all, is Lawrence? As what shall we primarily think of him? There has always been a readiness to think of him as a genius; but as what, above all, has he established his indisputable existence and his permanence?

The answer that T. S. Eliot made a point of disputing at the time when Lawrence, having died, was being dismissed to a long relegation from among living subjects would, I think, be now pretty generally accepted: Lawrence is a great artist, a creative writer. It is an answer I like, and, in fact, had myself proposed at that now distant time; but it is not delimiting enough. It does not exclude with sufficient finality the view, expressed by Desmond MacCarthy – expressed, then, not for the first or the last time (it is still not unlikely to recur in the *New Statesman* and the Sunday papers), that Lawrence has close affinities with Carlyle. Nor does it exclude the view that his genius is above all 'lyrical', and that in the novels it is to be found pre-eminently in the 'descriptive writing' and in the poetic evocation of scenes, environments, and atmospheres.

What needs to be said is this: Lawrence is before all else a great novelist, one of the very greatest, and it is as one of the major novelists of the English tradition that he will above all live. To give the proposition its due force I have to refer to a conception of the history of prose fiction in English that I have proposed elsewhere. It involves the view that, if depth, range, and subtlety in the presentment of human experience are the criteria, then in the work of the great novelists from Jane Austen to Lawrence – I think of Hawthorne, Dickens, George Eliot, Henry James, Melville, Mark Twain, Conrad – we have a creative achievement that is unsurpassed; unsurpassed by any of the famous phases or chapters of literary history. In these great novelists (I do not offer my list as exhaustive of the writers who might be relevantly adduced, but confine myself to those who present themselves as the great compelling instances) we have the successors of Shakespeare; for in the nineteenth century and later the strength – the poetic and creative strength – of the English language goes into prose fiction. In comparison the formal poetry is a marginal affair. And the achievement of T. S. Eliot, remarkable as it was, did not reverse the relation. This is a truth that adds an irony to the insistent leading part played by Eliot in retarding the recognition of Lawrence. I make elsewhere in this book some comparative comments on Lawrence's tale *St Mawr*, which deals with the 'Waste Land' aspect of modern civilization, and Eliot's poem.[1] The immense superiority as achieved creation that I note in Lawrence's tale has a representative significance. And *St Mawr*, though a classic, and major art, is only a minor thing in Lawrence's *œuvre*. The point I am making is that Lawrence is incomparably the greatest creative writer in English of our time – if I say, of Eliot's time, I make plain the phase of our civilization that is in question; he is one of the greatest English writers of any time; and, in the nature of his greatness, has his significant relation with what is most vital in the century before him.

His genius is distinctively that of a novelist, and as such he is as remarkable a technical innovator as there has ever been. It is *The Rainbow* and *Women in Love* that most demand attention. The need is to get recognition for the kind of major achievement they are. Together they constitute his greatest work, or perhaps it is better to say that, in their curious close relation and the separateness, they are his two greatest works. They represent the enormous labour, the defining of interests and methods, the exploration, the technical innovation, on which the ease of the later work is based. This is not to dismiss *Sons and Lovers*,

1. See p. 235 below.

which is certainly a work of striking original genius. But *Sons and Lovers* has not lacked attention; it has been widely appreciated, and the nature of its originality recognized. And for my purpose, which demands a close insistence on the essential, there would be little point in giving the book a fresh examination here. Remarkable as it is, its qualities and its achievement, on the one hand, are obvious enough, and, on the other, they are not, I think, such as to suggest that the author was going to be a great novelist. The earlier book, *The White Peacock*, is painfully callow.[1] In it Lawrence has no certain grasp of his emotional purpose, and is too much preoccupied with writing a novel: he feels obliged to transpose his experience into 'literature' (there is the significant shift into the cultivated middle class), and doesn't deal directly with what is at the centre of his own emotional life. There is a great deal of the literary and conventional in the style and the treatment; it is very much there, for instance, even in the gamekeeper theme, which provides one of the main interests of this extremely immature novel for a student of Lawrence who looks back from the later work. The advance to *Sons and Lovers* is one to the direct and wholly convention-free treatment of the personal problem: the immense improvement, the success, is bound up with the strict concentration on the autobiographical. The other early novel, *The Trespasser*, is also, it appears, autobiographically personal. It shows an unconventional power in the rendering of passion and emotion; the deadlock at Siegmund's home has an oppressive reality; but, short as the book is, it is hard to read through, and cannot be said to contain any clear promise of a great novelist.

With *Sons and Lovers* Lawrence put something behind him. Not for nothing did he warn Edward Garnett not to expect anything else of that kind: 'I shan't write in the same manner as *Sons and Lovers* again.'[2] Lawrence, of course, has more than one subsequent 'manner', but what he is recognizing here is that he has put something behind him for good. The acute emotional problem or disorder which queered his personal relations and the play of his intelligence has been placed – has been

1. 'I was very young when I wrote the *Peacock* – I began it at twenty. Let that be my apology.' *Letters*, p. 6.
2. *Letters*, p. 272.

conquered by intelligence, manifesting and vindicating itself in creative art. He is now freed for the work of the greatest kind of artist.

It is *The Rainbow* and *Women in Love*, written during the next few years – from early 1913 on – that prove him to be that. I should have said that they prove it triumphantly and incontestably if the depressing fact of history had not been what it is: they have had essentially no recognition at all. Not only has the supreme creative achievement they represent been ignored; the grossest untruths about Lawrence's attitudes – untruths running clean counter to the spirit and actuality of that achievement, as of his work everywhere – have been freely current, and accepted generally for the unquestioned truth about him. In fact, the record in respect of him stands out even in the annals of the treatment of great original writers. It is the more notable in that from the beginning Lawrence has been recognized to have 'genius' – 'genius' was the accepted word, and yet not only was his genius abusively denatured and its greatness denied while he lived; even after his death, which might have been expected to be followed by the irony of decisive recognition and a rapidly spreading enlightenment, the misrepresentation held the field for two decades.

This is partly to be explained by the fact that his death coincided with the opening of a peculiarly bad phase of English literary history – or of the English literary world. It coincided with the arrival of Auden. In the period in which Auden was so rapidly established as a major poet and remained one for so long, and Spender became overnight the modern Shelley, it was not to be expected that the portrayer of Rico would receive the sympathetic attention denied him in the emancipated twenties. The period of the Poetical Renaissance was as little favourable to intelligence about Lawrence as that dominated by the ethos of the old Bloomsbury had been. To see him as fostering the spirit of something akin to Nazism[1] – that was an easy way of dismiss-

1. This view had a long life, and could be advanced at the Metropolitan literary centre as unquestionable good sense till quite recently:

'Lawrence's teachings are interesting because they are a compendium of what a whole generation wanted to feel, until Hitler arose, just after Lawrence's death, and they saw where the dark unconsciousness was leading them. Seen in this light, Lawrence represented the last phase of the Romantic Movement: random, irresponsible egotism, power

ing the complications he would have introduced into the simple scheme of salvation adopted on the Left. To the Criterionic Right, whether Anglo-Catholic, Neo-Thomist, or Social-Crediting, he was of course no more congenial – the Editor of *The Criterion* could, and did, with a large generosity favour the Marxist and Fellow-Travelling poets as well as Joyce and Pound, but never Lawrence. And the spirit of Lawrence's dealings with the relations between men and women recommended itself no more to understanding than it had done in the days of Jix and Lytton Strachey. It was perhaps his supposed attitude in the matter of sex that mainly accounted for the ban on mention of him, or something approaching a ban, maintained by the B.B.C. for nearly twenty years. On the other hand, the sophisticated reaction is given by the writer in *The Times Literary Supplement*[1] who, reviewing a translation of *Bel-Ami*, contrasted Lawrence's 'crudities' with the mature wisdom of Maupassant.

For the grosser stupidities of our intellectual *élite* at Lawrence's expense the explanation must be discreditable to the English literary world of the last decades; but of course *The Rainbow* and *Women in Love* – to come back to these works in particular – can hardly have been altogether understood by anyone at first reading. They present a difficulty that is a measure of their profound originality. Lawrence's art in them is so original in its methods and procedures that at first we again and again fail to recognize what it is doing or what it is offering – we miss the point. And this technical originality was entailed by the originality of what Lawrence had to convey. The important truths about human experience are not necessarily at once obvious. The importance of some is to be measured by the difficulty with which we recognize them. They have no place in our habits of conscious thought, and what we say and what we believe with our conscious minds ignores or denies them.[2] Lawrence's insight was penetrating and clear, and he was marvellously intelligent, and the worst difficulty we have in

---

for power's sake, the blood cult of Rosenberg. And Lawrence was representative, because tens of thousands of people in England and Europe were uprooted people, like himself' (V. S. Pritchett, *The Living Novel*, Chatto & Windus, 1946).

1. *The Times Literary Supplement*, 18 December 1948.

2. A point made by Lawrence in an article reprinted in *Phoenix*, 'The Novel and the Feelings'.

coming to terms with his art is that there is resistance in us to what it has to communicate – if only the kind of resistance represented by habit; habit that will not let us see what is there for what it is, or believe that the door is open. And learning to recognize the success and the greatness of *Women in Love* – I speak for myself – was not merely a matter of applying one's mind in repeated re-readings and so mastering the methods of the art and the nature of the organization; it was a matter, too, of growing – growing into understanding.

Yet it remains true that the failure of criticism and of the cultivated in respect of Lawrence, the long unchecked prevalence of misrepresentation and malice, is a disgraceful chapter of English literary history. Even the book that makes the severest demand on the reader's intelligence and power of self-readjustment is rich in what should surely have been convincing manifestations of supreme creative genius. And there is the long succession of tales, the consummateness of so large a proportion of which, in all their wonderful originality, there can be no acceptable excuse for failing to perceive. And these things, the tales and all that should at once compel recognition in the novels, are enough and more than enough to dispose of the slanders that for decades have been current among the educated as the truth about Lawrence. He was certainly unfortunate in the phases of English literary culture and of the English literary world that have marked those decades. It has to be recorded, as among the adverse conditions, that he had against him the major personal influence of the time (and it was a peculiarly powerful and pervasive one for a good many years) – the major personal influence in the climate of literary opinion: that of T. S. Eliot. It was not merely that the literary and intellectual fashions promoted by Eliot were inimical to the appreciation of Lawrence's genius. The sad and undeniable fact is that Eliot did all that his immense prestige and authority *could* do to make the current stupidities about Lawrence look respectable. He talked of Lawrence's 'sexual morbidity' as of a *donnée* that needed no arguing. He made a point of denying that Lawrence could properly be called an artist.[1] It is in keeping with this denial that he should have been able to pronounce Lawrence incapable of 'what

1. e.g.: 'he never succeeded in making a work of art'. *The Criterion*, vol. x, p. 769.

we ordinarily call thinking',[1] subscribing thus to the general view that, wherever Lawrence's strength might lie, it was not, emphatically not, in intelligence. Of Lawrence's novels he spoke (addressing the public of *La Nouvelle Revue française*) as '*extrêmement mal écrits*'.[2] A quarter of a

1. *After Strange Gods*, p. 58. The context makes the intended force of the pronouncement quite plain:

'Lawrence has three aspects, and it is very difficult to do justice to all. I do not expect to be able to do so. The first is the ridiculous: his lack of a sense of humour, a certain snobbery, a lack not so much of information as of the critical faculties which education should give, and an incapacity for what we ordinarily call thinking. Of this side of Lawrence, the brilliant exposure by Mr Wyndham Lewis in *Paleface* is by far the most conclusive criticism that has been made. Secondly, there is the extraordinarily keen sensibility and capacity for profound intuition – intuition from which he commonly drew the wrong conclusions. Third, there is a distinct sexual morbidity.'

Lawrence has 'intuition'; Mr Wyndham Lewis has the intelligence that enables him to expose the muddles into which Lawrence's sensibility and intuition together lead him: the meaning is unmistakable. It may perhaps be suggested that, if Mr Wyndham Lewis's brilliance illustrates a capacity for 'what we ordinarily call thinking', then Lawrence's strength is to lack that capacity. But perhaps the conclusion should rather be that we ought to revise our notion of 'thinking' (Lawrence himself as critic actually shows the necessity for such a revision in his essay ' Why the Novel Matters' [*Phoenix*]).

2. *La Nouvelle Revue française*, Mai 1927 (vol. 28, p. 671).

The whole article, *Le Roman anglais contemporain*, is of great interest in the light it throws on the nature of the immense influence that Mr Eliot has exercised. There is the impressive distinction – the air of penetrating firsthandness, combined with (in this field which is remote from his own technical problems as a poet) actual conventionality of judgement: the valuations in general are essentially those of what was then the *chic* social-literary world. There is what would be distinguished intelligence if it were not stultified by the conventionality, and, where Lawrence is concerned, by grossly wrong preconceptions, blindly held, and the attendant unperceived contradictions. In the following passage he may be seen granting Lawrence, in the usual way, 'genius', and presenting this, at the same time, as something barbarous, inhuman, and boring. The account he gives of the novels, ludicrously false as it is, would have been widely accepted by the cultivated through the succeeding quarter of a century.

'*L'œuvre de M. Lawrence n'est jamais troublée par l'humeur, la gaîté ou le persiflage; aucune diversion politique, théologique ou artistique ne vient nous distraire. Dans la suite de ses romans splendides et extrêmement mal écrits – les presses vomissant chacun d'eux avant que nous ayons eu le temps de terminer le précédent – rien ne vient égayer la monotonie des "passions sombres" qui font que ses Mâles et ses Femelles se déchirent eux-mêmes et les uns les autres. Rien ne nous soutient, sauf l'évidente sincérité de l'auteur. M. Lawrence est un démoniaque, un démoniaque simple et naturel muni d'un évangile. Quand ses personnages font l'amour – ou du moins accomplissent ce qui chez M. Lawrence est l'équivalent de l'amour (et ils ne font pas d'autre chose) – non*

century later, having perhaps noted that this compact and memorable judgement had been challenged, he emended it to: 'To me, also, he seems often to write very badly: but to be a writer who had to write often badly in order to write sometimes well.'[1]

One wouldn't, it is true, call Lawrence, any more than one would call Shakespeare, a 'stylist'; but he seems to me to be plainly one of the

---

seulement ils perdent toutes les aménités, raffinements et grâces que plusieurs siècles ont elaborés afin de rendre l'amour supportable, mais ils semblent remonter le cours de l'évolution et de ses métamorphoses, rétrogradant au-delà du singe et du poisson jusqu'à quelque hideux accouplement de protoplasme.'

The odd significant inadvertence of that 'afin de rendre l'amour supportable' will have been noted.

The novels are 'splendid', it seems, because in spite of the 'progressive dégénérescence de l'humanité' in them, 'M. Lawrence ne le cède pour le génie descriptif à aucun auteur vivant; il peut non seulement reproduire le son, la couleur et la forme, l'odeur, mais tous les plus fins frémissements de la sensation.' Nevertheless, they are 'extrêmement mal écrits'.

Mrs Woolf, on the other hand (of whom we are told: 'Non seulement elle est civilisée, mais elle préfère la civilisation à la barbarie'), 'écrit avec grand soin, extrêmement bien, en suivant au moins l'une des grandes traditions de la prose anglais....'

Of David Garnett we are told: 'Il l'emporte sur tous les prosateurs contemporains pour l'habileté technique de "l'écriture".'

1. Foreword to D. H. Lawrence and Human Existence (1951), a book in which Fr William Tiverton argues that Lawrence may be properly admired and profitably cultivated by Anglo-Catholics. The Foreword as a whole is in keeping with the sentence I have quoted. There is no retraction, and no suggestion that the writer has anything to retract – that he ever lent himself to a view of Lawrence incompatible with Father Tiverton's. Simply, it appears, the time is 'now due' for serious criticism of Lawrence's work – something other than reminiscences by people who knew the man, and Mr Eliot commends this inaugural essay. (But think of the 'frightful consequences' that might have ensued if Lawrence had been a don at Cambridge, 'rotten and rotting others'!)

In Fr Tiverton's book we read:

'Writing to Murry in 1923, he [Lawrence] says: "This classiosity is bunkum, but still more, cowardice", and Mr Murry's Reminiscences show that the reference is to Mr Eliot himself. (Elsewhere he places the same writer in strange company: "All the Lynds and Squires and Eliots and Goulds instinctively dislike [me]!")'

But it is an undeniable fact of history that Mr Eliot put himself in that company, and made it immensely more effective in enmity to Lawrence than it could otherwise have been.

Lawrence's remark about 'classiosity' has an obvious bearing on my argument in the next pages.

I make my commentary on Mr Eliot's Foreword in a review reprinted at the end of this book.

greatest masters of what is certainly one of the greatest of languages; and I have already stated my conviction that as a creative writer he is of the greatest kind. There is no need to ask here how we can explain Mr Eliot's being able with so little misgiving to bring the charge of 'sexual morbidity' against him (or certain other charges that I shall refer to later). But it is, I think, worth inquiring at this point how, if I am right in sum about Lawrence's genius and achievement, a mind capable of Eliot's best criticism can have been so wrong in matters so important. It is worth inquiring because the challenge leads us to certain useful formulations regarding the nature of Lawrence's greatness and the significance of his work.

The answer, I think, is to be found in some things that Lawrence says about Flaubert and the conception of art Flaubert represents. He speaks, in a review of Thomas Mann,[1] of 'that will of the writer to be greater than and undisputed lord over the stuff he writes which is figured to the world in Gustav Flaubert'. It seems to him, he says, that 'this craving for form is the outcome, not of artistic conscience, but of a certain attitude to life'.

Thomas Mann seems to me the last sick sufferer from the complaint of Flaubert. The latter stood away from life as from a leprosy. And Thomas Mann, like Flaubert, feels vaguely that he has in him something finer than ever physical life revealed. Physical life is a disordered corruption, against which he can fight with only one weapon, his fine aestheticism, his feeling for beauty, for perfection, for a certain fitness which soothes him, and gives him an inner pleasure, however corrupt the stuff of life may be.

One may not have thought of comparing Eliot's creative work to Flaubert's, but Eliot's attitude to life is, not less than Flaubert's, one of distaste and disgust. His art, consequently, is involved in the contradiction of which Flaubert is the great example. For it is, surely, a contradiction that Flaubert's case presents classically – all that would-be creative intensity, that intensity of 'doing', devoted to expressing attitudes in which distaste, disgust, and boredom have so decisive a part; a cult of art that amounts to a religion, and the directing spirit of it a rejection of life. I am thinking of the Flaubert the stultifying nature of whose inner self-contradiction – art-defeating because life-defeating –

1. *Phoenix*, p. 308.

exposes itself so dismally in *L'Éducation sentimentale*. Flaubert is sup-posed to be pre-eminently the *intelligent* artist, but what we have here, as Henry James with his incisive and final delicacy points out,[1] is es-sentially a failure of intelligence (with eloquent effect he explicitly ab-stains from commenting on *Bouvard et Pécuchet*). The weakness that James diagnoses in *Madame Bovary*, Flaubert's greatest work, into which his romanticism enters so subtly as a creative force along with the dis-gust at *la platitude bourgeoise* – that is, at life as it surrounded him – is equally a failure of intelligence, for in making Emma Bovary the 'special conduit of the life he proposed to depict', and thus restricting himself so much by the limitations of her consciousness (which is 'really too small an affair'), Flaubert was clearly not altogether aware of what in effect he was doing, and of the criticism to which the book was exposed.

Eliot, of course, has, to complement the distaste for life and humanity, something other than the religion of art. But so has Flaubert too, in his romanticism of the exotic. Flaubert's romanticism and Eliot's Anglo-Catholicism are different things; but when we contemplate the religion of *The Cocktail Party* we may judge (if we think of the total case of each of the writers) that there is some analogy, and that the analogy has a bearing on the nature of Eliot's Christianity. And the plays in general to which Eliot has devoted himself since the completion of *Four Quartets* force us to recognize how little the genius of his personal poetry carried with it major creative powers – the creativity of a great creative writer. They exhibit something like a Flaubertian intensity of art: there is the slow meticulous labour of calculating judgement that clearly went to the doing; and, on the other hand, there is the sick poverty, the trivial-ity, and, finally, the nothingness, of the done – the human and spiritual nullity.

It is the significance of that lamentable record at Lawrence's expense, that persisting and grievous default of intelligence in a gifted writer, that I have in mind in these observations. And it is plain, I think, that the significance is what I pointed to in Lawrence's diagnostic placing of Flaubert's and Mann's kind of addiction to art. Eliot's 'standing-off'

1. In the essay on Flaubert that is most generally accessible in *The Art of Fiction*, a selection of Henry James's essays made by Morris Roberts.

from life – it can manifest itself when he is off his guard in that '*afin de rendre l'amour supportable*'[1] – is certainly not a less intense or a less radical sickness of the spirit than Flaubert's.[2] The addiction to art going with it is, equally with Flaubert's, involved in an inner contradiction, a defeat of intelligence. It is not after all surprising that, as a critic, Eliot, for all his distinction of mind, has shown himself incapable of sustained precision of thought, and, even in his best period, liable to shallowness and confusion. We should not expect such a writer to show up well in the major orders of value-judgement, those depending upon the critic's sense for the difference between what, in his time, makes for health and what makes against it; and Eliot's performance has been in its way consistent. Faced with the challenge of the great genius who is Flaubert's antithesis, the critic who can offer us Landor as exemplifying the impersonality of great art and find the true creative spirit in *The Black Book* and *Nightwood* tells us that Lawrence is morbid and without moral sense, 'never succeeded in making a work of art', and is incapable of what we ordinarily call thinking.

T. S. Eliot is distinguished enough, and has had influence enough, for this performance to be given classical status – as it will, I think. In that way, serving as it does, and so ironically, to bring out the nature of Lawrence's genius and achievement, it can be made to serve a good purpose. Particularly, and the more so because Eliot has been known as the vindicator of the function of criticism, it provides an apt occasion for insisting on the transcendent intelligence that is inseparable from Lawrence's creative genius. It is Lawrence's greatness that to appreciate him is to revise one's criteria of intelligence and one's notion of it. Eliot's finding him incapable of thinking is a failure of intelligence in himself.[3]

There is no profound emotional disorder in Lawrence, no obdurate major disharmony; intelligence in him can be, as it is, the servant of the whole integrated psyche. It is the representative in consciousness of the complex need of the whole being, and is not thwarted or disabled by

1. See footnote to p. 23 above.

2. And yet Eliot could talk about Lawrence's 'emotional disease' (Review of Murry's *Son of Woman* in *The Criterion*, July 1931).

3. 'A critic must be emotionally alive in every fibre, intellectually capable and skilful in essential logic, and then morally very honest' (D. H. Lawrence, essay on Galsworthy).

inner contradictions in him, whether we have him as artist, critic, or expositor. It is intensely active in his creative writing: we have on the one hand the technical originality of the creations, and on the other their organic wholeness and vitality. But the critic who cannot see a marvel of form, of significant organization, in *Women in Love*, finds the creative originality that really matters in the contrivances of Joyce, where insistent will and ingenuity so largely confess the failure of creative life, and in the technique of the *Cantos*, where, by Eliot's own account, he is not interested in what Pound says, but only in the way he says it.

The un-Flaubertian spirit of Lawrence's work, while producing its characteristic vital perfections, has of course its own tendencies to imperfection.

'Nothing outside the definite line of the book', is a maxim. But can the human mind fix absolutely the definite line of a book, any more than it can fix absolutely any definite line for a living being?[1]

Lawrence had not planned, or foreseen, the separating-out of *The Sisters* into *The Rainbow* and *Women in Love*. They represent, none the less, these novels, an immense labour of art, an untiring solicitude to get things right. His methods of work were characteristically un-Flaubertian (and un-Joycean). It is plain from the letters and other sources that he went forward rapidly once he had started on an enterprise, writing long stretches in remarkably little time as the creative flow carried him on. The first draft written, he revised, not by correcting locally or re-working parts, but by re-writing the whole with the same kind of creative *élan* as had gone to the earlier version (and this he habitually did yet again). His concern clearly was that the whole of himself should be engaged; that the book in its completeness should come from the living being. But, as he remarks in the passage I have just quoted, for a 'living being' it is not possible to fix 'any definite line'. Rapidly as he worked at *The Sisters*, he developed more rapidly and had to recognize that he had changed. It was that which determined the separating-off of *The Rainbow* as something complete and left behind. The conclusion with which, so to speak, he cut it loose is written

1. *Phoenix*, p. 308.

in a momentarily recaptured spirit; a spirit that *The Rainbow* itself in its later part has outgrown, so that these closing pages come with a certain incongruity.[1]

In *Women in Love* there is no such embarrassing development; but it might be said in criticism of that novel that the normative aspiration it clearly represents is not as fully realized as Lawrence (one guesses) had, in the first conception, hoped: the diagnosis represented by Gerald and Gudrun is convincing – terribly so; but Birkin and Ursula as a norm, contemplated in the situation they are left in at the close of the book, leave us wondering (and, it must in fairness be added, leave Lawrence wondering too). That is, if a certain symmetry of negative and positive was aimed at in *Women in Love*, Lawrence has been defeated by the difficulty of life: he hasn't solved the problems of civilization that he analyses. This criticism, if it *is* a criticism, is different in kind from that called for by the close of *The Rainbow*. And in any case, whatever criticisms may be urged against them, both books are, in sum, magnificently achieved great novels, major creations.

Lawrence never again worked at a novel in that way. He had embarked on the immense undertaking, the conception that was at first *The Sisters*, in the conviction that it challenged him with an inclusive significance the defining of which demanded, not only an originality of art locally and daring inventions of method in the part, but resources of organization in the whole as remarkable as any that had ever gone to a creative work. He doesn't seem to have been possessed again with a conviction of that kind – a conviction impelling him to a work of anything like that order. It might be said that the unsettled life foreshadowed in the close of *Women in Love* didn't favour such works. But the taking to such a mode of life is itself, of course, a significant fact.

To have had *The Rainbow* banned and to have been unable to publish *Women in Love* – this was a bad enough blow for Lawrence, isolated and without a public and unfriended among the powers of the contemporary literary world, and yet conscious of what he had achieved. But the major seismic experience was the war. The life dealt with in *The Rainbow* and *Women in Love* and the momentum carrying those works through belong to before the war. The spirit of *Women in Love*

1. See pp. 148–9 below.

belongs to a phase when the Bottomley horror, the nightmare hopelessness of the later years through which the war dragged on, had not
yet closed down on Lawrence. But already, before the war had made its
decisive impact on him, he had had, in order to bring *The Rainbow* to
a close, to recapture wilfully a buoyant note that, in his rapid development since beginning *The Sisters*, he had outgrown. The mood of
Women in Love is not buoyant or sanguine. And to this inevitable
growth – inevitable, with experience and advancing maturity, in a
Lawrence – into something remote at any rate from easy hopefulness
about modern civilization the years from the Somme to the Armistice
brought calamitous fostering.

But it was not in Lawrence's nature to rest in negation. He was ac-
quainted with horror and foreboding and a state bordering on despair,
but it was not possible for him to be defeatist. The affirmation of life
was always strong in him, and he had always that profound sense of
responsibility which, whatever one may conclude about some of its
manifestations, is of his strength and his genius. ('But in the novel', he
says in 'Why the Novel Matters', 'you can see, plainly, when the man
goes dead, the woman goes inert. You can develop an instinct for life,
if you will, instead of a theory of right and wrong, good and bad.')
The novels that succeed *Women in Love* are exploratory and experimental. In them Lawrence lives his problems in a tentative and immediately personal way that gives these books a different status as works
of art from that of *Women in Love* and *The Rainbow*.

The novels that I have in mind in this description are *Aaron's Rod*,
Kangaroo, and *The Plumed Serpent*. The last seems to me a bad book and
a regrettable performance, and I shall not seriously qualify these judgements. But the other two, though very much open to criticism as
novels and works of art, are yet most impressively the work of a
novelist of genius; they are full of life and interest. Nevertheless, I put
them apart from the works that show Lawrence's full creative power
and on which his position as one of the greatest of all novelists is firmly
based. These, I wish to insist, are *The Rainbow*, *Women in Love*, and
the tales; and on these I wish to place the emphasis unequivocally. I am
dealing, then, and dealing briefly, with the lesser novels – with the
things in general most open to adverse criticism – first, in order to put

them clearly apart from the work on which I would establish the claim for Lawrence.

I did not allow, in my summarizing account of the lesser novels, for *The Lost Girl*, which was actually the first novel of Lawrence's to come out after the banning of *The Rainbow*. I take it to be the work of which he writes to Lady Cynthia Asquith in 1918:

> I have begun a novel now – done 150 pages, which are as blameless as *Cranford*. It shall not have one garment disarranged, but shall be buttoned up like a Member of Parliament. Still, I wouldn't vouch that it is like *Sons and Lovers*: it is funny. It amuses me terribly.[1]

The Lost Girl is indeed equally unlike *Sons and Lovers* and *The Rainbow*; it is unlike any other novel that Lawrence wrote. It suggests the work of an unsentimental, more subtle and incomparably more penetrating Dickens, about whose humour, generous though it is, there is nothing soft, as there is nothing savage (though I find the Natcha Kee Tawara business irritating). As a rendering of English provincial life, it strikes one as what Arnold Bennett would have wished to have done, though, being the work of a great creative genius, it is utterly beyond Bennett's achievement. I am thinking of that main part of the book the scene of which is placed in England; the conclusion in the South Italian mountains (the note of it could not have been foreseen from the opening of the book) was obviously added after the war when Lawrence was in Italy or Sicily. What distinguishes *The Lost Girl*, then, is the lightness of Lawrence's personal engagement in it – the absence in it of

1. *Letters*, p. 427. I cannot be quite sure that it is *The Lost Girl* which is referred to here, but think it must be. In January 1920 (*Letters*, p. 497), he writes: 'The MS. which is now in the post, coming from Germany, has lain in Bavaria since early 1914. It is a novel, two-thirds finished – quite unlike my usual style – more eventual – I am very keen to see it.' The letter announcing the completion of *The Lost Girl* is dated the following May; Lawrence writes, again to Lady Cynthia Asquith: 'I've actually finished my new novel, *The Lost Girl*: not morally lost, I assure you.... I think *The Lost Girl* is quite passable, from Mudie's point of view.' This sounds like the novel referred to above, 'blameless as Cranford'. The first part of *The Lost Girl* strikes one as certainly written before the war. The part dealing with Alvina's experiences in war-time England might very well have been written in 1918. If so, Lawrence carried on from memory of the earlier part. The last part was clearly written in Italy or Sicily after the war. The book, at any rate, was written during widely separate phases of Lawrence's life.

the felt pressure of problems and personal urgencies: thinking of the prevailing comedy note, Lawrence himself, in a letter announcing that he has finished it, describes the book as 'amusing'. 'It amuses me terribly,' he says in that earlier letter (if we assume it to be about *The Lost Girl*), written in the last winter of the war.

It is amusing at a very high level. It contains plenty of acute social observation and of characteristic psychological insight. But, as the narrative proceeds and one thing comes after another, we realize that there is no compelling total significance in control.

In *Aaron's Rod*, which came out in 1921, we have again the full urgency of personal engagement, but we have it in a new way. Different as Laurentian art is from the Flaubertian, in *The Rainbow* and *Women in Love* Lawrence worked assiduously to achieve the impersonality of full creation. But in *Aaron's Rod* he is no longer so intently preoccupied with this, though what he offers us is art or nothing – art challenging the maxim: 'Never trust the artist; trust the tale.' A desperately personal urgency, we know, provided theme and impulsion for *Sons and Lovers*; but that work in the final achieved form in which we have it offers the achieved insight into the 'case', and the delicately verified exhibition of it; the author's judgement that the form is now right in his judgement that intelligence has successfully performed its office. *Aaron's Rod* is far more tentative, much more like an actual immediate living of the problem; something experimental embarked on in the expectation that the essential insight will have sufficiently clarified and established itself by the close, and that a sufficiently satisfactory close will present itself. The self-exploratory nature of the personal engagement is virtually stated at one point in the book, the occasion being the letter addressed by Aaron to Sir William Franks:

Well, here was a letter for a poor old man to receive. But, in the dryness of his withered mind, Aaron got it out of himself. When a man writes a letter to himself, it is a pity to post it to somebody else. Perhaps the same is true of a book. [Chapter XVIII]

That last sentence has its clear significance: in writing his letter Aaron discovers what he feels and thinks, and Lawrence is writing *Aaron's Rod* as a kind of 'letter' to himself.

The spirit of unembarrassed tentativeness in which he wrote the book proclaims itself in that lack of artistic providence which appears so unmistakably in the treatment of Jim Bricknell. So insistent a part do the oddities of this character play in the early pages of the book that we naturally assume that something is going to be done with him. But after punching Lilly in the wind in Chapter VIII he drops out. We remain convinced that Lawrence *had* been going to do something with him, but there has been a change of mind as the book has gone forward. Jim now figures merely as part of the representation of that artistic and intellectual Bohemia with which there is certainly some point in Aaron's having had his contacts. And of that representation in general we find that in other respects too it is calculated to prepare us for a development that actually we do not get. We come in fact to recognize in due course that in *Aaron's Rod* we are not reading a work of art of the order of *Women in Love*; there is nothing of that closeness of organization and density of significance, though what we are reading is certainly a most lively novel and a work of genius. The genius is irresistibly apparent in the rendering of the various scenes and episodes of Aaron's truancy. There are Sir William and Lady Franks and their house-party at Novara; there are the street-demonstration at Milan, and the meeting with Angus and Francis (Francis, that perfectly observed type of the artistic-intellectual nineteen-twenties in whom we recognize the Rico of *St Mawr*); there is Aaron's railway journey with this distinguished pair to Florence; and at Florence there is the English-speaking colony, done with that incomparable rightness of touch which is Lawrence's – comedy too intelligent and sensitive and poised for malice or the satirical note (and placing the callowness of Forster's treatment of the theme in *A Room with a View*). And as one goes on recalling the things in which the genius of the novelist especially compels recognition, one realizes that their power is not, as a rule, at the same time some inevitability of significance in relation to the themes of the novel. We may see in them a relevance to those themes, but this does not strike us as having compelled their presence, or as explaining their life. Lawrence, we feel, would not have been at a loss to substitute things that would have done as well. We recognize, in fact, that what we have here is for the most part recent actual experience of Lawrence's own, directly rendered: it

D.H.L. – 2

is just because its impact on him is fresh that it plays so large a part in the life of this novel.

We come to the questions: What, then, is the nature of the theme that is centred in Aaron, and what relation does Aaron bear to Lawrence himself? Like Lawrence he comes of a working-class family in the mining country. Like him, too, he has achieved education, but unlike him he has repudiated it. Having served three years' apprenticeship to school-teaching, he has 'thrown it up and gone into the pit'.

> He had the curious quality of an intelligent, almost sophisticated mind, which had repudiated education. On purpose he kept the Midland accent in his speech. He understood perfectly what a personification was – and an allegory. But he preferred to be illiterate. [Chapter VII]

A 'miner's checkweighman', but also a flautist of professional quality, he lives with a wife and family in one of a row of colliers' dwellings.

The facts about his education we learn when we know him. As he is introduced to us in the opening of the book, secretary to the Miners' Union for his colliery returning home late after an unsatisfactory meeting, met by the little girls at the door with the demand that he shall 'set' the Christmas tree at once, responding to children and wife with that steady amiability which is so curiously not genial, and playing the flute in his shirt-sleeves in the back kitchen, he is unquestionably there, as undeniably a distinctive individual and an actual person as if we were observing him in life. The whole evocation of Aaron Sisson *en famille* has a marvellous reality. The chapter by itself would be enough to establish that the author was a rare kind of genius. It is not merely the vivid intimacy with which the working-class home is done by a great writer who was brought up in one like it; it is the power with which the peculiar domestic tone is evoked: the domesticity without warmth; the Christmas festivity that brings no sympathetic flow and does nothing to soften the suggestion of hostile will; the prevailing undersense of grudge. There is the compelling and disconcerting truth with which this tone or ethos is focussed in the by-play of the little girls unpacking the Christmas-tree ornaments, the elder domineering, the younger protesting, and in the itching perverse will with which the elder (so insistent all the while on having her father's attention) finally breaks the blue glass ball.

The tone, we recognize, has for significance something that has gone wrong between husband and wife. Not that we are told this; the failure in their relations is given us in dramatic terms: her aggressively censorious and injured habit in talking to him, and his peculiar, quite unconciliatory way of not resenting it. She, we are told, 'was acutely aware of her husband', but 'he seemed not very much aware of her'. 'Seemed' carries a weight of positive definition; his 'unawareness' is withdrawal, and his unruffled passivity of good humour a profound will not to respond. She aggressively demands and he withholds. She calls him selfish, and it is impossible not to see that from her point of view it is a well-grounded judgement. With good-humoured indifference he goes off to the pub, leaving her resenting the freedom that *he* enjoys while *she*, as always, is confined to the house.

There is no need to analyse the ways in which we are made aware of Aaron's inner state – a state of which he himself could not give an account. He doesn't go home after the pub closes, and by the time when, after some days and nights of truancy, he sits in the shed at the bottom of the garden looking through the rainy darkness at his house, we know well enough what his state is. There he sits, watching the windows of his own house, and seeing those of the whole row of which it is one: 'a curious succession of lighted windows, between which jutted the intermediary back premises, scullery and outhouse, in dark little blocks'.

He heard the familiar sound of water gushing from the sink into the grating, the dropping of a pail outside the door, the clink of a coal-shovel, the banging of a door, the sound of voices. So many houses cheek by jowl, so many back yards, back doors giving on to the night. It was revolting.

What, as he sits in the dark, he is contemplating from the outside, focussing his sense of, we perceive, is the life – the twelve years of married life – that he cannot, he now knows, go on with. Stealing closer, for what purpose he doesn't quite know, he overhears his wife's account of him:

'Ah well,' sighed the doctor. 'Marriage is a mystery. I'm glad I'm not entangled in it.'

'Yes, to make some woman's life a misery. I'm sure it was death to live with him, he seemed to kill everything off inside you. He was a man you couldn't quarrel with, and get it over. Quiet – quiet in his tempers, and selfish through and through. I've lived with him twelve years – I know what it is. Killing! You don't know what he was –.'

It is a familiar situation, a familiar kind of life-frustrating deadlock. The presenting of it transcends ordinary moral judgements; to judge Aaron selfish and irresponsible for leaving his wife in the lurch with the children on her hands (though he provides for her financially), or to say that, whatever the total account of rights and wrongs might be, plainly the domineering, demanding, complaining woman was at fault, and had made his life intolerable, wouldn't, we know, be to the point. The presenting sensibility and the inquiring intelligence engaged are, of course, profoundly and essentially moral; the moral concern goes far deeper than the level of those judgements. What is wrong here? What laws of life have been ignored that there should be *this* situation, this dreadful deadlock, between a man and a woman? These questions give the informing preoccupation.

It is in the intellectual–artistic Bohemia into which his employment as flautist at Covent Garden takes the truant Aaron that he comes on Rawdon Lilly, who is the obvious enough direct presence of Lawrence himself in the book. In so far as Aaron is the centre of interest he appears to be, then Lilly's function is to help him to become duly conscious about what has gone wrong between him and his wife – to arrive at a diagnosis. This, in the course of his contacts and experiences, Aaron does, with Lilly's aid, achieve. An invalid supremacy assigned to the love motive and the love idea; the taking of love as a goal; the assumption that it is, or could be, the *raison d'être* of the man or the woman to make the other happy; possessive, or oppressively dependent love – the diagnosis, which cannot be adequately summarized, has a convincing presentment that is not, of course, merely a matter of the direct general statement. The correlated positive is stated by Lilly. It is that valid love and a permanent relation can be only between persons of whom each one knows that 'being with another person is secondary'

– knows that 'In so far as I am I, and only I am I, and I am only I, it is my last blessedness to know it and to accept it, and to live with this as the core of my self-knowledge' (end of Chapter XVII).

There is nothing new about this conclusion; it was presented with great force in *Women in Love*. What *is* new is the direct presence of Lawrence preaching it – the direct presence of Lawrence as a character in the novel, for Lilly must be judged to be that. And in confirming the identity of Lilly with Lawrence we recognize that Aaron Sisson, miner's checkweighman and professional flautist, is not so simply the centre of interest in *Aaron's Rod* as he might seem to be, and that Lilly's part in the book is not merely that of an accessory to the developing and resolving of Aaron's case. In fact, there are times when we ask whether Aaron is not the accessory – the accessory to the dominant part played by Lilly. It is plain at all events that in Lilly we have a self-questioning, or experimental self-testing, on the part of Lawrence, the consciously dominant personality who finds himself so prone to assume the role of 'saviour'. The promptings to it, the doubts and recoils, the fresh impulsions, are lived in the book, of which, it may be added, the most decided effect of development is that it closes with Lilly assuming more positively than ever before the function of 'leader' or 'heroic soul'.

But, as the book conveys it, Lawrence's total attitude in the matter is complex and unsure of itself – unaware of what it amounts to. One of the places where the uncertainty is plainly dramatized is the chapter called 'A Punch in the Wind'. The chapter (VIII) ends:

'You shouldn't try to make a little Jesus of yourself, coming so near to people, wanting to help them,' was Tanny's last word.

Rawdon Lilly and Tanny in their cottage, visited by Jim Bricknell, are unmistakably Lawrence and Frieda, and the chapter, we cannot doubt, registers the actual living relation between them. Tanny from the start disapproves of Lilly's 'helpful' response to Jim, a response in which he assumes a decidedly authoritative manner, and she tells him that he 'asked for' the blow in the wind that he gets. The disapproval would seem to be justified by the outcome of the episode, as he doesn't even tacitly deny. There is a remarkable integrity in Lawrence's registering of his relations with Frieda (an integrity not the less remarkable because it is essential, of course, to the experimental function, the self-testing, or self-exploration, that plays so large a part in the creative impulsion to *Aaron's Rod*). When Lilly makes what is certainly a called-for comment on Jim's 'wanting a woman always there, to hold his hand', Tanny strikes in characteristically:

'Don't be so spiteful,' said Tanny. '*You* see that you have a woman always there, to hold *your* hand.'

'My hand doesn't need holding,' snapped Lilly.

'Doesn't it! More than most men's! But you're so beastly ungrateful and mannish. Because I hold you safe enough all the time, you like to pretend you're doing it all yourself.'

'All right. Don't drag yourself in,' said Lilly, detesting his wife at that moment.

Tanny's retort, I say, is characteristic – it represents a note that, as we can tell from *Aaron's Rod* and *Kangaroo*, Lawrence heard a good deal from Frieda. And he doesn't, in those novels, disguise his sense that he has no convinced answer: he is concerned in them with evaluating the discomfiting truth admitted, with determining how seriously it affects the validity of the conviction that his genius seems to compel upon him. He confronts it with the positive promptings of that genius.

The complexity, the self-testing, is dramatized, too, in Lilly's contacts with Aaron. Having taken charge of the sick Aaron, Lilly wonders to himself why he does it:

'Jim ought to have taught me my lesson. As soon as this man's really better he'll punch me in the wind, metaphorically if not actually, for having interfered with him. And Tanny would say he was quite right to do it. She says I want power over them. What if I do? They don't care how much power the mob has over them, the nation, Lloyd George and Northcliffe and the police and money. They'll yield themselves up to that sort of power quickly enough, and immolate themselves *pro bono publico* by the million. And what's the *bonum publicum* but a mob power. Why can't they submit to a bit of healthy individual authority. The fool would die without me: just as that fool Jim will die in hysterics one day. Why does he last so long!

'Tanny's the same. She does nothing really but resist me: my authority, my influence, or just *me*. At the bottom of her heart she just blindly and persistently opposes me. God knows what it is she opposes: just me myself. She thinks I want her to submit to me. So I do, in a measure natural to our own two selves. Some-where, she ought to submit to me. But they all prefer to kick against the pricks. Not that *they* get many pricks. I get them. Damn them all, why don't I leave them alone?'

When Lilly tells the convalescent Aaron that he is slipping off to Malta, Aaron takes it as the signal for an insistent questioning:

'But what's the good of going to Malta? Shall *you* be any different yourself in another place? You'll be the same there as you are here.'

'How am I here?'

'Why you're all the time grinding yourself against something inside you. You're never free. You're never content. You can't stop chafing.'

As Aaron presses his questions, his doubts, and his ironies – and he does so pertinaciously in this chapter (X) – we have a sense that this is something very like a *dialogue intérieur*, and that Aaron is an *alter ego*. We come now once again to the question of Aaron's relation to Law-rence. When Lilly succours Aaron at Covent Garden, takes him in, puts him to bed, and looks after him, we don't question the existence of the two as separate identities and very different persons. We have formed a strong sense of Aaron as a physical presence and as a personality; and the personality – sardonic, phlegmatic, and rather taciturn – makes him as unlike Lawrence as the physical presence does. And yet if, especially towards the end of the book, we cast back reflectively, we feel that there is something equivocal about the unlikeness. Could a miner's checkweighman, even if also a flautist, really have got on so swim-mingly in cultivated, sophisticated, and distinguished society of all kinds as Aaron has done?

Lawrence himself was a genius of transcendent social gifts and irre-sistible personal fascination. Aaron, it is true, has had his three years' training as a teacher, but, apart from his flute-playing, he is not repre-sented as having any very striking gifts or social qualifications, and though we are told that he has charm, we hardly feel this when he is really present to us as the distinctive blond ex-checkweighman, Aaron Sisson. Not that, as we follow the story, we question the operation of the charm; his career has an irresistible actuality, and the things that are presented as happening happen, unquestionably, just so. But reflecting critically, we realize that, in our unanalysed sense of him, Aaron has not been as wholly distinct from Lawrence as the dramatic opposition of the ex-checkweighman flautist to the Laurentian Lilly affirms; he has had, in an equivocal way, the benefit of Lawrence's own genius, and has been, in his career, carried through the novel with an unquestioned ease on that. Thus, when at Sir William Franks's mansion at Novara he talks with Sir William or Lady Franks, he is indisputably the phlegmatic well-built flautist and *not* Lawrence. Nevertheless, our sense of him in sum is inseparable from our consciousness of the episodes and the milieux in which he has his experiences, and our consciousness of these is Lawrence's. We see Sir William and Lady Franks and the consummately done house-party with Lawrence's penetrating vision,[1] and this is not distinguishable from Aaron's; we take the impact of Novara, the beautiful foreign city exposed to the imminent, snow-streaked, tiger-like Alps, with Lawrence's sensibility, but we are consciously with the blond exploring Aaron when we take it. And so it is through the succession of Aaron's experiences and contacts; the view of the Lombard plain, the mob scenes at Milan, Angus and Francis, Florence, James Argyle (a genial rendering of Norman Douglas), Mr ffrench and Miss Wade, the nocturnal mystery of the Florentine streets.

How completely, without any jolt of transition, we can have an Aaron who in the profound reactions of his being is pure, immediate, and indisputable Lawrence the episode of the picked pocket illustrates. The whole episode – the way in which Aaron reacts to the suspected loss, and then verifies it, the accompanying emotional upheaval, the

1. How directly Lawrence's own experience figures in *Aaron's Rod* is illustrated by this passage from a letter to Lady Cynthia Asquith (*Letters*, p. 484): 'I stayed two nights on the way with rich English people – O.B.M. or O.B. something – parvenu, etc. – great luxury – rather nice people really – but my stomach, my stomach, it has a bad habit of turning a somersault when it finds itself in the wrong element, like a dolphin in the air. The old Knight and I had a sincere half-mocking argument, he for security and a bank-balance and power, and I for naked liberty. In the end he rested safe on his bank-balance, I in my nakedness; we hated each other – but with respect. But *c'est lui qui mourra*. He's going to die – *moi, non*. He knows that, the impotent old wolf, so he is ready in one half to murder me. I don't want to murder him – merely, leave him to his death.'

Compare this with Aaron's experience at Novara.

stocktaking, and the moral drawn – strikes us as the purest Laurentian autobiography. This is what the dazed Aaron, sitting in his chair in the hotel bedroom, thinks, 'not in his mind, but in his soul':

It serves you right. It is nothing but right, it serves everybody right who rushes enkindled through the street and trusts implicitly in mankind and in the life-spirit, as if mankind and the life-spirit were a playground for enkindled individuals. It serves you right. You have paid about twelve pounds sterling for your lesson. Fool, you might have known beforehand, and then you needn't have paid at all. You can ill afford twelve pounds sterling, you fool. But since paid you have, mind the lesson is learned. Never again. Never expose yourself again. Never again absolute trust. It is a blasphemy against life, is absolute trust. Has a wild creature ever absolute trust? It minds itself. Sleeping or waking it is on its guard. And so must you be, or you'll go under. Sleeping or waking, man or woman, God or the devil, keep your guard over yourself. Keep your guard over yourself, less worse befall you. No man is robbed unless he incites a rob-ber. No man is murdered unless he attracts a murderer. Then be not robbed: it lies within your own power. And be not murdered. Or if you are, you deserve it. Keep your guard over yourself, now, always and forever. Yes, against God quite as hard as against the devil. He's fully as dangerous to you.... [Chapter XVI]

What is the significance of this curious dual presence of Lawrence in *Aaron's Rod*? In the chapter already referred to, where the convales-cent Aaron, pressing Lilly with his questions and his criticisms, has the effect of a kind of ironical *alter ego*, we have the affinity between the two stated:

The two men had an almost uncanny understanding of one another – like brothers. They came from the same district, from the same class. Each might have been born into the other's circumstances. Like brothers, there was a pro-found hostility between them. But hostility is not antipathy. [Chapter X]

We might conclude at this point that Lawrence's intention bore some relation to Henry James's in *The Lesson of the Master*, and that Aaron, figuring what Lawrence might very well have been if he had married in his own class and things had gone more ordinarily, repre-sented a special imaginative effort on Lawrence's part to transcend the peculiarities of his actual situation. And it would seem that some such intention must, in some measure, have entered into the tentative conception with which Lawrence started on *Aaron's Rod*. If, however, we make this note, it must be to observe when we have read the book through that actually it fails to give full imaginative realization to Aaron's case as one different from Lawrence's own. And 'fails' seems the right word: that is, we are faced with an inadvertence, a default of imagination, which is very significant.

One essential respect in which, in the scene in Lilly's room at Covent Garden, Aaron is *not* Lawrence and Lilly *is* – and it is a respect in which, whenever the two are together, Aaron remains distinguished from Lilly – appears immediately after the passage last quoted:

> Lilly's skilful housewifery always irritated Aaron: it was so self-sufficient. But most irritating of all was the little man's unconscious assumption of priority. Poor Lilly was actually unaware that he assumed this quiet predominance over others. He mashed the potatoes, he heated the plates, he warmed the red wine, he whisked the eggs into the milk pudding, and served his visitor like a housemaid. But none of this detracted from the silent assurance with which he bore himself, and with which he seemed to domineer over his acquaintance.

The noting of Lilly's 'assumption of priority' as unconscious registers, of course, Lawrence's actual preoccupation with the trait. The preoccupation supplies, in fact, a major element among the interests and impulses that shape the novel, and, whatever Lawrence may have intended in beginning, Aaron himself has by the close become merely accessory to it. We have observed it in the form of Lilly's self-questioning about his role of 'saviour'. In the discussions that are staged at Florence it brings together the problems of marriage and the problems of politics. In the café discussion of the penultimate chapter Lilly, when the bomb explodes, is holding forth on 'power' and 'submission' in their political aspects. In his final colloquy with Aaron in the last chapter he tells him that there are 'two great life-urges' – the 'love-urge' and the 'power-urge'.

> 'That's where Nietzsche was wrong. His was the conscious and benevolent will, in fact the love-will. But the deep power-urge is not conscious of its aims: and it is certainly not consciously benevolent or love-directed. Whatever else happens, somewhere, sometime, the deep power-urge in man will have to issue forth again, and woman will submit lovingly, not subjectedly.'

'She never will,' persisted Aaron. 'Anything else will happen, but not that.'

'She will,' said Lilly, 'once the man disengages himself from the love-mode, and stands clear. Once he stands clear, and the other great urge begins to flow in him, then the woman won't be able to resist. Her own soul will wish to yield itself.'

'Woman yield –?' Aaron re-echoed.

'Woman – and man too. Yield to the deep power-soul in the individual man, and obey implicitly. I don't go back on what I said before. I do believe that every man must fulfil his own soul, every woman must be herself, herself only, not some man's instrument, or some embodied theory. But the mode of our being is such that we can only live and have our being whilst we are implicit in one of the great dynamic modes. We *must* either love, or rule. And once the love-mode changes, as change it must, for we are worn out and becoming evil in its persistence, then the other mode will take place in us. And there will be profound, profound obedience in place of this love-crying, obedience to the incalculable power-urge. And men must submit to the greater soul in a man, for their guidance: a woman must submit to the positive power-soul in man, for their being.'

'You'll never get it,' said Aaron.

'You will, when all men want it. All men say they want a leader. Then let them in their souls submit to some greater soul than theirs. At present, when they say they want a leader, they mean they want an instrument, like Lloyd George. A mere instrument for their use. But it's more than that. It's the reverse. It's the deep, fathomless submission to the heroic soul in a greater man.'

The transition from the marital to the political has been easily made, and it is from the political emphasis that Lilly goes on to the personal challenge:

'You, Aaron, you too have the need to submit. You, too, have the need lovingly to yield to a more heroic soul, to give yourself. You know you have. And you know it isn't love. It is life-submission. And you know it.'

The novel ends on the portentous note:

There was a long pause. Then Aaron looked up into Lilly's face. It was dark and remote-seeming. It was like a Byzantine eikon at the moment.

'And whom shall I submit to?' he said.

'Your soul will tell you,' replied the other.

Wherever the centre of interest was in the early part of *Aaron's Rod*, there can be no doubt where it is now. What bearing has Lilly's sufficiently explicit prescription on Aaron's problem? It is not suggested that Aaron is one of the 'greater men', and it is hardly to be supposed that his submitting to the 'heroic soul' in Lilly will reconcile Lottie, his wife, to forgoing the love he cannot give her. It might of course be suggested that the insolubility of the individual problem while the governing ideas of civilization remain what they are is just the moral. But actually nothing could be plainer than that Aaron is left so in the air because he is now for Lawrence a decidedly minor and subordinate interest – because, in fact, as a case different from Lawrence's own he is just not *there*.

He has become, in the course of his truancy, more conscious of the nature of the deadlock with his wife, and he has learnt that, though he cannot go back home to be made to 'love' and to 'care', he cannot love any other woman and remains married to Lottie. No further development is given us; we know nothing more about his state – the state of his problem. Though his sense of the finality of his marriage, the permanence of the tie that holds him to his wife, is insisted on, he has no feelings at all, it would seem, about his children. It is surely a significant inadvertence, a significant default of imagination, on Lawrence's part. And it has its relevance in a critical consideration of his wisdom, or doctrine (not to shirk the word). For to insist that the relation between a man and a woman is the supremely important one, to insist that the marriage for life is the relation necessary for the fulfilment of the 'deeper desires', and yet to be to this tune blank about the family – it is surely very odd? We may find the tacit admission of the oddity in Lawrence himself: there are the pages about marriage in that classical pamphlet (it should be), that superlatively fine personal statement and testament – it is a great piece of English prose, and it has been for years unobtainable – which he wrote at the end of his life: *À Propos of Lady Chatterley's Lover*. These sentences are to the point:

Do we want to be like the Romans, under the Empire, or even under the Republic? Do we want to be, as far as our family and our freedom is concerned, like the Greek citizens of a City State in Hellas? Do we want to imagine ourselves in the strange priest-controlled, ritual-fulfilled condition of the earlier Egyptians? Do we want to be bullied by a Soviet?

For my part, I have to say NO! every time. And having said it, we have to come back and consider the famous saying, that perhaps the greatest contribution to the social life of man made by Christianity is – marriage. Christianity brought marriage into the world: marriage as we know it. Christianity established the little autonomy of the family within the greater rule of the State. Christianity made marriage in some respects inviolate, not to be violated by the State. It is marriage, perhaps, that has given man the best of his freedom, given him his little kingdom of his own within the big kingdom of the State, given him his foothold of independence on which to stand and resist an unjust State. Man and wife, a king and queen with one or two subjects, a few square yards of territory of their own: this, really, is marriage. It is a true freedom because it is a true fulfilment, for man, woman and children.

That Lawrence should have been able so to slight the situation of his hero, so to ignore the pressures that an actual Aaron must surely have felt, shows how compellingly his own problems must have been pressing upon him when he wrote *Aaron's Rod*, and with how betraying an unawareness, therefore, he could fail to transcend his own personal situation. We have evidence enough that at this time not only was Lilly's kind of preoccupation with 'power', 'responsibility', and 'submission', and with the extra-literary implications of such genius as Lawrence's, very much Lawrence's own, but that the preoccupation as it absorbed Lawrence was at the same time a wrestling with the problem of his own most important personal relation – his relation with Frieda. It all comes out plainly enough in *Kangaroo*, the novel that appears a year after *Aaron's Rod*. The main figure in *Kangaroo*, Richard Lovat Somers, is clearly and without disguise Lawrence, and the book explores in a kind of fictional experiment the possibility for Lawrence of political action. It presents also, with an insight and an integrity that can be poignantly affecting, the drama of his relations with Frieda. And there is one place in particular that has a very significant bearing on his equivocal default of imagination in dealing with Aaron as the family man.

Somers engages in a political project, a 'conspiracy', with Jack Callcott. Harriet sees 'by the shut look on his face' that he is not going to tell her what it is.

And for two or three years now, since the war, he had talked about doing some work with men alone, sharing some activity with men. Turning away from the personal life to the hateful male impersonal activity, and shutting her out from this. [Chapter V]

It seems to her unnecessary, and a breach of faith on his part. 'If their marriage was a real thing, then anything very serious was her matter as much as his, surely.'

She continued bright through the day. Then at evening he found her sitting on her bed with tears in her eyes and her hands in her lap. At once his heart became very troubled: because after all she was all he had in the world, and he couldn't bear her to be really disappointed or wounded. He wanted to ask her what was the matter, and to try and comfort her. But he knew it would be false. He knew that her greatest grief was when he turned away from their personal human life of intimacy to this impersonal business of male activity for which he was always craving. So he felt miserable, but went away without saying anything. Because he was determined, if possible, to go forward in this business with Jack. He was also determined that it was not a woman's matter. As soon as he could he would tell her about it: as much as it was necessary for her to know. But, once he had slowly and carefully weighed a course of action, he would not hold it subject to Harriet's approval or disapproval. It would be out of her sphere, outside the personal sphere of their two lives, and he would keep it there. She emphatically opposed this principle of her externality. She agreed with the necessity for impersonal activity, but oh, she insisted on being identified with the activity, impersonal or not. And he insisted that it could not and should not be: that the pure male activity should be womanless, beyond woman. No man was beyond woman. But in his one quality of ultimate maker and breaker, he was womanless. Harriet denied this, bitterly. She wanted to share, to join in, not to be left out lonely. He looked at her in distress, and did not answer.

The delicacy of precision with which Somers's unresolved state of uncertainty is registered will have been noted. He doesn't suggest that Harriet disputes the 'necessity for impersonal activity'; on the contrary, he recognizes her acquiescence in it. He presents his refusal to let her share as a matter of complete and profound conviction, based on ultimate principle. Yet he manifestly has his hesitations about the nature of the conviction, and is certainly not confident about its ultimateness. He has conveyed his uneasy sense that she would in fact oppose the actual project, and that that in itself is an insuperable objection to letting her know what it is: 'But once he had slowly and carefully weighed a course of action, he would not hold it subject to Harriet's approval or disapproval.' The objection to having Harriet's disapproval to meet might (the whole context makes it plain that the possibility is tacitly recognized) prove on analysis to be disconcertingly complex. And, further, we have the evidence of Somers's painful capacity for realizing Harriet's point of view and the unanswerableness of her case. Then follows the supremely significant passage:

For the moment, however, he said nothing. But Somers knew from his dreams what she was feeling: his dreams of a woman, a woman he loved, something like Harriet, something like his mother, and yet unlike either, a woman sullen and obstinate against him, repudiating him. Bitter the woman was, grieved beyond words, grieved till her face was swollen and puffy and almost mad or imbecile, because she had loved him so much, and now she must see him betray her love. That was how the dream woman put it: he had betrayed her great love, and she must go down into an everlasting hell, denied, and denying him absolutely in return, a sullen, awful soul. The face reminded him of Harriet, and of his mother, and of his sister, and of girls he had known when he was younger – strange glimpses of all of them, each glimpse excluding the last. And at the same time in the terrible face some of the look of that bloated face of a madwoman which hung over Jane Eyre in the night in Mr Rochester's house.

The Somers of the dream was terribly upset. He cried tears from his very bowels, and laid his hand on the woman's arm saying:

'But I love you. Don't you *believe* in me? Don't you *believe* in me?' But the woman, she seemed almost old now – only shed a few bitter tears, bitter as vitriol, from her distorted face, and bitterly, hideously turned away, dragging her arm from the touch of his fingers; turned, as it seemed to the dream-Somers, away to the sullen and dreary, everlasting hell of repudiation.

He woke at this, and listened to the thunder of the sea with horror. With horror. Two women in his life he had loved down to the quick of life and death: his mother and Harriet. And the woman in the dream was so awfully his mother, risen from the dead, and at the same time Harriet, as it were, departing from this life, that he stared at the night-paleness between the window-curtains in horror.

'They neither of them believed in me,' he said to himself. Still in the spell of the dream, he put it in the past tense, though Harriet lay sleeping in the next bed. He could not get over it.

These pages bring us face to face with the abnormality of Lawrence's position – for it *is* as abnormality that we have to think of it in a writer whose preoccupation with the relations between men and women in marriage was so essentially normative in spirit. For all the emancipating triumph of intelligence represented by *Sons and Lovers*, the too-close relation established with him by his mother had its permanent consequences. The dream-confusion of the mother with Frieda is significant. Forcing himself to 'come right awake', Somers tells himself that when he is asleep and off his guard his old weaknesses, overcome in his full, day-waking self, rise up and take their revenge on the victorious healthy consciousness, 'like past diseases come back for a phantom triumph'. The dream 'means that the actual danger is gone'.

So he reasoned with himself. For he had an ingrained instinct or habit of thought which made him feel that he could never take the move into activity unless Harriet and his dead mother believed in him. They both believed in him terribly, in personal being. In the individual man he was, and the son of man, they believed with all the intensity of undivided love. But in the impersonal man, the man that would go beyond them, with his back to them, they did not find it so easy to believe.

We cannot help relating (as Lawrence himself does) the insistence that the 'pure male activity shall be womanless, beyond woman' with Lawrence's 'ingrained instinct or habit of thought which made him feel that he could never take the move into activity unless [Frieda] and his dead mother believed in him'. He had been brought up by his mother to live *for* her, and the effort to escape – the pain of growing out of – the corresponding dependence had been terrible. And we see how the dream associates his mother with Frieda, and with women in general who had played a part in his life. The considerations of personal history do not of themselves settle the questions; the questions that most exercised Lawrence. Yet, though he was supremely intelligent, with the intelligence that manifests itself in a rare degree of self-knowledge, clearly his peculiar experience of emotional forcing, strain, and painful readjustment had some lasting consequences that made it very difficult for him to be sure of his poise and centrality as a reporter on some of the most delicate problems his genius drove him to explore.

And again, there are the peculiarities of his own married life to be noted. He had no permanent home and no children. Frieda, of course, had children, and in regard to them Lawrence had had a phase (at any rate) of jealousy. There is a moment in *Aaron's Rod* when we recall this fact. It comes towards the end of Lilly's long *tête-à-tête* with the convalescent Aaron in Chapter IX. The discussion turns on the way in which, 'when a woman has got children, she thinks the world wags only for them and her'. This introduction of the theme comes from Lilly, who has just said that, though 'Tanny wants children badly', he doesn't, and is thankful they have none. In the kind of antiphonal exchange that the two then devote to the theme Lilly vies in emphasis with Aaron. Finally we come to this:

> 'Men have got to stand up to the fact that manhood is more than childhood – and then force women to admit it,' said Lilly. 'But the rotten whiners, they're all grovelling before a baby's napkin and a woman's petticoat.'
> 'It's a fact,' said Aaron. But he glanced at Lilly oddly, as if suspiciously. And Lilly caught the look.

What we have here, in the odd look and in Lilly's catching it, is surely Lawrence's characteristic recognition of something strained and suspect in the note, coming from him. To make the point is of course to pay tribute to that intelligence by which Lawrence so largely transcends the limiting and disabling effects of personal history and the accidents of situation. But it remains true, and significant, that he had no children, and that the existence of Frieda's had been for him a matter for jealousy.

And when we are taking stock of the disadvantages Lawrence had to contend with as a seeker after normative conclusions about the relations between men and women, we have to consider Frieda herself. She has, as Lawrence's wife, no home, and, having abandoned her children, no maternal function. She was, in fact, neither maternal in type nor intellectual; she had no place in any community, no social function, and nothing much to do – the request for novels for Frieda to read is a recurrent note in Lawrence's letters. No one would wish to question the evidence that the attraction that brought them together did not mislead them and that, essentially, the union justified itself. But it was hardly one that provided representative experience for pronouncing normatively about marriage. We see the great advantage enjoyed by the author of *Anna Karenina*.

There is what appears to be a clear illustration in *Aaron's Rod* of the way in which intelligence in Lawrence, marvellous as it was, could fail to transcend the special conditions of experience. The affair with the Marchesa forms a major episode in Aaron's Italian adventure. If one asks what significance it has in relation to his specific problem, his 'case', there doesn't seem to be any very impressive answer to hand. In it, one can say, he confirms his knowledge that he has remained married to Lottie, and that 'any other woman than his wife is a strange woman to him, a violation'; and one can add that, in declining finally to be Antony to the Marchesa's Cleopatra, he has learnt to place the love in which each uses the other as a 'mere magic implement'.

His famous desire for her, what had it been but the same attempt to strike a magic fire out of her, for his own ecstasy. They were playing the same game of fire.

But there is no inevitability about the episode as a part of Aaron's history. One is convinced, in fact, that it appears there because Lawrence himself had encountered the original of the Marchesa and been struck by her – been intrigued by her interest as a case. With her heavy eyes, her remoteness, and her 'muted' and 'numbed' way of speaking, she suffers from some soul-sickness. She was once very fond of music, but now 'can't stand' chords and harmonies:

'A number of sounds all sounding together. It just makes me ill. It makes me feel so sick.'

Aaron plays his flute to her, with an instant remedial effect:

'Good!' she said. 'Good!'

And a gleam almost of happiness seemed to light her up. She seemed like one who had been kept in a horrible enchanted castle – for years and years. Oh, a horrible enchanted castle, with wet walls of emotions and ponderous chains of feelings and a ghastly atmosphere of must-be. She felt she had seen through the opening door a crack of sunshine, and thin, pure, light outside air, outside, beyond this dank and beastly dungeon of feelings and moral necessity. Ugh! – she shuddered convulsively at what had been. She looked at her little husband.

Chains of necessity all round him: a little jailer. Yet she was fond of him. If only he would throw away the castle keys. He was a little gnome. What did he clutch the castle keys so tight for?

Aaron looked at her. He knew that they understood one another, he and she. Without any moral necessity or any other necessity. Outside – they had got outside the castle of so-called human life. [Chapter XVI]

Aaron's flute-playing draws directly on the spontaneous life below the level of 'ideas' and 'mental consciousness'. The flute represents that in him which made him know that he could no longer go on being made to 'love' and to 'care', and which prevailed in his act of desertion. His playing enables the Marchesa too to escape from the 'stone-tablets of consciousness'.[1] The theme is a familiar one in Lawrence, and he handles it again and again with wonderful subtlety and complete convincingness. But as exemplified in the Marchesa the diagnosis doesn't seem to have much point, since we haven't been given much case for it to explain. And it certainly seems to have very little point as leading to Aaron's Antony-and-Cleopatra affair with her. The whole episode, in fact, is irritatingly unsatisfying because not completely significant.

And anyone who has arrived at this judgement must have commented on an aspect of the treatment of the Marchesa that has yet to be mentioned. She is a cosmopolitan American, she is married to a dapper little Italian Marquis, she is forty and she is childless. She is an unintellectual, decidedly feminine woman, and her only *raison d'être* is to *be* that; there is no context, setting, purpose, or function suggested that might give her life meaning. If one remarks that she is as much at a loose end as Frieda, it must be to note also that she is not married to a genius (and Frieda believed in Lawrence and was truly devoted to him). Is it not astonishing – and significant – that Lawrence should take a woman so circumstanced, so obviously without the conditions of a satisfying life, as exemplifying the essential difficulties of establishing a permanent vital relation between a man and a woman in marriage? For that is what he implicitly does. He had no doubt observed the woman in life, observed too her husband's uneasiness about her, and arrived at some sound intuitions about their relations. But he could never have made of the Marchesa what he makes in *Aaron's Rod*, remaining so un-

1. See *The Ladybird* and p. 64 below.

aware of the major part that, for most responsive readers, her childless-
ness and general functionlessness must represent in the explanation of
her soul-sickness, if marriage had not been for him that migratory life
with Frieda, homeless and childless. The unsatisfactoriness of the episode, then, is significant as illustrating a tendency; an inherent tendency
of the special circumstances of Lawrence's life to affect his perception
of the problems in ways he is not sufficiently aware of.

The insidious effect appears with more ominous significance in one of
the finest of the tales, *The Captain's Doll*. Alexander Hepburn refuses to
marry Hannele on the basis of love; love conceived as a matter of the
man's devoting himself to adoring the beloved and making it the business of his life to make *her* life happy. The tale, with its vivacity and
variety of tone, is strikingly successful: it develops convincingly to the
close in which Hannele recognizes that she herself wants something
other than that, and agrees to 'honour and obey'. And yet, as I have
indicated in my detailed discussion of the tale,[1] the close leaves us with
a sense of there being some element of the equivocal that has to be
qualified away before full endorsement is possible. Hepburn is not
Lawrence; he hasn't genius, and doesn't pretend to it; he has no inner
urging to be a 'saviour', and, ostensibly at any rate, no sense of himself
as a 'greater soul'. His insistence on the necessity of an impersonal male
purpose or activity, something to be respected as more a man's *raison
d'être* than love can be, is to be taken as normative.

Hepburn, however, is not just any man. He has the 'dark, unseeing
eyes', the 'incalculable presence', the 'strange, fascinating physique' that
makes Hannele feel she 'can't help being in love' with him. He is the
antithesis, we may say, of Rico in *St Mawr*;[2] Rico, who is all face,
obvious good looks, well-groomed ostensible presence and personality,
and whose male activity, when he is not 'being an artist', is flirting with
the ladies. Hepburn has in him that which is represented by St Mawr;
he answers, in fact, to what Lou Carrington, talking with her mother,
Mrs Witt, desiderates when she says:

'Just think of St Mawr! I've thought so much about him. We call him an
animal, but we never know what it means. He seems a far greater mystery to

1. See p. 233 below.   2. See p. 235 *et seq.*

me than a clever man. He's a horse. Why can't one say in the same way, of a man: *He's a man?* There seems no mystery in being a man.'

Hepburn *is* a man – he is a man in the sense in which Rico isn't: that, and not any special gift, is his distinction – the mystery that fascinates Hannele.

St Mawr seems to me, in its treatment of its main themes, wholly convincing. The failure of Lou's marriage with Rico in the emptiness of a life of 'love' and good times has its clear significance. The significance is confirmed by the case of Lou's mother, Mrs Witt, who, as she moves on in her fifties, finds the meaninglessness left by her sardonic destructive will terrible to herself, and prays to God to conquer her before she dies. Of her we can perhaps say that it never was possible that she should make a successful marriage; possessed by the dominating female will, she was doomed to triumphant self-destruction. But the moral that the tale enforces in respect of Lou bears on the nothingness of Rico: in him, the husband, should have been focussed the purpose, the mystery, the deep impersonal urgency of life that will serves and that gives will and the individual life a meaning, and saves them from the horror of automatism.

To derive, however, from such perceptions and insights as are registered in *St Mawr*, and so many of the best tales, normative conclusions about the relation of the man and the woman in marriage, is obviously a delicate matter. Lawrence's complexity of attitude, characteristically conveyed in his work – as in (say) *Women in Love* and *Kangaroo*, shows how far from unaware he is of the delicacy; but the aspect of *The Captain's Doll* under consideration suggests that he doesn't sufficiently realize how insidious a tendency to unawareness or impercipience his own special circumstances of life can represent – how serious a default of intelligence they can foster. For we note at the close of the tale that, though Alexander Hepburn is not Lawrence, the married relations between him and Hannele are to be essentially those between Lawrence and Frieda. Hannele is suspiciously like Frieda; a German aristocrat of great vitality and charm, quite unbourgeois in moral habit, and not conceivably a Hausfrau. Alexander announces that he is 'going to East Africa to join a man who's breaking his neck to get his three thousand acres of land under control', and 'going to do a book on the moon'. Will Hannele, then, be a pioneering farmer's devoted wife, doing (in her own words) 'frightful housekeeping in Africa'? It seems improbable.

And actually, when we consider, it isn't very easy to think of Alexander Hepburn as a pioneering farmer. Once the doubt has been raised, we can't help suspecting that the plan must be taken as Alexander's way of saying that the life he proposes to lead will be as unlike the normal settled life as Lawrence's own. Lawrence had his genius and wrote with astonishing fertility till his death; but it is obviously impossible to take Alexander's amateur book on the moon as a sufficient 'male activity'. It doesn't, in fact, belong to the really imagined drama. Alexander's telescope and his interest in the moon have played their poetic and symbolic part in that; and when, at the close of the drama, Lawrence's imagination has slackened, he is content to use them as the cue for the alleged book. Since the book can't be taken very seriously, he adds the pioneering plan, which is equally unimagined (the dubious congruity therefore doesn't matter). Neither African farm nor married future belongs to the realized drama – to the area of Lawrence's focussed creative interest. What is significant is that at this comparatively inert moment, when intelligence and imaginative integrity no longer respond fully to the creative challenge, Lawrence should implicitly offer his life with Frieda as the type-marriage. That this is what he does, the point in which Hannele differs from Frieda only serves to emphasize. Hannele's art is necessary to the tale; it is necessary because it is involved in her having made the doll, which is an indispensable *donnée*. But as a part of Hannele's case and personal make-up it doesn't count; it is not something to be set against Alexander's book on the moon, and it is not thought of as anything sacrificed in her going to do (perhaps) 'frightful housekeeping in Africa'. In short, Hannele – her art (which implies a milieu of sophisticated culture) not sacrificed, but forgotten, as now an unnecessary *donnée* – is to be Frieda to Alexander's Lawrence; and the pair are to live homeless or not-belonging in the manner of the Lawrences. That this Frieda will have promised to 'honour and obey' doesn't strike us as portending any real difference, though we note it as perhaps a significant incongruity.

The 'honour and obey', in any case, brings up a major preoccupation of Lawrence's, involving (as *Aaron's Rod* adverts us) a good deal more than marriage: the preoccupation with 'obedience, faith, belief, responsibility, power. ....'[1] And it is time to note that if, in the enacted drama of *The Captain's Doll*, Alexander Hepburn is unquestionably someone quite other than Lawrence, nevertheless the difference between the two is equivocal. It is equivocal because, for Lawrence, in the nature of the case, the distinction between being a 'man' in the sense in which Rico is *not* a man and being a genius is a difficult one to make. That this is so is made plain in the prolonged examination of his relations with Frieda that we find in *Kangaroo* – an examination carried out with characteristic intelligence and integrity. Listening to Harriet's sarcasm about his contemplated political involvement, Richard Lovat Somers realized 'that most of what she said was true'. But

'None the less,' he reflected, 'I do want to do something along with men. I *am* alone and cut off. As a man among men, I just have no place. I have my life with you, I know; *et praeterea nihil.*'

'*Et praeterea nihil!* And what more do you want? Besides, you liar, haven't you got your writing? Isn't that all you want, isn't that *doing* all there is to be done? Men! Much *men* there is about them! Bah, when it comes to that, I have to be even the only man as well as the only woman.'

The voice is unmistakably Frieda's, and Lawrence doesn't make any show of finding an answer that wholly convinces himself. Yet it is *of* Lawrence's genius to be conscious of a responsibility – to be conscious of a power that *is* responsibility – such as makes him feel that writing is *not* doing all there is to be done; his writing is the writing of a man (a 'greater man' and a 'more heroic soul') who feels that. His problem is to determine what, in the concrete, the manifestation of the 'power' and the responsibility should be. And the three novels, *Aaron's Rod*, *Kangaroo*, and *The Plumed Serpent*, are preoccupied with the effort of determination.

Kangaroo might be described as a day-dream in which he tests the idea of his becoming a leader in political action – might, if 'day-dream' didn't suggest an indulgence in irresponsible fantasy and an

1. See p. 65 below.

evasion of the conditions of real life. Actually, imagining, in this fiction, is rather an exposure of the idea to something like the full test of reality. There is no evidence that there was in Australia, at the time of the Lawrences' stay there, any such movement as is described in *Kangaroo*. But Lawrence must have felt, at some time during that Australian sojourn, strongly possessed by the suggestion that something extra-literary was required of him – have felt that *here*, in Australia, if his writings meant anything, was surely the opportunity. Kangaroo, the leader of the Diggers, has read Somers's political essays, and appeals to him on the strength of them. Jack Callcott says to him: 'You're the only man I've met who seems to me sure of himself and what he means.'

Lawrence shows all his wonderful quickness and penetration in dealing with Australian characteristics, and civilization in Australia. The same intelligence forbids him to deceive himself with any gross simplification of the reality. It is an intelligence that is inseparable from the integrity with which he exposes all his urgencies and convictions to the presence of the real Frieda – we feel her there in the book – and doesn't disguise how unanswerable he finds her scepticism and how undeniable her claim. He registers all the complexities and delicacies and doubts; the upshot is that there is no resolution of them: Harriet (or Frieda) is, in a sense, proved right about the particular political project, but Richard Lovat remains convinced that the impulsion that led him to contemplate it seriously represents something profoundly valid.

The complexity of attitude that makes *Kangaroo* so unlike a daydream in the discreditable sense is manifested in the subtlety and variety of the tone. Here is a passage from the chapter, called 'At Sea in Marriage', in which Richard Lovat examines himself in his relation with Harriet (the dialogue is imaginary):

'You!' she exclaimed. 'You a lord and master! Why, don't you know that I love you as no man ever was loved? You a lord and master! Ah! you look it! Let me tell you I love you far, far more than ever you ought to be loved, and you should acknowledge it.'

'I would rather,' said he, 'that you deferred your loving of me for a while, and considered a new proposition. We shall never sail any straight course at all, until you realize that I am lord and master, and you my blissful consort. Supposing, now, you had the real Hermes for a husband, Trismegistus. Would you not hold your tongue for fear you lost him, and change from being a lover, and be a worshipper? Well, I am not Hermes or Dionysus, but I am a little nearer to it than you allow. And I want you to yield to my mystery and my divination, and let me put my flag of a phoenix rising from a nest in flames in place of that old rose on a field azure. The gules are almost faded out.'

'It's a lovely design!' she cried, looking at the new flag. 'I might make a cushion-embroidery of it. But as a flag it's absurd. Of course, you lonely phoenix, you are the bird and the ashes and the flames all by yourself! You would be. Nobody else enters in at all. I – I am just nowhere – I don't exist.'

'Yes,' he said, 'you are the nest.'

'I'll watch it!' she cried. 'Then you shall sleep on thorns, Mister.'

'But consider,' he said.

'That's what I'm doing,' she replied. 'Mr Dionysus and Mr Hermes and Mr Thinks-himself-grand. I've got one thing to tell you. Without *me* you'd be nowhere, you'd be nothing, you'd not be *that*,' and she snapped her fingers under his nose, a movement he particularly disliked.

'I agree,' he replied, 'that without the nest the phoenix would be – would be nowhere, and couldn't find a stable spot to resurrect in. The nest is as the body to the soul: the cup that holds the fire, and in which the ashes fall to take form again. The cup is the container and the sustainer.'

'Yes, I've done enough containing and sustaining of you, my gentleman, in the years I've known you. It's almost time you left off wanting so much mothering. You can't live a moment without me.'

That tone, so characteristic of Lawrence, is a more remarkable thing than may at first appear; it should be examined in the whole chapter. It expresses an extraordinary poise and completeness of attitude. What might seem to be levity or humorous disengagement is an absence of bitterness and partiality, and not an absence of depth or of seriousness. I picked on the given passage because of the sentence: 'Well, I am not Hermes or Dionysus, but I am a little nearer to it than you allow.' 'Dionysus' gives us a motif that Lawrence more often utters and develops with a complete gravity. It represents the profoundest prompting of his genius and his profoundest sense of 'power' and 'responsibility'. It has its solemn utterance in *Kangaroo* as in *Women in Love* and *Aaron's Rod*, but all three novels exemplify Lawrence's astonishing flexibility of tone: the solemnity is offset by (say) Frieda's voice; by the characteristic Laurentian recognition of the complex and indocile reality; by that Laurentian comedy which has never a touch of the complacent or insensitive but is always the expression of supreme intelligence, with the self-knowledge which that involves.

Lawrence, however, can practise modes of art that lay him more open to temptations and weaknesses of a kind ordinarily associated with the word 'day-dream'. An instance very relevant to the present discussion is to be seen in the tale called *The Ladybird*. I had thought of including this tale among those to be examined in detail, and if I had done so I should, for the sake of contrast, have dealt with it immediately after *The Daughters of the Vicar*.[1] The vicar's protest that I quote[2] in closing the discussion of this last tale sounds like unmistakable Jane Austen. In fact, though it comes with perfect rightness in *The Daughters of the Vicar*, it derives, one may hazard, from Jane Austen in the sense that if Lawrence had not read her, we should not have had just this touch. Flexible as his art is, nothing so suggestive of Jane Austen could well have appeared in *The Ladybird*. This tale is in a mode of solemn poetic – even prophetic – elevation that entails a much narrower range of tones than is common in Lawrence. There is a very pronounced frame-effect, limiting the freedom of the reader's implicit reference from the world of the tale to the expectations and habits of ordinary everyday actuality. The extent to which this is to be so doesn't announce itself at once; the tale hasn't an opening as clearly indicative as that (for example) of *The Man Who Loved Islands*: 'There was a man who loved islands.' The characteristic high solemnity establishes itself in the evocation of the dreadful historical reality of war – war, death, and grief, and the background of ruined Europe:

How many swords had Lady Beveridge in her pierced heart! Yet there always seemed room for another. Since she had determined that her heart of pity and kindness should never die. If it had not been for this determination she herself might have died of sheer agony, in the years 1916 and 1917, when her boys were killed, and her brother, and death seemed to be moving wide swaths through her family. But let us forget.

An actual milieu of English political history and actual historical persons are recognizable behind the setting and the English characters

---

1. See Chapter 2: 'Lawrence and Class'.   2. See p. 98 below.

of Lawrence's tale; one can say: 'Yes, he had met them; he had corresponded with *her*; and he clearly found his creative cue *there*.' The observation – this is typical of one of the various kinds of perversity of comment that Lawrence has suffered from – can be offered us in the form of an irrelevant (even if it were just) adverse criticism. Thus in a book on Lawrence in which *The Ladybird* is judged to be 'another of the early failures' we read:

The basis of the characterization is Lawrence's extremely superficial knowledge of Lady Cynthia Asquith and her husband, and the story can be put in the category of gossip, though it is irresponsible rather than malicious.

The critic quotes:

And she, Lady Beveridge, had for years as much influence on the tone of English politics as any individual alive. The close friend of the real leaders in the House of Lords, and in the Cabinet, she was content that the men should act, so long as they breathed from her as from the rose of life the pure fragrance of truth and genuine love.

On this we get the comment:

Even those who can give their unreserved admiration for the political and social lives of Campbell-Bannerman and Asquith cannot think of the function of political hostesses quite in those terms. The foundation of the story is in fact poppycock.

The critic goes on to attribute to Lawrence the kind of class-feeling he so notably lacks: 'the political country-house world to which Edward Marsh introduced him dazzled him and all he seemed to notice was the small splash he made in it'.[1]

To make that of *The Ladybird* is, in the way so common where Lawrence is concerned, to refuse to read it. His imagination had undoubtedly been struck by the governing-class world of birth, breeding, and patrician distinction he had glimpsed; but to have made of his glimpse what he did is not, it seems to me, to have imagined arbitrarily or superficially; and as for his being 'dazzled', one might as well say that of Shakespeare, contemplating *his* treatment of birth, breeding,

---

1. See the note, 'Being an Artist', on p. 310 below.

and patrician distinction – themes to which (and no one blames him for it) his imagination responded. The reference to Shakespeare has its point: Lawrence's dealing with these themes are means to a poetic licence and concentration in the treatment of his essential theme; means, that is, to a kind of creative art so remote from anything like gossip – or critical reflections – about the civilization of the political country house in the time of Campbell-Bannerman and Asquith that it suggests rather (affinities being in question) *The Winter's Tale*.

The mode has to be recognized before the relevant criticisms can be made, and this is not the less so because these criticisms bear, as I have suggested, on weaknesses that the mode made it possible for Lawrence to pass as something else. In so far as it is diagnostic, the tale is strong. In Lady Beveridge's philanthropic idealism and its effects we recognize a familiar Laurentian theme. She stands to her daughter (and to her husband) as Thomas Crich, the coal-magnate in *Women in Love*, stands to his proudly passionate wife. Of Lady Daphne we are told that she 'was not born for grief and philanthropy', and cannot, as her mother does, have her life 'in her sorrows, and her efforts on behalf of the sorrows of others'.

That was what ailed her: her own wild energy. She had it from her father, and from her father's desperate race. The earldom had begun with a riotous, dare-devil border soldier, and this was the blood that flowed on. And alas, what was to be done with it?

Daphne had married an adorable husband: truly an adorable husband. Whereas she needed a dare-devil. But in her *mind* she hated all dare-devils: she had been brought up by her mother to admire only the good.

So, her reckless, anti-philanthropic passion could find no outlet – and *should* find no outlet, she thought. So her own blood turned against her, beat on her own nerves, and destroyed her. It was nothing but frustration and anger which made her ill, and made the doctors fear consumption. There it was, drawn on her rather wide mouth: frustration, anger, bitterness. There it was the same in the roll of her green-blue eyes, a slanting, averted look: the same anger furtively turning back on itself. This anger reddened her eyes and shattered her nerves. And yet, her whole will was fixed in her adoption of her mother's creed, and in condemnation of her handsome, proud, brutal father, who had made so much misery in the family. Yes, her will was fixed in the determination that life should be gentle and good and benevolent. Whereas her blood was reckless, the blood of dare-devils. Her will was the stronger of the two. But her blood had its revenge on her.

– 'her handsome, proud, brutal father, who had made so much misery in the family': what we have to observe and appraise is the full subtlety, and the sum, of the implicit evaluative attitudes that define themselves in the course of the tale. The 'brutal' father, we note, without judging yet that the adjective doesn't properly apply, is 'condemned' as such from the point of view of the will that 'life shall be gentle and good and benevolent': we know that we have to ask what, more than handsomeness and pride, there may be to set against the 'brutality'. That there *is* more we know already: 'dare-devil' unmistakably covers positives, and 'energy' here is not a mathematico-physical concept. Moreover, as concretely there in Lady Beveridge, the opposed 'good' is seen to involve something more complex than the 'mind' makes it – Lady Beveridge's mind or Lady Daphne's. When we examine the irony with which Lady Beveridge is presented we find the most delicate evaluative precision. 'She had', we are told, 'no misgiving regarding her own spirit.' The sense in which misgiving would have been in place is not one that disposes of that spirit as impressive and admirable. And that we are to regard Lady Beveridge's 'influence on the tone of English politics' with unironical respect we cannot doubt. But there is more, we perceive, to her 'spirit' than her mind recognizes, and her influence is not merely a matter of her pure ideals and their intrinsic power. The picking-up of the word 'spirit' a dozen lines later is only apparently careless: the new impersonal context effects no disjunction; rather, the word as used in connexion with her acquires a stronger relevant charge:

The years 1916 and 1917 were the years when the old spirit died for ever in England. But Lady Beveridge struggled on. She was being beaten.

It was in the winter of 1917 – or in the late autumn. She had been for a fortnight sick, stricken, paralysed by the death of her youngest boy. She felt she *must* give in and just die. And then she remembered how many others were lying in agony.

So she rose, trembling, frail, to pay a visit to the hospital where lay the enemy sick and wounded, near London. Countess Beveridge was still a privileged woman. Society was beginning to jeer at this little, worn bird of an out-of-date righteousness and aesthetic. But they dared not think ill of her.

If they dared not think ill of her, that was not merely because of the intrinsic power of her ideals; and what in her personality awed them was, on the one hand, not mere benevolence, and, on the other, was associated with something impersonal. This becomes plain in the next paragraph:

So, on a sunny, warm November morning Lady Beveridge descended at the hospital, Hurst Place. The guard knew her, and saluted as she passed. Ah, she was used to such deep respect! It was strange that she felt it so bitterly, when the respect became shallower. But she did. It was the beginning of the end to her.

She is an aristocrat; in her philanthropy she is, without self-question, essentially that. In her will that men shall 'breathe from her as from the rose of life the pure fragrance of truth and genuine love' she affirms her profound allegiance to something other than these ideals. Her profound implicit belief is aristocratic. It is a belief so profound that she is not conscious of it; but she cares immensely about the 'deep respect' she has been used to. One can say that she values power and resents its loss, though the tale makes no such simple judgement. One can say that she values power because of the good it enables her to do; but this would be to simplify what is actually communicated. 'Power' is less the right word than 'authority', and this has to be associated with 'belief' and 'responsibility' – the later discussion between Basil and Count Dionys is very relevant:

'Obedience, submission, faith, belief, responsibility, power,' he said slowly, picking out the words slowly, as if searching for what he wanted, and never quite finding it.

In fact, Lady Beveridge doesn't represent so complete an antithesis to her husband as might appear. The Earl's pride, it has been made plain, is more than egotistic self-assertion; it is a conviction of sanctioned authority, and this conviction is inseparable from an impassioned sense of responsibility – responsibility for life, or, as the Earl might have put it, for honour and decency in the life of the country. These things may not be – they clearly are not – identifiable with his wife's 'truth' and 'love'; but her 'truth' and 'love' are less all-sufficient, she has implicitly to recognize, than her idealistic 'faith' and will have proposed to make them.

What, then, was this authority (this something more, surely, than mere privilege) which she herself, standing for 'truth' and 'love', has actually relied on, and which, in the England of the Horatio Bottomleys – to prescribe for whom 'truth' and 'love' would be obviously absurd – is now failing her? In what terms other than the merely negative are we, contemplating this malady of modern civilization, to express and explain the inadequacy of 'love'? The tale asks these questions; they are involved in its essential theme. For what *The Ladybird* gives us is not a narrowly personal drama, enacted by characters whom the author has chosen to make aristocrats because aristocracy is glamorous and lends itself to an exalted fairy-tale dignity of convention, or because, having (by favour of Eddie Marsh) glimpsed high life, he has a naïve and resentful bedazzlement to work off. That the English characters are governing-class and recall an actual milieu important in recent English history – these *données* are essential to the full intended significance, which registers Lawrence's preoccupation with the state of England (and Europe) at the end of the First World War.

It is in the largeness, the inclusiveness, of the preoccupation that we see the peculiar danger of the mode of the tale for Lawrence. The themes are those of *Aaron's Rod* and *Kangaroo*, but there is none of that supple freedom of treatment, none of that testing fulness of recognition of the complexities in his own experience and attitude, which, where in those novels the prophetic role is concerned, gives us for summary of the upshot: 'Well, I am not Hermes and Dionysus.' And we come now to Count Johann Dionys Psanek.

We cannot say he is Lawrence, if only because in Lawrence the 'Dionysus' has a great deal of varied company. And actually he is a convincing dramatic presence as someone other than Lawrence himself. The tale, in fact, has a large measure of success. In Lady Daphne's visits to the wounded Count in the hospital where her mother has discovered him we see a boldly poetic-symbolic art defining itself and defining its themes. There lies the dark, strange little enemy alien, recognizable as the dapper social figure of pre-war house-parties, but so different – so remote, it seems, from the human world in the border-land of death from which he has no will to return. The abnormality of his state of extreme weakness – 'he lay there a bit of loose, palpitating humanity, shot away from the body of humanity' – provides, to begin with, the licence for the poetic audacities of his speech (audacities of imagination, seeing that this is dialogue in modern prose fiction; and, addressed to Lady Daphne, unconventional liberties).

In the ensuing colloquies it is conveyed to us that the contrast (she being, in her famous beauty, tall and blonde) and the accompanying surface antagonism cover some deep understanding between them – the significance of which is symbolized in the scarab and snake of the thimble, his gift to her that she preserves from her girlhood. Repre-senting, in his dark unknownness, the profound energies and potentiali-ties of life that the conscious mind can only either serve or thwart, he represents, not the absence of 'consciousness', but rather the necessary vital intelligence that, serving the whole life, can detect and expose the usurpations of will and 'idea'. (There is something more to be said about what Count Dionys represents, but I leave that aside for the moment.) His influence, exerted first in her *tête-à-tête* encounters with him, and then when she visits him with Basil, her husband now back from the Turkish prison-camp, brings her to a recognition of the na-ture of her malady and enables her to free herself from the 'stone tab-lets of consciousness'. She realizes, not only that her mother's ideal love, which in her mind she has adopted, violates her nature, but that her husband's love-worship ('adoration-lust'), with which is associated her own worship of her own mirrored and photographed beauty, can pro-duce only worn nerves and intolerable life-exhausting unsatisfaction. She needs, not a 'spiritually intense' adoring husband, but one who stands for something other than love as an ultimate *raison d'être*.

The diagnosis of Lady Daphne's case is convincing. It is in the con-clusion, in so far as we seem to be offered something more positive than diagnosis, that we find ourselves moved to critical reflection. To what satisfactory conclusion, we cannot help asking at that point, could the tale in any case have been brought? Count Dionys, it is true, represents the dark 'power' that is lacking in Basil, and we are left in no doubt that Dionys and Daphne are fitting mates; but a resolution of the 'wicked triangle' by divorce and re-marriage is clearly out of the question. The tale doesn't move on the plane of such denouements; it is too portentous, too large, in the kind of significance it has proposed. And here we come to the further point to be made about Count Dionys.

It is not enough to say that he represents the dark potency of life that is denied in the 'white-faced, spiritually intense' Basil. There is the whole implication, the whole intention, that is focussed in the discussion between the two men. 'You must use another word than love,' he says to Basil, who talks of the 'extraordinary variety of forms' that love takes as the 'power that draws human beings together'; and, when Daphne 'blurts' 'What word then?' he replies: 'Obedience, submission, faith, belief, responsibility, power – picking out the words slowly, as if seeking for what he wanted, and never quite finding it.' He has just asked Basil: 'Do you think the old Egypt was established on love?' and the context makes it plain that he stands for all the promptings of 'power' in Lawrence's genius, those which will not let Lawrence escape from the sense that he has the responsibilities of a 'greater soul' and a leader.

Lawrence tries in *Kangaroo* to imagine a translation of these promptings into terms of action, and records the failure. Plainly, what he fails to do there cannot possibly be done in such a tale as *The Ladybird*; all he can do here, in fact, faced with the problem of concluding, is to move, finally, out of all ostensible relation to actuality. We have already seen a Hermes-Dionysus virtually accepted in his 'power' by a woman-aristocrat as Lawrence was *not* by Frieda; to marry Lady Daphne to Dionys wouldn't clinch any convincing significance. It could only expose the limitation of the tale in respect of its larger suggestion. To enforce that suggestion would be to have made us believe in a Dionys whose dark 'power' was going to engage on the problems of contemporary civilization in ways that, exploring them imaginatively in *Kangaroo*, Lawrence cannot believe in for his own genius. Dionys is not even a great writer.

Lawrence, then, cannot challenge the tests of reality so closely as to marry Daphne to Dionys. The tale early established a subtly equivocal relation to the world of the 'day-mood' – the 'day-mood of human convention', and the lapse into *märchen* and nocturnal incantation in the close of the tale, when the three, Daphne, Basil, and Dionys, are left alone together at Thoresway, the enchanted Elizabethan mansion, with its diamond-paned windows, its dark corridors, and its glamorous surroundings of English countryside, is easy and natural. Daphne, nerve-worn, suffers from insomnia. She overhears the Count, in the night, singing to himself the weird folksongs of his childhood, and irresistibly attracted, we are told, goes to his room. The song she has just heard, he tells her, is about a swan who became a woman and married a hunter by the marsh, and was finally, in the night, called back by the king of the swans. This figures plainly enough the actual close of the tale, and tells us to what order of reality the scene in the Count's room belongs: between Daphne's listening entranced to the incantation of the folk-theme and the trance in which, she being the swan-woman, the theme (as it were) is enacted there is no clear distinction. As he sits in the dark, an 'Egyptian King-god', she kneels at his feet, and what she hears him say defines (if that is the word) the more than personal relation between them:

'In the dark you are mine. And when you die you are mine. But in the day you are not mine, because I have no power in the day. In the night, in the dark, and in death, you are mine. And when you die you are mine. And that is forever. No matter if I must leave you. ...When the darkness comes I shall always be in the darkness of you.'

Again:

'If you are true to me, innerly true, he will not hurt us. He is generous, be generous to him. And never fail to believe in me. Because even on the other side of death I shall be watching for you. I shall be king in Hades when I am dead. And you will be at my side. You will never leave me any more, in the after-death. So don't be afraid in life. ... And so, in your heart of hearts be still, be still, since you are the wife of the lady-bird.'

This close of the tale, it can be said, completes the definition of the essential relations between the three main actors, a novelistic resolution of the theme being out of the question; and we have in *The Ladybird* – we have it in the insistence on the 'darkness' and in Dionys's references to 'the after-death' and to his being 'King in Hades' – a dimension that a novelistic treatment wouldn't permit. And certainly, the opening and middle of the tale are in their way remarkable achievements. Yet, in the close they lead to, we must feel there is something in the nature of evasion: instead of the frank inconclusiveness of *Aaron's Rod* and *Kangaroo*, we have this show of something positive and confident which, when we recall the larger suggestion of the tale, must affect us as something like an attempt to conjure the actual world, with its tests and problems, away. There is a betraying obviousness – it is of the order of sentimentality – about the quality of the final, would-be clinching, incantations.

Certain other tales of Lawrence's in modes that exclude his characteristic play of varied tone and prescribe a sustained solemnity are open to criticism of essentially the same order. *Glad Ghosts* and *The Border Line* may be instanced. But the supreme related case is the full novel, *The Plumed Serpent*.

Looking back from *The Plumed Serpent*, we can see how *Kangaroo* leads up to it. The exploration of the possibility of political action in *Kangaroo* is, in its characteristic intelligence, unillusioned, for all its spirit (so touching and warming) of a personal responsibility that impels to personal engagement:

> And yet he felt that preaching and teaching were both no good, at the world's present juncture. There must be action, brave, faithful action: and in the action the new spirit would arise.

The analysis of Australian democracy is penetrating, and the presentment of 'revolutionary' scheming and political discussion of very great interest, though I find Kangaroo himself, the leader who counts on Somers to take over, curiously unqualified to affect him (or Lawrence) as powerfully as we are asked to suppose him doing. We are not, however, asked to suppose Somers ever in imminent danger of committing himself to the 'revolution'; his disbelief in mere political movements is too profound. The attraction for him of the Diggers' movement is that it offers to be more than political. Kangaroo and Willie Struthers talk about the 'love of mates', and Somers responds to the extent that his heart is 'big within him, swollen in his breast', believing, as he does, the 'working people capable of a great, generous love for one another':

All this political socialism – all politics, in fact – have conspired to make money the only good. It has been a great treacherous conspiracy against the heart of the people. And that heart is betrayed: and knows it. [Chapter XI]

But here comes in the rejection of love as an absolute:

because every individuality is bound to react at some time against every other individuality, without exception – or else lose its individuality; because of the inevitable necessity of each individual to react away from any other individual, at certain times, human love is truly a relative thing, not an absolute. It *cannot* be absolute.

Yet the human heart must have an absolute. It is one of the conditions of being human. The only thing is the God who is the source of all passion. Once go down before the God-passion and human passions take their right rhythm. But human love without the God-passion always kills the thing it loves. Men and women are virtually killing each other with the love-will now. What would it be when mates, or comrades, broke down in their absolute love and trust? Because, without the polarized God-passion to hold them stable at the centre, break down they would. With no deep God who is source of all passion and life to hold them separate and yet sustained in accord, the loving comrades would smash one another, and smash all love, all feeling as well.

Willie Struthers argues that the movement *has* its religious basis:

'You see,' stammered Richard, 'it needs more than a belief of men in each other.'

'But what else is there to believe in? Quacks? Medicine-men? Scientists and politicians?'

'It *does* need some sort of religion.'

'Well then – well then – the religious question is ticklish, especially here in Australia. But all the churches are established in Christ. And Christ says Love one another.'

Richard laughed suddenly.

'That makes Christ into another political agent,' he said.

And in the next paragraph we have a statement of Richard's grounds for not coming into the revolutionary scheme; a statement the terms of which point straight on to *The Plumed Serpent*:

Richard was silent, his heart heavy. It all seemed so far from the dark god he wished to serve, the god from whom the dark, sensual passion of love emanates, not only the spiritual love of Christ. He wanted men once more to refer the sensual passion of love sacredly to the great dark God, the ithyphallic, of the first dark religions. And how could that be done, when each dry little individual ego was just mechanically set against any such dark flow, such ancient submission. As for instance Willie Struthers at this minute, Struthers didn't mind Christ. Christ could easily be made to subserve his egoistic purpose. But the first, dark, ithyphallic God whom men had once known so tremendous – Struthers had no use for Him.

The Plumed Serpent is an attempt to prove, in imaginative enactment, that the revival of the necessary religion is possible. There is no need to discuss the book in detail; it is the least complex of all Lawrence's novels (unless we bracket the very different *Lady Chatterley's Lover* with it), and it is the only one that I find difficult to read through. Not that there aren't good things in it, striking and characteristic manifestations of the author's genius. There is the bull-fight in the opening, with that presentment of Owen, Kate's American cousin, which throws so much light on Mr Witter Bynner's *Journey with Genius*; there is the tea-party in Tlacolula at which Kate meets Judge and Mrs Burlap and other 'old residents' of Mexico City; there is the attack on Jamiltepec. But *The Plumed Serpent* has none of that flexibility of mode and mood for which the preceding novels are remarkable; it is single-mindedly intent on imagining, as a piece of contemporary history, a revival of the ancient Mexican religion. The complexities of attitude in Lawrence are played down – for complexities there inevitably are, and the evidence of them has not been wholly eliminated from the book, of which 'single-minded' is a description that would have to be qualified in a full analysis. But the deeper governing intention or impulse has clearly been to escape as much as possible from that inner drama of doubts and self-questionings and partial recoils which, the evidence of *Aaron's Rod* and *Kangaroo* so amply proves, would have made sustained imaginative conviction in such an enterprise as *The Plumed Serpent* impossible.

And here we have an answer to a question that naturally occurs to anyone who reads the novels in succession: Why should the main character, the centre of sympathetic interest and the dramatized consciousness through which things are presented, be, in this book, a woman? A man as imaginative centre would inevitably have been a

Rawson Lilly or a Richard Lovat Somers, and inevitably have been involved in Lawrence's relations with Frieda – and so in all the disabling complexities of attitude. Kate Leslie, though not too distantly related to her, is not Frieda. She is a good-looking and impressive widow of forty whose second husband, married after her divorce from her first, was an Irish patriot. 'With Joachim', she tells Cipriano, 'I came to realize that a woman like me *can* only love a man who is fighting to *change* the world, to make it freer, more alive.'

But she has now come to realize also that fighting for Ireland, fighting for 'liberty', is not the right way of trying to 'change the world': and Mexico, Don Ramón tells her, 'is another Ireland'. She it is, then, who has to be persuaded to commit herself in the completest way to a belief in the possibility of restoring the old Gods and reviving the old ithyphallic religion. And she does, in fact, marry Cipriano, the living Huitzilopochtli, and enter into the pantheon. The dark little Cipriano, for all the ostensible difference between a barbaric Indian and a sophisticated European aristocrat, bears a very close resemblance to Count Dionys.[1] It is to be noted, however, that Cipriano is not himself the supreme world-saviour; he is second in command to Don Ramón, the living Quetzalcoatl, whom we certainly do not take for Lawrence, and in whom we are not very much interested (nor, in fact, are we in Cipriano himself).

Lawrence, then, in *The Plumed Serpent*, avoids the directness and obviousness of personal engagement that characterizes *Kangaroo*. A consequence that was not intended is that the book gives the effect of his not being *fully* engaged. The evoking of the pagan renaissance strikes one as willed and mechanical; at any rate, it is monotonous and boring. The descriptions of rituals and costumes and dances and ceremonies fill immense areas of print; and there are pages upon pages of chants and hymns that one feels Lawrence must have written very easily, and so

1. Cipriano's 'power' as the dominant 'Pan male' is evoked in Chapter XX in some peculiarly bad prose, the quality of which gets its implicit comment later in the same chapter in this passage, with its insistent 'must':

'"Shame?" laughed Ramón. "Ah, Señora Caterina, why shame? This is a thing that *must* be done. There must be manifestations. We *must* change back to the vision of the living cosmos. We *must*. The oldest Pan is in us, and he will not be denied."'

perhaps with pleasure – the reader tends to skip them. It is by a kind of incantation, a hypnotic effect figured in the endless pulsing of drums playing so large a part in Don Ramón's campaign, that Lawrence tries to generate conviction, and he produces boredom and a good deal of distaste. That he himself has his own recoils and repugnances we are made to feel unmistakably enough. They are expressed in his strongly conveyed sense of the sinisterness of this Mexican world. And they are expressed in Kate's own recoils and hesitations.

> 'Oh!' she cried to herself, stifling. 'For heaven's sake let me get out of this, and back to simple human people. I loathe the very sound of Quetzalcoatl and Huitzilopochtli. I would die rather than be mixed up with it any more. Horrible, really, both Ramón and Cipriano. And they want to put it over me, with their high-flown bunk.' [Chapter XXII]

Her alleged final conviction, when in the close she decides to stay in Mexico as the bride of the living Huitzilopochtli, is not convincing. And the ground that gives the decision what plausibility it has is too much a matter of Kate's recoiling from the fate of the ageing dominant woman:

> It is all very well for a woman to cultivate her ego, her individuality. It is all very well for her to despise love, or to love love as a cat loves a mouse that it plays with as long as possible, before devouring it to vivify her own individuality and voluptuously fill the belly of her own ego.
> 'Woman has suffered far more from the suppression of her ego than from sex suppression', says a woman writer, and it may well be true. But look, only look at the modern woman of fifty and fifty-five, those who have cultivated their ego to the top of their bent! Usually, they are grimalkins to fill one with pity or with repulsion.
> Kate knew all this. And as she sat alone in her villa she remembered it again. She had had her fling, even here in Mexico. And these men would let her go again. She was no prisoner. She could carry off any spoil she had captured.
> And then what! To sit in a London drawing-room, and add another to all the grimalkins? To let the peculiar grimalkin-grimace come on her face, the most weird grimalkin-twang come into her voice? Horror! Of all the horrors, perhaps the grimalkinwomen, her contemporaries, were the most repellent to her. Even the horrid old tom-cat men of the civilized roof-gutters did not fill her with such sickly dread.

'No!' she said to herself. 'My ego and my individuality are not worth *that* ghastly price. I'd better abandon some of my ego, and sink some of my individuality, rather than go like that.'

It is not merely that Kate has not struck us as having anything in her of the Mrs Witt of *St Mawr*; it is that to give this fear the decisive part in Kate's conquest of her repugnance to the 'high-flown bunk' and its accompaniments is not to promote the kind of convincingness that *The Plumed Serpent* clearly aims at. It suggests rather a failure in Lawrence to convince himself that the conquest would ever have been achieved. And in its sustained earnest intentness *The Plumed Serpent* as a whole rings false.

That the un-Flaubertian strength in art of Lawrence's genius should be offset by some related imperfections and defaults might seem to have been almost inevitable. And the way in which that genius found its challenge in the problems of contemporary civilized life necessarily involved failures. To have found, as he contemplated human life, or lives, in the contemporary world, the answers he was looking for, Lawrence would have had to be more than a great creative writer – he would have had to be something hardly conceivable. His diagnoses are almost always irresistible, and they involve, of course, the presentment and affirmation of norms and positives. But his art sometimes cherishes the illusion that it grasps and presents more in the way of positive 'answer' to the large issues raised than it actually does. It is then that we make our severest criticisms.

But for how little the things that call for such criticisms count in the whole body of Lawrence's work. It is an immense body of living creation in which a supreme vital intelligence is the creative spirit – a spirit informed by an almost infallible sense for health and sanity. Itself it educates for the kind of criticism that here and there it challenges – it provides the incitement and the criteria. And the marvellous creative intelligence continues in full activity to the end, for *The Plumed Serpent* is far from signifying the close of Lawrence's production of great art.

And the spirit that animates this later work, as it animates his work as a whole, is what is expressed with expository directness and simple lucidity in *À Propos of Lady Chatterley's Lover*, that final statement of position which, though its poise and vitality of intelligence yield no hint of it, he wrote when there was little between him and death.[1] The pamphlet, I ought to say, seems to me to compel more certainly a wholly approving judgement than the novel it defends. *Lady Chatterley's Lover* is a courageous, profoundly sincere, and very deliberate piece of work; if it errs, it is not through lack of calculation. The trouble lies in its being in certain ways *too* deliberate – too deliberate, at any rate, to be a wholly satisfactory work of art, appealing to imaginatively sensitized feeling. What may be called the hygienic undertaking to which it is devoted commands one's sympathy – the undertaking to cleanse the obscene words and to redeem from the smirch of obscenity the corresponding physical facts. But the willed insistence on the words and facts must, it seems to me, whatever the intention, have something unacceptable, something offensive, about it; it offends, surely, against Lawrence's own canons – against the spirit of his creativity and against the moral and emotional ethic that he in essence stands for. He felt that here there was something so urgent to be done that it *must* be done, whatever the cost. But that there *is* a cost – that, I think, needs to be said. I make some further observations that have relevance to this point in discussing, later in this book, *The Virgin and the Gypsy*.[2]

There is much that is admirable about *Lady Chatterley's Lover*. The spirit that animates the book is that strong vital instinct of health to which I have just referred as the spirit of Lawrence's genius. He relates his special theme with great power to the malady of industrial civilization. And the deep earnestness of his preoccupation appears in the description of Tevershall, seen (and heard) by Lady Chatterley as she passes through it in her car – a description that should be a *locus classicus* (I quote it along with the succeeding passage, 'England my England!' – the prose has a strong and nervous vitality of a kind that ought to be known as characteristically Laurentian):

The car ploughed uphill through the long squalid straggle of Tevershall, the blackened brick dwellings, the black slate roofs glistening their sharp edges, the mud black with coal-dust, the pavements wet and black. It was as if dismalness had soaked through and through everything. The utter negation of natural

1. It has now been reprinted in *Sex, Literature and Censorship*, edited by Harry T. Moore.

2. See pp. 304–5 below.

beauty, the utter negation of the gladness of life, the utter absence of the instinct
for shapely beauty which every bird and beast has, the utter death of the human
intuitive faculty was appalling. The stacks of soap in the grocer's shops, the
rhubarb and lemons in the greengrocers! the awful hats in the milliners! all
went by ugly, ugly, ugly, followed by the plaster and gilt horror of the cinema
with its wet picture announcements, 'A Woman's Love', and the new big
Primitive chapel, primitive enough in its stark brick and big panes of greenish
and raspberry glass in the windows. The Wesleyan chapel, higher up, was of
blackened brick and stood behind iron railings and blackened shrubs. The
Congregational chapel which thought itself superior, was built of rusticated
sandstone and had a steeple, but not a very high one. Just beyond were the new
school buildings, expensive pink brick, and gravelled play-ground inside iron
railings, all very imposing, and mixing the suggestion of a chapel and a prison.
Standard Five girls were having a singing lesson, just finishing the la-me-doh-la
exercises and beginning a 'sweet children's song'. Anything more unlike song,
spontaneous song, would be impossible to imagine: a strange bawling yell followed the outlines of a tune. It was not like savages: savages have subtle
rhythms. It was not like animals: animals *mean* something when they yell. It was
like nothing on earth, and it was called singing. Connie sat and listened with
her heart in her boots, as Field was filling petrol. What could possibly become
of such people, a people in whom the living intuitive faculty was dead as nails,
and only queer mechanical yells and uncanny will-power remained. ...

England my England! but which is *my* England? The stately homes of England
make good photographs and create the illusion of a connexion with the Eliza-
bethans. The handsome old halls are there, from the days of good Queen Anne
and Tom Jones. But smuts fall and blacken on the drab stucco, that has long
ceased to be golden. And one by one, like the stately homes, they are abandoned.
Now they are pulling down the stately homes, the Georgian halls are going.
Fritchley, a perfect old Georgian mansion, was even now, as Connie passed in
the car, being demolished. It was in perfect repair: till the war the Weatherleys
had lived in style there. But now it was too big, too expensive, and the country
had become too uncongenial. The gentry were departing to pleasanter places,
where they could spend their money without having to see how it was made.

This is history. One England blots out another. The mines had made the halls
wealthy. Now they were blotting them out, as they had already blotted out the
cottages. The industrial England blots out the agricultural England. One meaning blots out another. The new England blots out the old England. And the
continuity is not organic, but mechanical.

2

Of the shorter forms of prose fiction – short story and longer tale –
Lawrence is surely the supreme master. His genius manifests itself there
with an authority of original power, and an astonishing maturity, from
the start. And, before examining *The Rainbow*, I want to enforce this
judgement in a detailed study of one of the earlier tales: I want to show
what he can do (for oddly enough, it seems necessary) where, in that
early phase of *The White Peacock* and *Sons and Lovers*, his genius as a
creative writer is most undeniable.

The Prussian Officer came out in 1914, so that the stories it collects
were written during his first creative years. It is easy to understand that
the disturbing sensuous intensity with which the psychological insight
of such things as the title story and *The Thorn in the Flesh* is conveyed
should have made a great impression. But the tale that I wish to consider, *The Daughters of the Vicar*, seems to have escaped notice. I choose
it because it is representative of Lawrence's genius in a central and profound way, and because it provides a peculiarly effective answer to
some misconceptions about him that are still current.

One read in the *Listener* in 1953 (13 August) of an 'aspect' of Lawrence that had been 'quite adequately summed up by Mr Eliot'. The
summing-up then quoted is this: 'no man was ever more conscious of
class-distinctions'. *The Daughters of the Vicar*, I say, is profoundly representative of Lawrence, and class-distinctions enter as a major element
into its theme. The man who wrote it may certainly be said to have been
very conscious of them. But the consciousness of class-distinctions expressed in *The Daughters of the Vicar* is precisely a consciousness that we
have to define as wholly incompatible with snobbery or any related form
of class-feeling. Lawrence registers them as facts that play an important
part in human life. The part they play in the given tale is a sinister one,
and the theme is their defeat – the triumph over them of life.

It is one of the difficulties of criticism that the critic has to use such phrases as that last. It is one of the advantages of having such a creative achievement as *The Daughters of the Vicar* to deal with that the phrase gets its force in the tale, the movement and sum of which define 'life' in the only way in which it *can* be defined for the purposes of the critic: he has the tale – its developing significance and the concrete particulars of its organization – to point to. And I come now to two other charges (besides that of snobbery) brought against Lawrence in *After Strange Gods*. Adducing, as evidence, from the collection that contains *The Daughters of the Vicar*, a story called *The Shadow in the Rose Garden*, Mr Eliot attributes to Lawrence an 'alarming strain of cruelty'. In the same book he speaks of the 'absence of any moral or social sense' in the 'relations of Lawrence's men and women' – who, he says, 'are supposed to be recognizably human beings'. And the treatment in general of Lawrence in the book makes it plain that he means to convict Lawrence of crude insensitiveness and a certain subhumanity, to be in large measure explained (he suggests) by uncouthness of upbringing in conditions of cultural privation – cultural barbarity.

I recall these unpleasant things from that curious book of twenty years ago, because (apart from the major fact of history, that Mr Eliot's attitude towards Lawrence has had great influence – a fact that is not wholly of the past) they have their bearing on the charge of snobbery, and the exposure of their perversity is involved in the due treatment of that charge. For that *The Daughters of the Vicar* doesn't crudely indulge any snob bent is perhaps so plain that it doesn't need arguing; what may with profit be pondered is the intrinsic incompatibility of the radical and essential qualities of the tale, which are radical and essential qualities of Lawrence, with anything in the nature of snobbery.

Class, the villain of the drama, is represented by the proud classsuperiority of the impoverished vicar's family. We know of course that Lawrence grew up in a working-class environment. But the only evidence of that fact in *The Daughters of the Vicar* is the inwardness and the freedom from any form, direct or inverted, of sentimentality or idealization with which we are given the world of the cottage and the mine. And in the presentment of the vicarage too we have the same effect of classless truth. But it is not enough to say that, in this presentment, we can detect no faintest hint of animus: that doesn't suggest the poise and fineness of the actual attitude. The pride of class-superiority – and class at the vicarage is essentially that – appears as the enemy of life, starving and thwarting and denying, and breeding in consequence hate and ugliness. The mother, baulked in the assertion of her birthright of superiority, trapped in poverty and social isolation, humiliated, rages inwardly, sees herself hating her husband and becoming an uncontrollable destructive force, and finds a kind of safety from herself in invalidism. The vicar, hardly meeting even with resistance in this un-deferential collier-community which has no use for him, falls into 'conscious hatred of the majority and unconscious hatred of himself'. The superiority that exacts this terrible price is shown to us in all its nothingness. The ugliness bred in the clinging to it appear repellently for what they are. The unbeautiful pride places itself as hateful in its manifestations and as essentially destructive of all fineness and nobility. And yet it appears as having something heroic about it – something almost tragic. That is, the attitude implicit in the presentation of the drama is not one that goes with contemptuous exposure or satiric con-demnation; it is more subtle and poised – it is one that is incompatible with complacency or cruelty in any form. Of the vicar's children we are told:

> The children grew up healthy, but unwarmed and rather rigid. Their father and mother educated them at home, made them very proud and very genteel, put them definitely and cruelly in the upper classes, apart from the vulgar around them. So they lived quite isolated. They were good-looking, and had that curiously clean, semi-transparent look of the genteel, isolated poor.

Lawrence is the greatest kind of creative writer; it can be said of him, as of Flaubert or T. S. Eliot it cannot, that his radical attitude towards life is positive; looking for a term with which to indicate its nature, we have to use 'reverence'. But 'reverence' must not be allowed to suggest any idealizing bent; and if we say that the reverence expresses itself in a certain essential tenderness, we don't mean that Lawrence is 'tender-minded' or in the least sentimentally given. The attitude is one of strength, and it is clairvoyant and incorruptible in its preoccupation with realities. It expresses, of course, the rare personal adequacy of an individual of genius, but it is also the product of a fine and mature civilization, the sanctions, the valuations, and the pieties of which speak through the individual. So far from tenable is the view of Lawrence as an uncouth and arrogant genius brought up in cultural barbarism. And it is hard to respect the conception of proper training or of tradition that finds a superiority of moral sensibility over Lawrence in Wyndham Lewis, Pound, or Joyce.

'Reverence' and 'life', the large terms I have used in referring to the positive of Lawrence's attitude, get their definition in the course of the tale. As the ugliness bred by the thwarting of life takes on its most sinister form, at the same time the positive becomes insistent, and its significance begins to define itself for recognition. Mr Massy appears. 'What a little abortion!' – that gives the effect on Mrs Lindley, desperate mother of two daughters, when she first sees him. The eagerly awaited young clergyman of good family and private means who has in prospect a living with 'a good stipend' and is unmarried turns out to be this. Of Mrs Lindley we are told that 'for the first time for many days she was profoundly thankful to God that all her children were decent specimens'. This natural reaction – natural even in the warped and bitter Mrs Lindley – has a profounder significance than the conventional 'class' phrasing in which it expresses itself recognizes or suggests: that this is so is conveyed by the incongruous (if equally convincing and conventional) 'profoundly thankful to God', the weight of which we accept as truly appropriate. In the way in which the significance is developed and its profundity and scope are brought out we have the distinctive Laurentian insight. How early and how easily this seems to have achieved its full penetration, established its connexions – the relations between this aspect and that, and confirmed itself as a sure and full understanding! Here in *The Daughters of the Vicar*, before any statement in discursive and expository generalities, we have unmistakably, in the concrete presentment, the analysis that we associate with 'will', 'ideas', 'ideals', 'mental consciousness', and 'body'. There is no suggestion of the esoteric; it all seems, as we read, to be done in terms of ordinary observation.

Mrs Lindley readily overcomes the natural aversion she feels for Mr Massy, though besides his physical repulsiveness ('his body was unthinkable') he has also some non-physical characteristics that make him peculiarly trying company: he 'lacks the full range of human feelings', but has a decided philosophical mind, and a purely rational habit in conversation.

The little man would look at her, after one of her pronouncements, and then give, in his thin voice, his own calculated version, so that she felt as if she were tumbling into thin air through the flimsy floor on which their conversation stood.

She feels a fool, but has no difficulty in remembering, 'at the back of her mind', that he is 'an unattached gentleman, who will shortly have an income altogether of six or seven hundred a year'. This is the matron who, with all the mean righteousness of class-superiority, has commented on old Mrs Durant's grief at losing to the Navy Alfred, her youngest son, whom she wanted to keep at home: 'What does she care for her children's welfare? Their wages is all her concern.' Mr Massy, the 'little abortion', is a gentleman and he has money: 'What did the man matter if there was pecuniary ease?' The nothingness of the abstract superiority to which so much has been sacrificed, leaving a nothingness – the 'horrible nothingness of their lives' which chills and hardens the girls' hearts with fear, is here enacted by Mrs Lindley. It is enacted by her when she endorses as the salvation of the family Mr Massy, who is a gentleman and has money and for whom nothing else can be said – or for whom Mrs Lindley doesn't need to find anything else to say.

Miss Mary, the elder girl, with her 'proud, pure look of submission to a high fate', does, in fact, find that there is more to be said for him. If he is to figure as an escape from the 'horrible nothingness' for anyone, it must be for her, not for Miss Louisa. Louisa, plump and obstinate-looking, has 'more enemies than ideals': for her the natural aversion that Mr Massy inspires is, unequivocally, the essential and final fact; she cannot conceive any consideration that could cancel or qualify it. The positive aspect of what is presented here in negative terms appears in her strong feeling, which she characteristically admits to herself without shame, for Alfred Durant, the young collier who, to her grief as well as his mother's, goes off and joins the Navy. The nature of the attraction he has for her is defined with great delicacy and precision. He is significantly opposed to Mr Massy in the scene by his dying father's bedside.

The vicar's daughters escort Mr Massy on the visit of parish duty. 'Miss Louisa was crudely ashamed at being admitted to the cottage with the little clergyman.' While they are there Alfred arrives on leave to see his father. But though Mr Massy looks almost obliterated in the presence of the sunburnt sailor, he asserts himself as a force when he offers a prayer: he

prayed with a pure lucidity, that they might all conform to the higher Will. He was like something that dominated the bowed heads, something dispassionate that governed them inexorably. Miss Louisa was afraid of him. And she was bound, during the course of the prayer, to have a little reverence for him.

This is the Mr Massy in her reverence for whom Miss Mary can find strong enough grounds for discrediting her physical repugnance. Miss Louisa, on the other hand, her feeling centred upon Alfred, has, underneath, 'the deeper dread of the inhuman being of Mr Massy'. She feels 'she must protect herself and Alfred from him'. As for the attraction that Alfred has for her, it is certainly physical, but how little is said about it in saying that, this account of the effect of the episode on her brings out:

That evening she talked to Mary of the visit. Her heart, her veins were possessed by the thought of Alfred Durant as he held his mother in his arms; then the break in his voice, as she remembered it again and again, was like a flame through her; and she wanted to see his face more distinctly in her mind, ruddy with the sun, and his golden-brown eyes, kind and careless, strained now with a natural fear, the fine nose tanned hard by the sun, the mouth that could not help smiling at her. And it went through her with pride, to think of his figure, a straight, fine jet of life.

That 'pride' is to be set against the pride of class that produces Mary's marriage to Mr Massy. The class-superiority of the Lindleys has been exposed as a nothingness, yet the pride of it produces this horrible result. But the 'pride' attributed here to Louisa is a passionate sense for what is real, and a firm allegiance to it. 'Real', of course, is not a word of immediately determinate force, but it is a necessary word here, and it gets its definition concretely in the enactment of the drama. Louisa sums up the attraction that Alfred has for her in the appraisal of him as a 'fine jet of life'. The ordinary suggestion of 'physical' has in that phrase an enlargement in which, though we don't lose touch with the word, it is seen to be clearly inadequate, and misleading in its inadequacy. In fact, what, contemplating both the attraction and the complementary repugnance, we need to invoke is 'body' as Lawrence opposes it to 'mental consciousness' in the passage written many years later in À Propos of Lady Chatterley's Lover:

The body's life is the life of sensations and emotions. The body feels real hunger, real thirst, real joy in the sun or the snow, real pleasure in the smell of roses or the look of a lilac bush; real anger, real sorrow, real love, real tenderness, real warmth, real passion, real hate, real grief. All the emotions belong to the body, and are only recognized by the mind.

The 'body' here, we have to note, represents the deep spontaneous life over which the conscious mind and will have no dominion, and which they cannot control or replace though they can thwart it. And its frustration and impoverishment entail the frustration and impoverishment of life at what are thought of as the higher levels. Where the 'active emotional self has no real existence, but is all reflected downwards from the mind', the 'higher emotions are strictly dead':

And by higher emotions we mean love in all its manifestations, from genuine desire to tender love, love of our fellowmen, and love of God: we mean love, joy, delight, hope, true indignant anger, passionate sense of justice and injustice, truth and untruth, honour and dishonour, and real belief in *anything*; for belief is a profound emotion that has the mind's connivance.

This continuity of 'physical' and 'spiritual' Mary Lindley, with her 'proud, pure look of submission to a high fate', has learnt from her upbringing to deny. She has learnt what Louisa has shown herself incapable of learning – Louisa who, when she saw Mr Massy from behind, 'looking like a sickly lad of thirteen ... disliked him exceedingly, and felt a desire to put him out of existence'. Mary forces herself to overcome her shudders and to give honour to his 'genuine goodness'. Of him we are told that he 'seemed to have no sense of any person, any human being whom he was helping: he only realized a kind of mathematical working out, solving of given situations, a calculated well-doing'; and that 'his religion consisted in what his scrupulous, abstract mind approved of'. The significance of Mr Massy, horribly convincing as he is in himself, is what we have presented to us in Mary. It is left to Louisa to exclaim: 'What right has *that* to be called goodness!' Even Louisa can't explain why it has no right, and for Mary it *is*, unquestionably, goodness, so that, though 'her physical self disliked and despised him', her physical self must be overcome. There is 'a doggedness in her voice' when she defends him against Louisa. A force of will is felt, we are told, in Mr Massy: 'He had some curious power, some unanswerable right.' But the fatal will is Mary's; it is the will that strives to substitute the idea, the representative of mental consciousness, for the reality; to impose the ideal on the spontaneous life.

Mr Massy proposes. Mary feels 'as if her body would rise and fling him aside'. 'But she was in the grasp of his moral and mental being.' That is, her own will, embracing the idea of his moral and spiritual superiority, forces her to ignore the judgement of her 'body'. Mrs Lindley, referred to, would much rather not have to be explicit in assenting to what she has hoped for, but nevertheless replies, 'as if casually': 'Your father thinks it would not be a bad match.' The Reverend Ernest Lindley 'keeps out of sight'. And Mary accepts.

In marrying Mr Massy, we are told, she 'tried to become a pure reason such as he was, without feeling or impulse'. The association of 'reason' with will has now a very obvious inevitability: 'She *would* not feel, and she *would* not feel.' And the destructive aspect (Louisa felt she must protect herself and Alfred against Mr Massy) comes out more insistently, since, unlike Mr Massy, Mary has a body that will not be easily denied or subdued. And the process of subdual entails this irony:

She was a pure will, acquiescing to him. She elected a certain kind of fate. She would be good and purely just, she would live in a higher freedom than she had ever known, she would be free of mundane care, she was a pure will towards right. She had sold herself, but she had a new freedom. She had got rid of her body. She had sold a lower thing, her body, for a higher thing, her freedom from material things. She considered that she paid for all she got from her husband. So, in a kind of independence, she moved proud and free. She had paid with her body: that was henceforward out of consideration. She was glad to be rid of it. She had bought her position in the world – that henceforth was taken for granted. There remained only the direction of her activity towards charity and high-minded living.

The 'freedom from material things' is, actually, the sacrifice of everything that matters for the sake of mere material advantage. 'Whatever happens to *him*,' says her mother, 'Mary is safe for life.' Unlike her mother, Mary is high-minded; her 'safety' is terrible to her; and, if she could achieve such frankness with herself as to recognize material advantage as a motive, it would be the advantage of her family that she would plead – a motive that would still be also, at the same time and inseparably, the impulse to escape from 'this nothingness of their lives'. But whatever the difference between Mary and her mother, this high-mindedness, this idealism, is revealed as essentially not separable from its opposite – or its ostensible opposite.

Though the irony of Mary's purchase of freedom from material things is so mordantly rendered, our attitude towards her is not ironical. In fact, as the tale presents her, she is something like a tragic figure.

'I'd beg the streets barefoot first,' said Miss Louisa, thinking of Mr Massy. But evidently Mary could perform a different heroism.

And it *is*, we feel, a heroism. 'She suffered as if it were an insult to her own flesh,' we are told, 'seeing the repulsion which some people felt for her husband, or the special manner they had of treating him, as if he were a "case".' She seeks refuge in the isolation of the remote country rectory. But then, finding herself with child, she 'feels for the first time horror, afraid before God and man'.

Her heart hurt in her body, as she took the baby between her hands. The flesh that was trampled and silent in her must speak again in the boy. After all, she had to live – it was not so simple after all. Nothing was finished completely. She looked and looked at the baby, and almost hated it, and suffered an anguish of love for it. She hated it because it made her live again in the flesh, when she *could* not live in the flesh, she could not. She wanted to trample her flesh down, down, extinct, to live in the mind. And now there was this child.

Even Mr Massy responds in his way to the irrational fact of new life and fatherhood. His response takes the form of an obsessional and ridiculous fussing about the health of the child – later, of the children. ('But his children were the only beings in the world who took not the slightest notice of him.') The ugly comedy of his fatherhood plays its part in the gloom and misery of the Christmas visit to the vicarage. It shows him as positively insufferable in a new way. 'But,' we are told, 'no one said anything, because of the money that came into the vicarage from Mr Massy.'

In the same place as that in which he imputes cruelty to Lawrence, T. S. Eliot also speaks of an absence 'in all of the relations of Lawrence's men and women' of 'any moral or social sense'. A little further on in the same book, and again with intended application, it would seem, to Lawrence, he speaks of the disappearance both in poetry and prose fiction today of the idea of moral and spiritual struggle. Well, *The Daughters of the Vicar* is essentially characteristic of its author, and it expresses – how could anyone fail to see it – both an intense preoccupation on the part of the author with the manifestations of moral sense in the characters, and a profound and delicate moral sense in the author himself. One could fail to see it, I think, only if one approached with a 'moral sense' that approximated to the 'moral sense' with the aid of which Miss Mary enables herself to accept Mr Massy. One might in that case feel that the tale tended somehow to bring the moral sense into discredit. But what the tale brings into discredit is the spirituality of *The Cocktail Party*. It is preoccupied (being in this profoundly representative of Lawrence) with defining the nature of a true moral sense – one that shall minister to life.

As for moral and spiritual struggle, the determination of the most important and exacting kind of choice is what is enacted by both the sisters, and the contrast between them has for purpose to bring out the nature of right choice. Louisa reacts violently against Mary's acceptance of Mr Massy:

When Miss Louisa knew, she was silent with bitter anger against everybody, even against Mary. She felt her faith wounded. Did the real things to her not matter after all? She wanted to get away. She thought of Mr Massy. He had some curious power, some unanswerable right. He was a will that they could not controvert. Suddenly a flush started in her. If he had come to her she would have flipped him out of the room. He was never going to touch *her*. And she was glad. She was glad that her blood would rise and exterminate the little man, if he came too near to her, no matter how her judgement was paralysed by him, no matter how he moved in abstract goodness. She thought she was perverse to be glad, but glad she was. 'I would just flip him out of the room,' she said, and she derived great satisfaction from the open statement. Nevertheless, perhaps she ought still to feel that Mary, on her plane, was a higher being than herself.

The 'moral sense' in Louisa that prompts her with the idea that she ought still to feel that Mary is a higher being than herself is something to be defeated. Not that Louisa has any difficulty in defeating it. But what she defeats it with is not something antimoral or non-moral. The reality of the 'real' things that she invokes against the 'abstract goodness' endorsed by Mary is determined by the criteria that, in the depth and wholeness of herself, she knows to be the most authoritative and final. And it is difficult not to believe that they must be accepted as such by any reader of the tale who is qualified to read creative literature. The physical repugnance she feels for Mr Massy is related in a continuity with perceptions that anyone must agree to call spiritual, and judgements that no one would deny to be moral. We are told that 'at home in the dingy vicarage' she had 'suffered a great deal over her sister's wedding', but

she had been silenced by Mary's quiet: 'I don't agree with you about him, Louisa, I *want* to marry him.' Then Miss Louisa had been angry deep in her heart, and therefore silent. This dangerous state started the change in her. Her own revulsion made her recoil from the hitherto undoubted Mary.

'I'd beg the streets barefoot first,' said Miss Louisa, thinking of Mr Massy.

But evidently Mary could perform a different heroism. So she, Louisa, the practical, suddenly felt that Mary, her ideal, was questionable after all. How could she be pure – one cannot be dirty in act and spiritual in being. Louisa distrusted Mary's high spirituality. It was no longer genuine for her. And if Mary were spiritual and misguided, why did not her father protect her? Because of the money. He disliked the whole affair, but he backed away because of the money. And the mother frankly did not care: her daughters could do as they liked. Her mother's pronouncement:

'Whatever happens to *him*, Mary is safe for life' – so evidently and shallowly a calculation, incensed Louisa.

'I'd rather be safe in the workhouse,' she cried.

Her moral judgements are unmistakably vital judgements; they express a moral sense that speaks out of a fulness of life and is at the same time a fine sense of what makes for that and what makes against it. Her own attractiveness is that of someone who is essentially good, and the goodness that makes her attractive is that of someone in whom the life is strong. Unlike her sister she is not beautiful, but her vitality, we recognize at key-moments, is symbolized by her 'glistening, heavy, deep-blonde hair, which shone and gleamed with a richness that was not wholly foreign to her'. Her firm and deep attachment to Alfred is an expression of vitality (how much more than a 'physical' matter this is, the tale makes us recognize), and an attraction to it. Her recoil upon love is done with a convincing total truth that leaves no possibility of the sentimental. To her exclamation that she would rather be safe in the workhouse her mother replies: 'Your father will see to that.' This speech, we are told,

in its indirectness, so injured Miss Louisa that she hated her mother deep, deep in her heart, and almost hated herself. It was a long time resolving itself out, this hate. But it worked and worked, and at last the young woman said:

'They are wrong – they are all wrong. They have ground out their souls for what isn't worth anything, and there isn't a grain of love in them anywhere. And I *will* have love. They want us to deny it. They've never found it, so they want to say it doesn't exist. But I *will* have it. I *will* love – it is my birthright. I will love the man I marry – that is all I care about.'

'Love', here, is a richly charged word. It is focussed, for Louisa, upon Alfred Durant, a physically attractive young man. From a brief abstract account of the situation one might very well assume the attraction to be of a simple and elementary kind. And it certainly strikes us as a wholly normal attraction of a young and handsome man for a young woman. But the attraction represented by the description of the man as a 'fine jet of life' is not a simple thing; the implicit appraisal is complex, and the 'life' appraised, if it is certainly 'physical', is equally essentially 'spiritual'. And with the attraction, or the allegiance (for, though spontaneous, the feeling has won the full and deliberate approval of her mature judgement), Louisa associates all the livingness of life that the vicarage, with its dedication to the nothingness of class-pride, denies. In this love her will is engaged, the will figures in her 'heavy jaw' which now 'sets obstinately'. That is, will in Louisa represents, not the mental 'idea' stubbornly seeking to impose itself on the spontaneous life, but the wholeness of the being (in Louisa it *is* whole), in which the conscious mind does truly serve the life that transcends it.

She has need of all her stubbornness, for she cannot dispose of class merely by defying it as it confronts her at the vicarage; at the cottage it presents itself as a far more difficult problem. This she has to realize when she meets Alfred after the death of his father. He evades the embarrassing problem of personal relations by being the trained and deferential sailor, 'treating her not like a person, but as if she were some sort of will in command, and he a separate distinct will waiting in front of her'.

And that was how he would get away from her, that was how he would avoid all connexion with her: by fronting her impersonally from the opposite camp, by taking up the abstract position of an inferior.

The 'abstract position' he adopts denies the actuality, the sentient individual, in both.

But she was not going to submit. Dogged in her heart she held on to him.

The courage with which she adheres to this resolute election of love and life affects us as movingly noble and heroic. It is in the fullest sense moral courage that we witness – moral courage ensuing what is profoundly a moral decision. It is courage to live, and the way in which 'life' here – for it is the word in which what is at stake inevitably presents itself to us – gets its concrete definition is illustrated by the contrast between the vicarage and the cottage, the contrast impressed on us incidentally when Louisa slips away from the one to visit the other. Mary, her husband, and her children are at the vicarage for Christmas, the life-offending wrongness of things becomes almost insufferable, and the vicarage provides a décor in keeping:

The room was dull and threadbare, and the snow outside seemed fairy-like by comparison, so white on the lawn and tufted on the bushes. Indoors the heavy pictures hung obscurely on the walls; everything was dingy with gloom.

Without having consciously proposed that goal, Louisa finds herself outside the Durants' cottage, set snugly below the road in the old quarry by the railway crossing.

Peeping in, she saw the scarlet glow of the kitchen, and firelight falling on the brick floor and on the bright chintz curtains. It was alive and bright as a peep show.

There is nothing of romantic or sentimental illusion about this contrasting brightness and aliveness. What follows is Louisa's discovery of old Mrs Durant in the garden among the ragged cabbages, lying in great pain from some internal rupture by the uprooted stalk of brussels-sprouts that caused the disaster. And then comes the business of getting the old woman to bed in the primitive civilization of the cottage, with its bedroom that has no fireplace and a plaster floor. Louisa 'knows the ways of the working-people', and they are done, as always in Lawrence, with an intimacy of truth that has never been surpassed by any writer. He knows them from the inside, but his point of view and his feeling are not working class any more than they are middle class – upper-middle, middle-middle, or lower-middle. Class is an important human fact, and he is an incomparable master of it over the whole range of its manifestations. But – or therefore – no writer is more wholly without class-feeling in the ordinary sense of the term. When he presents working-class people or milieux, he doesn't write up or down; the people are first and last just human beings; his interest in them is an interest in them purely as such. The fact that they are working class doesn't affect in the least his feeling for them or his attitude towards them.

Again, though class-feeling shows itself in the Lindley parents in most hateful ways, the hatefulness of which is exposed in all its nakedness, there is no animus in the presentment. Class is a major fact in the case presented, but attention focusses on the essential humanity this fact conditions, and the interest informing the attention remains pure and undeflected. And always in Lawrence, whatever the circumstances of class or nationality or race that mark the drama in view, the interest he turns on it is incompatible with condescension, animus, or egotistic deflection of any kind; it has a quality that one has to call fundamental reverence, 'reverence' here being something that recommends itself no more to sentimentalists than to cynics, and will be found no more in T. S. Eliot's work than in Pound's or Wyndham Lewis's. Nor will it be found in Flaubert's.

This truth about the nature of Lawrence's treatment of class might perhaps seem to be so plain and indisputable as not to need insisting on. But actually the plainest truths about Lawrence have not been found indisputable; far from it; and the suggestion that his 'consciousness of class-distinctions' is other than the radical anti-snobbery it is, still keeps its currency. Every tale of his into which class enters provides an essential confutation; but, by way of giving the term 'reverence' as I have used it above its due force, I will adduce one tale in particular: *Fanny and Annie*. It opens with a well-dressed young woman, 'tall and distinguished', getting out of the train at a dismal wayside station in the industrial Midlands. She is a lady's maid, thirty years old, come back, defeated and unwilling, to marry her first love, a foundry-worker, after having kept him dangling, off and on, for a dozen years. He is there to meet her, and goes with her, carrying her bags, through the ugly little town to her aunt's, a little sweetshop in a side-street. 'When Fanny sat at tea her aunt looked at her, with an admiring heart, feeling bitterly sore for her.' For Fanny is 'such a lady', and seems doomed to bitterness and disappointment, and is now reduced to this – to marrying Harry. Harry is irremediably the foundry-hand he was twelve years ago.

That 'snobbery' is a word called for by any element in the situation it never occurs to us to suggest: the interest the situation has for the author is so essentially of a kind that implies a complete lack in him of the snob-tendency. (In those who too readily call 'snob', as in those who bring the charge against Lawrence, we may suspect that the snob-impulse is strong.) Lawrence sees Fanny's refinement as a real thing, knowing that a Fanny's refinement *can* be, and sees the plight that faces her, bitterly hesitant, with marriage to a Harry as one for full human sympathy. That the concrete circumstances of the plight are working class and lower-middle class, makes not the slightest difference to the nature of his interest or his attitude. He evokes those circumstances with his incomparable power, and the wonderful thing (on reflection) is that, though while reading we realize that they are such as we should find to a large extent ugly and vulgar, the element in our response represented by these adjectives is at most a very subordinate one. We don't ejaculate 'ugly!' or 'vulgar!', though we are conscious enough of the presence of the qualities. The attitude towards the characters – towards everything – that is conveyed by the art of the tale is too vitally positive; it is an attitude that finds the human beings it contemplates worthy of the fullest and most serious kind of interest, a kind that entails a profound sympathy – too profound and intelligent to permit of any sentimental leaning.

When we come to the scene in the Congregational chapel it is George Eliot we think of. The fulness of response to the beauty of the chapel, decked for the Harvest Festival, and still, for the industrial-town population, charged with the old emotional and vital significance, is peculiarly Lawrence. But it goes with his sense of the reality of the pieties that bring the congregation together.[1] It is in this sense, which is not in

---

1. He is drawing, of course, on his own childhood. And more than pieties are involved, as Lawrence makes clear in an article on 'Hymns in a Man's Life' in *Assorted Articles* (as he does, too, in this tale). Congregationalism was the religion of his mother, whose 'vague hymn-singing pietism' incurs Eliot's disdain in *After Strange Gods* (p. 39): 'nothing could be much drearier (so far as one can judge from his own account)'. Lawrence's own account of his debt to Congregationalism and 'hymn-singing' is to be found in that article. Its theme is not 'dreariness' but 'wonder'. And it contains a note on religion and class that should be pondered by the American Unitarian who became an Anglo-Catholic and charged Lawrence with snobbery; a note, too, on that essential history of English civilization and English religion of which the Anglo-Catholic exposes an ignorance so unsuspecting:

'At another time the last hymn was

"Fair waved the golden corn
In Canaan's pleasant land – "

And again I loved "Canaan's pleasant land". The wonder of "Canaan", which could never be localized.

'I think it was good to be brought up a Protestant: and among Protestants, a Nonconformist, and among Nonconformists, a Congregationalist. Which sounds pharisaic. But I should have missed bitterly a direct knowledge of the Bible, and a direct relation to Galilee and Canaan, Moab and Kedron, those places that never existed on earth. And in the Church of England one would hardly have escaped those snobbish hierarchies of class, which spoil so much for a child. And the Primitive Methodists, when I was a boy, were always having "revivals" and being "saved", and I always had a horror of being saved.

'So, altogether, I am grateful to my "Congregational" upbringing.'

the least sentimental or idealizing, but can turn without discomfort from the fruit and flowers to the Reverend Enderby, 'emotional, ugly, but very gentle' minister of the Morley Chapel, that we have the nearness to George Eliot. His seriousness, though, we note in the comparison, hasn't her touch of solemnity; and she couldn't conceivably have given us the highly characteristic resolution of the tale, with its comedy that is so wholly in resonance. There, in the choir gallery, is Harry the soloist, with his voice and his singing still beautiful, for all his ludicrous uncertainty about his aspirates.

But at the moment when Harry's voice sank carelessly down to his close, and the choir, standing behind him, were opening their mouths for the final triumphant outburst, a shouting female voice rose up from the body of the congregation. The organ gave one startled trump, and went silent; the choir stood transfixed.

'You look well standing there, singing in God's holy house,' came the loud, angry, female shout. Everybody turned electrified. A stoutish, red-faced woman in a black bonnet was standing up denouncing the soloist. Almost fainting with shock, the congregation realized it. 'You look well, don't you, standing there singing solos in God's holy house, you Goodall. But I said I'd shame you. You look well, bringing your young woman here with you, don't you? I'll let her know who she's dealing with. A scamp as won't take the consequence of what he's done.' The hard-faced, frenzied woman turned in the direction of Fanny. 'That's what Harry Goodall is, if you want to know.'

It *is* comedy, but with our response to it goes a profound recognition that the comedy is not the point. The significance of the episode concerns crucially the lives of two human beings who are fully realized as such and are not figures in a comedy, or in a story about the *mœurs* of the class that keeps small shops in provincial towns and attends Morley Chapels; the fully realized gravity of the issues for a man and a woman determines and informs our whole response.

Fanny and the minister wait at the door of the vestry, into which the gallery stairs descend.

At last Harry came – rather sheepish – with his hat in his hand.
'Well!' said Fanny, rising to her feet.
'We've had a bit of an extra,' said Harry.
'I should think so,' said Fanny.

'A most unfortunate circumstance – a most *unfortunate* circumstance. Do you understand it, Harry? I don't understand it at all.'

'Ay, I understand it. The daughter's goin' to have a childt, an' 'er lays it on to me.'

'And has she no occasion to?' asked Fanny, rather censorious.

'It's no more mine than it is some other chap's,' said Harry, looking aside.

If we are looking for 'moral struggle' and do not find it in Fanny now, it seems to me that our conception of 'moral struggle' is a very limited and unintelligent one. She walks away from the chapel with Harry.

'And it's yours as much as anybody else's?' she said.

'Ay,' he answered shortly.

And they went without another word, for the long mile or so, till they came to the corner of the street where Harry lived. Fanny hesitated. Should she go on to her aunt's? Should she? It would mean leaving all this for ever. Harry stood silent.

'Some obstinacy', we are told, makes her turn with Harry, and she goes home with him to his mother's, who doesn't like her. There is Sunday tea, 'with sardines and tinned salmon and tinned peaches, besides cakes and tarts'. The talk among the assembled clan turns on the scandal, Mrs Nixon the denunciatory woman, the history of her family, and the part she has played in driving the unfortunate girl 'to what she is'. It is matter-of-fact and unprudish, and, without being in the least sentimental, warmly humane: it is, in fact, humanly and decently moral. The tale ends:

So the talk went on after tea, till it was practically time to start off to chapel again.

'You'll have to be getting ready, Fanny,' said Mrs Goodall.

'I'm not going tonight,' said Fanny abruptly. And there was a sudden halt in the family. 'I'll stop with *you* tonight, mother,' she added.

'Best you had, my girl,' said Mrs Goodall, flattered and assured.

Fanny, whose 'superiority' Mrs Goodall had disliked, has taken her decision; it is a real and full choice, a self-committal, and as such wins a meeting response from Mrs Goodall. Fanny has always been genuinely attracted by Harry, and, without any simplifying or sentimentalizing of the situation, we are made to judge that she has chosen life. The sense in which she has done so it takes the tale to define, and in defining it the tale justifies that way of describing her decision. But the point I want to insist on is that, though the given class-circumstances and *mœurs* are so essentially of the story, Lawrence's attitude towards his characters is not in any way affected by class-feeling. Rendering the world of back-street homes, chapel, high-tea and vernacular talk, he turns on it no different kind or spirit of interest from that which informs his treatment of life anywhere, at any social level. In the stresses and hesitations of the lady's maid, returning unwillingly to her first love, the unambitious foundry-worker, he finds a theme demanding all the refinements and delicacies of his perception. Life for him is everywhere life, and he treats it always with the same sensitiveness and the same fulness of imaginative responsibility.

In *The Daughters of the Vicar*, I said, the contrast between the bright cottage and the gloomy vicarage has nothing sentimental about it. If we note it as a point made in favour of working-class life, then we have to note also the way in which we are told of old Mrs Durant that she would have liked to have this last of her sons, Alfred, 'a gentleman'. There is no touch of irony or criticism or amusement in the sympathy expected of us. What presents itself for our response is the situation, the pathos, of the sick but stoical old woman on her deathbed whose headstrong youngest boy has disappointed her by insisting on going into the pit as soon as he left school. We remember that Lawrence's mother had for him an aspiration like Mrs Durant's, and that if she hadn't had it he wouldn't, as he knows, have been writing this story. The significance for Lawrence of the aspiration has its commentary in the opening of *The Rainbow*, where again class claims attention as a major relevant fact, and where the presentment of it expresses a kind of interest in human life that might be described as a radical anti-snobbery.[1]

Class is a fact that Louisa has to contend with in herself, she finds, as, committed to tending the sick woman, she sees to the daily business of life in the cottage. Alfred has come home from the pit, and is washing on the hearthrug in front of the fire. This is routine, but 'Miss Louisa',

1. See pp. 103-4 below.

we are reminded, is 'strange in the house'; she has to 'brace herself to this also':

> 'Your mother said you would want your back washing,' she said.
>
> Curious how it hurt her to take part in their fixed routine of life! Louisa felt the most repulsive intimacy forced upon her. It was all so common, like herding. She lost her own distinctiveness. He ducked his face round, looking up at her in what was a very comical way. She had to harden herself.
>
> 'How funny he looks with his face upside down,' she thought. After all, there was a difference between her and the common people.

The way in which her difficulty resolves itself and the resistance vanishes is centrally Laurentian in its significance:

> The water in which his arms were plunged was quite black, the soap-froth was darkish. She could scarcely conceive him as human. Mechanically, under the influence of habit, he groped in the black water, fished out soap and flannel, and handed them backward to Louisa. Then he remained rigid and submissive, his two arms thrust straight in the panchion, supporting the weight of his shoulders. His skin was beautifully white and unblemished, of an opaque, solid whiteness. Gradually Louisa saw it: this also was what he was. It fascinated her. Her feeling of separateness passed away: she ceased to draw back from contact with him and his mother. There was this living centre. Her heart ran hot. She had reached some goal in this beautiful, clear, male body. She loved him in a white, impersonal heat. But the sun-burnt, reddish neck and ears: they were more personal, more curious. A tenderness rose in her, she loved even his queer ears. A person – an intimate being he was to her. She put down the towel and went upstairs again, troubled in her heart. She had only seen one human being in her life – and that was Mary. All the rest were strangers. Now her soul was going to open, she was going to see another. She felt strange and pregnant.

This was written nearly twenty years before the passage about the 'body' in *À Propos of Lady Chatterley's Lover*. The episode has its perfect dramatic inevitability; the 'body' here is in the most ordinary sense a body – a collier's body that has to be washed after work; the significance, without there being any suggestion of a special intention, makes itself felt with great power immediately. And when, considering the episode in relation to the whole context, we take stock of what the significance in its full development amounts to, we find that we could with relevance and felicity adduce the whole late passage about the 'body'. There is the obvious contrast with Mr Massy, whose body, we are told, is 'unthinkable' – a fact that should be present to us when Mary, who has chosen to ignore it (so far as she can), defines her attitude towards Alfred. He has been sent by Louisa on an errand to the vicarage:

> He felt abashed and humbled by the big house, he felt again as if he were one of the rank and file. When Miss Mary spoke to him, he almost saluted.
>
> 'An honest man,' thought Mary. And the patronage was applied as salve to her own sickness. She had station, so she could patronize: it was almost all that was left to her. But she could not have lived without having a certain position. She could never have trusted herself outside a definite place, nor respected herself except as a woman of superior class.

'Reality' and 'life' have both taken on a further defining charge when we say to ourselves at this point that the class-superiority for which Mary has renounced life is indeed unreal. It is an unreality that at the same time makes us recognize its sinister power: in its presence Alfred denies the reality in himself, assuming an unreal inferiority. And we may note here that the real superiority, the reality of life to which Louisa has just paid, mutely, her tribute, is seen (while not thereby taking on anything in the nature of a class-superiority) as associated with certain working-class conditions. These, in the cottage-born, have allowed the essential life to assert itself as in the slaves of impoverished gentility it could not. Alfred has insisted on going into the pit. We are made to feel the satisfyingness to the miners of the work there; the 'go-as-you-please about the day underground, a delightful cameraderie of men shut off alone from the rest of the world, in a dangerous place, and a variety of labour, holing, loading, timbering, and a glamour of mystery and adventure in the atmosphere, that made the pit not unattractive to him when he had again got over his anguish of desire for the open air and the sea'. There is no sentimentalizing of the miner's life, and we know that Alfred's choice of it was due, at least partly, to a certain self-distrust. But we can see that there is the closest relation between the satisfaction he gets from work in the mine and that delighted response of his to the 'upper world' which Lawrence conveys to us with such characteristic vividness:

He liked things about him. There was a little smile on his face. ... The upper world came almost with a flash, because of the glimmer of snow. Hurrying along the bank, giving up his lamp at the office, he smiled to feel the open about him again, all glimmering round him with snow. The hills on either hand were pale blue in the dusk, and the hedges looked savage and dark. The snow was trampled between the railway lines. But far ahead, beyond the black figures of miners moving home, it became smooth again, spreading right up to the dark wall of the coppice.

To the west there was a pinkness, and a big star hovered half revealed. Below, the lights of the pit came out crisp and yellow among the darkness of the buildings, and the lights of Old Aldecross twinkled in rows down the bluish twilight.

Durant walked glad with life among the miners, who were all talking animatedly, because of the snow. He liked their company, he liked the white dusky world. It gave him a little thrill to stop at the garden gate and see the light of home down below, shining on the silent blue snow.

This ability to be 'glad with life', which is so essentially a matter of the 'body' (Mr Massy is denied it and Mary has renounced it), is what, for Louisa, has its symbolic expression in the brightness of the cottage that strikes her, coming from the gloomy vicarage.

When Alfred enters the cottage, it is to find that his mother (he soon realizes) is on her deathbed. It is significant that the relations between him and his mother resemble those between Lawrence and *his* – significant because Lawrence was *not* the kind of boy to choose the pit, and *his* mother, like Fanny, but unlike Mrs Durant, was 'superior', so that her aspiration for her son was achieved: he emancipated himself from the conditions of working-class life. But the strength of vital reality exemplified in the young collier is something that Lawrence readily associates with himself and his own conditions of education and culture. The truth presented imaginatively in terms of the collier addresses itself to the educated reader of the tale, and he will know that he is not being incited to aspire to the life of a collier. But he will at the same time recognize that the truth, the significance conveyed, has the most immediate personal application.

The body feels real hunger, real thirst, real joy in the sun or the snow, real pleasure in the smell of roses or the look of a lilac bush; real anger, real sorrow, real love, real tenderness, real warmth, real passion, real hate, real grief. All the emotions belong to the body, and are only recognized by the mind. We may hear the most sorrowful piece of news, and only feel a mental excitement. Then hours after, perhaps in sleep, the awareness may reach the bodily centres, and true grief wrings the heart.

When Alfred, returning from the vicarage, stands at the gate of the cottage garden, 'looking northwards to the Plough climbing up the night, and at the far glimmer of snow in distant fields', and finds himself suddenly gripped by a fierce pain of grief, the reader who knows *À Propos of Lady Chatterley's Lover* cannot help recalling the whole passage about the 'body' and recognizing that the early tale could be taken for a concrete presentment of that generally stated burden.

The representative of 'real feelings' is as much Louisa as Alfred; she, in fact, is pre-eminently the vindicator of life and of the 'higher emotions':

This feeling only what you allow yourself to feel at last kills all capacity for feeling, and in the higher emotional ranges you feel nothing at all. …

And by higher emotions we mean love in all its manifestations, from genuine desire to tender love, love of our fellowmen, and love of God; we mean love, joy, delight, hope, true indignant anger, passionate sense of justice and injustice, truth and untruth, honour and dishonour, and real belief in *anything*: for belief is a profound emotion that has the mind's connivance.

That she is an educated women has its essential part in her significance. Her 'fixed will to love, to have the man she loves' is the resolution of her whole being. Her feeling that it would be morally wrong to be deflected by any such considerations as have determined Mary's marriage expresses the vital quality in her that is figured by her deep-gold hair, and it has her mind's full 'connivance'. It takes such wholeness of resolution – the steady certainty of profound emotions that complete themselves in conscious and deliberate judgement – to brave, with quiet inflexibility, the condemning righteousness of the vicarage. The pride, the self-respect, that meets the family's class-pride is that of an educated woman and a lady.

And, paradoxically, the lady is there in the heroism with which Louisa refuses to let her 'fixed will' to have the man she loves be defeated by his helplessness to overcome class in himself. For heroism is what it strikes us as in that scene in which, having called at the cottage to talk with the now solitary young collier (if *she* doesn't take the initiative, *he* plainly won't), and knowing that if she goes now, having failed to evoke in him the courage of his feeling and draw him from behind this cover of class-inferiority, she has failed for good, she says, finally: 'Don't you want me?' It is intensely moving, and, without any suggestion of the happy ending that promises a happy future, the climax affects us as a heroic triumph of life.

The strongly tender humanity of the tale comes out strikingly in the ironic closing scene at the vicarage. The scene is painful because of the force with which it presents the brutal class-consciousness, the utter lack of imaginative feeling, with which the Lindley parents treat the young collier. Yet the irony of the scene indulges in us no satiric animus against them, for we do not fail to see them as victims of a defeat of life. But the exposure of the class-superiority to which everything has been sacrificed is as final as it could be. Extracting from Alfred a promise to set up married life, not in the old family cottage but at a decent remoteness, Mr Lindley says: 'I have my position to maintain, and a position which may not be taken lightly.' And then:

'I cannot see why Louisa should not behave in the normal way. I cannot see why she should only think of herself, and leave her family out of count.'

This is addressed to Mary (she has protested that Alfred has his rights, and Louisa wants to marry him) – Mary, whose way the criterion of 'family' thus presents us as normal.

3

THE RAINBOW and *Women in Love* can be seen clearly enough to have emerged, by separation, out of what had been for Lawrence, at the outset, one; a single novel, if, in its pioneering audacity, a very complex one – the new and major thing proposed for achievement after *Sons and Lovers*. In the early references to *The Sisters*, the 'work in progress' that we begin to hear of in 1913, it is impossible not to see (along with whatever else) the shaping of *Women in Love*. But by 1915 *The Sisters* (or *The Wedding Ring*) has become *The Rainbow* – it was published in September of that year. Lawrence in 1916, speaks of *Women in Love* as a 'kind of sequel to *The Rainbow*'. Actually, the relation between the two novels is quite other than 'sequel' would ordinarily convey.

Women in Love is wholly self-contained, and, for all the carry-over of names of characters, has no organic connexion with *The Rainbow*. And, in a radical way, in fact, it refuses to be seen as establishing any continuity with the earlier-published novel: it represents, so decisively, a different phase of Lawrence's art. And, intimately related in conception and gestation as we can see the two books to have been, the order of publication puts them in their right places. *The Rainbow* is essentially a younger work, anterior in experience to *Women in Love*. Going back from *Women in Love* to *The Rainbow*, we can see that the later-published work, though not a sequel, does truly 'come after' and has *this* behind it: we can watch in the patently younger work Lawrence arriving at the themes and preoccupations and distinctive approaches to life of *Women in Love*.

But we have at the same time to recognize that 'anterior in experience' might suggest something too simple. Genius in Lawrence manifests itself in an astonishing richness and rapidity of development. Putting *Sons and Lovers* behind him even before the publishers have brought it out, he can tell Edward Garnett that he has written 'more than half' of a new book:

> But no one will dare to publish it. I feel I could knock my head against the wall. Yet I love and adore this new book. It's all crude as yet ... but I think it's great – so new, so really a stratum deeper than I think anybody has ever gone in a novel. But there, you see, it's my latest. It's all analytical – quite unlike *Sons and Lovers*, not a bit visualized.

We cannot but read this as pointing to *Women in Love*. That novel, if not 'all analytical' in being 'not a bit visualized', *is* 'all analytical' in that, though strongly dramatic, it everywhere renders, in the whole organization, in the part, and in all the subtleties of the method of presentment, a profound and comprehensive analysis of the kind indicated in the passages of the letters in which Lawrence explains the aim that is to characterize *The Sisters*. On the other hand, comparison with the later novel being in question, we may fairly distinguish *The Rainbow* by saying that it is notably less analytic. That is one of the differences that make it seem younger than *Women in Love*.

Another is that we don't find registered in it in any obvious way that experience of the advanced and sophisticated intellectual world – Chelsea, Garsington Manor, and the milieux where Lawrence associated with Russell – which figures so much in the letters contemporary with *The Sisters*, which played its part (we can see) in the striking development represented by the conception and rapid growth of that 'work in progress', and which has its clear manifestation in *Women in Love*. The fact is that the marvellous expansion of life and creativeness in the Lawrence of those years (we learn that he was also writing *The Lost Girl*) means a great complexity; we take note of phases of development, and 'phase' implies succession, but the contemplation of Lawrence's developing genius brings home to us how much it is in the nature of such complexity to entail 'anticipations' and concurrences. We may perhaps fairly judge that it is the Lawrence of *Women in Love* who determines the concluding of *The Rainbow* – its separating-off as the first published outcome of the 'work in progress'. By 1915 Lawrence, it seems reasonable to judge, was already predominantly the Lawrence of the later novel, though still sufficiently of the 'younger' one to be able to finish it. Or perhaps it is better to make the point by noting that, in an important sense, *The Rainbow* is not a finished work.

Lawrence's calling *Women in Love* a 'sequel' conveys his awareness that *The Rainbow* seemed to need one – or rather, that the final pause to which he had brought it was not an end but a cessation. The positive note on which the last chapter of the novel closes is significant; it has the effect of an arbitrary formal 'Finis', betraying in its declaratory emphasis the author's sense of an absence he cannot properly fill. The note is one that, in the phase of *Women in Love*, it would have been impossible for him to take up, and we suspect that, even while he was supplying it, he knew that he could not fulfil the promise in it. But that is a point to return to.

The Rainbow, then, is not a perfect work of art. I used to think *Women in Love* decidedly the less successful of the two novels. I now think *The Rainbow* that; but it nevertheless seems to me very much more successful than it once did. However much or little we judge it to fall short of complete success, it is certainly, and unmistakably (it seems to me now), a major work of a great writer. And it is unique. In spite of what I may have appeared to suggest, the methods and techniques are not those of *Women in Love* at a more rudimentary stage of development; they are different – different from those both of *Women in Love* and of *Sons and Lovers*. The creative impulsions and the determining interests are different.

How different *The Rainbow* is from *Women in Love* we may fairly convey by observing that there is much about *The Rainbow* that makes us see it as being, clearly and substantially, in a line from George Eliot; as belonging to the same tradition of art – and of more than 'art' immediately suggests. That there are, of course, the profoundest unlikenesses between the two great novelists even where they come closest can be very forcibly illustrated from the opening of the first chapter, in which Lawrence evokes, in a way at once so reminiscent and so original, the traditional country life that centres in the Midlands farm. This passage begins on the first page (that it is well known makes it the fitter for the illustrative purpose):

So the Brangwens came and went without fear of necessity, working hard because of the life that was in them, not for want of the money. Neither were they thriftless. They were aware of the last halfpenny, and instinct made them not waste the peeling of their apple, for it would help to feed the cattle. But heaven and earth was teeming around them, and how should this cease? They felt the rush of the sap in spring, they knew the wave which cannot halt, but every year throws forward the seed to begetting, and, falling back leaves the young-born on the earth. They knew the intercourse between heaven and earth, sunshine drawn into the breast and bowels, the rain sucked up in the daytime, nakedness that comes under the wind in autumn, showing the birds' nests no longer worth hiding. Their life and interrelations were such; feeling the pulse and body of the soil, that opened to their furrow for the grain, and became smooth and supple after their ploughing, and clung to their feet with a weight that pulled like desire, lying hard and unresponsive, when the crops were to be shorn away. The young corn waved and was silken, and the lustre slid along the limbs of the men who saw it. They took the udder of the cows, the cows yielded milk and pulse against the hands of the men, the pulse of the blood of the teats of the cows beat into the pulse of the hands of the men. They mounted their horses, and held life between the grip of their knees, they harnessed their horses at the wagon, and, with hand on the bridle-rings, drew the heaving of the horses after their will.

In autumn the partridges whirred up, birds in flocks blew like spray across the fallow, rooks appeared on the grey, watery heavens, and flew cawing into the winter. Then the men sat by the fire in the house where the women moved about with surety, and the limbs and the body of the men were impregnated with the day, cattle and earth and vegetation and the sky, the men sat by the fire and their brains were inert, as their blood flowed heavy with the accumulation from the living day.

It is not merely that George Eliot doesn't write this kind of prose. Lawrence is not indulging in descriptive 'lyricism', or writing poetically in order to generate atmosphere. Words here are used in the way, not of eloquence but of creative poetry (a wholly different way, that is, from that of *O may I join the choir invisible*): they establish as an actual presence – create as part of the substance of the book – something that is essential to Lawrence's theme. The kind of intense apprehension of the unity of life that they evidence is as decidedly not in George Eliot's genius as it is *of* Lawrence's. It goes with his ability to talk about – to evoke – 'blood-intimacy' and 'blood-togetherness'. It belongs, in short, to that aspect of his genius which has made him in general repute (however absurdly) the prophet of the Dark Gods – the partisan of instinct against intelligence, the humane, and the civilized.

The very theme of *The Rainbow* – the essential creative interest and the informing conception – confutes that fallacy. The quoted passage, so far from portending any Nazi-like doctrine of *Blut und Boden* has a directly opposed significance. The life of 'blood-intimacy' that it plays its part in creating is, in the novel, a necessary and potent presence as something to be transcended. The novel has for theme the urgency, and the difficult struggle, of the higher human possibilities to realize themselves – and no one who has read *The Rainbow* could call in question the legitimacy here of my 'higher'. Immediately on what I have quoted above follows this:

The women were different. On them too was the drowse of blood-intimacy, calves sucking and hens running together in droves, and young geese palpitating in the hands while the food was pushed down their throttle. But the women looked out from the heated, blind intercourse of farm-life, to the spoken world beyond. They were aware of the lips and the mind of the world speaking and giving utterance, they heard the sound in the distance, and they strained to listen.

It was enough for the men, that the earth heaved and opened its furrow to them, that the wind blew to dry the wet wheat, and set the young ears of corn wheeling freshly round about; it was enough that they helped the cow in labour, or ferreted the rats from under the barn, or broke the back of a rabbit with a sharp knock of the hand. So much warmth and generating and pain and death did they know in their blood, earth and sky and beast and green plants, so much exchange and interchange they had with these, that they lived full and surcharged, their senses full fed, their faces always turned to the heat of the blood, staring into the sun, dazed with looking towards the source of generation, unable to turn around.

But the woman wanted another form of life than this, something that was not blood-intimacy. Her house faced out from the farm-buildings and fields, looked out to the road and the village with church and Hall and the world beyond. She stood to see the far-off world of cities and governments and the active scope of man, the magic land to her, where secrets were made known and desires fulfilled. She faced outwards to where men moved dominant and creative, having turned their back on the pulsing heat of creation, and with this behind them, were set out to discover what was beyond, to enlarge their own scope and range and freedom; whereas the Brangwen men faced inwards to the teeming life of creation, which poured unresolved into their veins.

Looking out, as she must, from the front of her house towards the activity of man in the world at large, whilst her husband looked out to the back at sky and harvest and beast and land, she strained her eyes to see what man had done in fighting outwards to knowledge, she strained to hear how he uttered himself in his conquest, her deepest desire hung on the battle that she heard, far off, being waged on the edge of the unknown. She also wanted to know, and to be of the fighting host.

... What was it in the vicar that raised him above the common men as man is raised above the beast? She craved to know. She craved to achieve this higher being, if not in herself, then in her children. That which makes a man strong even if he be little, and frail in body, just as any man is little and frail beside a bull, and yet stronger than the bull, what was it? It was not money nor power nor position. What power had the vicar over Tom Brangwen – none. Yet strip them and set them on a desert island, and the vicar was the master. His soul was the master of the other man's. And why – why? She decided it was a question of knowledge.

... Why were her own children marked below those others? Why should the curate's children inevitably take precedence over her children, why should dominance be given them from the start? It was not money, nor even class. It was education and experience, she decided.

It was this, this education, this higher form of being, that the mother wished to give to her children, so that they too could live the supreme life on earth. For her children, at least, the children of her heart, had the complete nature that should take place in equality with the living, vital people in the land, not be left behind obscure and stifled among the labourers. Why must they remain obscured and stifled all their lives, why should they suffer from lack of freedom to move? How should they learn the entry into the finer, more vivid circle of life?

The mother's aspiration for her children is of its very nature indeterminate. What meaning it can take on by way of vindicating itself, what values may give it a meaning, will be discovered and created in the living – in the actual life of the individual. But the individual is both a child and a parent: the effort of realization and discovery starts again in each generation – is carried on by starting again (Lawrence feels with peculiar force this paradox of a continuity that is at the same time discontinuity); and it is an essential part of the undertaking of The Rainbow to deal with three generations. Here we have a major difference between the two novels that issued out of The Sisters. The Rainbow has not the inclusiveness of scope that, in the presentment of contemporary civilization, goes with profundity of treatment in *Women in Love*; but it has instead a depth of recession, a range, in time that distinguishes it.

To make this comparison is to recognize that *The Rainbow* too is (or was) a study of contemporary civilization. Lawrence's kind of insight entailed such a scope when he proposed a deep and sustained study of related individual lives – entailing it the more because of the advantage of his birth and upbringing in that Midland region where, as the opening chapter with its *mis en scène* conveys to us, the immemorial farm-life ('We've been here above *two* hundred years') and the England represented by the canal, the colliery, the colliery-town, and the advancing railway met one another and consorted in a challenging paradigm.

That the intuition of the oneness of life conveyed with such power at the beginning of *The Rainbow* is characteristic of Lawrence's genius doesn't need emphasizing; it is a commonplace. What perhaps may still be attested with some insistence is the other aspect of the given truth: the intensity of that intuition expresses itself in an intensity of preoccupation with the individual. No one could have been more profoundly possessed by the perception that life is a matter of individual lives, and that except in individual lives there is no life to be interested in or reverent about, and no life to be served. No one could have been more incapable than he in any mood of finding any felicity of meaning in 'the greatest good of the greatest number' (a phrase significantly associated with the failure in Anton Skrebensky). His sense of that truth which in *Women in Love* he emphasizes with the word 'disquality' makes itself felt everywhere in his work as a kind of steady religious passion.

The oneness of life; the separateness and irreducible otherness of lives; the supreme importance of 'fulfilment' in the individual, because here (if not here, nowhere) is life – the peculiar Laurentian genius manifests itself in the intensity, constancy and fulness of the intuition. We are given, towards the close of *The Rainbow*, the focussing image (it is as nearly a statement as the nature of the preoccupation of the book permits) when Ursula Brangwen, at Nottingham University College, looks through the microscope during a period consecrated to her (and Lawrence's) favourite study, Botany:

... as she focussed the light on her field, and saw the plant-animal lying shadowy in a boundless light, she was fretting over a conversation she had had a few days ago with Dr Frankstone, who was a woman doctor of physics in the college. ...

The conversation had ended on a note of uncertainty, indefinite, wistful. But the purpose, what was the purpose? Electricity had no soul, light and heat had no soul. Was she herself an impersonal force, or conjunction of forces, like one of these? She looked still at the unicellar shadow that lay within the field of light, under her microscope. It was alive. She saw it move – she saw the bright mist of its ciliar activity, she saw the gleam of its nucleus, as it slid across the plane of light. What then was its will? If it was a conjunction of forces, physical and chemical, what held these forces unified, and for what purpose were they unified.

For what purpose were the incalculable physical and chemical activities nodalized in this shadowy, moving speck under her microscope? What was the will which nodalized them and created the one thing she saw? What was its intention? To be itself? Was its purpose just mechanical and limited to itself?

It intended to be itself. But what self? Suddenly in her mind the world gleamed strangely, with an intense light, like the nucleus of the creature under the microscope. Suddenly she had passed away into an intensely-gleaming light of knowledge. She could not understand what it all was. She only knew that it was not limited mechanical energy, nor mere purpose of self-preservation and self-assertion. It was a consummation, a being infinite. Self was a oneness with the infinite. To be oneself was a supreme gleaming triumph of infinity.

Ursula's vision or intuition doesn't by itself immediately suggest that intense interest in personal relations, which in Lawrence it actually portends. The insistence on the individual, or 'fulfilment' in the individual, as the essential manifestation of life carries with it a corollary; one that points to the specific vocation of novelist (rather than, what is so often proposed to us as Lawrence's, the lyric poet's) more unmistakably: it is only by way of the most delicate and complex responsive relations with others that the individual can achieve fulfilment. This theme has its discursive exposition in the two treatises *Psychoanalysis and the Unconscious* and *Fantasia of the Unconscious*. In the novels it is explored dramatically with the marvellous technical inventiveness of a great artist. There, in the novels, the treatment of the theme has for a major part of its implicit moral this further insistence: except between 'ful-filled' individuals – individuals, that is, who are really themselves, recognizing their separateness or otherness, and accepting the responsi-bility of that – there can be no personal relations that are lasting and satisfactory.

The crucial relations, of course, are those between a man and a woman. And here, it will be said, we come to a matter in which the differences between Lawrence and George Eliot are great. That is true. But they are not so great as the widely accepted view of Lawrence would suggest. That becomes strikingly apparent when we consider the case of Tom Brangwen as it is given us in the early pages of *The Rainbow*. We can say that it is not merely because Tom Brangwen is a young man that George Eliot could not have dealt with the stresses of his sexual life as Lawrence does (though it is well to add at once that she has not in this matter the timidity often attributed to her). She would not have brought them insistently into full focus in this way, and she could not have achieved either this natural intimacy and direct-ness, or this inwardness, of treatment. But Lawrence's essential attitude is very far from exhibiting the kind of unlikeness to hers that his reputation invites the reader to expect: the point may be made by say-ing that they are not only equally unlike Maupassant in their attitudes towards sex; they are unlike in the same way. So much is this so that when, a few sentences back, for want of a substitute, I used the phrase 'sexual life' I did so under protest: it sorts as ill with Lawrence's kind of interest in the relations between men and women as it does with George Eliot's. It suggests that fling of Tom's which, though in his after-judgement intrinsically insignificant, nevertheless became a landmark in his life because it left him knowing so finally that *this* – mere satis-faction of the sexual impulse – was not what he wanted, and could not, in fact, bring him satisfaction.

'He was tormented now', says Lawrence, as George Eliot certainly could not have done, 'with sex desire, his imagination reverted always to lustful scenes.' But

the disillusion of his first carnal contact with woman, strengthened by his innate desire to find in a woman the embodiment of all his inarticulate, power-ful religious impulses, put a bit in his mouth. He had something to lose which he was afraid of losing, which he was not sure even of possessing. This first affair did not matter much: but the business of love was, at the bottom of his soul, the most serious and terrifying of all to him.

George Eliot herself could not have given us the intensities of Tom Brangwen's struggle to achieve a due relating of desire with the other needs that he could not in any long run, he found, consent to separate from it, but we can venture with some confidence that, if she could have read these pages of *The Rainbow*, she would have responded with a certain poignancy of understanding – if also, perhaps, with a certain enlightenment. For we recognize that in Tom Brangwen, here, Lawrence (though with so great an advantage in clairvoyance and freedom of presentment) is dealing, in terms of the life of a youth and a young man, with Maggie Tulliver's problem. The point is worth making as a way of calling attention to an important truth: Lawrence belongs to the same ethical and religious tradition as George Eliot. I say 'calling attention' to it, because, though it seems obvious to me, it would appear not to be so to everyone. It has been taken as obvious, for instance, that Lawrence exemplifies 'the crippling effect upon a man of letters of not having been brought up in the environment of a living and central tradition'.

That Lawrence was – for actually this way of putting it fits the case with a marked felicity – brought up in the environment of a living tradition *The Rainbow* offers the most compelling kind of evidence. The book might have been written to show what, in the concrete, a living tradition is, and what it is to be brought up in the environment of one. (As to whether the tradition qualifies as 'central' I will not argue; I am content with recording it to have been that in the environment of which George Eliot, too, was brought up.) We are made to see how, amid the pieties and continuities of life at the Marsh, the spiritual achievements of a mature civilization – the integrative sanctions, with the value-creating associations and forms that make possible the individual's attainment, above the level of mere response to basic instinct, of something rich and significant – are transmitted. We are shown how Tom Brangwen's problem has been created for him, the problem of satisfying desire in a less simple way than that of mere animal response to crude instinct; how, that is, he has become so different from a Norman peasant – or any character – of Maupassant (and so different, too, from any character of Wyndham Lewis):

> The thing was something of a shock to him. In the close intimacy of the farm kitchen, the woman occupied the supreme position. The men deferred to her in the house, on all household points, on all points of morality and behaviour. The woman was the symbol for that further life which comprised religion and love and morality. The men placed in her hands their own conscience, they said to her, 'Be my conscience-keeper, be the angel at the doorway guarding my outgoing and my incoming.' And the woman fulfilled her trust, the men rested implicitly in her, receiving her praise or her blame with pleasure or with anger, rebelling and storming, but never for a moment really escaping in their own souls from her prerogative.

But it is not the drift of *The Rainbow* to exalt this order of things – the order presented by the immemorial life at the Marsh and the 'close intimacy of the farm kitchen' – as finally adequate, the supreme fulfilment of life; the theme is rather the transcending of it. We watch the struggle towards self-responsibility in the individual – self-responsibility and a wider scope, things which entail a freer play of intelligence and a direct part in the intellectual culture and finer civilization of the age, the finer contemporary human consciousness. But the impulse to this development, as well as the vigour for it, comes from the life that is to be transcended. For that further life of which the woman is the symbol comprises, at any rate as she apprehends it and aspires to it, more than 'religion and love and morality'; the passage quoted above about the advantage enjoyed by the vicar's and the curate's children makes that plain. Lawrence has been called a snob; with what absurdity that passage sufficiently suggests. It gives an inkling, too, of the supreme qualifications of a great novelist for the work of a social historian, for it illustrates the subtlety of Lawrence's study of an actual civilization. In that civilization class differences play a great part, and of these Lawrence seems to me an incomparably sensitive and penetrating observer. But of class-feeling in the ordinary sense he has none. He can, as in *The Daughters of the Vicar*, show class as the deadly enemy of life. But he does this in no democratic spirit, and displays no animus against the upper-middle class as such – the class to which the unhappy family of

the vicar belong, and because of their tenacious belonging are condemned to a pinched, isolating and life-thwarting gentility. And he
can, on the other hand, record – with equal truth – another aspect of
class:

So the women of the village were fortunate. They saw themselves in the
lady of the manor, each of them lived her own fulfilment in the life of Mrs
Hardy. And the Brangwen wife of the Marsh aspired beyond herself, towards
the further life of the finer woman, towards the extended being she revealed,
as a traveller in his self-contained manner reveals far-off countries present in
himself. But why should a knowledge of far-off countries make a man's life a
different thing, finer, bigger? And why is a man more than the beast and the
cattle that serve him? It is the same thing.

The male part of the poem was filled in by such men as the vicar and Lord
William, lean, eager men with strange movements, men who had command of
the further fields, whose lives ranged over a great extent. Ah, it was something
very desirable to know, this touch of the wonderful men who had the power of
thought and comprehension. The women of the village might be much fonder
of Tom Brangwen, and more at their ease with him, yet if their lives had been
robbed of the vicar, and of Lord William, the leading shoot would have been
cut away from them, they would have been heavy and uninspired and inclined
to hate.

The imaginative values enjoyed by the women cannot be reduced to
snobbery, and the superiorities they see, with substantial truth, as
associated with class-differences are real.

Lawrence knows, and renders with the insight and art of a great
creative writer, what have been the conditions of his own individual
development; to be brought up in the environment of a living tradition – he is recording, in his rendering of provincial England, what in
the concrete this has meant in an actual civilization. As a recorder of
essential English history he is a great successor to George Eliot. I have
already intimated the tactical reasons for insisting on George Eliot's
name as properly to be associated with his. The propriety—the something very other than the incongruity that his general repute suggests
– is especially apparent in the opening part of *The Rainbow*. It is not
only that, in the life depicted, George Eliot would have recognized the
known and poignantly familiar; she would have found nothing un-

congenial in the ethical tone – the implicit moral and human valuations – of the presentment. Nor would she have found anything disconcerting about the art, though she would have been struck by its poetic intensity and resource and by the charged immediacy with which it evokes scenes and episodes that might (we can easily suppose her saying) have been imagined by herself.

Consider for instance the pages that show us Tom Brangwen – Tilly, the cross-eyed woman-servant, having been defeated – faced with subduing, soothing, and putting to bed his stepchild, the little Polish girl, unmanageable in her frenzy of terror and desolation at being denied her mother, who is in labour. George Eliot could not have given us, with that disturbing intensity, the child's blind sob-shaken stiffness, the controlled exasperation of the man, and the over-riding presence in the house of the long-drawn-out crisis, in relation to which he can only do what he feels he cannot do – wait. Nor could she have evoked with that sensuous immediacy the change to the wet night ('The child was suddenly still, shocked, finding the rain on its face and the darkness') and then to the 'other world' of the lantern-lit and warm-smelling barn, full of the tranquillizing wonder of its strangeness, when Brangwen goes with the child in his arms to feed the cows:

The light shed softly on the timbered barn, on the white-washed walls, and the great heap of hay; instruments cast their shadows largely, a ladder rose to the dark arch of a loft. Outside there was the driving rain, inside, the softly-illuminated stillness and calmness of the barn.

Holding the child on one arm, he set about preparing the food for the cows, filling a pan with chopped hay and brewer's grains and a little meal. The child, all wonder, watched what he did. A new being was created in her for the new conditions. Sometimes, a little spasm, eddying from the bygone storm of sobbing, shook her small body. Her eyes were wide and wondering, pathetic. She was silent, quite still.

In a sort of dream, his heart sunk to the bottom, leaving the surface of him still, quite still, he rose with the panful of food, carefully balancing the child on one arm, the pan in the other hand. The silky fringe of the shawl swayed softly, grains and hay trickled to the floor; he went along a dimly-lit passage behind the mangers, where the horns of the cows pricked out of the obscurity. The child shrank, he balanced stiffly, rested the pan on the manger wall, and tipped out the food, half to this cow, half to the next. There was a noise of chains run-

ning, as the cows lifted or dropped their heads sharply; then a contented soothing sound, a long snuffing as the beasts ate in silence.

The journey had to be performed several times. There was the rhythmic
sound of the shovel in the barn, then the man returned walking stiffly between
the two weights, the face of the child peering out from the shawl. Then the
next time, as he stooped, she freed her arm and put it round his neck, clinging
soft and warm, making all easier.

The beasts fed, he dropped the pan and sat down on a box, to arrange the
child.

'Will the cows go to sleep now?' she said, catching her breath as she spoke.

'Yes.'

'Will they eat all their stuff up first?'

'Yes. Hark at them.'

And the two sat still listening to the snuffing and breathing of the cows, feed-
ing in the sheds communicating with this small barn. The lantern shed a soft
steady light from one wall. All outside was still in the rain. He looked down at
the silky folds of the paisley shawl. It reminded him of his mother. She used to
go to church in it. He was back again in the old irresponsibility and security, a
boy at home.

The last touch in the passage brings out the point of insisting that,
great as are the differences, the relation to George Eliot is an essential
one. The presence of the associations introduced by the shawl – the
'mother', 'church', and the 'boy at home' – is not merely felt as an
emotional colouring, giving depth and richness to the recovered
serenity that marks this phase of the little drama. It is also felt, not as
something new, having a given dramatic and emotional felicity at this
point (which it has), but as a presence that is being continued and re-
emphasized; that of the pieties and sanctions that have played so essential a part in life as these early chapters of *The Rainbow* have evoked it.
We see the moral and religious tradition they engage working in Tom
Brangwen in his unpeasant-like lack of simplicity in relation to sex,
and in his stubborn and difficult unsatisfaction – his troubled sense (and
his power to act by it) of something more 'fulfilling' to be achieved
than mere day-to-day living with its routine and its relaxations:

Did he, or did he not believe that he belonged to this world of Cossethay and
Ilkeston? There was nothing in it he wanted. Yet could he ever get out of it?
Was there anything in himself that would carry him out of it? Or was he a

dunderheaded baby, not man enough to be like the other young fellows who drank a good deal and wenched a little without any question, and were satisfied.

Then Effie got married, and he was left in the house with only Tilly, the cross-eyed woman-servant who had been with them for fifteen years. He felt things coming to a close. All the time he had held himself stubbornly resistant to the action of the commonplace unreality which wanted to absorb him. But now he had to do something.

He was by nature temperate. Being sensitive and emotional, his nausea prevented him from drinking too much.

But, in futile anger, with the greatest of determination and apparent good-humour, he began to drink in order to get drunk. 'Damn it,' he said to himself, 'you must have it one road or another – you can't hitch your horse to the shadow of a gatepost – if you've got legs you've got to rise off your backside some time or other.'

So he rose and went down to Ilkeston, rather awkwardly took his place amongst a gang of young bloods, stood drinks to the company, and discovered he could carry it off quite well. He had an idea that everybody in the room was a man after his own heart, that everything was glorious, everything was perfect. When somebody in alarm told him his coat pocket was on fire, he could only beam from a red, blissful face and say 'Iss-all-ri-ight – iss-all-ri-ight – it's a'right – let it be, let it be – ' and he laughed with pleasure, and was rather indignant that the others should think it unnatural for his coat pocket to burn: – it was the happiest and most natural thing in the world – what?

This might seem to be far enough away from George Eliot. Yet the common tradition speaks emphatically in this comment on the drinking-bout – a comment that, if in its explicitness the novelist's, gives us Tom's implicit judgement too:

So, after three days of incessant brandy-drinking, he had burned out the youth from his blood. He had achieved this kindled state of oneness with all the world, which is the end of youth's most passionate desire. But he had achieved his satisfaction by obliterating his own individuality, that which it depended on his manhood to preserve and develop.

That the note here is specifically Laurentian makes the significance the clearer. For it is the nature of the Laurentian that I am insisting on – the essential relation of Lawrence's genius to an upbringing 'in the environment of a living tradition'. He is indeed different from George

Eliot, but not different in the way that seems widely taken for granted. An unrealizing glimpse of that truth, perhaps, can be detected behind the placing 'Puritan' so often applied to him. But what Lawrence brings from the civilization and the tradition that associate him with George Eliot is not a residual evangelizing earnestness, or a naïve provinciality of ethical temper, or a bent for insisting, in terms of a narrow untheological bigotry, that strait is the gate, and few there are that shall be saved. 'Upbringing' and 'environment' worked on him through the means by which (to quote Mr Eliot's account[1] of tradition) 'the vitality of the past enriches the life of the present'; and it is not anything merely residual he brings from them, but his very formation, something that lives and grows, and that expresses itself in his mature insight and wisdom, his creative impulse, and his criticism of the contemporary civilized world.

It has been said of George Eliot, by way of a limiting judgement, that the word for her is 'ethical' rather than 'religious'. This could not have been said of Lawrence, and a great difference lies there. In such places as the following, though the peculiar vibration is Lawrence, the difference doesn't look very great; George Eliot (we feel) could have responded as to something wholly congenial to her habit and sensibility:

But during the long February nights with the ewes in labour, looking out from the shelter into the flashing stars, he knew he did not belong to himself. He must admit that he was only fragmentary, something incomplete and subject. There were the stars in the dark heaven travelling, the whole host passing by on some eternal voyage. So he sat small and submissive to the great ordering.

But when such passages are read as they come in the book it will be found that what I have called the distinctive vibration is associated with the way in which they belong to their contexts. That just quoted comes as part of the rendering of the painful effort of resolution through which Brangwen has to go before he can bring himself to propose to Lydia, the 'Polish lady':

Gradually, even without seeing her, he came to know her. He would have liked to think of her as of something given into his protection, like a child

1. Also in *After Strange Gods*.

without parents. But this was forbidden him. He had to come down from this pleasant view of the case – she might refuse him. And besides, he was afraid of her.

She too, looking at 'the stranger who was not a gentleman, yet who insisted on coming into her life', resists the profound inner movement of response. Their coming together is felt as the contact between two utterly different pasts (for hers, too, is strongly present to us, evoked with a most poignant vividness). We have here the peculiar Laurentian sense of the paradox of personal relations, especially of those between a man and a woman which make and validate a marriage; the insistence that, the more intimate and essential the relations, the more must the intimacy itself be, for the two lives that are brought into so essential a contact, a mutual acceptance of their separateness and otherness. Love for Lawrence is no more an absolute than sex is his religion. What, in fact, strikes us as religious is the intensity with which his men and women, hearkening to their deepest needs and promptings as they seek 'fulfilment' in marriage, know that they 'do not belong to themselves', but are responsible to something that, in transcending the individual, transcends love and sex too.

This difference from George Eliot that strikes us simultaneously with the clear kinship comes out with great force in Tom Brangwen's courting, as Lawrence gives it, of Lydia. When, 'twenty-eight, a thick-limbed, stiff, fair man with fresh complexion and blue eyes staring very straight ahead', leading his horse, with the load clanking behind, down the steep hill homeward, he meets and passes in the road the strange foreign woman, and says involuntarily, 'That's her,' we have a very specific sense, even so early in the book, of the forces registered in the exclamation – the complexity speaking. Of what complex structure of needs love engages, and what marriage must involve for Brangwen, we know a good deal; and we know that what we have here is no drama of romantic love-at-first-sight. It might be said that the needs, as Lawrence presents Brangwen, are, *mutatis mutandis*, in a general way Maggie Tulliver's. But under that 'general' lies the immense difference between the two authors: it can be brought down here to the constatation that Lawrence sees what the needs are, and understands their nature, so much better than George Eliot. In the comparison, in fact, we have to judge that George Eliot doesn't understand them at all. Her strength doesn't lie here. When she most deliberately attempts this theme she produces her Dorotheas and her Daniel Derondas.

The point I want to make in stressing this obvious enough difference is that the given strength of Lawrence's is not something separable from that strength which (I suggested) would have struck George Eliot as the poetic intensity of his art. This intensity is an extraordinary sensuous immediacy (it is no more merely sensuous than the charged intensity of Shakespearian poetry is). We can take in illustration the peculiarly, and characteristically, moving power (more to the point, it is *specifically* moving) with which we are given Brangwen's courting visit to the vicarage. The world here is, in one sense, very much George Eliot's and we may be sure that she would have admired the rendering – admired, in recognizing the immense unlikeness to anything she herself could have done. And the unlikeness, examined, comes down to the difference between the writer of whom (as I recalled) it has been said that the word for her is 'ethical' rather than 'religious' and the writer of whom that could not have been said.

One evening in March, when the wind was roaring outside, came the moment to ask her. He had sat with his hands before him, leaning to the fire. And, as he watched the fire, he knew almost without thinking that he was going this evening.

'Have you got a clean shirt?' he asked Tilly.

'You know you've got clean shirts,' she said.

'Ay – bring me a white one.'

Tilly brought down one of the linen shirts he had inherited from his father, putting it before him to air at the fire. She loved him with a dumb, aching love, as he sat leaning with his arms on his knees, still and absorbed, unaware of her. Lately, a quivering inclination to cry had come over her, when she did anything for him in his presence. Now her hands trembled as she spread the shirt. He was never shouting and teasing now. The deep stillness there was in the house made her tremble.

He went to wash himself. Queer little breaks of consciousness seemed to rise and burst like bubbles out of the depths of his stillness.

'It's got to be done,' he said as he stooped to take the shirt out of the fender, 'it's got to be done, so why balk it?' And as he combed his hair before the mirror on the wall, he retorted to himself, superficially: 'The woman's not speechless dumb. She's not clutterin' at the nipple. She's got the right to please herself, and displease whosoever she likes.'

This streak of common sense carried him a little further.

'Did you want anything?' asked Tilly, suddenly appearing, having heard him speak. She stood watching him comb his fair beard. His eyes were calm and uninterrupted.

'Ay,' he said, 'where have you put the scissors?'

She brought them to him and stood watching as, chin forward, he trimmed his beard.

'Don't go an' crop yourself as if you was at a shearin' contest,' she said anxiously. He blew the fine-curled hair quickly off his lips.

He put on the clean clothes, folded his stock carefully, and donned his best coat. Then, being ready, as grey twilight was falling, he went across to the orchard to gather the daffodils. The wind was roaring in the apple-trees, the yellow flowers swayed violently up and down, he heard even the fine whisper of their spears as he stooped to break the flattened, brittle stems of the flowers.

'What's to-do?' shouted a friend who met him as he left the garden gate.

'Bit of courtin' like,' said Brangwen.

And Tilly, in a great state of trepidation and excitement, let the winds whisk her over the field to the big gate, whence she could watch him go.

He went up the hill and on towards the vicarage, the wind roaring through the hedges, whilst he tried to shelter his bunch of daffodils by his side. He did not think of anything, only knew that the wind was blowing.

Night was falling, the bare trees drummed and whistled. The vicar, he knew, would be in his study, the Polish woman in the kitchen, a comfortable room, with her child. In the darkest of the twilight, he went through the gate, and down the path where a few daffodils stooped in the wind, and shattered crocuses made a pale, colourless ravel.

There was a light streaming on to the bushes at the back from the kitchen window. He began to hesitate. How could he do this? Looking through the window, he saw her seated in the rocking-chair with the child, already in its nightdress, sitting on her knee. The fair head with its wild, fierce hair was drooping towards the fire-warmth, which reflected on the bright cheeks and clear skin of the child, who seemed to be musing, almost like a grown-up person. The mother's face was dark and still, and he saw, with a pang, that she was away back in the life that had been. The child's hair gleamed like spun glass, her face was illuminated till it seemed like wax lit up from the inside. The wind boomed strongly. Mother and child sat motionless, silent, the child staring with vacant dark eyes into the fire, the mother looking into space. The little girl was almost asleep. It was her will which kept her eyes so wide.

Suddenly she looked round, troubled, as the wind shook the house, and Brangwen saw the small lips move. The mother began to rock, he heard the slight crunch of the rockers of the chair. Then he heard the low, monotonous murmur of a song in a foreign language. Then a great burst of wind, the mother seemed to have drifted away, the child's eyes were black and dilated. Brangwen looked up at the clouds which packed in great, alarming haste across the dark sky.

This, of course, is to be taken as a reminder of the whole episode of the proposal. But in the passage as it stands the qualities in question are perhaps sufficiently present to make the point I am intent on. It is that the marvellous reality of the evocation cannot be distinguished from an intense specificity of dramatic significance: what is evoked is a given spiritual crisis, a crucial moment in a particular human life. The background of day-to-dayness against which the extreme and critical unordinariness of Brangwen's state stands out is given in the presence of Tilly – and in the 'Bit of courtin', like'. There is nothing routine or rustically usual about this courting. Brangwen can speak and act in scenes that, on the face of it, belong to the world of Mrs Poyser's kitchen, but he is the full complex human psyche, with all its potentialities.

'And as he watched the fire he knew almost without thinking that he was going this evening' – it is the arduously achieved wholeness of resolution in him that acts. And this state is what expresses itself in the poetic intensity of the episode, as we are given it. 'He did not think of anything, only knew that the wind was blowing.' What we have here, of course, is not relaxedness or distraction; he perceives 'out of the depths of his stillness', where the whole resolution is gathered – the stillness being set off by the outer stresses and disturbances. The needs and profound purposes that it unites are there in the intensity of the perceptions in which they register themselves, undistracted by his 'thinking of anything'; the intensity, on examination, we recognize to be a matter of their charge of significance.

He 'knows' that 'the Polish woman' will be in the kitchen with the child; and there, through the window, looking, with the glass between, from the darkness outside into the lighted interior, he sees them, and stands to watch. The foreignness is an important element. It emphasizes the theme of 'otherness', which has an aspect I have not yet touched on. Their mutual otherness is not just something that the man and woman in love and marriage must, with resignation, accept. True, the difficulty of the acceptance has its notation here: 'he saw, with a pang, that she was away back in the life that had been'. But, before being told, we know that he is glad she is a foreigner; the strangeness is for him a condition of depth and wholeness in the response. We have here a theme that recurs in *The Rainbow* as the experience of new love recurs in each new generation. Either lover is for the other a 'door'; an opening into the 'unknown', by which the horizon, the space of life, is immensely expanded, and unaccepted limits that had seemed final are 'transgressed'. Of Anna and Will, for example, we read:

> Without knowing it, Anna was wanting him to come. In him she had escaped. In him the bounds of her experience were transgressed; he was the hole in the wall, beyond which the sunshine blazed on an outside world.
>
> He came. Sometimes, not often, but sometimes, talking again, there recurred the strange remote reality which carried everything before it.

The sense of the door into the unknown and of the opening of horizons may turn out to be mainly illusion, as in Ursula's experience of Skrebensky:

> He brought her a strong sense of the outer world. It was as if she were set on a hill and could feel vaguely the whole world lying spread before her.

The 'outer' is merely outer; Ursula finds in Skrebensky no unknown that can be for her a real transcending of the banal. The relation between them manifests itself in due course as wholly a failure. And the failure is there in the beginning:

> And he kissed her, asserting his will over her, and she kissed him back, asserting her deliberate enjoyment of him. Daring and reckless and dangerous they knew it was, their game, each playing with fire, not with love. A sort of defiance of all the world possessed her in it – she would kiss him just because she wanted to. And a dare-devilry in him, like a cynicism, a cut at everything he pretended to serve, retaliated in him. ...
>
> So shaken, afraid, they went back to her parents in the kitchen, and dis-

simulated. But something was roused in both of them which they could not now allay. It intensified and heightened their senses, they were more vivid, and powerful in their being. But under it all was a poignant sense of transience. It was a magnificent self-assertion on the part of both of them. ... And, after all, what could either of them get from such a passion but a sense of his or her own maximum self, in contradistinction to all the rest of life? Wherein was something finite and sad, for the human soul at its maximum wants a sense of the infinite.

Nevertheless, it was begun now, this passion, and must go on, the passion of Ursula to know her own maximum self, limited and so defined against him.

I cite these later pages of *The Rainbow* here (the passages quoted are not in themselves extraordinary, the 'love' between Ursula and Skrebensky being a very ordinary kind of thing) in order to bring out by contrast the effect of the passage we are examining, that giving us Tom Brangwen's visit to the vicarage. What is defined in that passage is so much more than sensual passion (though that has its part), and it is something that entails the opposite of any assertion of will or of self. In the 'depths of his stillness' Brangwen contains, and lives, a resolution of the whole being; a state that sees its meaning out there in the lighted interior; in the scene that is separated by the glass from the windy night and contained in a stillness for contemplation. The Polish woman is not merely a lady and a foreigner, an object of awe and wondering conjecture; she is a mother with a child upon her knee. The symbol is a familiar one, but there is nothing banal or sentimental about its use here, nothing of the cliché about its relation to tradition:

> The fair head with its wild, fierce hair was drooping towards the fire-warmth, which reflected on the bright cheeks and clear skin of the child, who seemed to be musing, almost like a grown-up person. The mother's face was dark and still, and he saw, with a pang, that she was away back in the life that had been. The child's hair gleamed like spun glass, her face was illuminated till it seemed like wax lit up from the inside. The wind boomed strongly. Mother and child sat motionless, silent, the child staring with vacant dark eyes into the fire, the mother looking into space. The little girl was almost asleep. It was her will which kept her eyes so wide.

The tenderness, reverence, and wonder that are defined here have an utterly unsentimental strength. And this is not the less so because of the directness of the presence of Brangwen's own past, as we know it. We recall the cultural role of 'the woman' at the Marsh Farm. With the mother are associated, for Brangwen, not only the pieties, the sanctions, and the ethical standards, but also the aspiration to 'learn the entry into the finer, more vivid circle of life'. This aspiration of the mother for her children, we noted, is a wholly different thing from snobbery. What she values in the superiority of outward fineness is the promise of a 'higher form of being', and that this is no mere phrase, Lawrence's art leaves it impossible for us to question:

Looking out, as she must, from the front of her house towards the activity of man in the world at large, whilst her husband looked out to the back at sky and harvest and beast and land, she strained to see what man had done in fighting outwards to knowledge. She strained to hear how he uttered himself in his conquest, her deepest desire hung on the battle that she heard, far off, being waged on the edge of the unknown. She also wanted to know, and to be of the fighting host.

This 'deepest desire' of the mother is there in Brangwen's being drawn to a foreigner and a lady. We note in the passage just quoted the part played by the 'unknown' and the 'beyond': words that figure so significantly in Lawrence's rendering of the relations between men and women. Life is 'fulfilled' in the individual or nowhere; but without a true marital relation, which is creative in more than the sense of producing children, there can be no 'fulfilment': that is the burden of Lawrence's art. It is in the establishment of a sure relation with the 'beyond' that the creativeness of a valid marriage has its inclusive manifestation. What the word 'beyond', with the associated 'fulfilment' and the associated symbol, the rainbow, points to is what all the varied resources of Lawrence's dramatic poem are devoted to defining.

The particular concrete terms of the state of 'fulfilment' vary from individual to individual. To have achieved 'fulfilment' is to find meaning in life in the sense of having found immunity against the torments of the question, 'What for?', and found it, not by falling into inert day-to-dayness, the anaesthesia of habit or automatism, but by achieving what Lawrence elsewhere (and both the context of discourse in *Psychoanalysis and the Unconscious* and the art of *The Rainbow* and *Women in*

Love make it very much more than a phrase) calls 'spontaneous-creative fulness of being'. General descriptive terms might seem to suggest the day-dreams of Maggie Tulliver and the consummation represented by Daniel Deronda (justified in his 'sweet irresistible hopefulness that the best of human possibilities might befall him – the blending of a complete personal love in one current with a larger duty' – this duty representing the 'higher, the religious life, which holds an enthusiasm for something more than our own appetites and vanities'). But what Lawrence's art defines is something very different from an idealizing 'personal love' associated with ethical exaltation – emotion-and-devotion, passionate and high-principled. The complex and delicate relations that form a marriage involve, in themselves, the recognition of something beyond love – the recognition that love is 'not an end in itself':

> Dorothy pondered, rather angry and afraid.
> 'Then what *do* you care about?' she asked, exasperated.
> 'I don't know,' said Ursula. 'But something impersonal. Love – love – love – what does it mean – what does it amount to? So much personal gratification. It doesn't lead anywhere.'
> 'It isn't supposed to lead anywhere, is it?' said Dorothy, satirically. 'I thought it was the one thing which is an end in itself.'
> 'Then what does it matter to me?' cried Ursula. 'As an end in itself, I could love a hundred men, one after the other. Why should I end with a Skrebensky?'

That is after Ursula's failure with Skrebensky. These two, in their affair, have treated love as an end in itself; an end to which Skrebensky, by way of answering the question, 'What for?', proposed to add another 'end in itself', ethical devotion, figuring as the good of humanity. The case presented in Brangwen as he stands outside the kitchen window at the vicarage is of another order. What I have called the wholeness of his resolution is focussed on the scene he contemplates through the window; the distinguishable positives other than love that are associated with the 'something impersonal' that love, for him, involves – pieties, sanctions, ethical values, and the Brangwen mother's divinations (as they have affected him) of a 'higher form of being' – are there, so to speak, in what he sees. They are there in the impersonality that is dramatically realized as his 'stillness' – the 'stillness' out of the 'depths' of which his perceiving comes.

I have spoken of the tumult of the outer world as serving to set off the inner stillness (and the stillness behind the glass). But its action is more than that:

Suddenly she looked round, troubled, as the wind shook the house, and Brangwen saw the small lips move. The mother began to rock, he heard the slight crunch of the rockers of the chair. Then he heard the low, monotonous murmur of a song in a foreign language. Then a great burst of wind, the mother seemed to have drifted away, the child's eyes were black and dilated. Brangwen looked up at the clouds which packed in great alarming haste across the dark sky.

Then there came the child's high, complaining, yet imperative voice:

'Don't sing that stuff, mother; I don't want to hear it.'

The singing died away.

Here, plainly, the effect is that of a passage I quoted earlier:

But during the long February nights with the ewes in labour, looking out from the shelter into the flashing stars, he knew that he did not belong to himself. ...

The effect is to reinforce directly, giving an added depth to its suggestion, a presence, already strongly evoked, of what is registered later as absent in Ursula's relations with Skrebensky:

She knew him all round, not on any side did he lead into the unknown. Poignant, almost passionate appreciation she felt for him but none of the rich fear, the connexion with the unknown, or the reverence of love.

No more, perhaps, need be said to justify the observation that Lawrence's treatment of the relations between men and women – his central interest – illustrates something in his art to indicate the distinctive nature of which we have to use the word 'religious'. I have made the point that this characteristic is not something separable from the poetic intensity that distinguishes him from George Eliot. When we examine this intensity, as in the episode of Brangwen's courtship, what we find ourselves analysing is an effect to which a religious resonance inseparably belongs. In fact, we are led by the analysis of such passages to the recognition that the poetic intensity that characterizes Lawrence's art in general, and leads to the mistaken view that his genius is essentially 'lyrical', derives from a depth and wholeness of response in him of the kind that he illustrates, with a specific dramatic propriety, in Brangwen. In Lawrence's wholeness, of course, there is the marvellous intelligence of the great artist: his capacity for an impersonal depth of response has an immensely wide and varied application. But the vividness in his rendering of all the varieties of life, human and non-human, *is* this depth – depth that involves an impersonal wholeness.

Love between man and woman in the three generations of *The Rainbow* is most successful in the first. Between Tom and Lydia there are, of course, the inevitable difficulties: 'Such intimacy of embrace, and such utter foreignness of contact.' He learns painfully – a recurrent theme in Lawrence – that though the relation springs from mutual need, there is a dependence that cannot be permitted:

When, in November, the leaves came beating against the window shutters, with a lashing sound, he started, and his eyes flickered with flame. The dog looked up at him, he sunk his head to the fire. But his wife was startled. He was aware of her listening.

'They blow up with a rattle,' he said.

'What?' she asked.

'The leaves.'

She sank away again. The strange leaves beating in the wind on the wood had come nearer than she. The tension in the room was overpowering, it was difficult for him to move his head. He sat with every nerve, every vein, every fibre of muscle in his body stretched on a tension. He felt like a broken arch thrust sickeningly out from support. For her response was gone, he thrust at nothing. And he remained himself, he saved himself from crashing down into nothingness, from being squandered into fragments, by sheer tension, sheer backward resistance.

This is at the time of Lydia's pregnancy, during which 'he went out more often to the Red Lion again, to escape the madness of sitting next to her when she did not belong to him, when she was as absent as any woman in indifference could be'. These strains, with the other disharmonies and the deep antagonisms inevitable when two complex beings with such different pasts are committed to such mutuality in living, are rendered by Lawrence with many varieties of power and subtlety: the endless resource of his art is profound psychological insight. But the marriage prospers, the relation is established:

What did it matter that Anna Lensky was born of Lydia and Paul? God was her father and her mother. He had passed through the married pair without fully making Himself known to them.

Now he was declared to Brangwen and to Lydia Brangwen, as they stood together. When at last they had joined hands, the house was finished, and the Lord took up his abode. And they were glad. ...

Anna's soul was at peace between them. She looked from one to the other, and she saw them established to her safety, and she was free. She played between the pillar of fire and the pillar of cloud in confidence, having the assurance on her right hand and the assurance on her left. She was no longer called upon to uphold with her childish might the broken end of the arch. Her father and her mother now met to the span of the heavens, and she, the child, was free to play in the space beneath, between.

Primarily I picked on this passage, where the traditional religious upbringing is so significantly apparent (the abridged quotation comes from the close of Chapter III), because of the way in which the child, Anna, comes in. Lawrence, I have remarked, feels with a peculiar responsiveness the paradox of a continuity that is at the same time discontinuity: lives are separate, but life is continuous – it continues in the fresh start by the separate life in each generation. No work, I think, has presented this perception as an imaginatively realized truth more compellingly than *The Rainbow*, or given more subtly in related particular lives the complex movement, or pattern in time, of succeeding (and co-existent) generations. The passage just quoted registers the point in the action at which we begin to know that Anna will be a major representative of our second cycle of life. She starts for us as involved in the earlier, that of Tom Brangwen and her mother. Brangwen (a characteristic Laurentian observation) has turned to her ('for her sympathy and her love') in his own emotional insecurity – 'they were like lovers, father and child'. And the past weighs on her; she has been strained and distorted to support her mother. But after the birth of the baby and the establishment of the marriage, 'gradually the child was freed'; she 'became an independent, forgetful little soul, loving from her own centre'.

Now, as the new life-cycle emerges, the theme becomes predominantly Anna's growing-up. It is not a sudden complete shift of focus. Of all the vaunted effects of the kind in fiction, none, I think, surpasses what Lawrence has achieved here and elsewhere in *The Rainbow*. The thing is done in very little space; but it is as if, given in day-to-day living, we had the large onward movement of life. We see Anna growing up in that George Eliot world – *mœurs de province* – which is done with more than George Eliot's range and with a subtler and more penetrating, as well as a more vivid, notation. As she drives to Nottingham or Derby market in the trap with Brangwen, we see Anna still as playing a major part in *his* life; but, the developing interest has become very much the part he plays in hers. But, when the great moment in the new life-cycle comes, and she meets her cousin Will, we have it at the same time as, to another effect, a critical moment in the 'father's' life too – the moment when he must take the full impact of the truth that 'there is a generation between them'.

The moment is that at which, looking up into the lighted fowl-loft, he sees, 'blurred through the rain', the 'youth and the girl together, the youth with his back against the wall, his head sunk over the head of the girl', and remembers 'the child he had carried out at night into the barn, while his wife was in labour with the young Tom'. The page of Chapter IV that gives the episode might well be noted as illustrating, in relation to that earlier passage (quoted above, p. 111), what replaces, in Lawrence's drama, the familiar kinds of organization (plot, fable, climax-and-resolution, and so on) the lack of which has led experienced novel-readers to find that *The Rainbow* has no form and no logic of development – has in sum no dramatic or narrative point (though it obviously offers dramatic and narrative value in great variety). Brangwen's pang, then, thus conveyed, has its part in defining the complex rhythm organizing the book – the movement that, by recurrence along with newness, brings continually a significant recall of what has gone before. The episode of the fowl-loft conveys a rending anguish. Yet this crucial experience in the life-cycle is the occasion for Brangwen's recognizing that his marriage has been a success (if that word belongs in this region):

What was missing in his life that, in his ravening soul, he was not satisfied? He had had that friend at school, his mother, his wife, and Anna. What had he done? He had failed with his friend, he had been a poor son; but he had known satisfaction with his wife, let it be enough; he loathed himself for the state he was in over Anna. Yet he was *not* satisfied. It was agony to know it.

Was his life nothing? Had he nothing to show, no work? He did not count his work, anybody could have done it. What had he known, but the long marital embrace with his wife! Curious, that this was what his life amounted to! At any rate it was something, it was eternal. He could say so to anybody, and be proud of it.

The recognition of success is there in the word 'eternal', as an examination of its use in *The Rainbow*, and of its relation to the rainbow symbol and to the term, 'fulfilment' will show. Success in a later generation, if there is to be success again, will not be just this success repeated. The questions will demand a more difficult, or a less reductive, answer; satisfaction will be something more complex. That is indicated in the 'bitterness, underneath, that there still remained an unsatisfied Tom Brangwen, who suffered agony because a girl cared nothing for him'. Much more than the feeling of a man for someone of the opposite sex, and much more than any personal relation, is involved:

He loved his own sons – he had them also. But it was the further, the creative life with the girl, he wanted as well.

'Further' and 'creative' – here we have the 'beyond' and the 'rainbow'. This is no mere romantic yearning in Brangwen. If the charge that the words have for the reader who has duly taken what has come before in the book is indeterminate, it is not vague in that way. It is indeterminate in the way in which, we noted, the Brangwens' mother's aspiration for her children was indeterminate. There are values, there is a meaning, to be discovered and created in the living, but not, now, by Tom Brangwen. 'She also wanted to know, and to be of the fighting host.' 'How should they learn the entry into the finer, more vivid circle of life?' Tom Brangwen's life, by the measure of those suggestions has been a very limited one. There is a logic (as it were) of development implicit in the presented theme as we have it in the opening of *The Rainbow*.

And in the significantly different history of civilization in England. An interest like his in the deeper life of the psyche cannot be an interest in the individual abstracted from the society to which he belongs.

The conflict that develops rapidly upon the young love of Anna and Will and breaks in upon the honeymoon days (these given in pages that surely form the incomparable classic of the theme in literature) provides pages of *The Rainbow* that have probably been found among the most difficult. Since the conflict is one that they do not themselves understand, and the rendering of it entails the evoking of blind forces in the unconscious, there are indeed what may strike any reader as difficult places. Yet the nature of the conflict should not, after all, be found defeatingly obscure. Anna, on the face of it, might seem to be the aggressor. The relevant aspect of her has its clear dramatization in the scene that led to the banning of the book; the scene in which she is surprised by Will dancing the defiant triumph of her pregnancy, naked in her bedroom. She is the Magna Mater, the type-figure adverted to so much in *Women in Love* of a feminine dominance that must defeat the growth of any prosperous long-term relation between a man and a woman.

But we have to recognize that this dominance in Anna has for its complement a dependence in Will. There are passages that convey to us with the most disturbing force the paradoxical insufferableness to Anna of such a dependence, and its self-frustrating disastrousness. This inability to stand alone constitutes a criticism of a positive trait of Will's towards which Anna feels a deep antipathy. In a sense that Lawrence's art defines very clearly, he is religious. It is a religiousness that provokes in Anna a destructive rationalism, and the scenes that give us the clash leave us in no doubt that both attitudes are being criticized. The whole treatment of religion in this chapter, called 'Anna Victrix', which deals with it directly in a sustained way, is very subtle in its distinctions and its delicacies.

When Anna, in church, sees Will absorbed in contemplation of the lamb that, in the stained-glass window, holds a flag in the cleft of its foot, 'dark, violent hatred of her husband' sweeps up in her. She reacts so violently because she has found herself responding to the spell worked by the symbol on her husband: 'the power of the tradition seized on her, she was transported to another world'. She sees that 'the church teaching in itself means nothing to him':

'Why do you never listen to the sermon?' she asked, seething with hostility and violation.
'I do,' he said.
'You don't – you don't hear a single word.'

Yet she herself, we are told, had got no satisfaction from the sermon or the doctrine:

Was this what she had come to hear: how, by doing this thing, and by not doing that, she could save her soul? She did not contradict it. But the pathos of her face gave the lie. There was something else she asked for from the church.

Nevertheless, she doesn't find it in her husband's religion, which strikes her as dark, and 'caring nothing for humanity'. We cannot take her as, in anything like totality, endorsed, but it is impossible not to register that, however we may judge her own attitudes, Will's religion emerges from the conflict criticized – criticized by the total effect. Nothing would be gained by trying to summarize the argument acted out between them. It is a very impressive illustration of the originality of Lawrence's genius, and its effect is unmistakable enough. The culmination comes in the visit to Lincoln Cathedral that is recorded in the next chapter. The sustained stretch of prose that renders Will's ecstacy is not 'poetic prose' in any ordinary suggestion of that phrase. It is a poem rising easily and naturally out of the almost incredibly flexible prose in which *The Rainbow* is written – prose characteristically Lawrence's, but different from that of any book of his before or after. It 'creates the concepts' with which it is concerned. It occupies several pages, and its effect depends upon the sustained exaltation and the significant changes that this makes possible. I must, however, represent it by a detached and abridged passage in order to make an essential critical point:

Then he pushed open the door, and the great, pillared gloom was before him, in which his soul shuddered and rose from her nest. His soul leapt, soared up into the great church. His body stood still, absorbed by the height. His soul leapt up into the gloom, into possession, it reeled, it swooned with a great escape, it quivered in the womb, in the hush and the gloom of fecundity, like seed of procreation in ecstasy.

She too was overcome with wonder and awe. She followed him in his progress. Here, the twilight was the very essence of life, the coloured darkness was the embryo of all light, and the day. Here, the very first dawn was breaking, the very last sunset sinking, and the immemorial darkness, whereof life's day would blossom and fall away again, re-echoed peace and profound immemorial silence.

Away from time, always outside of time! Between east and west, between dawn and sunset, the church lay like a seed in silence, dark before germination, silenced after death. Containing birth and death, potential with all the noise and transition of life, the cathedral remained hushed, a great involved seed, whereof the flower would be radiant life inconceivable, but whose beginning and whose end were the circle of silence. Spanned round with the rainbow, the jewelled gloom folded music upon silence, light upon darkness, fecundity upon death, as a seed folds leaf upon leaf and silence upon the root and the flower, hushing up the secret of all between its parts, the death out of which it fell, the life into which it has dropped, the immortality it involves, and the death it will embrace again.

Here in the church, 'before' and 'after' were folded together, all was contained in oneness. ...

And there was no time nor life nor death, but only this, this timeless consummation, where the thrust from earth met the thrust from earth, and the arch was locked on the keystone of ecstasy. This was all, this was everything. Till he came to himself in the world below. Then again he gathered himself together, in transit, every jet of him strained and leaped, leaped clear into the darkness above, to the fecundity and the unique mystery, to the touch, the clasp, the consummation, the climax of eternity, the apex of the arch.

So the poem goes on, and we might suppose that Will's religion, offered us at its most impressive in this ecstasy, was being endorsed. But Anna, merged at first into the absoluteness of the exaltation, begins to be a qualifying presence:

After all, there was the sky outside, and in here, in this mysterious half-night, when his soul leapt with the pillars upwards, it was not to the stars and the crystalline dark space, but to meet and clasp with the answering impulse of leaping stone, there in the dusk and secrecy of the roof. The far-off clinching and mating of arches, the leap and thrust of the stone, carrying a great roof overhead, awed and silenced her.

But yet – yet she remembered that the open sky was no blue vault, no dark dome hung with many twinkling lamps, but a space where stars were wheeling in freedom, with freedom above them always higher.

Her soul too was carried forward to the altar, to the threshold of Eternity in reverence and fear and joy. But ever she hung back in the transit, mistrusting the culmination of the altar.

Her qualifying withdrawal, at first itself exalted, becomes more inimically critical: she 'caught at little things, which saved her from being swept forward headlong in the tide of passion that leaps on into the Infinite in a great mass, triumphant and flinging its own course'. The little things that arrest her are the carved faces.

These sly little faces peeped out of the grand tide of the cathedral like something that knew better. They knew quite well, these little imps that retorted on man's own illusion, that the cathedral was not absolute. They winked and leered, giving suggestion of the many things that had been left out of the great concept of the church. 'However much there is inside here, there's a good deal they haven't got in', the little faces mocked.

Will himself cannot ignore the criticism. Angrily, and hating her, he admits to himself that there is much outside the church. 'Strive as he would, he could not keep the cathedral wonderful to him.' It is impossible not to register, in the upshot of the argument, that criticism has been established against both parties to the conflict – against both sides of the enacted argument. Her seizing on the carved faces (which are, and very relevantly, there) becomes a lapse into the jeering vein. ('The deep root of his enmity lay in the fact that she jeered at his soul.')

There is no need here to analyse further the delicacies and subtleties of the whole poetic-dramatic debate (which surely ought to be a *locus classicus*). What we have to note is that the debate is a conflict in the inner life of the married pair, and that the defeat or failure on both sides has its significance in a failure of complete 'fulfilment' in marriage; a failure to 'create' (in a phrase used later of Ursula), here in marriage, 'a new knowledge of Eternity in the flux of time'. The positive religious preoccupation of *The Rainbow* is *there*: a 'fulfilled' life has achieved its religious validity. But for Will and Anna the experience at Lincoln is in large measure defeat. Will in the main subsides into an inert day-to-dayness of home, work, and church:

His life was shifting its centre, becoming more superficial. He had failed to become really articulate, failed to find real expression. He had to continue in the old form. But in spirit, he was uncreated.

Anna subsides into motherhood:

Anna was absorbed in the child now, she left her husband to take his own way. She was willing now to postpone all adventure into unknown realities. She had the child, her palpable and immediate future was the child. If her soul had found no utterance, her womb had.

It is the burden of *The Rainbow*, dealing as it does with the generations, that *this* is not fulfilment. The problem is *here* – it is here now in Anna and in Will – and to bring into the world another life that will be faced with it is not to solve it.

Again, as in the child the new life-cycle begins, we feel it at first mainly as something that happens in the father's. Anna's absorption in her baby will be followed by her absorption in turn in its successors; it marks her lapsing from the foreground of the drama; she is the serene mother in the background. But between Will and his first child there is a very special relation.

From the first, the baby stirred in the young father a deep, strong emotion he dared scarcely acknowledge, it was so strong and came out of the dark of him. When he heard the child cry, a terror possessed him, because of the answering echo from the unfathomed distances in himself. Must he know in himself such distances, perilous and imminent?

The rendering of Will's awe, terror, and delight is very intensely Laurentian. What we have in these pages, at the opening of Chapter VIII ('The Child'), is something more than the imaginative divination of a young father's response. It is dramatically appropriate; but we cannot help feeling that it comes with peculiar directness from the centre of Lawrence himself. Here is that Lawrence whose genius is to be the antithesis of the inventor of the Houyhnhnms and the Yahoos. It is in such places as these that we realize with special force how inseparable from such creativeness as Lawrence's, how essentially *of* so un-Flaubertian an art, is the un-Flaubertian attitude towards life; the reverence that, in its responsiveness, is courage and vitality. And as we read we tell ourselves that certainly there *is* something that is neither the optimistic enlightenment detested by the author of *Four Quartets* and *The Cocktail Party* nor, on the other hand, the spirituality of Baudelaire; those are not exhaustive alternatives:

One evening, suddenly, he saw the tiny living thing rolling naked in the mother's lap, and he was sick, it was so utterly helpless and vulnerable and extraneous; in a world of hard surfaces and varying altitudes, it lay vulnerable and naked at every point. Yet it was quite blithe. And yet, in its blind, awful crying was there not the blind, far-off terror of its own nakedness, the terror of being so utterly delivered over, helpless at every point. He could not bear to hear it crying. His heart strained and stood on guard against the whole universe.

But he waited for the dread of these days to pass; he saw the joy coming. He saw the lovely, creamy, cool little ear of the baby, a bit of dark hair rubbed to a bronze floss, like bronze-dust. And he waited, for the child to become his, to look at him and answer him.

It had a separate being, but it was his own child. His flesh and blood vibrated to it. He caught the baby to his breast with his passionate, clapping laugh. And the infant knew him.

As the newly-opened, newly-dawned eyes looked at him, he wanted them to perceive him, to recognize him. Then he was verified. The child knew him, a queer contortion of laughter came on its face for him. He caught it to his breast, clapping with a triumphant laugh.

The pages that follow give us the child's dawning consciousness, its growing awareness of the world, its development into a person, all the freshness of experience in the beginning life. And here too, as again and again in *The Rainbow* with respect to other things, we find ourselves asking whether *that* has ever been done so well by any other writer. As experience, with its wonders and shocks and pains, becomes more and more complex for Ursula we realize that the theme now is coming to have its main force in her. Yet for a while the father might seem to be retaining his old proportionate claim on our attention; the part played by her in *his* life to be weighing fairly evenly against the part played by him in hers. Will's abnormal intensity of relation with his daughter is an outcome of the failure between him and Anna; in it the drama of the second generation continues. But we very soon settle down to the recognition that the consequences for Ursula matter more, in the sense that she, now, represents the major developing interest.

'She was wakened too soon': what is stated here summarizes what we see, and take the vibration of, in the direct concrete presentment. And as the too intense and rousing interchange between father and child is given us it is in the child's experience that we find ourselves the more inwardly and respondingly.

The child ran about absorbed in life, quiet, full of amusement. She did not notice things, nor changes, nor alterations. One day she would find daisies in the grass, another day apple-blossoms would be sprinkled white on the ground, and she would run among it, for pleasure because it was there. Yet again the birds would be pecking at the cherries, her father would throw cherries down from the tree all round her on the garden. Then the fields were full of hay.

She did not remember what had been nor what would be, the outside things were there each day. She was always herself, the world outside was accidental. Even her mother was accidental to her: a condition that happened to endure.

Only her father occupied any permanent position in the childish consciousness. When he came back she remembered vaguely how he had gone away, when he went away she knew vaguely that she must wait for his coming back. Whereas her mother, returning from an outing merely became present, there was no reason for connecting her with some previous departure.

The return or the departure of the father was the one event which the child remembered. When he came something woke up in her, some yearning. She knew when he was out of joint or irritable or tired: then she was uneasy, she could not rest.

The consequences for Ursula of her father's making on her something too like the demand of one adult on another are felt in the intensity, for her, of the common strains of childhood. The experience in all its varieties is recaptured with wonderful immediacy:

'Not so close,' he said, stooping over her potatoes, taking some out and re-arranging the others. She stood by looking on, with the painful terrified help-lessness of childhood. He was so unseeing and confident, she wanted to do the thing and yet she could not. She stood by looking on, her little blue overall fluttering in the wind, the red woollen ends of her shawl blowing gustily.

Then he went down the row, relentlessly, turning the potatoes in with his sharp spade-cuts. He took no notice of her, only worked on. He had another world from hers.

She stood helplessly, stranded on his world. He continued his work. She knew she would not help him. A little bit forlorn, at last she turned away, and ran down the garden, away from him, as fast as she could go away from him, to forget him and his work.

He missed her presence, her face in her red woollen bonnet, her blue overall fluttering. She ran to where a little water ran trickling between grass and stones. That she loved.

When he came by her he said to her:

'You didn't help me much.'

The child looked at him dumbly. Already her heart was heavy because of her own disappointment. Her mouth was dumb and pathetic. But he did not notice, he went his way.

And she played on, because of her disappointment persisting even the more in her play. She dreaded work, because she could not do it as he did. She was conscious of the great breach between them. She knew she had no power. The grown-up power to work deliberately was a mystery to her.

Then there are the occasions when Will, with that unregarding ferocity which the relation (a comment on it) permits him, turns on her – as in the episode of the trampled seed-bed:

It had shocked him in his intent world to see the zig-zagging line of deep little footprints across his work. The child was infinitely more shocked. Her vulnerable little soul was flayed and trampled. Why were the footprints there? She had not wanted to make them. She stood dazzled with pain and shame and unreality. ...

'I'll break your obstinate little face,' he said, through shut teeth, lifting his hand.

The child did not alter in the least. The look of indifference, complete glancing indifference, as if nothing but herself existed to her, remained fixed.

Yet far away in her, the sobs were tearing her soul. And when he had gone, she would go and creep under the parlour sofa, and lie clinched in the silent, hidden misery of childhood.

When she crawled out, after an hour or so, she went rather stiffly to play. She willed to forget. She cut off her childish soul from memory, so that the pain, and the insult, should not be real. She asserted herself only. There was now nothing in the world but her own self. So very soon, she came to believe in the outward malevolence that was against her. And very early she learned that even her adored father was part of this malevolence.

Now this of course is not in every way the notorious relation between Lawrence himself and his mother: Will is a man, the failure in his life is of a different kind from that in Mrs Lawrence's, and his blind rages and his perversities (as exemplified in the incidents of the jumping from the bridge with Ursula on his back into the canal, and of the swing-boat at the fair) have no equivalent in *Sons and Lovers*. Yet that we have here pretty directly the insight brought from Lawrence's personal misfortune is pretty plain. And this general statement from *The Rainbow* clearly covers both cases:

> Still she set towards him like a quivering needle. All her life was directed by her awareness of him, her wakefulness to his being. And she was against her mother.
> Her father was the dawn wherein her consciousness woke up. But for him, she might have gone on like the other children, Gudrun and Theresa and Catherine, one with the insects and flowers and playthings, having no existence apart from the concrete object of her attention. But her father came too near to her. The clasp of his hands and the power of his breast woke her up almost in pain from the transient unconsciousness of childhood. Wide-eyed, unseeing, she was awake before she knew how to see. She was awakened too soon. Too soon the call had come to her, when she was a small baby, and her father held her close to his breast, her sleep-living heart was beaten into wakefulness by the striving of his bigger heart, by his clasping her to his body for love and for fulfilment, asking as a magnet must always ask. From her the response had struggled dimly, vaguely, into being.

Replace 'father' by 'mother', and 'he' by 'she', and this is Lawrence describing what happened to him in his childhood. I spoke above of his 'misfortune'; but the question forced upon us by the comparison between *Sons and Lovers* and *The Rainbow* is: What, for a genius, *is* misfortune? The personal note of the earlier (but not so very much earlier) book has vanished in *The Rainbow*; the catharsis was complete and final; and those who talk as if Lawrence had been warped for life or in some way disabled by the strain set up in babyhood would be hard put to it to assemble any weight of critical evidence from the writings. There is in fact no more impressive mark of his genius than what he did with his 'misfortune'; he turned it into insight. It was a triumph of supreme intelligence – the intelligence that is inseparable from imagination and self-knowledge.

In its use in *The Rainbow* the experience is wholly impersonalized (and, in being impersonalized, extended). There is nothing about it diagnostic in relation to the writer; it is experience that understands itself. When Tom Brangwen marries Lydia, older, foreign and a lady, we think of Lawrence and Frieda: the parallel is clearly not accidental. But, again, the element belongs as much and as inevitably to the impersonal dramatic whole as any other in it; we shouldn't, if we hadn't had the special knowledge, have guessed at any special relation here to the author's personal history. Lawrence uses this experience because, duly transformed, it presents itself as right for the development of his theme, and, more generally, because he finds himself free to use all his experience for the definition of the significances he has discerned: none is especially difficult or painful or compulsive.

In Anna Lensky too, it has been noted, we had a very young child 'wide-eyed, unseeing ... awake before she knew how to see' because of the demand made upon her by a parent, here the mother. Further than this there is nothing that recalls the Lawrence history, and we have here the extremely clear clinching instance of the general truth: what Lawrence derived from the strain and disturbance he had suffered was a quick sense for the excessive demand by parent on child, and, in each concrete case, a sure insight into the dangers.

Of the lives dealt with in *The Rainbow*, that nearest to Lawrence's own is Ursula's, and in important ways it is very near. The impersonalizing process has its overt manifestation in the sex – the she protagonist. One can imagine cases in which such a manifestation, the substitution of the other sex for the author's, might be the mark of an impersonality unachieved or insecure, a disguise prompted by a sense of danger. But in Lawrence it is clearly not that; it is rather the mark of creative genius, the impulse and the power to transcend the merely personal predicament by the intelligence that is imagination – or the imagination that is intelligence. To a masculine reader, at any rate, Ursula is astonishingly *there* – certainly not less convincingly a girl, or less inwardly done, than George Eliot's Maggie Tulliver.

In fact, in this matter too Lawrence has marked advantages over George Eliot. And the comparison has a special point, for there is point, it seems to me, in saying that in Ursula we have the Maggie Tulliver theme. So insistent, indeed, at times, in Chapters X and XI ('The Widening Circle' and 'First Love') is the suggestion of Maggie herself as to prompt the observation that *The Mill on the Floss* had certainly made a profound impression on Lawrence. But his insight he brings from life, from his experience and observation, and it is more penetrating that George Eliot's, whose Maggie, the comparison reminds us, is too much Maggie's. Ursula's adolescent ardours and earnestnesses and confusions are inwardly enough evoked, but they are evoked by an intelligence that is immensely more mature than Ursula's. Not that Lawrence, in understanding better, shows less sympathy than George Eliot. And nowhere does it appear more plainly than in these chapters that he was brought up in the 'environment' of the same 'living tradition' ('living and central' – surely the whole of Mr Eliot's phrase applies). For, in presenting Ursula's wrestlings with the problems with which life faces the adolescent, Lawrence gives us also the 'environment' from which they are inseparable – gives us the particular relevant 'environment', of course; and anyone who wishes to know what, in the concrete, in the matter of religion, a living tradition is – or has been in provincial England – would do well to consider these pages of *The Rainbow*.

There is the confusing problem, for Ursula, of the relation between the Sunday world and the week-day world (a problem bound up with the kind of confusion that, without fully realizing its nature, George Eliot presents in Maggie Tulliver):

Early in the year, when the lambs came, and shelters were built of straw, and on her uncle's farm the men sat at night with a lantern and a dog, then again there swept over her this passionate confusion between the vision world and the week-day world. Again she felt Jesus in the countryside. Ah, she would lift up the lambs in his arms! Ah, and she was the lamb. Again, in the morning, going down the lane, she heard the ewe call, and the lambs came running, shaking and twinkling with new-born bliss. And she saw them stooping, nuzzling, groping to the udder, to find the teats, whilst the mother turned her head gravely and sniffed her own. And they were sucking, vibrating with bliss

on their little, long legs, their throats stretched up, their new bodies, quivering
to the stream of blood-warm, loving milk.

Oh, and the bliss, the bliss!

Ursula comments on herself, with shame, that she confuses the
spiritual with the carnal, and uses the idea of Jesus 'to pander to her own
carnality'. The conditions of her ability to distinguish this much in
respect of her 'passionate yearning' are there in what we have been
shown of traditional religion as a concrete presence. There is that
evocation, in 'The Widening Circle', of the Brangwen Sunday. Mr
Eliot once referred suggestively to Lawrence's 'hymn-singing' mother;
Lawrence himself, it is said, was a puritan; and the most adverse impressions have been recorded of the Victorian English Sunday. For adverse impressions, undoubtedly, there has been much justification. But
if it should be necessary to show that there is more to be said about the
place of the English Sunday in the history of English civilization, it
would be enough to adduce this chapter of *The Rainbow*, so illustrating
once again the incomparable wealth of the novel as social and cultural
history.

Lawrence here is unmistakably writing out of experience – remembering the life at home of his childhood:

On this day of decorum, the Brangwen family went to church by the high-
road, making a detour outside all the garden-hedge, rather than climb the wall
into the churchyard. There was no law of this, from the parents. The children
themselves were the wardens of the Sabbath decency, very jealous and instant
with each other.

It came to be, gradually, that after church on Sundays the house was really
something of a sanctuary, with peace breathing like a strange bird alighted in
the rooms. Indoors, only reading and tale-telling and quiet pursuits, such as
drawing, were allowed. Out of doors, all playing was to be carried on un-
obtrusively. If there were noise, yelling and shouting, then some fierce spirit
woke up in the father and the elder children so that the younger were subdued,
afraid of being excommunicated.

The children themselves preserved the Sabbath. If Ursula in her vanity sang:

Il était une bergère
Et ron-ron-ron petit patapon,

Theresa was sure to cry:

'*That's* not a Sunday song, our Ursula.'

'You don't know,' replied Ursula, superior. Nevertheless, she wavered. And her song faded down before she came to the end.

Because, though she did not know it, her Sunday was very precious to her. She found herself in a strange, undefined place, where her spirit could wander in dreams, unassailed.

The white-robed spirit of Christ passed between olive trees. It was a vision, not a reality. And she herself partook of the visionary being. There was the voice in the night calling, 'Samuel, Samuel!' And still the voice called in the night. But not this night, nor last night, but in the unfathomed night of Sunday, of the Sabbath silence.

That something valid and of great value has its record here is established as only the art of a great novelist *could* establish it (I am thinking, of course, of the passage in its whole context). But no one reading Lawrence will be tempted to simplify or sentimentalize; with an astringent delicacy that is peculiarly his, and a clear-eyed subtlety, he explores in terms of Ursula's experience the question, the lived question, of what the relations should be, or can be, between that something and the week-day world. But to put it in this way, of course, is itself to simplify; the question at the same time regards the nature of the something, and the complexity, calling for discriminations, of the 'Sunday world'.

But in how full a sense a *living* tradition informed the environment in which Ursula Brangwen grew up has yet to be suggested. A quotation of some length is necessary. Again the power of the great artist provides the testimony that could have been provided in no other way.

Still, it was there, even if it were faint and inadequate. The cycle of creation still wheeled in the Christian year.

The statement has behind it an evocation that is astonishing in its poetic force. It is indisputably enough 'there' in Lawrence's prose to make the statement indisputable, the 'rhythm of eternity' – 'this rhythm of eternity in a ragged inconsequential life' – taking us back to the England of *Sir Gawayne and the Green Knight*. The 'old mystery play of St George and Beelzebub' makes its significant appearance in the first of the quoted paragraphs; the older than Christian traditions that it represents, traditions constituting (as the passage itself testifies) so much of the strength of the traditional religion, are a potent presence in the whole passage, with its evocation of the 'Church year'. It strikes one now as astonishing that the England of the late nineteenth century could have produced *this* – I speak of the whole burden and effect – for Lawrence to record; for that, with his intuitive creative genius, he is recording an actual 'environment' no one capable of reading *The Rainbow* can doubt:

Gradually there gathered the feeling of expectation. Christmas was coming. In the shed, at nights, a secret candle was burning, a sound of veiled voices was heard. The boys were learning the old mystery play of St George and Beelzebub. Twice a week, by lamplight, there was choir practice in the church, for the learning of old carols Brangwen wanted to hear. The girls went to these practices. Everywhere was a sense of mystery and rousedness. Everybody was preparing for something.

The time came near, the girls were decorating the church, with cold fingers binding holly and fir and yew about the pillars, till a new spirit was in the church, the stone broke out into dark rich leaf, the arches put forth their buds, and cold flowers rose to blossom in the dim, mystic atmosphere. Ursula must weave mistletoe over the door, and over the screen, and hang a silver dove from a sprig of yew, till dusk came down, and the church was like a grove.

In the cow-shed the boys were blacking their faces for a dress-rehearsal; the turkey hung dead, with opened, speckled wings, in the dairy. The time was come to make pies, in readiness.

The expectation grew more tense. The star was risen into the sky, the songs, the carols were ready to hail it. The star was the sign in the sky. Earth too should give a sign. As evening drew on, hearts beat fast with anticipation, hands were full of ready gifts. There were the tremulously expectant words of the church service, the night was past and the morning was come, the gifts were given and received, joy and peace made a flapping of wings in each heart, there was a great burst of carols, the Peace of the World had dawned, strife had passed away, every hand linked in hand, every heart was singing.

It was bitter, though, that Christmas day, as it drew on to evening, and night, became a sort of bank holiday, flat and stale. The morning was so wonderful, but in the afternoon and evening the ecstasy perished like a nipped thing, like a bud in a false spring. Alas, that Christmas was only a domestic feast of sweet-meats and toys! Why did not the grown-ups also change their everyday hearts, and give way to ecstasy? Where was the ecstasy? ...

Still it was there, even if it were faint and inadequate. The cycle of creation still wheeled in the Christian year. ...

So the children lived the year of Christianity, the epic of the soul of mankind. Year by year the inner, unknown drama went on in them, their hearts were born and came to fulness, suffered on the cross, gave up the ghost, and rose again to unnumbered days, untired, having at least this rhythm of eternity in a ragged, inconsequential life.

This 'environment' doesn't represent the England in which Ursula, as she grows up, will have to achieve her 'fulfilment'. It is in the logic of Lawrence's theme that for the third generation the problem should pose itself in more complex terms, as the cultural conditions become more sophisticated. This development follows from the mother's aspiration for her children, in so far as that takes effect:

It was this, this education, this higher form of being, that the mother wished to give to her children, so that they too could live the supreme life on earth. For her children, at least the children of her heart, had the complete nature that should take place in equality with the living, vital people in the land, not be left behind obscure among the labourers. Why must they remain obscured and stifled all their lives, why should they suffer from lack of freedom to move? How should they learn the entry into the finer, more vivid circle of life?

But the change has at the same time a representative quality; we watch the movement of civilization in England. Ursula has to live *her* problem in the England of D. H. Lawrence. In fact, her life, though she is convincingly a girl and a young woman, bears something closely approaching an autobiographical relation to Lawrence's own. In Ursula's experience as a teacher in St Philip's School, and then as a student at University College, Nottingham, we have, unmistakably (though without incongruity), some direct transcription.

It is significant that the problems of personal relations as they are now dealt with involve explicit reference to the state or tendency of the civilization in which they are staged. Thus Anton Skrebensky's inadequacy has for a major aspect this:

He went about at his duties, giving himself up to them. At the bottom of his heart his self, the soul that aspired and had true hope of self-effectuation, lay as dead, still-born, a dead-weight in his womb. Who was he, to hold important his personal connexion? What did a man matter personally? He was just a brick in the whole great social fabric, the nation, the modern humanity. .... One had to fill one's place in the whole, the great scheme of man's elaborate civilization, that was all.

He believed in the greatest good of the greatest number, unable to see that 'the highest good of the community as it stands is no longer the highest good of even the average individual'.

He thought that, because the community represents millions of people, therefore it must be millions of times more important than any individual, forgetting that the community is an abstraction from the many, and is not the many themselves.

And so 'there came over Skrebensky a nullity, which more and more terrified Ursula'.

It will not, however, do to suggest that the essential exposition of Skrebensky's case is a matter of statement and explicit analysis. These are altogether secondary; they owe their force, as they come in the book, to the dramatically and poetically rendered significances they resume. We have here, in fact, one of the characteristic methods (a triumphantly successful one) of *Women in Love*. The statement or analysis relates immediately to what has been said in discussion of the same themes between the actors, discussion that comes with perfect dramatic naturalness and has its completion and main force in some relevant episode or enactment. We have an instance in the episode of the barge in the chapter, 'First Love'.

The lovers are walking together, and the setting is evoked in a passage that might well be adduced as illustrating a kind of power that critics are very ready to credit Lawrence with, though neither the nature of what is in front of them, nor, consequently, the genius at work in it, gets as a rule anything that can properly be called recognition:

The blue way of the canal wound softly between the autumn hedges, on towards the greenness of a small hill. On the left was the whole black agitation of colliery and railway and the town which rose on its hill, the church tower topping all. The round white dot of the clock on the tower was distinct in the evening light.

That way, Ursula felt, was the way to London, through the grim, alluring seethe of the town. On the other hand was the evening, mellow over the green water-meadows and the winding alder trees beside the river, and the pale stretches of stubble beyond. There the evening glowed softly, and even a pee-wit was flapping in solitude and peace.

Ursula and Anton Skrebensky walked along the ridge of the canal between. The berries on the hedges were crimson and bright red, above the leaves. The glow of evening and the wheeling of the solitary pee-wit and the faint cry of the birds came to meet the shuffling noise of the pits, the dark, fuming stress of the town opposite, and they two walked the blue strip of water-way, the ribbon of sky between.

What we have here is no mere 'lyrical' description, functional in the sense that the lovers' walk has to take place somewhere, and may fitly be made the occasion for some poetically evocative writing. The point of the passage, in terms of significance, comes in that close: 'and they two walked the blue strip of water-way, the ribbon of sky between'. The symbolism is unobtrusive, but, clinched in that 'between', quite unmistakable. There are the lovers with life before them, the world (its contrasts and complexities represented in local terms) around them, and the great decisions (they must feel) still to take. Skrebensky talks about his work in the service, and Ursula asks him: 'Do you like to be a soldier?' She wants a real answer, and presses him, and he replies, yes, if there were a war he would want to go:

'I should be doing something, it would be genuine. It's a sort of toy-life as it is.'

Ursula continues to press him, and the exchange goes on through a page to this conclusion:

'I hate soldiers, they are stiff and wooden. What do you fight for, really?'
'I would fight for the nation.'
'For all that, you aren't the nation. What would you do for yourself?'
'I belong to the nation and must do my duty by the nation.'
'But when it didn't need your services in particular – when there *is* no fighting? What would you do then?'
He was irritated.
'I would do what everybody else does.'
'What?'

'Nothing. I would be in readiness for when I was needed.'

The answer came in exasperation.

'It seems to me,' she answered, 'as if you weren't anybody – as if there wasn't anybody there, where you are. Are you anybody really? You seem like nothing to me.'

At this point they come to the barge and see the man sitting on a box outside the cabin, nursing a baby. There follows the scene between Ursula, the bargee, and the bargee's wife, which ends with the decision on the part of these two, the parents, to name the baby after Ursula, and with her leaving her necklace round the baby's neck for a gift. The whole, one can confidently venture, would have compelled the warmest admiration from George Eliot, such are the touch and the tone; yet the tone – which, when one examines it, leads one to the analysis of a delicately complex poise – is not George Eliot at all; it is pure Lawrence. And of the whole effect it is enough here to say that when we read the paragraphs that follow they merely give explicitness to a significance that we have already taken:

> She went hastening on, gladdened by having met the grimy, lean man with the ragged moustache. He gave her a pleasant warm feeling. He made her feel the richness of her own life, Skrebensky, somehow, had created a deadness round her, a sterility, as if the world were ashes.
>
> They said very little as they hastened home to the big supper. He was envying the lean father of three children, for his impudent directness and his worship of the woman in Ursula, a worship of body and soul together, the man's body and soul wistful and worshipping the body and spirit of the girl, with a desire that knew the inaccessibility of its object, but was only glad to know that the perfect thing existed, glad to have had a moment of communication.
>
> Why could not he himself desire a woman so? Why did he never really want a woman, not with the whole of him: never loved, never worshipped, only just physically wanted her.

The relation between Skrebensky's inadequacy as a lover and what may be called his 'public spirit', his good-citizen acceptance of the social function as the ultimate meaning of life, has been fully *done* – bodied forth, one might say. Ursula's judgement, 'You seem like nothing to me,' has its full charge of significance. And the reader recalls here how Ursula (see the beginning of the chapter) having concluded that 'only the week-day world mattered', found nevertheless a 'residue of the Sunday world' persisting within her:

> One was responsible to the world for what one did.
>
> Nay, one was more than responsible to the world. One was responsible to oneself. There was some puzzling, tormenting residue of the Sunday world, some persistent Sunday elfs, which insisted on a relationship with the now shut-away vision world.

In personal relations with Skrebensky, however, she manifests an inadequacy answering to his. The essential relation between them is given in their dancing, as they dance together at Frederick Brangwen's wedding-supper, which is also a celebration of harvest; the whole thing – the supper, the dance, and the subsequent scene in the moonlit stackyard – being done with a sensuous and disturbing force that is intensely Lawrence, and not for a moment suggestive of anyone else (least of all George Eliot).

When Skrebensky has gone away (he goes to the South African war, and an absence of years follows), the passionate attachment dealt with in the chapter called 'Shame' forms between Ursula and her class-mistress Miss Inger. Winifred Inger is intellectually superior, and her cultured enlightenment is impressive enough to have at first a great effect on Ursula:

> It was a strange world the girl was swept into, like a chaos, like the end of the world. She was too young to understand it all. Yet the inoculation passed into her, through her love for her mistress.

The love itself is diagnostic in respect of Miss Inger, whose passion for Ursula goes with an attitude towards men that she states in terms of advanced feminist thought. For Ursula, we are told later, in the teaching days at St Philip's School, when her friend is Maggie,

> the vote was never a reality. She had within her the strange, passionate knowledge of religion and living far transcending the limits of the automatic system that contained the vote. But her fundamental, organic knowledge had as yet to take form and rise to utterance.

More and more she feels (as we are made to do) that, deep within, life has somehow been thwarted, and gone wrong, in Winifred Inger, that 'rather beautiful woman of twenty-eight, a fearless-seeming, clean type of modern girl whose very independence betrays her sorrow'. The significance in terms of the environing modern world, a significance that, in relating her feminism to Skrebensky's Benthamism (as it might be called) relates her inadequacy to his, comes out when she marries Tom Brangwen, Ursula's uncle:

> He too was at the end of all his desires. He had done the things he had wanted to. They had all ended in a disintegrated lifelessness of soul, which he hid under an utterly tolerant good-humour. He no longer cared about anything on earth, neither man nor woman, nor God nor humanity. He had come to a stability of nullification.

He is now a scientifically efficient colliery-manager, and the failure of life in him expresses itself in a worship of the machine, and an acquiescence in the surrender of life to the industrial or social function; in subordination to the function as the only meaning that, for miner or manager, life can have. Introduced by Ursula to Winifred, he 'looked at the athletic, seemingly fearless girl, and detected in her a kinship with his own dark corruption'.

> 'But is this place as awful as it looks?' the young girl asked, a strain in her eyes.
> 'It is just what it looks,' he said. 'It hides nothing.'

A long discussion of the place and the people follows between them:

> Ursula sat black-souled and very bitter, hearing the two of them talk. There seemed something ghoulish even in their very deploring of the state of things. They seemed to take a ghoulish satisfaction in it. The pit was the great mistress. Ursula looked out of the window and saw the proud, demon-like colliery with her wheels twinkling in the heavens, the formless, squalid mass of the town lying aside. It was the squalid heap of side-shows. The pit was the main show, the *raison d'être* of all.
>
> How terrible it was! There *was* a horrible fascination in it – human bodies and lives subjected in slavery to that symmetric monster of the colliery. There was a swooning, perverse satisfaction in it. For a moment she was dizzy.
>
> Then she recovered, felt herself in a great loneliness, wherein she was sad but free. She had departed. No more would she subscribe to the great colliery, to the great machine which has taken us all captives. In her soul, she was against it,

she disowned even its power. It had only to be forsaken to be inane, meaningless. And she knew it was meaningless. But it needed a great, passionate effort of will on her part, seeing the colliery, still to maintain her knowledge that it was meaningless.

The colliery, of course, is not merely the colliery; it is 'the great machine that has taken us all captives'. We have, in this later part of *The Rainbow*, the very world of *Women in Love*; the distinctive themes and tones of the later book, and the same sense of the plight of human life in an industrial civilization. In the relations between Miss Inger and Tom Brangwen, added to those between Ursula and Skrebensky, we have well-developed notes – clear, if only rough and tentative – for the drama of Gerald Crich and Gudrun, all the extra-personal significance of Gerald being plainly forecast.

Themes are proposed that clearly cannot be dealt with in this book. Further, they involve a sense of contemporary civilization, a perception of the problems, that has developed since the enterprise of *The Rainbow* was conceived. No real conclusion of the book, only a breaking-off, is possible – if only because the Lawrence who started it has changed too much.

It is not likely that Lawrence *said* this to himself. What he was most conscious of, probably, was the desire to get this book somehow finished and done with, in order that he might get on with the one he now wanted to write. There is something oddly desperate about that closing page and a half; the convalescent Ursula's horrified vision, from her windows, of the industrial world outside, and then that confident note of prophetic hope in the final paragraph – a note wholly unprepared and unsupported, defying the preceding pages:

And the rainbow stood on the earth. She knew that the sordid people who crept hard-scaled and separate on the face of the world's corruption were living still, that the rainbow was arched in their blood and would quiver to life in their spirit, that they would cast off their horny covering of disintegration, that new clean naked bodies would issue to a new germination, to a new growth, rising to the light and the wind and the clean rain of heaven. She saw in the rainbow the earth's new architecture, the old, brittle corruption of houses and factories swept away, the world built up in a living fabric of Truth, fitting to the overarching heaven.

The Lawrence of *Women in Love* could not have written that paragraph. And it was not really written by the Lawrence of the last part of *The Rainbow*; the note is one recaptured, momentarily, for the occasion. That this should be so constitutes, in a sense, an implicit criticism of *The Rainbow* by Lawrence himself. The spirit or radical mood represented (as that closing paragraph illustrates) by the symbol that gives its name to the book was one that he had left behind (as, again, the incongruity of the paragraph when it comes forces upon our notice) before he had fully worked out the conception and seen his way to bring the book to a close. But who can but be grateful that he committed himself to the book? There it is, the wonderfully original work of a great genius. It is not the less something solidly achieved (and there is nothing like it) because it is open to the kind of commentary provoked by that ending. In fact, the imperfection that can be urged against it as a 'work of art' is really in and of the essential achievement, and can properly be described as – more than a condition – an aspect of the unique positive value, the achieved significance, of what has been done.

For *The Rainbow* exemplifies in a special way the peculiar Laurentian genius: the extraordinary power of the impersonalizing intelligence to maintain, while the artist, in an intensely personal exploratory way, is actually living the experience that goes into the art, the conditions that make creative impersonality possible. When Lawrence started *The Rainbow* he knew that it was only by further living – not by mere further pondering of experience already lived – that he could complete it; he hadn't the end then in his mind, already fully conceived. This meant that, in fact, he found himself faced later with a problem in art that he couldn't solve because he had grown into a more daunting perception of the problem in life; but it meant also that we have a great work that we shouldn't otherwise have had. For it is hard to see how we could have had this marvellous rendering of the movement of life through the generations in any other way. (How non-significant in its externality does Arnold Bennett's much-praised evocation of the passage of life and time show itself to be when we go to *The Old Wives' Tale* from *The Rainbow*!) The Lawrence of the opening of *The Rainbow* himself saw the rainbow spanning the day: that, patently, was *of* the creative impulsion to the undertaking. He was very close in feeling to the aspiration of the Brangwen mother at the Marsh Farm. The Lawrence who developed in the writing of it found himself compelled to another mood; he expresses in the later part of the book that sense of human problems as they were in contemporary civilization which has its profound and complete expression in *Women in Love*. And so the development of the theme through the successive life-cycles has at the same time its poignant immediacy in all its phases and its representative historical quality.

The Lawrence of *Women in Love* no longer wants to contemplate the past that goes back to the Marsh Farm and its rainbow. His mood is that expressed by the Ursula of *Women in Love*:

A flash of a few lights on the darkness – Ghent Station! A few more spectres moving outside on the platform – then the bell – then motion again through the level darkness. Ursula saw a man with a lantern come out of a farm by the railway, and cross to the dark farm-buildings. She thought of the Marsh, the old, intimate farm-life at Cossethay. My God! how far she was projected from her childhood, how far was she still to go! In one life-time one travelled through aeons. The great chasm of memory from her childhood, in the intimate country surroundings of Cossethay and the Marsh Farm ... was so great that it seemed she had no identity, that the child she had been, playing in Cossethay churchyard, was a little creature of history, not herself.

As for the imperfection of *The Rainbow*, the absence of an inevitable close matters, when one sees what the book does, not at all. A more serious criticism, perhaps, bears on the signs of too great a tentativeness in the development and organization of the later part; signs of a growing sense in the writer of an absence of any conclusion in view. Things very striking in themselves haven't as clear a function as they ought to have. Above all, the sterile deadlock between Ursula and Skrebensky – a theme calling, we can see, for the development it gets in *Women in Love*, but cannot have here – seems too long-drawn-out.

Yet how small a sum these criticisms amount to when one takes stock of what has been achieved. This is enough to make *The Rainbow* a classic, and a major one. The rendering of the continuity and rhythm of life through the individual lives has involved a marvellous invention of form, and no one who sees what is done will complain of the absence of what is not done. It is the same life, and they are different lives, living differently the same problems – the same though different – in three interlinked generations: that is how the form is felt.

And how much of England that can have no other record than the creative writer's there is in *The Rainbow*. The wealth of the book in this respect is such as must make it plain to any reader that, as social historian, Lawrence, among novelists, is unsurpassed. Actually he is, in the strict sense, incomparable. *The Rainbow* shows us the transmission of the spiritual heritage in an actual society, and shows it in relation to the general development of civilization. Where *Women in Love* has that astonishing comprehensiveness in the presentment of contemporary England (or the England of 1914) *The Rainbow* has instead its historical depth. These two books would by themselves have been enough to place Lawrence among the greatest English writers.[1]

1. Lawrence himself again and again expressed his sense of their being his greatest achievements. His characteristic tone about their reception is given in this note on the suppression of *The Rainbow* (it comes from his introduction to McDonald's *A Bibliography of D. H. Lawrence* and it can be found in *Phoenix*):

'In print my fellow-authors kept scrupulously silent, lest a bit of the tar might stick to them. Later Arnold Bennett and May Sinclair raised a kindly protest. But John Galsworthy told me, very calmly and *ex cathedra*, he thought the book a failure as a work of art. They think as they please. But why not wait till I ask them, before they deliver an opinion to me. Especially as impromptu opinions by elderly authors are apt to damage him who gives as much as him who takes.

'There is no more indecency or impropriety in *The Rainbow* than there is in this autumn morning – I who say so ought to know. And when I open my mouth let no dog bark.

'So much for the first edition of *The Rainbow*. The only copy of any of my books I ever keep is my copy of Methuen's *Rainbow*. Because the American editions have all been mutilated. And this is almost my favourite among my novels: this, and *Women in Love*. And I should really be best pleased if it were never reprinted at all, and only those blue, condemned volumes remained extant.

'Since *The Rainbow*, one submits to the process of publication as to a necessary evil: as souls are said to submit to the necessary evil of being born into the flesh. The wind bloweth where it listeth. And one must submit to the processes of one's day. Personally, I have no belief in the vast public. I believe that only the winnowed few can care. But publishers, like thistle, must set innumerable seeds on the wind, knowing most will miscarry.'

4

I HAVE not always thought *Women in Love* one of the most striking works of creative originality that fiction has to show – I have not always thought it successful enough to make such a judgement reasonable. When, at the time of the novel's first appearance, I read Middleton Murry's review of it in the *Nation and Athenaeum* I saw no reason for protesting. Even ten years later, when I came on the pages of *Son of Woman* that deal with *Women in Love*, I was not moved to protest that Murry was ignoring all those immediately impressive aspects of the book which should make it at first reading an unquestionable and astonishing work of genius. If then I adduce Murry for disagreement, that is by way not of exhibiting superiority but of making a convenient approach to the peculiar difficulties that Lawrence presents to literary criticism.

For Lawrence is, I have to contend, a case for literary criticism, in a way that Murry would seem to deny. Murry himself, of course, is a literary critic in *Son of Woman*; for the purposes of that study he has to be one. But the interest he takes there in Lawrence's writings is of a special kind that leads him to treat them as documentation; as evidence of Lawrence's personal case and inner history. He concerns himself in particular with the difficulties resulting for Lawrence throughout his life from the relation established with him in childhood by his mother. And it is true that Lawrence is for us a man and a life as well as a writer and true that the writings yield the kind of personal and psychological interest that Murry specializes in. To elicit it safely, however, one must be a better critic than Murry permits himself to be, and one will not then be able to ignore the fact that Lawrence is an artist, and a great one. It is this aspect of Lawrence that I am concerned with.

Murry denies that it exists. 'To charge him with lack of form,' he says, 'or of any other of the qualities that are supposed to be necessary to art, is to be guilty of irrelevance. Art was not his aim' (*Son of Woman*, p. 173). Against this we may bring Lawrence's own dictum: 'Art speech is the only speech.' His own emotional and personal problems may have tormented him, in the way Murry describes, all his life, and made him at times a difficult husband and an 'impossible' man. But anyone who needs convincing that Murry's perverse, tortured, and hate-possessed Lawrence is not the whole truth, or the most important part of it, need only read *Psychoanalysis and the Unconscious*, or *À Propos of Lady Chatterley's Lover*, or even the *Fantasia*. Here we have unmistakably the serenely triumphant reign of intelligence – intelligence that, in creative understanding, transcends the personal plight that feeds it. It is the intelligence of a great creative artist, whose imaginative achievements *are*, at the same time, achievements of intelligence.

They are not always, everyone can see, achieved enough to be wholly impersonal works of art, containing within themselves the reason why they are so and not otherwise, and leading one, for their significance, not back to the author, but into oneself and out into the world. *Look, we have come through!*, the sequence of poems, is fairly treated by Murry as registering in a directly personal way the graph of Lawrence's experience, in his early life with Frieda, of the problem of marital relations – for him a peculiarly difficult one. *St Mawr*, on the other hand, seems to me to be, in its poised imaginative range, as impersonal as the serene and lucid essay, *Psychoanalysis and the Unconscious*. But there are creative works of Lawrence's that are not so easily classified. The novels succeeding *Women in Love* are neither simply autobiographical in the way of *Look, we have come through!*, nor have they the complete and impersonal significance of highly organized works of art. They were written at great speed in a tentative and self-exploratory spirit, and something like a direct involvement of the author is so evident in them on so large a scale as to give much colour, here, to Middleton Murry's kind of documentary reduction.

Women in Love, however, is another matter. Lawrence worked hard at it over a period of years; and these years belonged to the phase of his life when he still believed that he would before long win recognition as the great contemporary novelist. There were new things to be done in fiction, conceived as a wholly serious art, and it was for his peculiar genius to do them. No artist could be more consciously and pertinaciously preoccupied with problems of method, technique, and form. His genius moved him to creation, and his was the most profoundly original kind of genius. *Women in Love* is the work of the writer who, in undertaking *The Rainbow*, had explained that another *Sons and Lovers* must not be looked for from him, but that the original treatment of life he was now proposing required a formidable originality of method and style.[1] It is the work of the novelist whose intentness on his art as he conceives it leads him to say:

> Tell Arnold Bennett that all rules of construction hold good only for novels that are copies of other novels. A book which is not a copy of other books has its own construction, and what he calls faults, he being an old imitator, I call characteristics.[2]

Nevertheless, after forming a higher opinion of *Women in Love* at each re-reading in the course of nearly thirty years, I still do not question that the book *has* faults. The most obvious and the worst, it seems to me, is that exemplified in the passages quoted by Murry from the chapter called 'Excurse'. Here is one of them:

> She knew there was no leaving him, the darkness held them both and contained them, it was not to be surpassed. Besides, she had a full mystic knowledge of his suave loins of darkness, dark-clad and suave, and in this knowledge there was some of the inevitability and the beauty of fate, fate which one asks for, which one accepts in full.
> He sat still like an Egyptian Pharaoh, driving the car. He felt as if he were seated in immemorial potency, like the great carven statues of real Egypt, as real and as fulfilled with subtle strength as these are, with a vague inscrutable smile on their lips. He knew what it was to have the strange and magical current of force in his back and loins, and down his legs, force so perfect that it stayed him immobile, and left his face subtly, mindlessly smiling. He knew what it was to be awake and potent in that other basic mind, the deepest physical control, magical, mystical, a force in darkness, like electricity.

I see here a fault of which I could find worse examples in *Women in Love*, though it is a fault that I do not now see as bulking so large in the

1. *Letters*, pp. 172 and 197.   2. *Letters*, p. 295.

book as I used to see it. It seems to me that in these places Lawrence betrays by an insistent and over-emphatic explicitness, running at times to something one can only call jargon, that he is uncertain – uncertain of the value of what he offers; uncertain whether he really holds it – whether a valid communication has really been defined and conveyed in terms of his creative art ('Art speech is the only speech').

For Murry, however, these places which I see as marginal in their unsatisfactoriness represent the centre of significance. On the passage just quoted he comments: 'This is the reassertion of his masculinity, of which he is always dreaming.' That is, Murry treats *Women in Love* as if it were a document of essentially the same order as *Look, we have come through!* 'To the working out of this personal argument in the imaginary consummation of Birkin and Ursula', he says, 'all else is really subsidiary in the novel.'

This is just not true. By way of beginning to show that it obviously isn't, one might point to the wealth of vivid dramatic creation for which the book should be found remarkable at first reading – the astonishing variety and force of the enacted life. It should not be too difficult to see that these memorable scenes, episodes, and images are not random. Even a reader who is still far from having grasped the full thematic development must be aware by the time he reaches the end of the book that it contains a presentation of twentieth-century England – of modern civilization – so first-hand and searching in its comprehensiveness as to be beyond the powers of any other novelist he knows of.

The novelist who achieves this is one whose treatment of the individual life, for him the inevitable focus of preoccupation, is incomparably inward and subtle – the individual life in its essential and inescapable relations with others. 'No human being can develop save through the polarized connexion with other beings.' This might perhaps seem to be a truism: in nothing does Lawrence's genius show itself more than in the originality and profundity with which he explores and demonstrates the truth the proposition sums up. The same essay, *Psychoanalysis and the Unconscious*, contains – to choose one of many eligible sentences – what might have served as an epigraph for *Women in Love*:

The tortures of psychic starvation which civilized people proceed to suffer, once they have solved the bread-and-butter problem of alimentation, will not bear thought.

Positively, the preoccupations of the novel are put here:

The amazingly difficult and vital business of human relationship has been almost laughably underestimated in our epoch. All this nonsense about love and unselfishness is more crude and repugnant than savage fetish-worship. Love is a thing to be *learned*, through centuries of patient effort. It is a difficult, complex maintenance of individual integrity throughout the incalculable processes of interhuman polarity.

Psychoanalysis and the Unconscious is obviously, and very impressively, a work of poised and sober intelligence. Together with the companion treatise, *Fantasia of the Unconscious*, which in its 'fantasia' mode has equally the poise of lucid and assured intelligence, it is closely related to *Women in Love*, that novel which has so often been supposed to represent a repudiation of mind in an extreme of abandonment to frenzied sexuality and the Dark Gods. That Lawrence can write a convincing expository treatise on his themes will not, perhaps, be held against him as a novelist.

That he *is* a novelist it should have been impossible to doubt after reading the first few pages of *Women in Love*. The opening, though it can hardly be alleged to have the personal-documentary vibration that announces the significant for Murry, proclaims the master. The reader, wholly engaged at once, cannot doubt that this novel is *about* something, as few novels are:

Ursula and Gudrun Brangwen sat one morning in the window-bay of their father's house in Beldover, working and talking. Ursula was stitching a piece of brightly-coloured embroidery and Gudrun was drawing upon a board which she held on her knee. They were mostly silent, talking as their thoughts strayed through their minds.

'Ursula,' said Gudrun, 'don't you *really want* to get married?' Ursula laid her embroidery in her lap and looked up. Her face was calm and considerate.

'I don't know,' she replied. 'It depends how you mean.' Gudrun was slightly taken aback. She watched her sister for some moments.

'Well,' she said ironically, 'it usually means one thing! But don't you think anyhow, you'd be –' she darkened slightly – 'in a better position than you are in now?'

A shadow came over Ursula's face.

'I might,' she said. 'But I'm not sure.'

Again Gudrun paused, slightly irritated. She wanted to be quite definite.

'You don't think one needs the *experience* of having been married?' she asked.

'Do you think it need *be* an experience?' replied Ursula.

'Bound to be, in some way or other,' said Gudrun, coolly. 'Possibly undesirable, but bound to be an experience of some sort.'

'Not really,' said Ursula. 'More likely to be the end of experience.'

Gudrun sat very still, to attend to this.

'Of course,' she said, 'there's *that* to consider.'

As the two girls continue their conversation the novel is decisively launched. There they are, educated, intelligent, and conscious, no longer belonging to the working class into which they were born, or to any class or context that can give life bearings or direction, or in which (say) marriage has its significant and unquestionable place. And yet, if not marriage – what? 'The sisters found themselves confronted by a void, a terrifying chasm, as if they had looked over the edge.'

They worked on in silence for some time, Gudrun's cheek was flushed with repressed emotion. She resented its having been called into being.

'Shall we go out and look at that wedding?' she asked at length, in a voice that was too casual.

'Yes,' cried Ursula, too eagerly, throwing aside her sewing and leaping up, as if to escape something, thus betraying the tension of the situation and causing a friction of dislike to go over Gudrun's nerves.

The way to the church is through representative English scenes, the 'amorphous ugliness of a small colliery town in the Midlands', and, evoked with all Lawrence's peculiar genius, the spoilt and blackened countryside. The wedding is a conventional one, very different from any in which we can imagine the Brangwen girls being involved – that of course is a large part of its dramatic and poetic point. At the church we are introduced to most of the other main characters of the novel: the Crich family, one of whom is being married; Birkin; and Hermione Roddice, a Baronet's daughter and 'a woman of the new school, full of intellectuality, and heavy, nerve-worn with consciousness', having, for all her external overbearing assurance, a void within her that she feels Birkin alone can fill. It doesn't matter in the least that Hermione is supposed to be modelled on a well-known Georgian intellectual hostess; what does matter is that she at once becomes a convincing presence and that she has her essential part in the organized significance of the novel.

The problem of discussing *Women in Love* is that the organization is so rich and close. From the moment the Brangwen girls begin their conversation about marriage, the dramatic poem unfolds – or builds up – with an astonishing fertility of life. This life, so much of which commands the imagination at the first encounter, is all significant life; not a scene, episode, image, or touch but forwards the organized development of the themes. To discuss this development point by point as the dramatic action advances would take a volume. One can only hope to do some sufficiently representative illustrating that will convey the nature of the themes and of the whole organization.

I will consider the treatment of Gerald Crich's case. There we have peculiarly well exemplified the way in which, in Lawrence's art, the diagnosis of the malady of the individual psyche can become that of the malady of a civilization. Moreover, to consider *Women in Love* as it focusses on Gerald, as so much of it does, is to expose with great force the fallacy of Murry's approach. 'To the working out of this personal argument in the imaginary consummation of Birkin and Ursula all else is really subsidiary in the novel': no one who had read the novel disinterestedly as a novel – as the dramatic poem that it so impressively is – could think that; and for such a reader it must seem perversely arbitrary to assert that the movement of the action towards Gerald's death draws its significance and its power from its relation to a major and central drama of Birkin and Ursula.

We see Gerald first through Gudrun's eyes ('her interest was piqued'), at the wedding in the first chapter, a blond and handsome young Englishman of the ruling class. A reception follows at Shortlands, the Crich home, where, deputizing for his ailing father, he takes command with a poised and easy adequacy. Yet in the same chapter we are made aware that he is more interesting than the ostensible type suggests. We gather, and the effect is to establish a sense of some strain or self-distrust beneath the confident surface, that when a boy he had accidentally killed his brother. This effect is reinforced by the conversation with which Gerald and Birkin bring the chapter to a close – the conversation about the enactment of marriage by capture that has so oddly qualified the conventionality of the wedding. We have here an admirable small-scale illustration of Lawrence's power of introducing direct discussion of his themes into dialogue that remains convincingly dramatic in every respect. Gerald disapproves of the unconventional episode. Birkin, who is obviously very near to a self-dramatization of Lawrence, replies:

'I think it was perfect good form in Laura to bolt from Lupton to the church door. It was almost a masterpiece in good form. It's the hardest thing in the world to act spontaneously on one's impulse – and it's the only really gentlemanly thing to do – provided you're fit to do it.'

'You don't expect me to take you seriously, do you?' asked Gerald.

'Yes, Gerald, you're one of the very few people I do expect that of.'

'Then I'm afraid I can't come up to your expectations here, at any rate. You think people should just do as they like.'

'I think they always do. But I should like them to like the purely individual thing in themselves, which makes them act in singleness. And they only like to do the collective thing.'

'And I,' said Gerald grimly, 'shouldn't like to be in a world of people who acted individually and spontaneously, as you call it. We should have everybody cutting everybody else's throat in five minutes.'

'It's a nasty view of things, Gerald,' said Birkin, 'and no wonder you are afraid of yourself and your own unhappiness.'

'How am I afraid of myself?' said Gerald; 'and I don't think I am unhappy.'

'You seem to have a lurking desire to have your gizzard slit, and imagine every man has his knife up his sleeve for you,' Birkin said.

'How do you make that out?' said Gerald.

'From you,' said Birkin.

There was a pause of strange enmity between the two men, that was very near to love.

But still more has been done to qualify our sense of Gerald's perfectly poised 'strong man' normality by Birkin's encounter, earlier in the chapter, with Gerald's mother. Her disturbing queerness is evoked with that power of Lawrence's which sometimes reminds us of Dickens, though it is a power that serves a profound psychological insight, and conveys characteristically the vibration of inner significances. Mrs Crich, in her outdoor things, comes noiselessly into the room and makes straight for Birkin:

'I don't know half the people here,' she said, in her low voice. Her son-in-law moved uneasily away.

'And you don't like strangers?' laughed Birkin. 'I myself can never see why one should take account of people, just because they happen to be in the room with one: why *should* I know they are there?'

'Why indeed, why indeed!' said Mrs Crich, in her low, tense voice. 'Except that they *are* there. *I* don't know people whom I find in the house. The children introduce them to me – "Mother, this is Mr So-and-so." I am no further. What has Mr So-and-so to do with his own name? – and what have I to do with either him or his name?'

She looked up at Birkin. She startled him. He was flattered too that she came to talk to him, for she took hardly any notice of anybody. He looked down at her tense clear face, with its heavy features, but he was afraid to look into her heavy-seeing blue eyes. He noticed instead how her hair looped in slack, slovenly strands over her rather beautiful ears, which were not quite clean. Neither was her neck perfectly clean. Even in that he seemed to belong to her, rather than to the rest of the company; though, he thought to himself, he was always well washed, at any rate at the neck and ears.

He smiled faintly, thinking of these things. Yet he was tense, feeling that he and the elderly, estranged woman were conferring together like traitors, like enemies within the camp of the other people. He resembled a deer, that throws one ear back upon the trail behind, and one ear forward, to know what is ahead.

'People don't really matter,' he said, rather unwilling to continue.

The mother looked up at him with sudden, dark interrogation, as if doubting his sincerity.

'How do you mean, *matter*?' she asked sharply.

'Not many people are anything at all,' he answered, forced to go deeper than he wanted to. 'They jingle and giggle. It would be much better if they were just wiped out. Essentially, they don't exist, they aren't there.'

She watched him steadily while he spoke.

'But we don't imagine them,' she said sharply.

'There's nothing to imagine, that's why they don't exist.'

'Well,' she said, 'I would hardly go as far as that. There they are, whether they exist or no. It doesn't rest with me to decide on their existence. I only know that I can't be expected to take count of them all. You can't expect me to know them, just because they happen to be there. As far as *I* go, they might as well not be there.'

'Exactly,' he replied.

'Mightn't they?' she asked again.

'Just as well,' he repeated. And there was a little pause.

'Except that they *are* there, and that's a nuisance,' she said. 'There are my sons-in-law,' she went on, in a sort of monologue. 'Now Laura's got married, there's another. And I really don't know John from James yet. They come up to me and call me mother. I know what they will say – "How are you, mother?" I ought to say, "I am not your mother, in any sense." But what is the use? There they are. I have had children of my own. I suppose I know them from another woman's children.'

'One would suppose so,' he said.

She looked at him, somewhat surprised, forgetting perhaps that she was talking to him. And she lost her thread.

She looked round the room, vaguely. Birkin could not guess what she was looking for, nor what she was thinking. Evidently she noticed her sons.

'Are my children all there?' she asked him abruptly.

He laughed, startled, afraid, perhaps.

'I scarcely know them, except Gerald,' he replied.

'Gerald!' she exclaimed. 'He's the most wanting of them all. You'd never think it, to look at him now, would you?'

What lies behind Mrs Crich's queerness we learn later in the chapter (XVII) called 'The Industrial Magnate'. The account there of what has gone wrong between her and her husband, and consequently to both of them, is a profound study of individual psyches. As their son Gerald's case assumes its relation to the past and becomes for us a significant part of the family history, we realize that, in the rendering of this, we have seen at the same time – and seen as revealed by a profoundly diagnostic insight – the large movement of civilization.

The surveying sweep, the history, and the exposition of 'The Industrial Magnate', which comes half-way through the book, bring to full explicitness what has been conveyed in the complex course of the preceding action by dramatic and poetic means – all the resources of a great poet-novelist. That we have in *Women in Love* astonishing imaginative power should be granted at once by any reader, so largely compact is the book of effects that work an irresistible spell immediately, even when their full significance is very far from being taken. What is manifested in the organization that commands such a variety of resource and method with such seeming ease, so that they work together to serve a complex significance, is a remarkable intellectual grasp: the novelist's imaginative grasp is at the same time that.

To suggest the range and flexibility of Lawrence's art one may set over against 'The Industrial Magnate' the earlier chapter (IX), 'Coaldust', in which Gerald forces his terror-stricken Arab mare to stand while the colliery-train passing the level-crossing does its worst with wheels, brakes, buffers, chains, and whistle. The whole thing is rendered with shattering immediacy; with Ursula and Gudrun we stand, tortured by hideous noise and clenched in violent protest, while the rider compels the frantic mare back against herself and into the assaulting terrors. The significance of the episode needs no eliciting or developing by anything in the nature of comment from the novelist. The little drama – the image of Gerald, 'a glistening and half-smiling look on his face', as he 'bites down' on the mare, and strikes his spurs into her bleeding sides – crystallizes our sense of Gerald and gives it a new sharp edge. It picks up and brings to a focus of significance a multitude of intimations that have been conveyed to us earlier in different ways. We now realize the energy of will in Gerald as something more cruelly and dangerously ruthless than, for instance, it appears as Ursula and Gudrun discuss it in Chapter IV, 'The Diver'. Walking by Willey Water, they see in the distance Shortlands, 'Dorothy Wordsworth and Jane Austen' in its charm, but, says Ursula, being ruthlessly modernized inside by Gerald:

'Certainly, he's got go,' said Gudrun. 'In fact I've never seen a man who showed signs of so much. The unfortunate thing is, where does his *go* go to, what becomes of it?'

'Oh I know,' said Ursula. 'It goes in applying the latest appliances.'

Where Gerald's 'go' goes to ultimately is self-destruction: the novel shows us the process, in all its aspects, with inexorable convincingness.

To analyse step by step the process of art by which this is done would take inordinate space. And it is unnecessary; for once the reader has grasped the general nature of Gerald's case he should find that the subtleties of the art tell sufficiently at a first current reading to make the development of the themes, and the ways in which they are organized, clear. The best commentator on Gerald's case is Lawrence himself; the discussion of will and 'ideas' in *Psychoanalysis and the Unconscious* is illuminatingly relevant. To say this may perhaps be to invite the suspicion that Lawrence, for a poet-novelist (as I have called him), is dangerously a theorist. But the intelligence that makes his generalized exposition of his theme so lucid and convincing is precisely that which qualified him to be a great novelist. He experiences, perceives, and understands, and the strength of his thought lies in its sensitive adequacy to the perceptions, insights, and realizations that it orders and states in epitomizing abstraction.

It is because he has the genius of a great creative writer that he has been capable of this thinking; and that he has done it, achieving the appropriate expression in discursive form, has certainly its consequences for his art. But this is not to say that in *Women in Love* (for example) he has written a novel to illustrate a theory. That would be to suggest that an abstract system of schematic simplifications has been imposed on life. But his discursive thought itself is governed by a distrust of abstractions that, positively, is a rare power of maintaining a living fidelity to the concrete; and the mind that has done this thinking brings to the artist's creative work a sharpened perception of the significance and a strengthened grasp of it – brings the ability to achieve such an organization as that of *Women in Love*.

Here, then, is a passage of *Psychoanalysis and the Unconscious* immediately relevant to Gerald's case:

True, we must all develop into mental consciousness. But mental consciousness is not a goal; it is a cul-de-sac. It provides us only with endless *appliances* which we can use for the all-too-difficult business of coming to our spontaneous-creative fulness of being. It provides us with means to adjust ourselves to the external universe. It gives us further means for subduing the external, materio-mechanical universe to our great end of creative life. And it gives us plain indications of how to avoid falling into automatism, hints for the *applying* of the will, the loosening of false, automatic fixations, the brave adherence to a profound soul-impulse. This is the use of the mind – a great indicator and instrument. The mind as author and director of life is anathema.

– But that is what it has become in Gerald; hence the destructiveness of his 'go', as the following passage from the same essay explains:

The mind is the dead end of life. But it has all the mechanical force of the non-vital universe. It is a great dynamo of super-mechanical force. Given the *will* as accomplice, it can even arrogate its machine-motions and automatizations over the whole of life, till every tree becomes a clipped tea-pot and every man a useful mechanism. So we see the brain, like a great dynamo and accumulator, accumulating *mechanical* force and presuming to apply this mechanical force-control to the living unconscious, subjecting everything spontaneous to certain machine-principles called ideals or ideas.

And the human will assists in this humiliating and sterilizing process. We don't know what the human will is. But we do know that it is a certain faculty belonging to every living organism; the faculty for self-determination.

The significance of these propositions reveals its full force and scope in the life and death of Gerald. A certain verbal identity may have been noticed between what Ursula says of his 'go' and what Lawrence says of 'mental consciousness'. Gerald's 'go', says Ursula, goes 'in applying the latest appliances': 'Mental consciousness', says Lawrence, 'provides us only with endless *appliances* which we can use for the all-too-difficult business of coming to our spontaneous-creative fulness of being.' But mind, with its accomplice, will, does not, in Gerald, serve; it has established itself in the saddle, and its 'appliances' work the psyche from above. He suffers an attendant disadvantage, the lack of something that will and idea cannot supply: the sense of a meaning in life. 'I wish you'd tell me something that *did* matter,' he says suddenly in one of his intimate talks with Birkin. But he has his 'go': he can cultivate a sense of purposive activity in 'applying the latest appliances'.

In Gerald, in fact, we see the malady of the individual psyche as the essential process of industrial civilization. Gerald, when *Women in Love* begins, has virtually taken over the direction of the mines from his father. What lies behind this we are shown in the chapter 'The Industrial Magnate'. Thomas Crich has been an idealist all his life:

He had been so constant to his lights, so constant to charity, and to his love for his neighbour. Perhaps he had loved his neighbour even better than himself – which is going one further than the commandment. Always, this flame had burned in his heart, sustaining him through everything, the welfare of the people. He was a large employer of labour, he was a great mine-owner. And he had never lost this from his heart, that in Christ he was one with his workmen. Nay, he had felt inferior to them, as if they through poverty and labour were nearer to God than he. He had always the unacknowledged belief that it was his workmen, the miners, who held in their hands the means of salvation. To move nearer to God, he must move towards his miners, his life must gravitate towards theirs. They were, unconsciously, his idol, his God made manifest. In them he worshipped the highest, the great sympathetic, mindless Godhead of humanity.

The domination of this idea is something that Mrs Crich's very being repudiates. The relation between her husband and her recalls in its way the episode of Gerald and the mare; for in Christiana Crich we see 'spontaneous-creative' life cruelly constrained and violated by a will-enforced idea:

And all the while his wife had opposed him like one of the great demons of hell. Strange, like a bird of prey, with the fascinating beauty and abstraction of a hawk, she had beat against the bars of his philanthropy, and like a hawk in a cage, she had sunk into silence. By force of circumstance, because all the world combined to make the cage unbreakable, he had been too strong for her, he had kept her prisoner. And because she was his prisoner, his passion for her had always remained keen as death. He had always loved her, loved her with intensity. Within the cage, she was denied nothing, she was given all licence.

But she had gone almost mad. Of wild and overweening temper, she could not bear the humiliation of her husband's soft, half-appealing kindness to everybody.

But it is in the logic of the development of son out of father that Thomas Crich's ideal receives its critical exposure. Gerald as a boy had 'hated remorselessly the circumstances of his own life, so much that he never really saw Beldover and the colliery valley'. He had 'turned his face entirely away from the blackened mining region that stretched away on the right hand of Shortlands, he turned entirely to the country and the woods beyond Willey Water'. Yet, after a young-manhood spent in unsatisfying quest for adventure, he had 'discovered a real adventure at last in the coal-mines'. Asked by his father to help in the firm, he has settled down to finding the meaning of life in them. The meaning they actually represent for him, however, differs radically, not only from his father's ideal, but from what, when challenged, he says it is. Here is a conversation between him and Birkin as they travel together to London in the train (Chapter V):

'Can't you see,' said Birkin, 'that to help my neighbour to eat is no more than eating myself. "I eat, thou eatest, he eats, we eat, you eat, they eat" – and what then? Why should every man decline the whole verb. First person singular is enough for me.'

'You've got to start with material things,' said Gerald. Which statement Birkin ignored.

'And we've got to live for *something*, we're not just cattle that can graze and have done with it,' said Gerald.

'Tell me,' said Birkin. 'What do you live for?'

Gerald's face went baffled.

'What do I live for?' he repeated. 'I suppose I live to work, to produce something, in so far as I am a purposive being. Apart from that, I live because I am living.'

'And what's your work? Getting so many more thousands of tons of coal out of the earth every day. And when we've got all the coal we want, and all the plush furniture, and pianofortes, and the rabbits are all stewed and eaten, and we're all warm and our bellies are filled and we're listening to the young lady performing on the pianoforte – what then? What then, when you've made a real fair start with your material things?'

Gerald sat laughing at the words and the mocking humour of the other man. But he was cogitating too.

'We haven't got there yet,' he replied. 'A good many people are still waiting for the rabbit and the fire to cook it.'

'So while you get the coal I must chase the rabbit?' said Birkin mocking at Gerald.

'Something like that,' said Gerald.

Birkin watched him narrowly. He saw the perfect, good-humoured callousness, even strange, glistening malice, in Gerald, glistening through the plausible ethics of productivity.

The 'callousness' and the 'glistening malice' betray the deep anti-human drive in which Gerald has found the solution of his personal problem – in so far as he *has* found a solution. The 'plausible ethics of productivity' is not only an irrelevance in the face of this problem ('What do you live for?' is the way of putting it here): it represents, by the criterion that Lawrence's creative genius compels us to apply, a refusal of responsibility – of self-responsibility, or responsibility towards life. But so equally does Thomas Crich's idealism:

Perhaps he had loved his neighbour even better than himself – which is going one further than the commandment.

Against this we may put Birkin's:

Can't you see that to help my neighbour to eat is no more than to eat myself?

Thomas Crich attributes to eating as done by others a significance that it hasn't for himself as eater, for he attributes to the having, in charity, helped others to eat, a significance that can dispose for him of the question, 'What do you live for?' The fallacy, the idealism, is not only a sentimental self-indulgence and an evasion of responsibility; we are made to see it as positively inimical to life, which, victim of the malign inescapable logic, suffers a cruel disaster in Christiana Crich.

But there is a wider-reaching defeat of life, one that involves the miners themselves. Thomas Crich's benevolent idealism could not establish permanent peace in the mines. Moved by 'the last impulses of the last religious passion left on earth, the passion for equality' – and 'how disentangle the passion for equality from the passion of cupidity, when begins the fight for equality of possessions?' – the miners take the field:

The idea flew through them: 'All men are equal on earth,' and they would carry the idea to its material fulfilment. After all, is it not the teaching of Christ? And what is an idea, if not the germ of action in the material world. 'All men are equal in spirit, they are all the sons of God. Whence then this obvious *disquality*?' It was a religious creed pushed to its material conclusion. Thomas Crich at least had no answer.

That word 'disquality' is no mere ill-bred wantonness on Lawrence's part, a pointless substitute for 'inequality'. It registers an essential insistence. The truth it insists on is one that no great novelist, I imagine, could have thought of denying. Lawrence insists on it in *Women in*

Love because it is peculiarly important for the diagnostic presentment of industrial civilization and of the political ideas prevailing in the society to which his characters belong. The challenging word, when it occurs in the chapter called 'The Industrial Magnate', picks up certain immediately relevant earlier passages in the novel. One of them is a discussion that takes place at the house-party in Chapter VII ('Breadalby') – a chapter in which the dramatic power, the penetration and the flexibility of a great novelist's art are wonderfully exemplified. Since the discussion suggests peculiarly well the ways in which the different aspects of Lawrence's themes are related – how the personal question about marrying with which the novel opens is related to the examination of social and political ideas and to the industrial revolution effected by Gerald – a quotation of some length will be in place:

The great social idea, said Sir Joshua, was the *social* equality of man. No, said Gerald, the idea was, that every man was fit for his own little bit of a task – let him do that, and then please himself. The unifying principle was the work in hand. Only work, the business of production, held men together. It was mechanical, but then society *was* a mechanism. Apart from work they were isolated, free to do as they liked.

'Oh!' cried Gudrun. 'Then we shan't have names any more – we shall be like the Germans, nothing but Herr Obermeister and Herr Untermeister. I can imagine it – "I am Mrs Colliery-Manager Crich – I am Mrs Member of Parliament Roddice. I am Miss Art-Teacher Brangwen." Very pretty that.'

'Things would work very much better, Miss Art-Teacher Brangwen,' said Gerald.

'What things, Mr Colliery-Manager Crich? The relations between you and me, *par exemple?*'

'Yes, for example,' cried the Italian. 'That which is between men and women –!'

'That is non-social,' said Birkin, sarcastically.

'Exactly,' said Gerald. 'Between me and a woman, the social question does not enter. It is my own affair.'

'A ten-pound note on it,' said Birkin.

'You don't admit that a woman is a social being?' asked Ursula of Gerald.

'She is both,' said Gerald. 'She is a social being, as far as society is concerned. But for her own private self, she is a free agent, it is her own affair, what she does.'

'But won't it be rather difficult to arrange the two halves?' asked Ursula.

'Oh no,' replied Gerald. 'They arrange themselves naturally – we see it now, everywhere.'

'Don't you laugh so pleasantly till you're out of the wood,' said Birkin.

Gerald knitted his brow in momentary irritation.

'Was I laughing?' he said.

'*If*,' said Hermione at last, 'we could only realize, that in the *spirit* we are all one, all equal in the spirit, all brothers there – the rest wouldn't matter, there would be no more of this carping and envy and this struggle for power, which destroys, only destroys.'

This speech was received in silence, and almost immediately the party rose from the table. But when the others had gone, Birkin turned round in bitter declamation, saying:

'It is just the opposite, just the contrary, Hermione. We are all different and unequal in spirit – it is only the *social* differences that are based on accidental material conditions. We are all abstractly or mathematically equal, if you like. Every man has hunger and thirst, two eyes, one nose and two legs. We're all the same in point of number. But spiritually, there is pure difference and neither equality nor inequality counts. It is upon these two bits of knowledge that you must found a state. Your democracy is an absolute lie – your brotherhood of man is a pure falsity, if you apply it further than the mathematical abstraction. We all drank milk first, we all eat bread and meat, we all want to ride in motor-cars – therein lies the beginning and the end of the brotherhood of man. But no equality.

'But I, myself, who am myself, what have I to do with equality with any other man or woman? In the spirit, I am as separate as one star is from another, as different in quality and quantity. Establish a state on *that*. One man isn't any better than another, not because they are equal but because they are intrinsically *other*, [so] that there is no term of comparison. The minute you begin to compare, one man is seen to be far better than another, all the inequality you can imagine is there by nature. I want every man to have his share in the world's goods, so that I am rid of his importunity, so that I can tell him: "Now you've got what you want – you've got your fair share of the world's gear. Now, you one-mouthed fool, mind yourself and don't obstruct me."'

Birkin here enunciates the truth registered in the term 'disquality', and does so in a context that explains the insistence. No great novelist can be a Benthamite; for him the fact that we can be said to be 'all abstractly and mathematically equal' has little to do with his interest in mankind. It is a fact that Lawrence is concerned with by way of protest and warning; his study of the individual psyche has led him to the diagnosis of a civilization in which the idealism he condemns (it amounts, he points out, to the same thing as materialism) has become a deadly enemy to life. The truth that 'disquality' insists on has, he knows, to be insisted on in the modern world – and he was writing *Women in Love* thirty years ago, when Lenin's revolution was contemporary news ('Bliss was it in that dawn to be alive'). In *Psychoanalysis and the Unconscious* he insists on it characteristically when, desiderating a 'science of the creative unconscious', he adds that such a science will need 'a super-scientific grace'; for

mark, the first naked unicellular organism is an *individual*. It is a specific individual, not a mathematical unit, like a unit of force.

Thomas Crich's idealism, denying the essential truth, and traitorous to life, gets him

trapped between two half-truths and broken. He wanted to be a pure Christian, one and equal with all men. He even wanted to give away all he had, to the poor. Yet he was a great promoter of industry, and he knew perfectly that he must keep his goods and keep his authority. This was as divine a necessity to him as the need to give away all he possessed – more divine, even, since this was the necessity he acted upon. Yet because he did *not* act on the other ideal, it dominated him. He wanted to be a father of loving kindness and sacrificial benevolence. The colliers shouted to him about his thousands a year. They would not be deceived.

The new conditions call for a new kind of master, and as the son takes over we see the issue of Thomas Crich's idealism in the triumph of mechanism. For Gerald the 'whole Christian attitude of love and self-sacrifice is old hat': he acts consistently and without misgiving on the half-truth that even his father had *acted* on. Confident of grasping reality, 'he knows that position and authority are the right thing in the world':

They were the right thing, for the simple reason that they were functionally necessary. They were not the be-all and the end-all. It was like being part of a machine. He himself happened to be a controlling part, the masses of men were the parts variously controlled.

The logic, when the truth of 'disquality' is left out, is irresistible. His father's dilemma is resolved; and as Gerald goes ahead with his 'life-work ... to extend over the earth a great and perfect system in which the will of man ran smooth and unthwarted, timeless, a God-head in process', we see in the good-humoured common sense of his part in the discussion quoted above a ruthless inhuman force, and a terrifying reality of the modern world. In some moods, the account of the process may very well strike us as something like the essential human history of the decades since *Women in Love* was written. The supreme end that commands Gerald is the efficiency of the 'great social productive machine': 'let it produce a sufficiency of everything, let every man be given a rational portion ... and then, provision made, let the devil supervene, let every man look after his own amusements and appetites, so long as he interfered with nobody'. The beneficent-sounding end entails, ironically, the conception in which the father's dilemma is resolved: 'the pure instrumentality of mankind'. This, of course, for Lawrence is a destructive blasphemy; and the novel gives us a vivid glimpse of the consequences for the lives of the miners, who hate Gerald, but nevertheless accept what they 'really want': 'the first great step in undoing, the substitution of the mechanical principle for the organic ... the subordination of every organic unit to the great mechanical purpose'.

Then we have the focus again on the individual psyche. In Gerald himself we see life as the victim of the triumph of mechanism – the usurping dominance of idea and will. It was the sense of an inner lack that drove him to find meaning and purpose in the triumphant activity ('he was a pure and exalted activity'), and the outcome of it is a more terrible void:

But now he had succeeded – he had finally succeeded. And once or twice lately, when he was alone in the evening and had nothing to do, he had suddenly stood up in terror, not knowing what he was. And he went to the mirror and looked long and closely at his own face, at his own eyes, seeking for something. He was afraid, in mortal dry fear, but he knew not what of. He looked at his own face. There it was, shapely and healthy and the same as ever, yet somehow it was not real, it was a mask. He dared not touch it, for fear it should prove to be only a composition mask. His eyes were blue and keen as ever, and as firm in their sockets. Yet he was not sure that they were not blue false bubbles that would burst in a moment and leave clear annihilation. He could see the darkness in them, as if they were only bubbles of darkness. He was afraid that one day he would break down and be a purely meaningless babble lapping round a darkness.

But his will yet held good, he was able to go away and read, and think about things.

The breakdown actually comes at the death of his father. The long-drawn-out process of the death is done with profoundly disturbing power (we are reminded of the death of the mother in *Sons and Lovers*). In Chapter XXIV, 'Death and Love' (*not* 'Love and Death'), we are made to realize the horror of the process for Gerald, as he can less and less disguise from himself the fact of the dependence of his own life, for meaning and the sense of reality in things, on the existence of his father – the father whom he has superseded. We see him turning, more and more compulsively, to Gudrun to save him from the void. The thing is done in dramatic immediacy, through the concrete presence, the evoked action and gesture, and the dramatic utterance; let the reader turn up, for example, the half-dozen pages following the opening two of Chapter XXIV ('Death and Love') by way of correcting any impression I may possibly have conveyed of a preponderant reliance on more distant modes – on the expository and historical – in Lawrence's presentment of his themes.

When the father at last dies, Gerald takes the desperate plunge into the salvation of 'love'. In a kind of somnambulistic automatism – the whole episode is uncannily evoked – he goes cross-country through the dark to the churchyard, recoils from the smell of the raw earth and the flowers on his father's grave, pushes on with a blind purpose, enters the house that is his goal, and in his muddy boots climbs the stairs to Gudrun's room. Now begins the see-saw battle between them that ends in his death. His 'love' is desperate need and utter dependence, and these make him a deadly oppression to her. Her 'love' for him takes on more and more of malice. The sense of his dependence, and the knowledge that there is no dominance to be achieved that will ensure his safety, makes him hate her.

This drama acts itself out in the high Tyrolese valley where Gerald and Gudrun, with Birkin and Ursula, go for a holiday, and it ends, closing the whole action of the novel, in Gerald's death in the snow. This end in a world of snow, inhumanly cold and white, has its significance. We shall not appreciate fully what this is unless we have recognized the symbolic and emotive function of the primitive carving about which Gerald challenges Birkin so pressingly in the early chapter (VII) called 'Totem'.

The episode takes place during Gerald's initiatory visit, as Birkin's guest, to 'London Bohemia' (for this representative world of the intelligentsia, pungently evoked, has its place in Lawrence's wonderfully comprehensive presentment of contemporary England). In the house in Soho there are 'several statues, wood-carvings from the West Pacific, strange and disturbing ...'. Gerald takes Birkin up to one of these and demands his opinion on it:

'Why is it art?' Gerald asked, shocked, resentful.

'It conveys a complete truth,' said Birkin. 'It contains the whole truth of that state, whatever you feel about it.'

'But you can't call it *high* art,' said Gerald.

'High! There are centuries and hundreds of centuries of development in a straight line, behind that carving; it is an awful pitch of culture, of a definite sort.'

'What culture?' Gerald asked, in opposition. He hated the sheer barbaric thing.

'Pure culture in sensation, culture in the physical consciousness, really ultimate *physical* consciousness, mindless, utterly sensual. It is so sensual as to be final, supreme.'

But Gerald resented it. He wanted to keep certain illusions, certain ideas like clothing.

The figure that repels him draws him with a certain fascination too; that is made plain to us. 'He saw Minette in it,' we are told, significantly. Minette is the artist's model with whom he is carrying on a casual *liaison*. And a Minette, we come to learn, is one of the habitual remedies to which Gerald resorts when, as happens more and more, the drive fails in him, and he is 'emptily restless, utterly hollow', 'suspended motionless, in an agony of inertia, like a machine that is without power'.

The significance is sharpened and developed in various ways as the chapters succeed one another. There is, notably, the passage in Chapter XIX ('Moony') that Middleton Murry cites as supporting the argument of *Son of Woman*. The figure from West Africa that Birkin recalls has the same intended force as the figure that fascinated Gerald:

He remembered her vividly; she was one of his soul's intimates. Her body was long and elegant, her face crushed tiny like a beetle's, she had rows of round heavy collars, like a column of quoits, on her neck. He remembered her; her astonishing cultured elegance, her diminished, beetle face, the astounding long elegant body, on short, ugly legs, with such protruberant buttocks, so weighty and unexpected below her slim long loins. She knew what he himself did not know. She had thousands of years of purely sensual, purely unspiritual knowledge behind her. It must have been thousands of years since her race died, mystically: that is, since the relation between the senses and the outspoken mind had broken, leaving the experience all in one sort, mystically sensual. Thousands of years ago, that which was imminent in himself must have taken place in these Africans; the goodness, the holiness, the desire for creation and productive happiness must have lapsed, leaving the single impulse for knowledge in one sort, mindless progressive knowledge through the senses, knowledge arrested and ending in the senses, mystic knowledge in disintegration and dissolution, knowledge such as the beetles have, which live purely within the world of corruption and cold dissolution. That was why her face looked like a beetle's. ...

Murry sees nothing here but Lawrence's personal 'case', the significance being self-diagnosis or self-exposure: 'Birkin shrinks back from the lapse from goodness in himself.' And it is true that Lawrence (as he is fully aware) knows the general human plight because he himself is part of contemporary civilized humanity. But to be able, in reading through *Women in Love*, to ignore the whole presentment of the general plight! – it shows what blindness can be induced by a predetermined and stubborn misdirection of interest. For, as I hope I have sufficiently demonstrated, all the resources of a marvellously·vital and intelligent art are devoted, in that book, to transcending, not only the author's personal case, but that of any presented individual.

The presence of impersonal themes, in their significant relations, is plain enough (one would have thought) on the page from which Murry takes his diagnostic passage. The West African statuette (this we are actually told, and the local explicitness merely picks up what has been done in drama, imagery, and poetic organization) represents something that we are to see as a default, a failure, antithetical – and so significantly related – to the human disaster enacted by Gerald Crich. A strong normative preoccupation, entailing positives that are concretely present in many ways (we have them above in the phrases, 'the goodness, the holiness, the desire for creation and productive happiness') informs the life of *Women in Love* – the life that manifests itself in the definition and 'placing' of these opposite human disasters. If Lawrence's art exposes so cogently the malady of a civilization in which will and 'idea', controlling from above, have usurped the direction, and the smooth-running of an almost inconceivably intricate interlocking of mechanisms has become the supreme end, that is not by way of recommending a flight from intelligence and responsibility.

In fact, we are made to see the cult of the primitive as a symptom of the malady. This significance gets its completed definition in that final act which has for setting the high, remote world of inhuman cold and snow. As Gerald and Gudrun 'stepped out on the naked platform', at the end of the tiny valley railway,

with only snow around and above, Gudrun shrank as if it chilled her heart.

'My God, Jerry,' she said, turning to Gerald with sudden intimacy, 'you've done it now.'

We have had a plain enough hint of what is coming, and of the relation between the significance of the West African carving and that of the snow, in the self-same meditation of Birkin's from which Murry snips out the piece that fits his account. Birkin reflects:

There is a long way we can travel, after the death-break: after that point when the soul in intense suffering breaks, breaks away from its organic hold like a leaf that falls. We fall from the connexion with life and hope, we lapse from pure integral being, from creation and liberty, and we fall into the long, long African process of purely sensual understanding, knowlege in the mystery of dissolution. ...

There remained this way, this awful African process to be fulfilled. It would be done differently by the white races. The white races, having the arctic north behind them, the vast abstraction of ice and snow, would fulfil a mystery of ice-destructive knowledge, snow-abstract annihilation. ...

Was this then all that remained. ... Is our day of creative life finished?

Birkin thought of Gerald. He was one of those strange, white wonderful demons from the north fulfilled in the destructive frost mystery. And was he fated to pass away in this knowledge, this one process of frost-knowledge, death by perfect cold? Was he a messenger, an omen of the universal dissolution into whiteness and snow?

I grant that this kind of explicitness might seem to go with an element in *Women in Love* that is open to criticism. Yet the significances pointed to here are conveyed concretely in the work as a whole with the living cogency of great art. In the closing act in the world of snow we have the process completed.

To go through even this relatively short part of the whole in a detailed analysis is out of the question: it is too densely and subtly organized. But consider the part played by Loerke, the German sculptor whom the English party find at the hostel among the guests already there. He is a small, strange underworld creature: Gudrun, whom he attracts, 'could see in his brown, gnome's eyes the blank look of inorganic misery', though he is intelligent, and, in his uneasy way, contemptuously self-sufficient. Taking the hint of the name Gudrun we can't help seeing in Loerke a suggestion of Loki. For in calling this sister Gudrun Lawrence can't have been unmindful of the destructive part played by Gudrun in the saga of the Niblungs. And that in imagining the snow-death, with its symbolic significance, Lawrence was consciously, as well as profoundly, affected by his knowledge of northern mythology (in which we know him to have been intensely interested) is beyond doubt – northern mythology with its vision of the end of life in the cold of the dreadful final winter that heralds the last battle of the Gods. Birkin tells Gerald that Loerke is a 'gnawing little negation at the roots of life'. We have here the clear presence of Niðhögg, the evil power who gnaws at the roots of Yggdrasil, the tree of life. 'Loerke' blends the suggestion of 'Loki' with that of the evil 'lurker'.

Loerke tells Gudrun about a great granite frieze he has made for a factory in Cologne:

It was a representation of a fair, with peasants and artisans in an orgy of enjoyment, drunk and absurd in their modern dress, whirling ridiculously in roundabouts, gaping at shows, kissing and staggering and rolling in knots, swinging in swing-boats, and firing down shooting galleries, a frenzy of chaotic motion.

The discussion that follows between him and Gudrun has its clear part in the thematic exposition and development:

'Sculpture and architecture must go together. The day for irrelevant statues, as for wall-pictures, is over. ... And since churches are all museum stuff, since industry is our business now, then let us make our places of industry our art – our factory-area our Parthenon, *ecco* !'

'And do you think then,' said Gudrun, 'that art should serve industry?'

'Art should *interpret* industry, as art once interpreted religion,' he said.

'But does your fair interpret industry?' she asked him.

'Certainly. What is man doing when he is at a fair like that? He is fulfilling the counterpart of labour – the machine works him, instead of he the machine. He enjoys this mechanical motion in his own body !'

'But is there nothing but work – mechanical work?' said Gudrun.

'Nothing but work !' he repeated, leaning forward, his eyes two darknesses, with needle-points of light. 'No, it is nothing but this, serving a machine, or enjoying the motion of a machine – motion, that is all. You have never worked for hunger, or you would know what god governs us.'

The relation of this attitude to Gerald's doesn't need labouring: both artist and industrialist accept, from their different points of view, the triumph of mechanism and the implicit reduction of human life to mere instrumentality. And the conception of art expressed by Loerke doesn't stand by itself, unrelated; it has its part in the comprehensive examination of the nature and function of art that the reader, once adverted, will find to have been performed in the course of *Women in Love*. Loerke himself goes on to provoke the explicit statement of the conception that we recognize to be Lawrence's own – one illuminated and supremely vindicated by the book. The sculptor produces the photogravure of a statuette, a 'more popular' work of his. It represents a girl, slight and naked, sitting 'exposed on the flank' of a horse – 'a massive, magnificent stallion, rigid with pent-up power'. Gudrun, we are told, 'went pale, and a darkness came over her eyes, like shame, she looked up with a certain supplication, almost slave-like'.

Nevertheless, and significantly, she stands by Loerke in the sharp battle that follows with Ursula. Ursula asks why the horse should have been made 'so stock and stupid and brutal', and Loerke retorts, insultingly *de haut en bas*, that the horse is a 'piece of form':

'Wissen sie, gnädige Frau, that is a Kunstwerk, a work of art. It is a work of art, a picture of nothing, of absolutely nothing: it has no relation with the everyday world of this and other, there is no connexion between them, absolutely none, they are two different and distinct planes of existence, and to translate one into the other is worse than foolish, it is a darkening of all counsel, a making confusion everywhere. Do you see, you *must not* confuse the relative world of action with the absolute world of art. That you *must not* do.'

But Ursula refuses to be quenched:

'It isn't a word of it true, of all this harangue you have made me,' she replied flatly. 'The horse is a picture of your own stock stupid brutality, and the girl was a girl you loved and tortured and then ignored. ...

'As for your world of art and your world of reality ... you have to separate the two because you can't bear to know what you are. You can't bear to realize what a stock, stiff, hide-bound brutality you *are* really, so you say "it's the world of art". The world of art is only the truth about the real world, that's all – but you are too far gone to see it.'

Ursula's indignant *naïveté* is far from discrediting what she says; she affirms, in fact, the conception of art that is exemplified by the work of genius that contains her. We see her as opposing plain and profound truth to shallow sophistication and sophistry. The pregnant and subtle relevance of the whole episode to the main themes of the book become apparent as we consider the pages that follow. Loerke is not a major character, and he appears only in this closing act; but there is nothing gratuitous or loose about his appearance. Lawrence's art seems fed by an inexhaustible creative flow, but he organizes with a corresponding closeness. Ursula's personal charge against Loerke is borne out by what he himself tells about his relations with his model, and what he avows about his taste in the other sex (the sinister effect, as of a deep-seated perversion, inimical to life, conveyed by his avowal – 'at sixteen, seventeen, eighteen – after that, they are no good to me' – cannot be missed by the reader and hardly needs analysis).

Nevertheless, Gudrun finds herself oddly drawn to him, and the attraction is mutual. As in the intensifying seclusion of the snow-world the strain between her and Gerald – the oppression, for her, of his need, and the torturing humiliation of it for him – becomes intolerable, she takes more and more to spending her time in conversation with Loerke. What attracts in him is the antithesis of Gerald. It is, in appearance, a qualified antithesis, for Loerke doesn't bother about consistency. But the antithesis is there, and Birkin explains it to Gerald:

'He's a gnawing little negation, gnawing at the roots of life.'
'But why does anybody care about him?' cried Gerald.
'Because they hate the ideals also in their souls. They want to explore the sewers, and he is the wizard rat that swims ahead.'

Loerke and Gudrun talk together about art. 'They were almost of the same ideas', and 'he liked the West African figures, the Aztec art, Mexican and Central American'. At the same time – and it is no diffi-cult paradox at this point in *Women in Love* – 'they took a sentimental, childish delight in the achieved perfections of the past'. And then comes this remarkable passage (written, we remind ourselves, nearly forty years ago):

They played with the past, a sort of little game of chess, or marionettes, all to please themselves. They had all the great men for their marionettes, and they two were the God of the show, working it all. As for the future, that they never mentioned except one laughed out some mocking dream of the destruc-tion of the world by a ridiculous catastrophe of man's invention: a man in-vented such a perfect explosive that it blew the earth in two, and the two halves set off in different directions through space, to the dismay of the inhabitants; or else the people of the world divided into two halves, and each decided that it was perfect and right, and the other half was wrong and must be destroyed; so another end of the world. Or else, Loerke's dream of fear, the world went cold, and snow fell everywhere, and only white creatures, polar-bears, white foxes, and men like awful white snow-birds, persisted in ice-cruelty.

Apart from these stories, they never talked of the future.

The relation between the taste for the West African, the taste for the 'achieved perfections of the past', and the characteristics of contemporary civilization represented by Gerald hardly needs expounding. Loerke and Gudrun are artists, but of art as serving 'spontaneous-creative fulness of being' – a fulness impossible without 'mental consciousness' and a creativity in which intelligence has its indispensable part – they know nothing. Repelled by the world of usurping 'idea' and will with its triumphs of automatism and mechanical order, they can only react to the other extreme, or cultivate the finished perfections of the past in a subtler denial of creative life in the present. In these two 'the goodness, the holiness, the desire for creation and productive happiness' have essentially lapsed.

The contact with Loerke gives the Gudrun-Gerald relation its complete definition. For Gudrun, 'art', we have been made to recognize in full explicitness, is a very different thing from 'art' for the creator of *Women in Love*. It is significant that she does, we are told, only small things – for instance, a carved wagtail (Lawrence, we note, knew Katherine Mansfield). We see, in this last act, that the intolerableness for her of Gerald's need has for its other aspect the need in her, now finally disappointed, that had made him so strongly attractive till now. She lies awake, thinking of Gerald's 'force of will and his power of comprehending the actual world':

Her heart beat fast, she flew away on wings of elation, imagining a future. He would be a Napoleon of peace, or a Bismarck – and she the woman behind him. She had read Bismarck's letters, and had been deeply moved by them. And Gerald would be freer, more dauntless than Bismarck.

And even as she lay in fictitious transport, bathed in the strange false sunshine of hope in life, something seemed to snap in her, and a terrible cynicism began to gain upon her, blowing like a wind.

Her answer to the question, 'What for?' – and the irony is that she comes to the full recognition now, when the emptiness of the answer surrounds her inescapably in the form of the snow-world – was to have been Gerald's, made for her, a satisfying answer by being vicariously acted. What speaks in the question is the thwarted need for 'spontaneous-creative fulness of being':

And at the same instant came the ironical question: 'What for?' She thought of the colliers' wives, with their linoleum and their lace-curtains and their little girls in high-laced boots. She thought of the wives and daughters of the pit-managers, their tennis-parties, and their terrible struggles to be superior each to the other, in the social scale. There was Shortlands with its meaningless distinction, the meaningless crowd of the Criches. There was London, the House of Commons, the extant social world. My God!

Young as she was, Gudrun had touched the whole pulse of social England!

This last sentence is no mere statement. It evokes for us in an epitomizing presence what the whole book has so potently done. We are told only that we may sharply recall; for after reading *Women in Love* we do feel that we have 'touched the whole pulse of social England'. It is one of the astonishing manifestations of Lawrence's genius that he can, with easy mastery, achieve this – he, the miner's son and the ex-elementary schoolteacher. By the time we come to Gudrun's definitive collapse we seem to have experienced, in unanswerable actuality, the representative varieties of English life. What other English novelist commands such a range? – and Lawrence *commands* it, for his penetration is incomparably deep and his perception of significance keeps everything duly functional to the development of his themes.

The realization that will and idea and dominant masculinity in Gerald can supply no answer to the question that gnaws from within leaves Gudrun unable to evade the failure, in herself, of 'spontaneous-creative life'. The failure manifests itself to her in an experience that, suffered from time to time by different actors, recurs in *Women in Love*: an obsessed and tormenting awareness of time as measured by the clock, an endless succession of minutes and hours and days.

The thought of the mechanical succession of day following day, day following day, *ad infinitum*, was one of the things that made her heart palpitate with a real approach of madness. The terrible bondage of this tick-tack of time, this twitching of the hands of the clock, this eternal repetition of hours and days – oh God, it was too awful to contemplate. And there was no escape from it, no escape.

She almost wished Gerald were with her to save her from the terror of her own thoughts. Oh, how she suffered, lying there alone, confronted by the terrible clock, with its eternal tick-tack. All life, all life resolved itself into this: tick-tack, tick-tack, tick-tack; then the striking of the hour; then the tick-tack, tick-tack, and the twitching of the clock-fingers.

Gerald could not save her from it.

Gerald, of course, could not save himself. But in him, at this stage, failure of that life which cannot be commanded, though it can be thwarted, by will and 'mental consciousness' manifests itself in his rapid assimilation into the snow-world. After the departure of Birkin and Ursula, followed as it is by the overt breach with Gudrun, he spends his days on skis in a frenzied coursing of the slopes of endless snow. Finally, after the violent scene with Gudrun and Loerke, in which he behaves like an angry automaton, he goes off on his skis, mere unseeing 'go' now, and ends in the hollow near the top of the pass, where his life fades out into the cold. His body is brought back to the hostel frozen.

The drama as it centres in Gerald, involving as it does the diagnostic presentment of the large movement of civilization, has the effect – one difficult, in the nature of the case, to test in a count of pages – of bulking a good deal more largely in the whole than the Birkin–Ursula theme. No separation, of course, can really be made: the total drama is a closely organized whole, and the significance depends upon (among other things) the interplay between the two halves of the quarter.

In Birkin's married relations with Ursula the book invites us to localize the positive, the conceivable and due – if only with difficulty attainable – solution of the problem; the norm, in relation to which Gerald's disaster gets its full meaning. The stretch of the chapter 'Moony' from which Murry quotes, for misuse, the passage in which Birkin recalls the African carving – a passage followed immediately, as we have seen, by the paragraphs in which Birkin thinks of Gerald as the omen of the 'universal dissolution into whiteness and snow', 'snow-abstract annihilation' – brings us next to this:

Suddenly his strained attention gave way, he could not attend to these mysteries any more. There was another way, the way of freedom. There was the paradisal entry into pure, single being, the individual soul taking precedence over love and desire for union, stronger than any pangs of emotion, a lovely state of free proud singleness, which accepted the obligation of the permanent connexion with others, and, with the other, submits to the yoke and leash of love, but never forfeits its own proud individual singleness, even while it loves and yields.

Murry quotes this too, and interprets it in terms of his damning account of Lawrence the man, and of Lawrence's intimate relations with Frieda. Birkin, for him, is nothing but the self-vindicating, self-deceiving presence of Lawrence himself in the book. That Birkin is substantially Lawrence there can be little temptation to deny; for one of the most striking proofs of creative power, with its transcendent impersonalizing intelligence, in *Women in Love* is the way in which the author's direct presence is given a dramatic status among the other characters.

Some of the means by which Birkin is 'placed', and we are reminded that, as special representative of Lawrence's conscious and formulated attitudes, he is exposed to the implicit criticism of the whole creative context ('Never trust the artist, trust the tale'), offer themselves plainly for examination. We may take for example the chapter 'Gudrun and the Pompadour', and the letter, a Laurentian self-parody, that, hearing it intoned parsonically by Halliday for public derision, Gudrun snatches from his hand and walks off with. This episode reinforces the criticism, implicitly admitted by Birkin, that Ursula brings against him from time to time. In the chapter called 'An Island', for instance, we are told that she 'hated the Salvator Mundi touch. It was something diffuse and generalized about him, which she could not stand.' Again: 'There was a certain Sunday-school stiffness about him, priggish and detestable.'

But we may see a more significant clue to the nature of Lawrence's success with Birkin in the following (it comes in the chapter called 'Mino'), which is a very fine example of Lawrence's command of the methods he invented to meet the originality of his purpose – consider what is done in the episode of the cats:

'Ha!' she cried bitterly. 'It is the old dead morality.'

'No,' he said, 'it is the law of creation. One is committed. One must commit oneself to a conjunction with the other – for ever. But it is not selfless – it is a maintaining of the self in mystic balance and integrity – like a star balanced with another star.'

'I don't trust you when you drag in the stars,' she said. 'If you were quite true it wouldn't be necessary to be so far-fetched.'

'Don't trust me then,' he said, angry. 'It is enough that I trust myself.'

'And that is where you make another mistake,' she replied. 'You *don't* trust yourself. You don't fully believe yourself what you are saying. You don't really want this conjunction, otherwise you wouldn't talk so much about it, you'd get it.'

Taking this hint, we realize that in Birkin, who is far from being co-extensive with the 'spontaneous-creative fulness of being' out of which *Women in Love* comes, Lawrence, the whole creative artist, enacts a tentative or kind of experimental process – a testing and exploring of the conscious and formulated conclusions that Birkin thinks he has settled in securely enough to act upon. *Has* he? What in the concrete do they really amount to? Do they involve any self-deception or illusion or unreality? These questions the thoroughly dramatic Birkin enacts. Self-dramatized in Birkin, the Lawrence who formulates conclusions ('doctrines') and ponders them suffers exposure to the searching tests and the impersonal criteria that the artist's creative genius, which represents an impersonal profundity and wholeness of being, implicitly and impartially applies to them. The creative work itself is not to be taken as offering any such conclusions, except in so far as the reader feels that the 'tale' does in fact endorse, concretely define, and convey them. The tentative note on which *Women in Love* ends should leave us recognizing Lawrence's full awareness of this truth, and recognizing the sensitive integrity with which he serves it.

Actually, it seems to me, the position for which Birkin contends in his wooing of Ursula does emerge from the 'tale' vindicated, in the sense that the norm he proposes for the relations of man and woman in marriage has been made, by the varied resources of Lawrence's art, sufficiently clear, and, in its intelligibility, sufficiently cogent, to compel us to a serious pondering. The long drama of Birkin's relations with Ursula, which lends itself so little to dramatic presentation in the ordinary sense of the adjective, illustrates, in the doing, the astonishing originality of the novelist's genius. The drama takes its decisive start in the early chapter (III) called 'Classroom'. This chapter opens with that tenderly beautiful evocation of the late-afternoon school-room which tells us that Lawrence's memories of his school-teaching days were far from wholly distasteful (he was too creative a spirit for that); while Ursula's self-forgetful intentness on the botany lesson gives us Lawrence's own capacity for absorption, and conveys too the delighted and reverent wonder associated for him – so characteristically – with the study of botany. Upon the scene comes the threat of electric violence as first Birkin and then Hermione arrive, and the embarrassed triangle fills the school-room with odd tensions.

In this scene Hermione's function of parodying Lawrence is peculiarly manifest:

'Do you really think, Rupert,' she asked, as if Ursula were not present, 'do you really think it is worth while? Do you really think the children are better for being roused to consciousness?'

A dark flush went over his face, a silent fury. He was hollow-cheeked and pale, almost unearthly. And the woman, with her serious, conscious-harrowing question tortured him on the quick.

'They are not roused to consciousness,' he said. 'Consciousness comes to them, willy-nilly.'

'But do you think they are better for having it quickened, stimulated? Isn't it better that they should remain unconscious of the hazel, isn't it better that they should see as a whole, without all this pulling to pieces, all this knowledge?' ...

'Doesn't it destroy all our spontaneity, all our instincts? Are not the young people growing up today really dead before they have a chance to live?'

'Not because they have too much mind, but too little,' he said brutally.

'Are you *sure*?' she cried. 'It seems to me the reverse. They are over-conscious, burdened to death with consciousness.'

'Imprisoned within a limited, false set of concepts,' he cried. ...

'You are merely making words,' he said; 'knowledge means everything to you. Even your animalism, you want it in your head.'

What Hermione utters – and she persists in her line through the painful duel with Birkin that follows – is what the world has been content to take for the pure Laurentian doctrine. Birkin repudiates it, with the violence of exasperation and disgust, and there is no need to stress the significance of his having been given the opportunity. But the dramatic projection remains wholly undisturbed, and what we have is more than a simple dissociation. Hermione, as Birkin himself (we recognize) could tell us, doesn't merely represent someone else's perversion of his 'doctrine'; the perversion is one he has had to take note of in his own inner experience. As he says of the school-children, 'Consciousness comes to them, willy-nilly; intelligence has its indispensable part.' Birkin's 'prophetic' conclusions, or general formulations, in their very nature as such, testify to the vital function of 'mental consciousness' in the attainment of 'spontaneous-creative fulness of being'. But mental consciousness brings with it the inevitable danger, and only a constant delicate concern for wholeness can ensure against the perversion that means a usurping domination from above. What Birkin denounces so brutally in Hermione is what he knows as a dangerous potentiality in himself.

Hermione's case, we can see, has a close affinity with Gerald's, with whom, significantly, she maintains a kind of sympathetic antagonism; they 'were always strangely but politely and evenly inimical'. Their relations are given us (to take one of the many ways) in the chapter called 'Sketchbook', when, together in the one boat, they both, in a pointless (and therefore expressive) encounter of wills, stretch out an insistent hand for Gudrun's sketch-book, with the result that it falls in the mere. Their relations have already been overtly stated in the chapter called 'Carpentry', where, the episode of the Arab mare being under discussion, Hermione supports Gerald: 'If only we could learn to use our will we could do anything,' she says, adducing her own self-cures (nail-biting and so on). She exemplifies, in fact, dominating will in the intellectual, as Gerald represents it in the 'executive type'; and we see how, in the whole presentment of the human case offered by the drama, she relates Gerald and Birkin.

After the scene in the classroom, though Birkin has yet to escape from an embarrassing residual relation with Hermione, all his hopes, it soon becomes plain, are fixed on Ursula. With her his problem, a tough one (for she offers a natural and femininely tenacious resistance), is to win her to an acquiescent understanding of the norm he propounds as what, in the relation of man to woman, is to be realized between them. The exposition involves some violent offence against her ideas of love:

'We want to delude ourselves that love is the root. It isn't. It is only the branches. The root is beyond love, a naked kind of isolation, an isolated me, that does not meet and mingle, and never can.'

In these places Birkin stands convicted of being what, on Ursula's retaliatory challenge, he can't but deprecate: the preacher – the preacher whom he too, in the mirror she holds up, readily sees as a prig. In fact, an experimental process of exploring, testing, and defining does seem really to be enacted, dramatically, in the 'tale'; so little are we affected as by any doctrine formulated in advance, and coming directly from Lawrence. For all Birkin's misgivings ('Was it only an idea, or was it the interpretation of a profound yearning?'), and his unsettling ability to hear his own accents as they affect Ursula, he is nevertheless confirmed in the position he stands for. He puts it to himself as he lies in bed, recovering from illness (Chapter XVI, 'Man to Man'):

Man must be added on to a woman before he had any real place or wholeness.

And why? Why should we consider ourselves, men and women, as broken fragments of one whole? It is not true. Rather we are the singling away into purity and clear being of things that were mixed. Rather the sex is that which remains in us of the mixed, the unresolved. And passion is the further separating of this mixture, that which is manly being taken into the being of the man, that which is womanly passing to the woman, till the two are whole and clear as angels, the admixture of sex in the highest sense surpassed, leaving two single beings constellated together like two stars. ...

There is now to come the new day, when we are beings each of us, fulfilled in difference. The man is pure man, the woman pure woman, and they are perfectly polarized. But there is no longer any of the horrible merging mingling self-abnegation of love. There is only the pure duality of polarization, each one free from any contamination of the other. In each, the individual is primal, sex is subordinate, but perfectly polarized. Each has a single separate being, with its own laws. The man has his pure freedom, the woman hers. Each recognizes the perfection of the polarized sex-circuit. Each admits the different nature in the other.

This may strike the reader as Laurentian prophetic 'preaching'. But the need of some norm for the relations between men and women other than what Gerald and Gudrun enact is cogently presented by the 'tale'. Birkin posits a relation that shall be, in its vitality, stable and permanent because the terms between which it subsists are real; the need or demand of neither of the two individuals who find fulfilment in the relation is of such a kind as to deny the individual being of the one or of the other.

In Ursula, Birkin finds something to be fought before the hope of a permanent relation can be assured – something he calls the 'Magna Mater':

> Did he not know it in Hermione. Hermione, the humble, the subservient, what was she all the while but the Mater Dolorosa, in her subservience, claiming with horrible, insidious arrogance and female tyranny her own again, claiming back the man she had borne in suffering. By her very suffering and humility she bound her son with chains, she held him her everlasting prisoner.
>
> And Ursula. Ursula was the same – or the inverse. She too was the awful, arrogant queen of life, as if she were a queen bee on whom all the rest depended. ... She was unconscious of it herself. She was only too ready to knock her head on the ground before a man. But that was only when she was so certain of her man that she could worship him as a woman worships her own infant, with a worship of perfect possession.

The possessiveness he divines in Ursula is what (though that, we may feel, is not all) he sees in the reflected moon which, in the uncanny scene (Chapter XIX) where she watches from among the dark trees, he shatters with stone after stone, starting again and again with a kind of possessed frenzy each time it re-forms. It does, of course, re-form finally; Birkin, appealed to by Ursula, gives up his stoning, sits down by her, and responds at last to her plea that he shall say he 'loves' her. This might seem to portend for Birkin ineluctable defeat in the end. Actually, the observation called for at this point is that significance in Lawrence's art is never a matter of a mere intended 'meaning' symbolized; it works from profounder levels and in more complex ways. It is enough here to say that, in beginning to reflect back over the whole dramatic poem, the perceptive reader will not assume any simple identity between Birkin's own formulated view of his relations with Ursula and what is conveyed by the 'tale' (even though Ursula endorses Birkin's normative conclusions in her parting talk with Gudrun). On the other hand, we sufficiently see their union as successful to take, and take as significant, the contrast it presents to the disaster of the other pair. The question-mark on which with characteristic Laurentian integrity the book ends, regards the implications of Birkin's failure with Gerald. For the relation with Gerald was to have been an essential condition of a successful 'polarity'. Contemplating the frozen corpse of his friend, Birkin is left with nothing to disguise from him the question that faces him and Ursula: the question of the kind of success possible in marriage, and in life, for a pair that have cut themselves finally adrift. The society in which, if they had a place, their place would be, represents the civilization that has been diagnosed in Gerald.

So substantially and wonderfully is *Women in Love* an achieved thing that the faults seem to me very minor. I have spoken of the worst, the element of jargon, which is the more irritating because it so often comes when the uncertainty it betrays is unnecessary: what Lawrence offers to reinforce by *saying* and insisting, though saying could in any case be of no avail, his art has sufficiently done. The other fault is of a kind that might look like strength, for in it are certainly manifested, in a striking way, the powers of a highly gifted novelist. It is represented pre-eminently by Chapters VI and VII ('Crème de Menthe' and 'Totem') and Chapter XXVIII ('Gudrun in the Pompadour'). Lawrence here does some astonishingly vivid history: he re-creates, giving us the identifiable individuals, the metropolitan Bohemia he had known after the success of *Sons and Lovers*. A great deal of what he renders with such force is clearly there because it was once actual; he recalls the scene, the detail, and the face. The episode that made so deep an impression on him goes in, for that reason – even when it was one he only heard about, as for instance that of the impounding of the letter by Katherine Mansfield at the Café Royal. But all that doesn't owe its presence to the needs of thematic definition and development would have been better excluded; a point to be made with the more emphasis since *Women in Love* has so complex and subtle an organization, and we have to assume in general, as we read, that everything is fully significant.

How, we have now to inquire, was it possible to bring against Lawrence's art in *Women in Love* the kind of criticism brought with such violence by Middleton Murry when the novel came up for review? –

we can discern no individuality whatever in the denizens of Mr Lawrence's world. We should have thought that we should be able to distinguish between male and female, at least. But no! Remove the names, remove the sedulous catalogue of unnecessary clothing ... and man and woman are as indistinguishable as octopods in an aquarium tank.[1]

1. J. Middleton Murry, *Reminiscences of D. H. Lawrence*, p. 223.

If what we have here were merely an astonishing capacity for aberration in a given critic, there would be no point in asking how such a pronouncement should have been possible. But Murry's reaction has in fact a representative quality. It expresses in an extreme form a kind of dislike that one met with among the sophisticated in the nineteen-thirties when advancing the claims of Lawrence ('I've no use for a novelist who can't create characters you can get hold of'). Where *Women in Love* has been in question I am not sure that Murry's verdict wouldn't at any time up till now have been very generally endorsed. No one, of course, could say of the great body of short stories and *nouvelles* that they were remarkable for any lack of gift or bent they showed for the evoking of distinguishable *dramatis personae*. And – though how account for the almost complete neglect suffered by such a masterpiece as *St Mawr*? – that an original creative genius appears convincingly in some of them has been very widely recognized. Yet the power of making human individuality livingly present, which is in fact one of the striking manifestations of that genius in the tales, is not less undeniably there in *Women in Love*. By 'undeniably' I mean that one could, without research, produce abundant and varied illustration of the thing's being done, in ways that the ordinary novel-reader might have been expected to find irresistible – if, that is, *Women in Love* hadn't offered so much more than the dramatic play of 'character'.

Here, of course, in this last clause, we have the answer to the question why so patently false a judgement as that of Murry's quoted above should have been possible. These recognizable manifestations of the 'art of the novelist' are, like everything else in *Women in Love* (with the minor qualifications suggested), wholly significant, and significant in relation to a drama of a different order from that of *Madame Bovary* or of *Adam Bede* – or of *Sons and Lovers*. The habit-conditioned novel-reader brings to the book expectations that certainly do not open him to the possibility of that kind of significance; he merely feels that such local life as he may acclaim is unexplained, or wantonly stultified, by the offered context; he is left with a general impression of meaningless chaos. Murry, demanding a familiar 'significance', and responding with exasperation to a challenge he doesn't understand, but is sure he hates, declares the whole book altogether devoid of any life that is distinguishably human: 'We can discern no individuality whatever in the denizens of Mr Lawrence's world.'

Yet consider Hermione Roddice. I pick on her because she so indisputably has all the qualifications for being recognized as triumphantly a character even by the novel-reader who is repelled by the hint of Laurentian significances. With her introduction at the wedding, in the first chapter, she becomes for us a potent specific presence. We see her first through Ursula Brangwen's eyes:

a tall slow, reluctant woman with a weight of fair hair, and a pale, long face. This was Hermione Roddice, a friend of the Criches. Now she came along with her head held up, balancing an enormous flat hat of pale yellow velvet, on which were streaks of ostrich feathers, natural and grey. She drifted forward as if scarcely conscious, her long blanched face lifted up, not to see the world. ... People were silent when she passed, impressed, aroused, wanting to jeer, yet for some reason silenced. Her long, pale face, that she carried lifted up, somewhat in the Rossetti fashion, seemed almost drugged, as if a strange mass of thoughts coiled in the darkness within, and she was never allowed to escape.

Her physical presence and her manner are as vividly evoked as those of any character in fiction, and they transmit to us the resonance of her inner personality. The highly and convincingly individual Hermione, who is 'there' beyond question even for the reader who doesn't take kindly to the hint of significances that are not to be expressed in the climaxes and resolutions of the drama of 'characters', is nevertheless wholly significant in terms of the deep informing themes of the book.

'I was a very queer and nervous girl. And by learning to use my will, simply by using my will, I *made* myself right.'

Ursula looked all the while at Hermione, as she spoke in her slow, dispassionate, and yet strangely tense voice. A curious thrill went over the younger woman. Some strange, dark, convulsive power was in Hermione, fascinating and repelling.

'It is fatal to use the will like that,' cried Birkin harshly, 'disgusting. Such a will is an obscenity.'

Hermione looked at him for a long time, with her shadowed, heavy eyes. Her face was soft and pale and thin, almost phosphorescent, her jaw was lean.

'I'm sure it isn't,' she said at length. There always seemed an interval, a strange split between what she seemed to feel and experience, and what she actually said and thought. She seemed to catch her thoughts at length from off the surface of a maelstrom of chaotic black emotions and reactions. Birkin was always filled with repulsion, she caught so infallibly, her will never failed her. Her voice was always dispassionate and tense, and perfectly confident. Yet she shuddered with a sense of nausea, a sort of sea-sickness that always threatened to overwhelm her mind. But her mind remained unbroken, her will was still perfect. It almost sent Birkin mad. But he would never, never dare to break her will, and let loose the maelstrom of her unconsciousness, and see her in her ultimate madness. Yet he was always striking at her.

The penultimate sentence is not an instance of a Laurentian lapse into jargon. It has behind it the blow that Birkin has suffered from Hermione's paper-weight. That episode represents the radical disconcertingness with which *Women in Love* has defeated so many readers and left them ready to endorse some such judgement as Murry's; it gives us the preoccupation with significances that are not to be conveyed by crises and resolutions of the familiar kind, at the level of the drama of 'characters'. And yet, as a matter of fact, the blow dealt by Hermione issues with a sufficiently clear inevitability (one would have thought) out of a preceding exoteric drama in which the powers of a great novelist manifest themselves in ways that offer nothing to baffle, and everything to engage and convince, the reader who comes to Lawrence from George Eliot and Tolstoy. Since the instance has a very convenient representative value I will examine at some length the circumstances of the blow.

The chapter (VIII, called by the name of the Roddice country house, 'Breadalby') opens with Hermione's reception of the two Brangwen sisters, which makes us feel at the outset the peculiar oppressive insistence with which her presence pervades the house-party. We recognize this reception as wholly significant – Hermione's personality in action: this is what, as hostess, she inevitably is:

'The motor-car ran down the hill and up again in one breath, and they were curving to the side-door. A parlour-maid appeared, and then Hermione, coming forward with her pale face lifted, and her hands outstretched, advancing straight to the newcomers, her voice singing:

'Here you are – I'm so glad to see you –' she kissed Gudrun – 'so glad to see you' – she kissed Ursula and remained with her arm round her.

'Are you very tired?'

'Not at all tired,' said Ursula.

'Are you tired, Gudrun?'

'Not at all, thanks,' said Gudrun.

'No –' drawled Hermione. And she stood and looked at them. The two girls were embarrassed because she would not move into the house, but must have her little scene of welcome there on the path. The servants waited.

'Come in,' said Hermione at last, having fully taken in the pair of them.

Ursula was glad when she could be left alone in her room. Hermione lingered so long, made such a stress on one. She stood so near to one, pressing herself near upon one, in a way that was most embarrassing and oppressive. She seemed to hinder one's workings.

It is the idealistic intellectuality going with the insistent will that we are next reminded of. As the party sit on the lawn after lunch, 'round the bushes comes the tall form of Alexander Roddice, striding romantically like a Meredith hero who remembers Disraeli'. Since he has just come from London, from the House, and has the resignation of the Minister of Education to report, the talk (the very recognizable advanced thinker Sir Joshua Mattheson being present) naturally turns on education. Hermione rhapsodizes characteristically, provoking from Birkin a retort the personal animus of which brings in as a disturbingly immediate presence the tense history of their personal relations:

'M-m-m – I don't know. .... But one thing was the stars, when I really understood something about the stars. One feels so *uplifted*, so *unbounded*.'

Birkin looked at her in a white fury.

'What do you want to feel unbounded for?' he said sarcastically. 'You don't want to *be* unbounded.'

Hermione recoiled in offence.

'Yes, but one does have that limitless feeling,' said Gerald. 'It's like getting on top of the mountain and seeing the Pacific.'

'Silent upon a peak in Dariayn,' murmured the Italian, lifting her face for a moment from her book.

'Not necessarily in Darien,' said Gerald, while Ursula began to laugh.

Hermione waited for the dust to settle, and then she said, untouched:

'Yes, it's the greatest thing in life – to *know*. It is really to be happy, to be *free*.'

'Knowledge is, of course, liberty,' said Mattheson.

Hermione, we know, is *not* happy and *not* free; to what extent not, the culmination of this chapter will bring out. Her love of 'knowledge' is the desperate sense of insufficiency that determines also her attachment to Birkin – makes him, that is, so terribly necessary to her; and the sense of insufficiency is indistinguishable from the unrelaxed insistence of her will. The will asserts itself now, after the affront, in what is on the surface an episode of comedy:

> After tea, they were all gathered for a walk.
> 'Would you like to come for a walk?' said Hermione to each of them, one by one. And they all said yes, feeling somehow like prisoners marshalled for exercise. Birkin only refused.
> 'Will you come for a walk, Rupert?'
> 'No, Hermione.'
> 'But are you *sure*?'
> 'Quite sure.' There was a second's hesitation.
> 'And why not?' sang Hermione's question. It made her blood run sharp, to be thwarted in even so trifling a matter. She intended them all to walk with her in the park.
> 'Because I don't like trooping off in a gang,' he said.
> Her voice rumbled in her throat for a moment. Then she said, with a curious strong calm:
> 'Then we'll leave a little boy behind, if he's sulky.'
> And she looked really gay, while she insulted him.

This leaves things at a new pitch of tension between them. Hermione's behaviour as she conducts the walk is given us with all the economy of Lawrence's most vivid art. We see her as a figure of comedy, the domineering female. But, at the same time, if we have really been reading the book, we see her as enacting the case that, by a variety of creative means, has been diagnosed for us and presented with such potency:

> They all went through the park. Hermione wanted to show them the wild daffodils on a little slope. 'This way, this way,' sang her voice at intervals. And they had all to come this way. The daffodils were pretty, but who could see them? Ursula was stiff all over with resentment by this time, resentment of the whole atmosphere. Gudrun, mocking and objective, watched and registered everything.

They looked at the shy deer, and Hermione talked to the stag as if he too were a boy she wanted to wheedle and fondle. He was male, so she must exert some kind of power over him. They trailed home by the fish-ponds, and Hermione told them about the quarrel of two male swans, who had striven for the love of one lady. She chuckled and laughed as she told them how the ousted lover had sat with his head buried under his wing, on the gravel.

It is not to comedy that this, in its full significance, belongs; we feel too disturbingly beneath the comedy surface, in the feminine will and the malice, the thwarted life and the torments of the starved psyche. That Gudrun, 'mocking and objective, watched and registered everything', we register against *her* as characteristic (for, in spite of Murry, the sisters are strongly differentiated, and Gudrun, in being evoked as a highly specific personality, is critically 'placed').

The insistent will makes itself felt more menacingly as a blind and sinister force in the obsessed intensity with which Hermione, returned from the walk, seeks Birkin out:

'Where is Mr Birkin, Alice?' asked the mild, straying voice of Hermione. But under the straying voice, what a persistent, almost insane *will*.

'I think he is in his room, madam.'

'Is he?'

Hermione went slowly up the stairs, along the corridor, singing out in her high, small call:

'Ru-oo-pert! Ru-oo-pert!'

She came to his door, and tapped, still crying: 'Roo-pert.'

'Yes,' sounded his voice, at last.

'What are you doing?'

The question was mild and curious.

There was no answer. Then he opened the door.

'We've come back,' said Hermione. 'The daffodils are *so* beautiful.'

'Yes,' he said. 'I've seen them.'

She looked at him with her long, slow impressive look, along her cheeks.

'Have you?' she echoed. And she remained looking at him. She was stimulated above all things by this conflict with him, when he was like a sulky boy, helpless, and she had him safe at Breadalby. But underneath she knew the split was coming, and her hatred of him was subconscious and intense.

It is not a mere matter of our being *told* that 'her hatred of him was subconscious and intense'; the destructive animus has been defined and conveyed by a variety of inexplicit evocative means. It is there in the hunger of possession with which she besieges him:

'What were you doing?' she reiterated, in her mild, indifferent tone. He did not answer, and she made her way, almost unconsciously into his room. He had taken a Chinese drawing of geese from the boudoir, and was copying it, with much skill and vividness.

'You are copying the drawing,' she said, standing near the table, and looking down at his work.

'But why do you copy it?' she asked, casual and sing-song. 'Why not do something original?'

'I want to know it,' he replied. 'One gets more of China, copying this picture, than reading all the books.'

'And what do you get?'

She was at once roused, she laid as it were violent hands on him, to extract his secrets from him. She *must* know. It was a dreadful tyranny, an obsession in her, to know all he knew. For some time he was silent, hating to answer her. Then, compelled, he began:

'I know what centres they live from – what they perceive and feel – the hot, stinging centrality of a goose in the flux of cold water and mud – the curious bitter stinging heat of a goose's blood, entering their own blood like an inoculation of corruptive fire – fire of the cold-burning mud – the lotus mystery.'

She *must* know; her will is not her instrument, a power by which she commands: she is under its compulsion, the slave of a malign automatism that is inimical to life in herself as in Birkin. To 'know' is to possess, and to possess is to destroy; it is a self-defeating process. This, far down in herself, Birkin's reply forces her to realize; his 'knowing' is so obviously a different kind of thing, and different in a way that proclaims, implicitly, the impossibility of satisfying her own hunger to 'know': hence the strange quality of her reaction.

It is here, it might be said, that the drama becomes decidedly esoteric; no longer, that is, immediately intelligible and convincing to the novel-reader who approaches in good faith but with no special apparatus of interpretation. And yet, actually, what we have here demands of the reader, for its effect, no interpretive capacity beyond the power of recognition and response that is generated in an intelligent reading of what has gone before. It is not for nothing that the highly recognizable

Sir Joshua Mattheson figures in the house-party (he alone, 'whose mental fibre was so tough as to be insentient, seemed to be thoroughly happy'). Birkin, we are counted on to recognize, is consciously resorting to a use of language directly opposed to that of which Sir Joshua is the distinguished representative – Sir Joshua, the 'famous sociologist', whose approach to human problems, we have reason for supposing, very closely resembles Bertrand Russell's. Birkin here, with the Chinese drawing in view, is forcing Hermione to admit to herself an awareness of 'unknown modes of being'. To understand him is to recognize her awareness of such modes in herself; unknown and unknowable, in the sense that they cannot be reduced to terms of the 'mental consciousness'.

This recognition is insufferable to her; it is a recognition that the reality of life is something she can have no command over and cannot take into her possession. As for Birkin, not only is he brutally defying her need of him; he has made her, for the moment at least, unable not to realize that he couldn't in any case be the cure for her insufficiency that she so desperately wants him to be, since to possess him is in the nature of things impossible. Forced by the essential failure of life in herself to live by her will and her possessiveness (a process that confirms the failure), she now finds these annulled – for that is what, for the moment, her sense of their futility amounts to. There is nothing unintelligible about the rendering, here, of her state and its significance, even though the language is not Sir Joshua's, any more than the state represents any problem that could interest him:

Hermione looked at him along her narrow, pallid cheeks. Her eyes were strange and drugged, heavy under their heavy drooping lids. Her thin bosom shrugged convulsively. He stared back at her, devilish and unchanging. With another strange, sick convulsion, she turned away, as if she were sick, could feel dissolution setting-in in her body. For with her mind she was unable to attend to his words, he caught her, as it were, beneath all her defences, and destroyed her with some hideous occult potency.

This, then, is Hermione when her will has lost its illusion of command, her 'personality' has collapsed, and she feels herself for the moment nothing but the play of chaotic forces that the 'mental consciousness' had excluded. We should have found ourselves ready enough to take the significance, since the art of *Women in Love* is, with such endless resource, preoccupied with evoking the deeper life of the psyche; that life which, under the drama of relations between the characters at the level of the social 'personality', makes itself felt as a kind of latent drama of fields of force, a drama out of which disconcerting effects may emerge at the upper level, where the characters feel themselves to be wills and consciousnesses.

Hermione, we are told, immediately after the passage last quoted, 'came down to dinner strange and sepulchral, her eyes heavy and full of sepulchral darkness'. In the atmosphere of social-intellectual talk at the brilliant dinner-table her possessive will – her personality – rallies. 'She took very little part in the conversation, yet she heard it all, it was all hers.' The talk continues after dinner in the drawing-room, and, sensitized as we are, we take the potent suggestion that all this excited intellectuality has beneath it energies of a wholly different order from the interest in ideas that the talkers are conscious of:

> The talk was very often political or sociological, and interesting, curiously anarchistic. There was an accumulation of powerful force in the room, powerful and destructive. Everything seemed to be thrown into the melting pot, and it seemed to Ursula they were all witches, helping the pot to bubble. There was an elation and a satisfaction in it all, but it was cruelly exhausting for the newcomers, this ruthless mental pressure, this powerful, consuming, destructive mentality that emanated from Joshua and Hermione and Birkin and dominated the rest.

The pressure of destructive mentality, or the main incitement to it, we realize, derives from Hermione, and registers her desperate effort of self-recovery. The significance is clear enough when we are told:

> But a sickness, a fearful nausea gathered possession of Hermione. There was a lull in the talk, as it was arrested by her unconscious but all-powerful will.

She proposes dancing, rings the bell for costumes, tells off the dancers, and it begins. It is dance-miming, and I need not analyse the ways in which it conveys the deep accompaniment that underlies the overt drama – underlies the play, in and between the characters, of conscious intention, feeling, and thought. But since what we have in view is the climax to come between Hermione and Birkin, there is a passage that should be quoted:

> Birkin, when he could get free from the weight of the people present, whom he disliked, danced rapidly and with a real gaiety. And how Hermione hated him for this irresponsible gaiety.
>
> 'Now I see,' cried the Contessa excitedly, watching his purely gay motion, which he had all to himself. 'Mr Birkin is a changer.'
>
> Hermione looked at her coldly, and shuddered, knowing that only a foreigner could have seen and have said this.
>
> 'Cosa vuol' dire, Palestra?' she asked, sing-song.
>
> 'Look,' said the Contessa in Italian. 'He is not a man, he is a chameleon, a creature of change.'
>
> 'He is not a man, he is treacherous, not one of us,' said itself over in Hermione's consciousness. And her soul writhed in the black subjugation to him, because of his power to escape, to exist, other than she did, because he was not consistent, not a man, less than a man. She hated him in a despair that shattered her and broke her down. ...

The changeableness perceived in Birkin is a capacity for surrender to the spontaneous life that will cannot command. Hermione feels it as something lethal and insufferable, because it denies the competence of will and idea for the role assigned to them in her psyche, and denies it in the most disturbing way, by assuring her that she cannot hope to take that possessive hold of Birkin which alone, she feels, could remedy the insufficiency from which will cannot save her.

To take note of everything in this highly complex and brilliantly successful chapter would demand inordinate space. Enough has been said to suggest how the discussion, towards its close, of political and social ideas, in which Gerald expounds his functionalism, reducing human life to instrumentality, and in which Hermione proclaims that 'in the *spirit* we are all one', can be at the same time, and be convincingly, so intense a personal crisis between Hermione and Birkin that it can end in the murderous violence of that blow upon the head.

The discussion comes convincingly as in the natural course of an intellectual house-party. The ideas expressed in it engage immediately, such is the force of Lawrence's art and his mastery of organization, the essential themes of the book (themes that are presented in terms of individual lives). Birkin, in contradicting Hermione, as, out of intense conviction as well as exasperation, he is bound to do, makes, characteristically, and with wholly felicitous relevance to the general discussion, his affirmation of the Laurentian truth that 'One man isn't any better than another, not because they are equal, but because they are intrinsically *other*.' He is not only affronting Hermione's idealism; in asserting 'otherness' he asserts the vanity of the will that seeks after possessive 'knowledge'.

In the same way, though the major event in which the whole action of *Women in Love* resolves itself, Gerald's death in the snow, doesn't belong to the familiar kind of dramatic climax, but is a resolution below the level of personality, it nevertheless comes as the inevitable upshot of a drama enacted by human individuals as recognizable and as intelligibly motivated as any in fiction. And Gerald's case reminds us that it is the scope as well as the depth of Lawrence's significances that has led to the kind of incomprehension typified by Murry: Lawrence's preoccupation with relating the overt expressions of personal life to the impersonal depths goes with his power of presenting in the disorder of the individual psyche the large movement of civilization. It is because it gives so much, and gives the unexpected, that *Women in Love* has been judged to give less than the reader has the right to demand.

No one could be in less danger than Lawrence of forgetting the truth that life is a matter of individual lives. In fact, as his affirmation of 'otherness' implies (together with his hatred of 'merging'), he lays peculiar stress on individuality. And not only are the main characters of *Women in Love*, *pace* Murry, thoroughly individualized; Lawrence's natural genius for the rendering of character shows itself, as a kind of Dickensian creativeness, in the rendering of the minor figures. The German party at the hostel in Chapter XXIX ('Continental') seems to be done with a gusto of appreciative response. Then take the episode (Chapter XXVI) of the woman and her captive man to whom Birkin and Ursula give the chair they have just bought: we have here something very different from gusto, but in an equally notable degree we have that specific kind of creative power which is generally supposed to constitute a novelist.

There is no need, however, to enforce the point by multiplying illustrations or to show in detail how completely (and significantly) Gudrun and Ursula are differentiated. The facts are manifestly and abundantly what they are, and only the kind of wrong-headed approach, with the consequent exasperation, exemplified in an extreme form by Murry, can account for any report to the contrary. Rather, in closing this examination of *Women in Love*, I will revert to those aspects of Lawrence's astonishingly original art which, in the rendering of the manifestations of life in the actors, are *not* concerned with 'character'. The ways in which Lawrence brings into the drama the forces of the psyche of which the actors' wills have no cognizance, and which, consequently, do not seem to belong to their selves, are very various. There may, however, be some point in adducing a major illustration of a kind of thing for which ordinary notions of what should be found in a novel have no place.

There is the episode of the rabbit in the chapter (XVIII) called after it. How does this chapter advance the action of the novel? readers have no doubt asked. What can it be said to do to justify its presence, which is a very emphatic one? The vividness and the disturbing quality are beyond question; but in what ways are they relevant in *Women in Love*? Do they not belong rather to an independent and highly Laurentian short story or sketch that is loosely brought in here – as (it might be alleged) so much is brought into *Women in Love* in default of any pressure of significance? The child, Winifred Crich, is wonderfully done, here and elsewhere – in the rendering of children Lawrence, it seems to me, has no rival. We are given the French governess – her 'neat, brittle finality of form', 'like some elegant beetle with thin ankles ... how repulsive her completeness and her finality was' – with characteristic vivid economy. The storm of frenetic violence emanating from the rabbit has a disturbing immediacy of effect as we read. But the only major characters figuring in the chapter are Gerald and Gudrun, to whom falls the problem of dealing with the possessed resistance of the brute, and for them the episode seems wholly incidental and marginal. In what way does it leave them or their relations different from what they were before? The question cannot be satisfactorily replied to at the level of the expectations going with the drama of 'characters'. Yet in relation to the essential themes of *Women in Love* the episode is charged with significance. There is no need to analyse here how, in the violence of response engendered in Gerald and Gudrun by the struggle with the rabbit, there is engendered too an effect as of a dangerous field of force between the lovers – an intimation, not even now taken by their conscious minds, of latent tensions and potential conflict. The nature of the significance is suggested well enough in such places as these:

The long, demon-like beast lashed out again, spread on the air as if it were flying, looking something like a dragon, then closing up again, inconceivably powerful and explosive. The man's body, strung to its efforts, vibrated strongly. Then a sudden sharp, white-edged wrath came up in him. Swift as lightning he drew back and brought his free hand down like a hawk on the neck of the rabbit. Simultaneously, there came the unearthly abhorrent scream of a rabbit in the fear of death. It made one immense writhe, tore his wrists and his sleeve in a final convulsion, all its belly flashed white in a whirlwind of paws, and then he had slung it round and had it under his arm, fast. It cowered and skulked. His face was gleaming with a smile.

'You wouldn't think there was all that force in a rabbit,' he said, looking at Gudrun. And he saw her eyes black as night in her pallid face, she looked almost unearthly. The scream of the rabbit, after the violent tussle, seemed to have torn the veil of her consciousness. He looked at her, and the whitish, electric gleam in his face intensified.

'Isn't it a *fool*!' she cried. 'Isn't it a sickening *fool*?' The vindictive mockery in her voice made his brain quiver. Glancing up at him, into his eyes, she revealed again the mocking, white-cruel recognition. There was a league between them, abhorrent to them both. They were implicated with each other in abhorrent mysteries.

'How many scratches have you?' he asked, showing his hard forearm, white and hard and torn in red gashes.

'How really vile!' she cried, flushing with a sinister vision. 'Mine is nothing.'

She lifted her arm and showed a deep red score down the silken white flesh.

'What a devil!' he exclaimed. But it was as if he had had knowledge of her in the long red rent of her forearm, so silken and soft. He did not want to touch her. He would have to make himself touch her, deliberately. The long, shallow red rip seemed torn across his own brain. ...

Gudrun's wanton provocation of the Highland cattle in Chapter XIV ('Water-party') is the last instance I can allow myself to refer to. The general bearings of the incident on the potentialities of her relations with Gerald should be plain enough. To sum up the significance is another matter: the whole remarkable chapter is very complex, closely organized, and highly charged. It will be noticed that I have avoided the terms 'symbol' and 'symbolism' in this discussion: to suggest that the rabbit and the cattle 'stand for' this and that would be to suggest much simpler ways of constructing and conveying significance and much simpler significances than we actually have. The point may be made by turning for comparison to instances of what can, without mis-leading effect, be called symbolism. We have such an instance when, after the episode of the Highland cattle, Gerald and Gudrun sit at either end of the canoe they have elected to share, returning to the other end of the lake:

'You like this, do you?' she said, in a gentle solicitous voice.

He laughed shortly.

'There is a space between us,' he said, in the same low, unconscious voice, as if something were speaking out of him. And she was as if magically aware of their being balanced in separation, in the boat. She swooned with acute com-prehension and pleasure.

'But I'm very near,' she said caressingly, gaily.

'Yet distant, distant,' he said.

What is symbolized is that normative relation between the man and the woman which Birkin ultimately achieves with Ursula, and in which alone Gerald can escape disaster. A little further on we are given Gerald's new sense – for him new and unprecedented – of spontaneous life in the relaxed whole psyche:

He was listening to the faint near sounds, the dropping of water-drops from the oar-blades, the slight drumming of the lanterns behind him, as they rubbed against one another, the occasional rustling of Gudrun's full skirt, an alien land noise. His mind was almost submerged, he was almost transfused, lapsed out for the first time in his life, into the things about him. For he always kept such a keen attentiveness, concentrated and unyielding in himself. Now he had let go, imperceptively he was melting into oneness with the whole. It was like pure, perfect sleep, his first great sleep of life. He had been so insistent, so guarded, all his life. But here was sleep, and peace, and perfect lapsing out.

And, symbolically, too, this transcending of that sense of imminent disaster which underlies Gerald's characteristically tensed will breaks when the stillness of the serene night is shattered:

And again they were still. The launch twanged and hooted, somebody was singing. Then, as if the night smashed, suddenly there was a great shout, a confusion of shouting, warring on the water, then the horrid noise of paddles reversed and churned violently.

Gerald sat up, and Gudrun looked at him in fear. 'Somebody in the water,' he said angrily and desperately, looking keenly across the dusk. ...

'Wasn't this *bound* to happen?' said Gudrun, with heavy hateful irony. .... She glanced at his face. He was looking fixedly into the darkness, very keen and alert and single in himself, instrumental. Her heart sank, she seemed to die a death. 'Of course,' she said to herself, 'nobody will be drowned. Of course they won't. It would be too extravagant and sensational.' But her heart was cold, because of his sharp impersonal face. It was as if he belonged naturally to dread and catastrophe, as if he were himself again.

Then there came a child's voice, a girl's high, piercing shriek:

'Di – Di-Di-Di – Oh Di – Oh Di – Oh Di!'

The blood ran cold in Gudrun's veins.

Then, when Gerald dives into the black depths of the lake, seeking in vain for the vanished pair, Diana Crich and her would-be rescuer, there is, for the reader who recalls the earlier chapter (IV), 'Diver', a clear symbolism. On that earlier occasion Gerald's man-of-action mastery on the surface of the water, the plane of will and mental consciousness, had evoked in Gudrun a passionate envy – and evoked too Ursula's account (the sinister resonance of which is amplified now) of Gerald's boyhood: 'You know he shot his brother?' He now, with a horribly disturbing and chilling effect, conveys his sense of the strange vast world beneath the surface, a world where he is helpless and hopeless:

'If you once die,' he said, 'then when it's over, it's finished. Why come to life again? There's room under that water there for thousands.'

'Two is enough,' she said murmuring.

He dragged on his second shoe. He was shivering violently, and his jaw shook as he spoke.

'That's true,' he said, 'maybe. But it's curious how much room there seems, a whole universe under there; and as cold as hell, you're as helpless as if your head was cut off.' He could scarcely speak, he shook so violently. 'There's one thing about our family, you know,' he continued. 'Once anything goes wrong, it can never be put right again – not with us. I've noticed it all my life – you can't put a thing right once it has gone wrong.'

They were walking across the high-road to the house.

'And do you know, when you are down there, it is so cold, actually, and so endless, so different really from what it is on top, so endless – you wonder how it is so many are alive, why we're up here.'

Then again, replacing with an ironical response the suggestion of the balanced pair in the canoe, there is an anticipatory symbolism in this:

The bodies of the dead were not recovered till towards dawn. Diana had her arms tight round the neck of the young man, choking him.

But these effects work subtly in with the whole complex organization of poetic and dramatic means that forms this wonderful chapter, means that, in sum, are no more to be brought helpfully under the limiting suggestion of 'symbolism' than the Shakespearian means in an act of *Macbeth.*

5

IT illustrates the flexibility of Lawrence's art that *The Captain's Doll* should be as different in mode from either of the other tales in the volume (*The Ladybird*) in which it appeared as they are from one another. Flexibility is strikingly illustrated within the tale itself; for when we examine what we at once note as its distinctive tone it is a very remarkable flexibility that we have to analyse – a sure rightness of touch in conveying the shifts of poise and tone that define an extremely delicate complexity of attitude. The success of *The Ladybird* depends on the maintaining of a grave and noble seriousness, earnestly and prophetically poetic. The immediately relevant point may be made by saying that if Lawrence had always written in the mode of *The Ladybird* the view that he is 'without humour' would not have been as absurd as it is. And *The Fox*, in establishing so perfectly the homely lower-middle-class ordinariness upon which its effect depends, doesn't go in for humour or irony. But that humour and irony and all the liveliness of a refined and highly civilized comedy are to be essential to the mode of *The Captain's Doll* we know at the very outset.

That is given us in the perfection of touch of that opening scene between the Countess Johanna zu Rassentlow and the Baroness Anna-maria von Prielau-Carolath – between Hannele and Mitchka. Once again we are made to reflect, with a fresh wonder, that never was there a greater master of what is widely supposed to be the novelist's distinctive gift: the power to register, to evoke, life and manners with convincing vividness – evoke in the 'created' living presence that compels us to recognize the truth, strength, and newness of the perception it records. To say that he exercises it incomparably over the whole social range doesn't suggest the full marvel. The women in the opening of *The Captain's Doll* are aristocrats and Germans, and these foreign ladies of high birth and breeding are, as such, immediate actual presences for

us; they are *there*, in their intimate encounter, authentic and real beyond question; done – established and defined in our sense of them – by
an economy of art that looks like casualness.

In that economy Lawrence's marvellous ear for speech, we note at
once, plays a great part. This aspect of his genius is, of course, an aspect
of it, and not something separable, a special mimetic gift, as the phrase
'ear for speech' might suggest. The speech that is so irresistibly right,
and carries so subtle a charge of significance, testifies to the profundity
of the whole perception it registers, the insight it is of a piece with. So
Lawrence's ostensible dramatic range is in fact something very remarkable indeed; it is the range of a truly great dramatic poet. There is
point, then, in insisting on the more obvious and undeniable manifestations.

Here, but for a half-dozen words of German, is the opening of *The
Captain's Doll* (coming in the original volume, it should be noted, immediately after *The Fox* – from which Witter Bynner[1] quotes a piece
of dialogue to enforce his contention that there is something radically
peasant in Lawrence, betrayed here in his crude humour):

Hannele did not lift her head from her work. She sat in a low chair under a
reading-lamp, a basket of coloured silk pieces beside her, and in her hands a doll,
or mannikin, which she was dressing. She was doing something to the knee of
the mannikin, so that the poor little gentleman flourished head downwards
with arms wildly tossed out. And it was not at all seemly, because the doll was
a Scotch soldier in tight-fitting tartan trews.

There was a tap at the door, and the same voice, a woman's, calling:

'Hannele?'

'Ja-a!'

'Are you here? Are you alone?' asked the voice, in German.

'Yes – come in.'

Hannele did not sound very encouraging. She turned round her doll as the
door opened, and straightened his coat. A dark-eyed young woman peeped in
through the door, with a roguish coyness. She was dressed fashionably for the
street, in a thick cape-wrap, and a little black hat pulled down to her ears.

'Quite, quite alone!' said the newcomer, in a tone of wonder. 'Where is he,
then?'

'That I don't know,' said Hannele.

1. In *Journey With Genius*.

'And you sit here alone, and wait for him? But no! That I call courage! Aren't you afraid?' Mitchka strolled across to her friend.

'Why shall I be afraid?' said Hannele curtly.

'But no! And what are you doing? Another puppet? He is a good one, though! Ha-ha-ha! *Him*! It is him! No-no-that is too beautiful, Hannele. It is him – exactly him. Only the trousers.'

'He wears these trousers too,' said Hannele, standing her doll on her knee. It was a perfect portrait of an officer of a Scottish regiment, slender, delicately made, with a slight, elegant stoop of the shoulders, and close-fitting tartan trousers. The face was beautifully modelled, and a wonderful portrait, dark-skinned, with a little close-cut dark moustache, and wide-open dark eyes, and that air of aloofness and perfect diffidence which marks an officer and a gentleman.

How, one may ask, would one know this was Lawrence? There is that last sentence: 'that air of aloofness and perfect diffidence which marks an officer and a gentleman' – one can put one's finger there and say with conviction that only Lawrence could have written that. But it wouldn't be easy to justify the conviction to anyone who should then ask: 'Why do you say that?' One can of course reply by pointing to just such a use of 'diffidence' elsewhere in Lawrence to describe the air and bearing of a gentleman. But of course it is as clinching the whole description of the doll that those phrases produce the effect that makes one put one's finger down there. And if one asks why every phrase, every touch, in that description – in the whole of the quoted passage, in fact – seems to tell, so that the whole page wonderfully *lives*, the life is seen to be very largely a matter of what is revealed in the analysis of the 'tone' (as I have called it): a complexity of total attitude, conveyed in the shifts of expectation and evaluative response – the sympathetic, the amused, the impressed, the critical, the wondering and waiting, and so on – the reader goes through as his attention is carried forward down the page.

If one says that this complexity of attitude, as we take it first, is focussed on the doll, it will be to note that the doll is – and 'is' here, it will be seen, itself gives us a complexity – the Scottish officer, Hepburn (we soon learn his name). Captain Hepburn, then, as he is introduced to us in the opening scene of the tale, is both a doll and impressively a gentleman. The essential tendency of the doll-presentation gets strong explicit emphasis at the very start: the 'poor little gentleman', as the curtain lifts, is revealed in a position and a posture of ludicrous indignity:

And it was not at all seemly because the doll was a Scotch soldier in tight-fitting tartan trews.

These are freedoms inconceivable in the world of Count Dionys and Lady Daphne. Yet the officer and gentleman, with his impressive dignity, is there too. As a presence commanding respect he is strongly established for us in the appreciative description of the doll as portrait: the elegant distinction, the beautiful modelling, the wide-open dark eyes – here is not merely outward distinction but a personality able to inspire 'a wonderful portrait'. By the time we have the description (which owes some of its life to that fact) he has already been evoked for us as a formidable reality existing in the background. He is certainly formidable, but he is also unknown, unpossessed (no doll) and unplaced: the strong field of force, the tension, of the exchange between the two women refers us to him, and he is qualified to inspire awe in the roguish and elegant young woman (we learn very soon without surprise that she is handsome and an aristocrat) who is *not*, it seems, the one in love with him:

'Quite, quite alone?' said the newcomer, in a tone of wonder. 'Where is he, then?'

'That I don't know,' said Hannele.

'And you sit here alone, and wait for him? But no! That I call courage! Aren't you afraid?' Mitchka strolled across to her friend.

'Why shall I be afraid?' said Hannele curtly.

That 'curtly' says a great deal.

To return now to the question raised above: it is the peculiar livingness, of which we have glanced at some of the conditions and manifestations, that tells us the quoted passage is Lawrence – the fresh and easy (it seems) creative, or poetic, power and sensitiveness of the prose, with the unpondered inevitability of its rightness, and the way in which the dialogue, itself so right, works with it. But if what is looked for is something one can put a finger on, to say convincingly, 'There you have Lawrence,' a better answer to the question than I first suggested can be found: it is to point, with the commentary they call for, to the 'tight-fitting tartan trews'. They are decidedly, it will be seen, insisted on in this passage quoted. And if we extend the quotation a few lines we have this:

> Mitchka bent forward, studying the doll. She was a handsome woman with a warm, dark golden skin and clear black eyebrows over her russet-brown eyes.
>
> 'No,' she whispered to herself, as if awestruck. 'That is him. That is him. Only not the trousers. Beautiful, though, the trousers. Has he really such beautiful fine legs?'
>
> Hannele did not answer.

– '"Why shall I be afraid?" said Hannele curtly': it is the same effect again, with the same significance; Mitchka's question this time, with silence – curtness intensified to that – for an answer, leaves us knowing that the relations between Hannele and the foreign officer have indeed been intimate. But that is not all. The question 'Has he really such beautiful fine legs?' brings us to the distinctively Laurentian significance of the tight-fitting trews.

I have spoken of the doll as making present a personality such as can inspire a 'wonderful portrait'. That is a proposition to which the artist, Hannele, would no doubt have assented. But the insistence on the tight-fitting trews gives us a clear intimation that the theme of *The Captain's Doll* carries with it a characteristic Laurentian challenge to 'personality' – to the place and valuation of 'personality' in the accepted understanding of personal relations, especially those between a man and a woman. The involvement of 'personality' with 'ideals', 'ideas', and 'will' – that insight is central to the creative preoccupation. And we recognize that the significance of the trews and the legs they insist on is one with the significance of the Laurentian 'body'.[1]

It is a significance that Hannele herself cannot recognize: if she had been capable of recognizing it there would have been no doll. But, obeying an impulse the meaning of which gets its definition in the drama as a whole, she *has* made the doll, and at the same time she has represented the Captain in those tight-fitting trews which are not his

1. See p. 241 below.

normal wear. That there is a pregnant paradox here, a profound contradiction, becomes clear enough when, Mitchka having departed (the departure is wonderfully done), Alexander Hepburn himself enters:

He was like the doll, a tall, slender, well-bred man in uniform. When he turned, his dark eyes seemed very wide open.

We somehow feel the contradiction in this very account: it is as if his being 'like the doll' meant at the same time something very different – as if in some way the suggestion of 'doll' were being annulled. The part of the 'dark eyes ... very wide open' in this effect lends itself to analysis as we go forward. And the significance of the paradox that acts itself out in the drama can be pointed to here:

'Do you want to see it?' she asked, in natural English.
'Yes,' he said.
She broke off her thread of cotton and handed him the puppet. He sat with one leg thrown over the other, holding the doll in one hand and smiling inscrutably with his dark eyes. His hair, parted perfectly on one side, was jet black and glossy.
'You've got me,' he said at last, in his amused, melodious voice.
'What?' she said.
'You've got me,' he repeated.
'I don't care,' she said.
'What – you don't care?' His face broke into a smile. He had an odd way of answering as if he were only half-attending, as if he were thinking of something else.

His 'You've got me' recognizes the nature of the impulse to make a portrait-doll. But she clearly *hasn't* got him. Her sense in his presence when she can see him and hear him speak that what communicates with her through the voice and the dark eyes is something unknown and unpossessable imposes itself on us with compelling force. Troubled and baffled, she rebels, and yet has to reckon with the fact that what she rebels against is what irresistibly attracts her:

He lifted his brows and looked at her. Her heart always melted when he looked straight at her with his black eyes, and that curious, bright unseeing look that was more like second-sight than direct human vision. She never knew what he saw when he looked at her.

She never knew what *she* saw when she looked at *him* – that, as the last sentence of the quotation intimates, is only one aspect. There is another, a complementary one, though she tends to be much less conscious of it: she too – she betrays her sense of this, even while her attention focusses upon him and it is *his* perception she is thinking of – she too, in her reality, is an unknown, for all the ostensible definitiveness of her outward presence, her face and her 'personality'. The problem that preoccupies her, and the enactment of which provides the dramatic tension of the tale, is that of determining whether the spell exercised upon her by the man owes its power to reality or illusion. What *is* Alexander Hepburn? The problem has this form too:

And she was heavy and spell-bound, and she loved the spell that bound her.
Also she didn't love it.

And the solution, the denouement, is her tacit recognition of her own deepest desire or need. *The Captain's Doll* gives us her *éducation sentimentale* – if a phrase so bound up with conventional ideas of love will pass here.

For the tale expresses Lawrence's profoundest insights into the relations between men and women, and his accompanying convictions about the nature of a valid marriage, and those insights and convictions challenge established ideas so radically that they are resisted – resistance often taking the form of a refusal, or an inability, to attend to them for what they are. They are resisted by Hannele as she meets them in Alexander Hepburn. He, it must be said at once, is a wholly dramatic *dramatis persona*, and not at all like Lawrence. Nor is he like Count Dionys Psanek – in a work of this mode and intention he couldn't be (the point has, in effect, already been made). The inspiration, the *raison d'être*, of *The Captain's Doll* entails the convincing presentment of the Laurentian themes in an action that shall affect us as belonging, not to a poetic-prophetic Sabbath-world, as *The Ladybird* does, but to the everyday reality in which we live, though, unlike *The Fox*, to a milieu of educated and sophisticated people. To have made Hannele's final capitulation credible and right, then, is to have brought off a remarkable creative feat: that of making Alexander, with the spell he exercises and inner reality that validates the demand he makes on her, a compellingly concrete presence.

The Alexander of the 'Alexander doll' – the Alexander who can be doubled in so extraordinary a likeness – is evoked with that characteristic power which should from the outset have made it plain that, if Lawrence's novels and tales weren't immediately intelligible and satisfying, he nevertheless had the genius of a very remarkable novelist. The doll might be taken as representing the kind of treatment of 'character' that the cultivated novel-reader expected, or hoped, to find – and still for the most part does. What more, it might be asked, can a novelist do in the presentment of human beings than produce such likenesses and make them talk (and act) with correspondingly lifelikeness? It is because Lawrence's art answers so little to this kind of expectation – because it is so essentially concerned with going below the level of 'personality' and 'character' and so far transcends the customary kind of interest in human life – that it still receives so little understanding and intellectuals can safely betray the blankest incomprehension in print (consider the recent reviews of Witter Bynner's book – and consider the book itself).

The 'dark eyes' in *The Captain's Doll* do not, as they would in any other writer, give us a trait, a quality, a fascination of personality; they go with the tartan trews (which the Captain himself, in our presence, never wears), and the tartan trews, as it has already been intimated, signalize what is most profoundly and strikingly original in Lawrence's preoccupation. Hannele's complex and varying apprehension of the charm and the speech portends, not romantic love, but her tacit agreement to base her marriage with Alexander on a relation so unlike romantic love as to do violence to accepted Western ideas. This, of course, Hannele doesn't know. What she is aware of is Alexander's odd fascination and its varying effect on her. Our own apprehension of him, to begin with, is wholly hers – which is not to say that we seem not to have direct access: we have him through her shared perceptions with the most convincing immediacy. But as we enact the drama of her wondering response, exasperation, recoil and resubmission, the time comes when our apprehension of him no longer coincides with hers. We perceive, by then, the significance of the doll better than she does.

So that our reaction to his proposing marriage while 'leaving aside the question of whether you love me or I love you' is not hers.

But this is to anticipate. It is essential that we should have shared Hannele's fascinated sense of something strange, indefinable, yet supremely real in Alexander Hepburn – the more real because indefinable. And what we have to observe is how we are taken beyond the mere evocation of a glamorous unknownness, so that, though the evoked deep reality behind the 'black, unseeing eyes' and the 'mask-like face' and under the voice must remain, of its nature, indefinable, yet it becomes for us unquestionably a supreme reality, qualified for the supreme part it has to play in the drama. His incalculable presence, if it cannot be said to be 'defined', is nevertheless given a strong positiveness by the particularity with which the strange, fascinating physique and all the idiosyncrasies of the observable living presence are conveyed to us. The fascination associates with the distinctiveness of the large attic he inhabits – the large beautiful room, soft-lighted, with its white-vaulted ceilings, its 'very little furniture, save large peasant cupboards or presses of painted wood', its huge writing-table, 'on which were writing materials and some scientific apparatus and a cactus plant with fine scarlet blossoms', and its two telescopes, one mounted on a stand near a window. But it is in his talk that the effect registered by her as the 'dark, strange vacancy of his brow, his not-thinking', gets its decisive development.

> The soft, melodious, straying sound of his voice made her feel helpless. She felt that he never answered her. Words of reply seemed to stray out of him in the need to say *something*. But he himself never spoke. There he was, a contained blank silence in front of her.

That she should feel like this seems to us, as we read, the inevitable outcome of the preceding conversation between them. He has come in at last, with the explanation that, 'as a matter of fact', he has been kept talking with his Colonel, and talking about her: the wife at home has made trouble. The manner and tone in which he recounts this news – and nothing could sound less like news, and news of moment – would be hard to define; which is a way of saying that they are defined with great precision in his actual speech (with its context). And they are in perfect accord with the odd suggestion of his presence. After having made, in his way, his highly disturbing communication (and, on the Colonel's advice, he is going, he supposes, home on leave), he hangs up his belt, changes his tunic, replaces his shoes by slippers, and resumes his chair, stretching luxuriously:

'There,' he said, 'I feel better now.' And he looked at her. 'Well,' he said, 'and how are you?'

'Me?' she said. 'Do I matter?' She was rather bitter.

'Do you matter?' he repeated, without noticing her bitterness. 'Why, what a question! Of course you are of the very highest importance. What? Aren't you?' And smiling his curious smile – it made her for a moment think of the fixed sadness of monkeys, of those Chinese carved soapstone apes – he put his hand under her chin, and gently drew his finger along her cheek. She flushed deeply.

'But I'm not as important as you, am I?' she asked defiantly.

'As important as me! Why bless you, I'm not important a bit. I'm not important a bit!' – the odd straying sound of his words mystified her. What did he really mean?

'And I'm even less important than that,' she said bitterly.

'Oh no, you're not. Oh no, you're not. You're very important. You're very important indeed, I assure you.'

'And your wife?' – the question came rebelliously. 'Your wife? Isn't she important?'

'My wife? My wife?' he seemed to let the word stray out of him as if he did not quite know what it meant. 'Why, yes, I suppose she is important in her own sphere.'

'What sphere?' blurted Hannele, with a laugh.

'Why, her own sphere, of course. Her own house, her own home, and her two children: that's her sphere.'

'And you? – where do you come in?'

'At present I don't come in,' he said.

'But isn't that just the trouble,' said Hannele. 'If you have a wife and home, it's your business to belong to it, isn't it?'

'Yes, I suppose it is, if I want to,' he replied.

'And you *do* want to?' she challenged.

'No, I don't,' he replied.

'Well, then?' she said.

'Yes, quite,' he answered. 'I admit, it's a dilemma.'

This odd casualness is certainly not flippancy, for all the effect of that, now and then, as the words 'stray' out of his apparent 'not-thinking'. And is it merely out of an absence of something – an absence of thought, or purpose, or concentration – that they 'stray'? The elusive nonchalance, so baffling and even frightening to Hannele, seems to be at the same time a profound seriousness. The key-word is given us at the end of the scene between them, all of which goes to engender this peculiar exasperating and ambiguously disturbing effect as of a lack of directed responsive tension in him (there is a quiet poise, which she is aware of at the same time, and under which she detects a restlessness):

'What are you thinking about tonight?' he said. 'What are you thinking about?'

'What did your Colonel say to you exactly?' she replied, trying to harden her eyes.

'Oh, that!' he answered. 'Never mind that. That is of no significance whatever.'

'But what *is* of any significance?' she insisted. She almost hated him.

'What is of any significance? Well, nothing to me, outside of this room, at this minute. Nothing in time or space matters to me.'

'Yes, *this minute*!' she repeated bitterly. 'But then there's the future. *I've* got to live in the future.'

'The future! The future! The future is used up every day. The future to me is like a big tangle of black thread. Every morning you begin to untangle one loose end – and that's your day. And every evening you break off and throw away what you've untangled, and the heap is so much less: just one thread less, one day less. That's all the future matters to me.'

'Then nothing matters to you. And I don't matter to you. As you say only an end of waste thread,' she resisted him.

'No, there you're wrong. You aren't the future to me.'

'What am I then? – the past?'

'No, not any of those things. You're nothing. As far as all that goes, you're nothing.'

'Thank you,' she said sarcastically, 'if I'm nothing.' But the very irrelevancy of the man overcame her.

That 'irrelevancy' is the clue: the word seems to be left with us, a kind of precipitate, by the just-quoted conclusion of the exchange, with its closing, 'As far as that goes, you're nothing' (clinched by the retort:

'Thank you,' she said sarcastically, 'if I'm nothing.'). The terms of her conscious expectation of the 'man', the ideas that determine it, are irrelevant to the reality that, at bottom, attracts her: his presence is a challenge to the assumptions and the moulds of thought and feeling, especially those concerning love and happiness, in which she has grown up. She finds him, then, in his strange elusive fascination, 'meaningless' – irrelevant to the just and inevitable demand of her nature as a woman:

And the meaninglessness of him fascinated her and left her powerless. She could ascribe no meaning to him, none whatever.

The arrival of the wife, with its consequences, immensely complicates and intensifies the paradox, leaving Hannele more desperately unable to say what, in sum, her attitude towards him is, but leaving us with a much enriched perception of the significance of the doll. There is the odd, perverse impulse that, in the opening of this phase of the story, makes her show the 'Alexander doll' to the unidentified 'little lady' who visits the studio kept by Hannele and Mitchka. Alexander has been away some days on business, and he 'seems to have quite disappeared out of her'.

And was he real? Why had she made his doll? Why had his doll been so important if he was nothing? Why had she shown it to that funny little woman this afternoon? ... In actual life, her own German friends were real. ... But this other, he was simply not there. He didn't really exist. He was a nullus, in reality. A nullus – and she had somehow got herself entangled with a nullus.

But when she hears his voice on the stairs outside, talking (though she doesn't know it) to the 'funny little woman',

instantly she was afraid again. She knew there was something there.

When, however, she finds herself in presence of the actuality, the question, '*What* is there?' takes on a new and baffling force. We feel directly with her his unpredictable strangeness, so that, at the close of the scene, we have, for the moment, little advantage over her as interpreters and assessors. His tone and what he says are so utterly inappropriate by the standards of ordinary expectation, so unrelated to the crucial matters that are being discussed. Yet the extraordinariness offers itself as an unanswerable ordinariness – offers itself with such quiet conviction that it has partly the effect of that. Have we to do here with an unknown dimension, something real that forces us to recognize the invalidity of our routine assumptions and concepts, or merely an extravagant and irresponsible oddity, disqualifying the man for serious human relations?

The impressive strangeness is given in the situation in which she finds him when, unable to sleep, she goes to look. There he is, on the little roof-platform outside the landing window, squatting motionless on a stool at the end of a telescope, peering up at the moon. She taps at the window and he 'looked round, like some tom-cat staring with wide night-eyes'. After inviting her to have a look at the moon (she declines), he tells her casually that yesterday's visitor was his wife.

'Your wife!' – she looked up really astonished.

It is an essential condition of the effect of the scene that to all he says, in his quiet, conversational way, astonishment would be the natural response, while he shows himself, by his tone and trend, wholly un-aware of that. Yet we are aware that, in this disconcerting oddity, he is not giving proof of insensitiveness; we have taken, in the earlier course of the tale, all the suggestions that establish a sense of there being something really *there*, behind and beneath – something positive and vital, but indefinable, in relation to which these appearances have their significance.

But Hannele, of course, is an actor in the drama, not the reader of it. Her sense (we note as we register it) is less impersonal and inclusive than ours. She hears her lover tell her in his casual way, 'looking with dilated, blank and black eyes at nothing', that he is going to spend a week or so with his wife at the hotel:

Was this a man? – or what was it? It was too much for her, that was all.

'Well, good-bye,' she said. 'I hope you will have a nice time at the Vier Jahreszeiten.'

There follows, at the hotel, the *tête-à-tête* between Hannele and Mrs Hepburn, who have met in the street. Mrs Hepburn, it turns out, assumes without question that the woman who has seduced her hus-band is Mitchka, the beautiful and aristocratic brunette: 'she's just the type I always knew would attract him, if he hadn't got me'. Confronted with her confiding assurance, Hannele is 'almost indignant at being slighted so completely herself'. But she listens to the little lady's long account of Alec's perfection as a devoted husband:

'Oh, but he's been perfect to me, perfect. Hardly a cross word. Why, on our wedding night he kneeled down in front of me and promised, with God's help, to make my life happy. And I must say, as far as possible, he's kept his word.'

Hannele can 'see her being a heroine, playing the chief part in her life-romance' – which is 'such a feminine occupation', we are told, 'that no woman takes offence when she is made an audience'. The way in which, as we attend to the preposterous, vivacious, and irresistibly convincing comedy of the little lady, the doll gets its significance developed and generalized is subtle and unobtrusive – we have no sense of there being any symbolic designs upon us; but it has told decisively by the end of the scene. There are touches that keep the doll sufficiently present. Towards the middle of the *tête-à-tête* Mrs Hepburn says: 'But when you showed me his doll, then I knew.' And she closes it on the insistence that *she* must have the doll:

'You'll send it round – will you? – if you will be so kind.'
'I must ask my friend, first.'
'Yes, of course. But I am sure she will be so kind as to send it to me. It is a little – er – indelicate, don't you think!'
'No,' said Hannele. 'No more than a painted portrait.'
'Don't you?' said her hostess coldly. 'Well, even a painted portrait I think I should like in my own possession. This *doll* –'
Hannele waited, but there was no conclusion.
'Anyhow,' she said, 'the price is three guineas: or the equivalent in marks.'
'Very well,' said the little lady, 'you shall have your three guineas when I get the doll.'

Hannele's 'Alexander doll' doesn't represent so absurd a triumph of 'will' and 'idea' over reality as Mrs Hepburn's does. Nevertheless, it is a doll; and the impulsion to the making of a doll has now been associated with the expectation of 'love' as adoration and as the self-devotion of the lover to making the loved one happy; with which expectation, it has been brought home to us, goes an essential possessiveness, and, inseparably from that, a denial of the living reality (which is unpossess-able) of the possessed.

... the picture of Alec at his wife's feet on his wedding night, vowing to devote himself to her life-long happiness – this picture strayed across Hannele's mind time after time, whenever she thought of her dear captain. With disastrous consequences to the captain. Of course, if it had been at her own feet, then Hannele would have thought it almost natural: almost a necessary part of the show of love. But at the feet of the other little woman! And what was that other little woman wearing?

Hannele's recoil, then, though she doesn't know it, involves an implicit criticism of herself: it is not till the close of the long process of Alexander's formal proposal of marriage (that is, till the end of the drama) that she is brought to recognize this. At present her attitude may be represented by a retort of hers thrown out in the course of the proposal:

'Why shouldn't I make a doll of you? Does it do you any harm? And *weren't* you a doll, good heavens! You *were* nothing but a doll. So what hurt does it do you?'

How, she asks herself, could she have been in love with the devoted husband of that little lady: the hero of that ridiculous wedding-night scene; the husband who, in her own presence, had acted the doll his wife had made of him?

Ach! Ach! Hannele wrung her hands to think of *herself* being mixed up with him. And he had seemed to her so manly. He seemed to have so much silent male passion in him. And yet – the little lady! 'My husband has *always* been *perfectly sweet* to me.' Think of it! On his knees too. And his 'Yes dear! Certainly. Certainly.' Not that he was afraid of the little lady. He was just committed to her, as he might have been committed to gaol, or committed to paradise.

She sees him now as a limited, rather vulgar, and inferior person. And yet she cannot forget the spell:

Nevertheless. If it had existed, it did exist. And if it did exist, it was worth having. You could call it an illusion if you liked. But an illusion which is a real experience is worth having. Perhaps this disillusion was a greater illusion than the illusion itself. Perhaps all this disillusion of the little lady and the husband of the little lady was falser than the brief moments of real illusion.

Significantly, her settling to this – to the state indicated here – at the centre of her shifting and balancing expresses itself in a resolution *not* to send the doll; the little lady shall never have the doll. The final note of the scene is:

What a doll she would make herself! Heavens, what a wizened jewel!

Signalled by this, there follows a further developing and generalizing of the significance of the doll, given us in Hepburn's talk to Hannele about his wife, after the fatal fall from the hotel-bedroom window. His talk also does a great deal to enrich our sense of the indefinable reality – our apprehension of it as something positive – that attracts her in his charm. There is the way in which he taps at her door after the dreadful event and asks her to 'come over for a chat', and the curious, untense, matter-of-fact way in which he does chat about the accident and his wife.

Hannele's ears were sharp. But strain them as she might she could not catch the meaning of his voice.

And he goes on to give her his incredible account of his wife as herself a mysterious unknown, something quite other than her 'personality'. But *is* it incredible? When we hear that 'she was like a fairy who is condemned to live in houses and sit on furniture and all that, don't you know', we don't dissociate ourselves from his confidante's reaction: '"No?" said Hannele, herself sitting in blank amazement.' And yet his description is not without its point of coincidence with our own observed 'little lady':

'Like some sort of delicate creature you take out of a tropical forest the moment it is born, and from the first moment teach it to perform tricks. You know what I mean. All her life she performed the tricks of life, clever little monkey she was at it too. Beat me into fits.'

We remember the little lady as we have seen and heard her; wonderfully done, with her 'rather lardy-dardy middle-class English', her ruthless imitation upper-class authority, and the femininity of her determination to 'protect our men'. And it is of this rather vulgar and decidedly limited person that Hepburn, answering the challenge, 'You loved her, then?' can speak in these terms:

'Yes. But in this way. When I was a boy I caught a bird, a black-cap, and I put it in a cage. And I loved that bird. I don't know why, but I loved it. I simply loved that bird. All the gorse, and the heather, and the rock, and the hot smell of yellow gorse-blossom, and the sky that seemed to have no end to it, when I was a boy, everything that I almost was *mad* with, as boys are, seemed to me to be in that little, fluttering black-cap. And it would peck its seed as if it didn't quite know what else to do; and look round about, and begin to sing. But in quite a few days it turned its head aside and died. Yes, it died. I never had the feeling again that I got from that black-cap when I was a boy – not until I saw her. And then I felt it all again. I felt it all again. And it was the same feeling. I knew, quite soon I knew, that she would die. She would peck her seed and look round in the cage just the same. But she would die in the end. Only it would last much longer. But she would die in the cage, like the black-cap.'

It is the reality, not of the wife thus presented to us, but of Hepburn himself on which our wonderment focusses during the astonishing presentment. As far as the little lady is concerned, we grant with real assent the application of the general truth to her: the reality of a human being is not exhausted in his or her 'personality'. But the main effect on us of the scene is to confirm our sense of the valid claim – claim to key-significance – of the unknown in Hepburn. Hannele, of course, who can no longer think of him as 'rather awful – stupid – an ass – a limited, rather vulgar person', is left in a new phase of baffled indetermination. The scene ends:

'And perhaps I was to blame. Perhaps I ought to have made some sort of a move. But I didn't know what to do. For my life, I didn't know what to do, except try and make her happy. She had enough money – and I didn't think it mattered if she shared it with me. I always had a garden – and the astronomy. It's been an immense relief to me watching the moon. It's been wonderful. Instead of looking inside the cage, as I did at my bird, or at her – I look right out – into freedom – into freedom.'

'The moon, you mean?' said Hannele.

'Yes, the moon.'

'And that's your freedom?'

'That's where I've found the greatest sense of freedom,' he said.
'Well, I'm not going to be jealous of the moon,' said Hannele at length.
'Why should you? It's not a thing to be jealous of.'

We can now tell ourselves more about the significance of the telescopes and Alexander's interest in the moon. They point, we see here,
to that impersonal purpose (if 'purpose' is the word) which an individual human being must have while he has his integrity and his *raison
d'être*; that 'purpose' which cannot, without disaster, be abdicated in
favour of anything else. One cannot live to make another person happy; and to propose to do so, to take that for a *raison d'être*, is a denial
of life that can only breed ill. Again, what we have had presented to us
by the whole scene is the fact of *otherness*: we cannot possess one another,
and the possibility of valid intimate relations – the essential lasting relations between a man and a woman, for instance – depends on an
acceptance of this truth.

We cease for a while to be given Alexander Hepburn through Hannele's apprehension of him; we have him directly. He is not now a
fascinating unknown; he is just a man, with his problems, and with no
more mystery about him than there is about any man – he is ordinary,
we might say, if we felt ourselves to be ordinary. He goes back to
England to settle his affairs, feeling that 'the emotional flow between
him and all the people he knew and cared for' is broken. He is 'profoundly thankful' his wife is dead ('It was an end of pity now'). During the long winter he neither, though free to do so, goes back to
Germany, nor writes to Hannele; he 'cannot even think of her'.
Nevertheless, 'Alexander Hepburn was not the man to live alone':

We must be *able* to be alone, otherwise we are just victims. But when we *are*
able to be alone, then we realize that the only thing to do is to start a new
relationship with another – or even the same – human being. That people
should all be stuck up apart, like so many telegraph poles, is nonsense.
So with our dear captain. He had his convulsion into a sort of telegraph-pole
isolation: which was absolutely necessary for him. But then he began to bud
with a new yearning for – for what? For love?

Hannele does not 'exactly represent rosy love' to him; rather, 'a hard
destiny'; but he writes to her, but gets no answer. Finally he goes to

Germany, fails to find either of the two women, but suddenly, in Munich, sees his doll in a shop window, 'lounging with his back against a little Japanese lacquer cabinet, with a few old pots on his right hand and a tiresome brass ink-tray on his left, while pieces of not very nice filet lace hung their length up and down the background ... it was like a deliberate satire'. Between two of his fascinated visits to the shop window the doll is sold ('Five hundred marks'). He gets no clue to Hannele's whereabouts till he reads, under 'Studio Comments', in the *Muenchner Neue Zeitung*, about Theodor Worpswede's latest picture, a 'still-life, containing an entertaining group of a doll, two sun-flowers in a glass jar, and a poached egg on toast'. The doll is of a Scottish officer and the same paragraph reports the rumour of its original creator's engagement to the Herr Regierungsrat of a summer resort in the Tyrol. Alexander buys the picture, and hurries off with it across the Austrian frontier to Kaprun.

We now see him again through Hannele's eyes. Walking with the Herr Regierungsrat across the 'space of sunshine', she suddenly finds Alexander there in front of her.

She did not notice till he had taken off his hat and was saluting her. Then what she saw was the black, smooth, shining head, and she went pale. His black, smooth, close head – and all the blue Austrian day seemed to shrivel before her eyes.

'How do you do, Countess! I hoped I should meet you.'

She heard his slow, sad-clanging, straying voice again, and she pressed her hand with the umbrella stick against her breast. She had forgotten it – forgotten his peculiar, slow voice. And now it seemed like a noise that sounds in the silence of the night. Ah! how difficult it was, that suddenly the world could split under her eyes, and show this darkness inside. She wished he had not come.

We recall what Count Dionys tells Lady Daphne about the light of the sun:

'And the true sunbeams coming towards us flow darkly, a moving darkness of the genuine fire. The sun is dark, the sunshine flowing to us is dark. And light is only the inside-out of it all, the lining, and the yellow beams are only the turning away of the sun's directness that was coming to us. Does that interest you at all?'

'Yes,' she said dubiously.

'Well, we've got the world inside out. The true living world of fire is dark, throbbing, darker than blood. Our luminous world that we go by is only the reverse of this.'

'Yes, I like that,' she said.

'Well! Now listen. The same with love. This white love that we have is the same. It is only the reverse, the whited sepulchre of the true love. True love is dark. …'

But what follows here is nothing like the nocturnalities – mystery and incantation – of *The Ladybird*. It is the expedition to the glacier, a strenuous daylight affair, in which the challenging strangeness of the mountains is not more in evidence than the reminders of the ordinary day-to-day human world, in the form of tourists, motor-coaches, hotels, and so on – done with Lawrence's incomparable genius. It is astonishing how, in all this part of the tale, that post-war Austria is brought before us. It provides, with its indisputable and constantly obtruding actuality, the setting in which the lovers negotiate. For it seems inevitable, and it is certainly not misleading now, to call them lovers: as they set off together on this holiday excursion (it manifests itself later as a kind of ordeal or *rite de passage*) we know that, in their deeper psyche, they are intent on coming to terms.

But, as they climb into the upper world, they are 'not in good company together'. Alexander's unconcealed revulsion against 'this Bergheil business', and the whole cult of mountains it represents, jars on Hannele: 'if you don't like it, why must you spoil it for me?' When, as they emerge in the upper valley, below the glacier, he exclaims in wonder ('as if to himself') –

She looked quickly at his face, saw the queer, blank, sphinx-look with which he gazed out beyond himself. His eyes were black and set, and he seemed so motionless, as if he were eternal, facing these upper facts.

She thrilled with triumph. She felt he was overcome.

She is mistaken; his attitude towards 'these upper facts' is very remote indeed from the sanctioned exaltation or awe. This soon becomes plain. But first, as they lunch under a rock, he pulls out the picture from his shoulder-sack, so bringing up at last the question of their past relations. To his saying that he didn't quite like it that she sold the doll she replies that, when his wife appeared, and *he* disappeared, she felt he had sold *her*. In an intensified antagonism, then, they go on; and revert to the theme of the mountains. Why, she asks 'with an ice-bitter fury', turning round on him in the cold rain, why has she come here? – to see the mountains, not to see *him*.

'You came to see the glacier and the mountains *with* me,' he replied.

'Did I? Then I made a mistake. You can do nothing but find fault even with God's mountains.'

A dark flame suddenly went over his face.

'Yes,' he said, 'I hate them, I hate them. I hate their snow, and their affectations.'

'*Affectations*!' she laughed. 'Oh! Even the mountains are affected for you, are they?'

'Yes,' he said. 'Their loftiness and their uplift. I hate their uplift. I hate people prancing on mountain-tops and feeling exalted. I'd like to make them all stop up there, on their mountain-tops, and chew ice to fill their stomachs. I wouldn't let them down again, I wouldn't. I hate it all, I tell you; I hate it.'

The relation of his vehement feeling to the antagonism between them is now pretty plain: he associates the sentimental idealism of the mountain-cult with the unrealities of ideal 'love'. And he gets, soon, an endorsement straight out of the tale (so to speak); for the following – it comes during their halt for shelter in the restaurant of the uppermost hotel – comes neither as his reflection nor hers:

Certainly they were lords of the Alps, or at least lords of the Alpine hotels this summer, let prejudice be what it might. Jews of the wrong sort. And yet even they imparted a wholesome breath of sanity, disillusion, unsentimentality, to the excited 'Bergheil' atmosphere. Their dark-eyed, sardonic presence seemed to say to the maidenly-necked mountain youths: 'Don't sprout wings of the spirit too much, my dears.'

Yet that is not all; Alexander's revulsion against the mountains, 'their loftiness and their uplift', is no mere negation. What gives it its vehemence, as the close of that angry exchange with Hannele brings out, is an affirmation of life:

'You must be a little mad,' she said superbly, 'to talk like that about the mountains. They are so much bigger than you.'

'No,' he said. 'No! They are not.'

'What!' she laughed aloud. 'The mountains are not bigger than you? But you are extraordinary.'

'They are not bigger than me,' he cried. 'Any more than you are bigger than me if you stand on a ladder. They are not bigger than me. They are less than me.'

'Oh! Oh!' she cried in wonder and ridicule. 'The mountains are less than you.'

'Yes!' he cried, 'they are less.'

He seemed suddenly to go silent and remote as she watched him. The speech had gone out of his face again, he seemed to be standing a long way off from her, beyond some border-line. And in the midst of her indignant amazement she watched him with wonder and a touch of fascination. To what country did he belong then? – to what dark, different atmosphere?

Hannele herself, even in her fierce antagonism, cannot dismiss it wholly as rhodomontade or megalomania, and this is altogether credible to us; so convincingly, in this drama which affects us so largely as comedy – and in which (to illustrate a characteristic tone) the 'mule had to stand exactly at that spot to make his droppings' – has the deep centre of life in Alexander been established for us as a potent reality. The affirmation, and the reality that affirms, have their significance enforced by the opposing 'upper facts', the terribleness of which is borne in upon us with all Lawrence's marvellous power:

The wonder, the terror, and the bitterness of it. Never a warm leaf to unfold, never a gesture of life to give off. A world sufficient unto itself in lifelessness, all this ice.

To Hannele it still seems 'to hold the key to all glamour and ecstasy, the great silent, living glacier', though, we get the hint, a sense of a more frightening reality is dawning:

'Are you glad that you came?' she said, looking at him triumphant.

'Very glad I came,' he said. His eyes were dilated with excitement that was ordeal or mystic battle rather than the Bergheil ecstasy. The curious vibration of his excitement made the scene strange, rather horrible to her. She too shuddered.

The significance of the ordeal gets its explicit pointer when, as she watches from below, he makes the final desperate scramble on to the face of the glacier, and stands there with the 'little cluster of people facing the uphill of sullen, pure, sodden-looking ice': they were 'all afraid', but 'being human, they all wanted to go beyond their fear'. The admonition of this inhuman and lifeless world is terrible; Alexander's affirmation of life, 'They [the mountains] are less than me', is made in the face of a full apprehension of 'these upper facts': there is nothing romantic about it. Safely down again from the ice, he says:

'I've been far enough. I prefer the world where cabbages will grow on the soil. Nothing grows on glaciers.'

The effect of the holiday-excursion is to confirm the positiveness and the validity of Hepburn's ostensibly negative attitude – his repudiation of 'love' and his 'meaninglessness'. This attitude is truly one of insistence on reality, and the insistence, negative as it may have seemed to Hannele, the 'idea'-bound, expresses an ultimate – an unsentimental and unideal – vital faith, a profound assertion of life and wholeness.

When Hepburn begins his proposal, as they wait, on the way down, at the coach-terminus, Hannele is still, in outer seeming, as she was. The essential choice stands there clearly before her – at least, one term of it is clear, made present by Alexander's characteristic opening: 'Do you think you will marry the Herr Regierungsrat?' The Herr Regierungsrat, impressively mature and very distinguished, offers her homage, and makes her feel like 'a queen in exile'. On the other hand there is the insufferably inappropriate matter-of-factness of Alexander, who 'suggests', simply, that she should marry *him*, 'leaving aside the question of whether you love me or I love you'. It is the same 'incalculable' Alexander, with the same voice and manner, and yet *we* do not feel the characteristic odd matter-of-factness to be inappropriate. Nor do we feel that she, though she looks at him 'with amazement, ridicule, and anger in her face', is really, now, baffled, or would describe him as 'incalculable'. So he impresses us as being right when, to her 'I really think you must be mad', he replies:

'I doubt if you think that. It is only a method of retaliation, that is. I think you understand my point very clearly.'

When he produces from his knapsack the 'famous picture', it is merely to bring to a focus – to present sharply for recognition – the upshot of the whole argument or demonstration that has been enacted between them (the wife having had her major part too). All the essential things that cannot be explained – and can least of all in a tense altercation between two lovers in a public place – are represented by the doll, which for both Hannele and Alexander as well as for us, is now a fully charged symbol. It gives the due force to his remark that 'All this about love is very confusing, and very complicated.' When Hannele says, 'Love to me is simple enough,' he replies: 'And was it simple love which made you make that doll of me?' Her 'amazement and rage' at his insisting on the doll, and that it *does* him harm ('It does me the greatest possible damage'), betray her unwilling recognition of the force of his references to it.

'Why? Pray why? Can you tell me why?'

'Not quite, I can't,' he replied, taking up the picture and holding it up in front of her. She turned her face from it as a cat turns its nose away from a lighted cigarette.

'But when I look at this – then I *know* that there's no love between you and me.'

In the rushing and swerving motor-coach, where, having failed to find another seat, she has to sit next to him, he 'finishes what he has to say': that is, he gives her – shouting when necessary against the noise – a sober statement of his position. It is perfectly dramatic, and it is at the same time an explicit statement of the burden ('moral', one might say) of the tale or drama. It contains the passage, already quoted from, in which he sums up the full charge of significance the doll now has:

'My wife might have done it. She did do it, in her mind. ... If a woman loves you, she'll make a doll of you. She'll never be satisfied till she's made your doll. And when she's got your doll, that's all she wants. And that's what love means. And so I won't be loved. And I won't love.'

There is point in his bringing it to the stage of blunt explicitness with her: the upshot of the enacted vicissitudes of their relations has been to have established (and for us as well as for him) that there is, between them, the basis for something permanent and unillusory – for a marriage that shall not commit anyone to adoring or possessive 'love', or, as an ultimate, to the undertaking to make an adored one happy. This is to say that his negative is the other face of a positive: his belief in the possibility (and – for him – the need) of a lasting relation with a woman. And this belief the 'incalculable' Alexander Hepburn, with the 'strange, dark vacancy of his brow, his not-thinking', conveys in the most old-fashioned of traditional terms – terms going with what might seem to be an outmoded common sense:

'It isn't very easy to put into words,' he said. 'But I tried marriage once on a basis of love, and I must say it was a ghastly affair in the long run. And I believe it would be so, for me, whatever woman I had.'

'There must be something wrong with you, then,' said she.

'As far as love goes. And yet I want marriage. I want marriage. I want a woman to honour and obey me.'

For a further formulation we have:

'Honour and obedience: and the proper physical feelings,' he said. 'To me that is marriage. Nothing else.'

'But what are the proper physical feelings but love?' asked Hannele.

'No,' he said. 'Any woman wants you to adore her, and be in love with her – and I shan't. I will not do it again, if I live a monk for the rest of my days. I will neither adore you nor be in love with you.'

There is nothing merely and crudely reductive about the attitude; that, even locally, is apparent enough:

'If a woman honours me – absolutely from the bottom of her nature honours me – and obeys me because of that, I take it, my desire for her goes very much deeper than if I was in love with her, or if I adored her.'

'It's the same thing. I love you, then everything is there – all the lot: your honour and obedience and everything. And if love isn't there, nothing is there,' she said.

'That isn't true,' he replied. 'A woman may adore you, but she'll neither honour you nor obey you. The most loving and adoring woman today could any minute start and make a doll of her husband – as you made of me.'

Coming as they do for the reader who brings to them the charge of what has gone before, the forthright – seemingly blunt – terms of the formulation define, for all the 'nothing else', a conception of the relations between a man and a woman that cannot readily be convicted of impoverishment. Their use by Alexander Hepburn now is wholly convincing. That it should be so is a wonderful triumph of creative art

and a significant pointer to the nature of Lawrence's genius. The traditional terms are no more paradoxically wrested than they are used
naïvely to express a crude or simple attitude: they are revitalized in the
service of a profound insight into the deeper human needs and desires.

Of course, very far from every reader of Lawrence testifies to this
genius: critics give us the most surprising reports of his best things, and
The Captain's Doll itself is invoked to prove that he preached – what
he itched, it is alleged, to practise – a bullying male dominance. Such
commentaries betray a resistance closely related to the kind that Hannele ultimately relinquishes. She, of course, has a direct personal
involvement, but her resistance, nevertheless, is a resistance of 'ideas'
to a deep vital truth – a truth that, recognized, must sap their power.
And such 'ideas' cannot be overcome by logic. And, as the history of
his reception shows, even such genius as Lawrence's – even in those who
formally salute the genius – cannot be counted on to overcome the
implicit resistance to the recognition.

In defining the norm with which he is preoccupied (and the creative
impulse in *The Captain's Doll* cannot be separated from a normative
concern – with which fact is bound up the dramatic impersonality of
the art), it is with a significant propriety that he makes Alexander Hepburn invoke the traditional formulation. A man is a man and not a
woman, and a woman is a woman and not a man: the difference is not
superficial or inessential. Hepburn uses 'honour and obey' to point to
the positive aspect of the profound conviction to which experience has
brought him – the conviction that he has 'always made a mistake,
undertaking to love'.

'And you?' she cried. 'You! Even suppose you *were* honoured and obeyed. I
suppose all you've got to do is to sit there like a sultan and sup it up.'

'Oh no, I have many things to do. And woman or no woman, I'm going to
start to do them.'

'What, pray?'

'Why, nothing very exciting. I'm going to East Africa to join a man who's
breaking his neck to get his three thousand acres under control. And when I've
done a few more experiments and observations, and got all the necessary facts,
I'm going to do a book on the moon. Woman or no woman, I'm going to do
that.'

A man's *raison d'être* cannot be to adore a woman, or to make her, or anyone else, happy (an illusory aim); his meaning is not exhausted in the service of wife and children. And unless he is there, vindicated in his full meaning as a man, he is not there to establish with the woman the vital polarity without which there cannot be a lasting relation that doesn't thwart the life in either. It is for the man, Hepburn intimates, to vindicate himself as such by having, in the world, an impersonal, non-domestic purpose and activity. If he does not, whatever the woman may think she desires, she is let down; however adoring, he has failed her.

The Captain's Doll does not propound or generalize; we do not find it laid down there, nor are we forced to deduce, that the mode of the manifestation of the difference between men and women must always and everywhere be this, which Alexander defines cogently enough for Hannele's conviction with the help of the marriage service. We have to note of course that theme and creative impulsion are, as I have said, essentially normative. And again and again Lawrence's art deals with the woman, nerve-worn and strained or lethally sardonic, in whom life has gone wrong because she is committed to the man's part, or to contempt for it, or to living in a mode that gives it no place. Or his theme sometimes (as in *England, My England*) is the man who, declining the life-responsibility represented by the male activity and purpose, fails his wife in a way no love or goodwill can forgive or condone. But there are, it is plain, possibilities that are not recognized in *The Captain's Doll*. And it might be made a criticism of that tale that it raises questions in a way of which the author can be supposed to be unaware. Hannele, it might be pointed out, has her art, the expression (we are given to understand) of a real talent. If Alexander's amateur dealings with the moon are to be taken so seriously, doesn't Hannele's talent represent something that shouldn't have dropped so easily out of the account? And, plainly enough, situations can be imagined in which such questions should pose themselves forcibly and poignantly, providing a great novelist with a different kind of theme from Lawrence's, and with a vision of a different kind of partnership between a man and a woman. On the other hand, Lawrence may well be implying that Hannele's doll-making belongs with Mrs Bodoin's and Mrs Witt's wit – that it is a perverting into work of sardonic destructiveness (determined by her attitude towards men) of the woman's gift of creating and sustaining life, and that in the changed conditions Hannele will not be impelled to that mode of self-expression.

But the normative preoccupation of Lawrence's theme starts from the mischievousness of the 'ideas' the tale deals with – the 'ideas' of 'love' and adoration and 'making happy'; and the positive aspect of the theme is inseparable from the negative one. It may be a point of adverse criticism that Hannele's talent has, ostensibly, no more significance in the drama than that it enables her to make the doll. But it *is*, ostensibly, just that limited kind of *donnée*, asking to be given no more than just that value. And in Hannele's anger against Alexander no part is played by any sense in her of gifts or powers for which he proposes to leave no place.

Her attitude and her change have their significance strictly in relation to what has become focussed in the doll. We recognize before she does the signs of the imminent surrender; the conviction is substantially there before she admits it to herself: we have watched it forming as the inevitable outcome of the demonstration they enact between them. When, near the beginning of the proposal, he says, 'I think you understand my point very clearly,' we know (I have already remarked) that, for all her genuine indignation, he is right. The inner shifts in her have been rendered with convincing subtlety. Immediately after his outburst about the 'affectations' and 'uplift' of the mountains, she has recognized that her relations with him are different from any she has had with other men, and unwittingly testifies that they are supremely important to her:

'Is he mad? What does he mean? Is he a madman? He wants to bully me into something. What does he want to bully me into? Does he want me to love him?' ...

So this was the conclusion to which Hannele came. And it pleased her, and it flattered her. And it made her feel quite warm towards him as they walked in the rain. ... He wanted her to love him. Yes, that was how she had to put it. He didn't want to *love* her. No. He wanted *her* to love *him*.

But then, of course, woman-like, she took his love for granted. So many men had been so very ready to love her. And this one – to her amazement, to her indignation, and rather to her secret satisfaction – just blackly insisted that *she* must love *him*. Very well – she would give him a run for his money.

The indignant anger that accompanies the 'giving him a run for his money' subsides during the proposal and the discussion into which this turns, but she gives no sign of acquiescence till the very end, when he is leaving her at the landing-stage outside the villa where she lives. Then it is hardly a surrender: the fact of their accord stands there fully formed between them, revealed as they part. The shift from antagonism is made easy for her by the shouted matter-of-fact exchange with the friends in the garden.

> From the villa they were running down the steps to meet Hannele.
> 'But won't you have me even if I love you?' she asked him.
> 'You must promise the other,' he said. 'It comes in the marriage service.'
> 'Hat's geregnet? Wie war das Wetter? Warst du auf dem Gletscher?' cried the voices from the garden.
> 'Nein – kein Regen. Wunderschön! Ja, er war ganz auf dem Gletscher,' cried Hannele in reply. And to him, *sotto voce*:
> 'Don't be a solemn ass. Do come in.'
> 'No,' he said, 'I don't want to come in.'
> 'Do you want to go away tomorrow? Go if you *do*. But anyway, I won't say it *before* the marriage service. I needn't, need I?'
> She stepped from the boat on to the plank.
> 'Oh,' she said, turning round, 'give me that picture, please, will you? I want to burn it.'
> He handed it to her.
> 'And come tomorrow, will you?' she said.
> 'Yes, in the morning.'
> He pulled back quickly into the darkness.

With the reign of sanity and profound common sense established, we must end on the reminder of 'darkness' – 'darkness', with all its associations: the 'dark, wide-open eyes'; the moment when, walking with the Herr Regierungsrat, she saw Alexander in front of her, and suddenly the world 'split under her eyes' and showed 'this darkness inside'; and the 'curious, dark, masterful force that supplanted thought in him', while she pondered 'Is he mad?' The effect here is validating: this common sense *is* profound.

6

St Mawr, I suppose, would commonly be described as a long short-story – a *nouvelle*, rather than a novel. Actually, that description, with its limiting effect, has a marked infelicity. It certainly doesn't suggest the nature or weight of the astonishing work of genius that Lawrence's 'dramatic poem' is. *St Mawr* seems to me to present a creative and technical originality more remarkable than that of *The Waste Land*, being, as that poem is not, completely achieved, a full and self-sufficient creation. It can hardly strike the admirer as anything but major.

The comparative reference isn't random: *St Mawr*, too, has the Waste Land for theme. To say this is to suggest scope as well as intensity, and the suggestion isn't idle. There are, besides the horse and the two grooms, only three main actors, but, at the end of the hundred and eighty-odd pages, it is as if we had had a representative view of the civilized world. Lawrence's art, then, commands a pregnancy and a concentrated force not suggested by 'tale' or '*nouvelle*'. Yet what strikes us in the opening of *St Mawr* is not a portentousness or any kind of tension, but a freedom – something extraordinarily like careless ease:

Lou Witt had had her own way so long, that by the age of twenty-five she didn't know where she was. Having one's own way landed one completely at sea.

To be sure for a while she had failed in her grand love affair with Rico. And then she had had something really to despair about. But even that had worked out as she wanted. Rico had come back to her, and was dutifully married to her. And now, when she was twenty-five and he was three months older, they were a charming married couple. He flirted with other women still, to be sure. He wouldn't be the handsome Rico if he didn't. But she had 'got' him. Oh yes! You had only to see the uneasy backward glance at her, from his big blue eyes: just like a horse that is edging away from its master: to know how completely he was mastered.

She, with her odd little *museau*, not exactly pretty, but very attractive; and her quaint air of playing at being well-bred, in a sort of charade game; and her queer familiarity with foreign cities and foreign languages; and the lurking sense of being an outsider everywhere, like a sort of gipsy, who is at home anywhere and nowhere: all this made up her charm and her failure. She didn't quite belong.

Of course she was American: Louisiana family, moved down to Texas. And she was moderately rich, with no close relation except her mother. But she had been sent to school in France when she was twelve, and since she had finished school, she had drifted from Paris to Palermo, Biarritz to Vienna and back via Munich to London, then down again to Rome. Only fleeting trips to her America.

So what sort of American was she, after all?

And what sort of European was she either? She didn't 'belong' anywhere. Perhaps most of all in Rome, among the artists and the Embassy people.

It was in Rome she had met Rico. He was an Australian, son of a government official in Melbourne, who had been made a baronet. So one day Rico would be Sir Henry, as he was the only son. Meanwhile, he floated round Europe on a very small allowance – his father wasn't rich in capital – and was being an artist.

The economy of those opening pages, establishing the present from which the drama starts, is very remarkable. For what looks like carelessness – the relaxed, idiomatic, and even slangy familiarity – is actually precision and vivid firsthandness. And we soon discover that there is no limit to the power of easy and inevitable transitions. For Lawrence writes out of the full living language with a flexibility and a creative freedom for which I can think of no parallel in modern times. His writing seems to have the careless ease of extraordinarily fluent and racy speech; but you see, if you stop to cast a critical eye back over the page, that everything is precisely and easily *right* – the slangy colloquialism, the flippant cliché given an emotional intensity, the 'placing' sardonic touch, and, when it comes (as it so marvellously can at any moment), the free play of poetic imagery and imaginative evocation, sensuous and focally suggestive.

The opening pages are sardonic comedy, and it looks as if we are going to have merely a variant of that admirable short story, *Mother and Daughter*.[1] Rico and Lou, though 'they reacted badly on each other's

1. See p. 287 below.

nerves', and he 'couldn't stand Mrs Witt, and Mrs Witt couldn't stand him',

... couldn't get away from one another, even though in the course of their rather restrained correspondence he informed her that he was 'probably' marrying a very dear girl, friend of his childhood, only daughter of one of the oldest families in Victoria. Not saying much.

He didn't commit the probability, but reappeared in Paris, wanting to paint his head off, terribly inspired by Cézanne and by old Renoir. He dined at the Rotonde with Lou and Mrs Witt, who, with her queer democratic New Orleans sort of conceit looked round the drinking-hall with savage contempt, and at Rico as part of the show. 'Certainly,' she said, 'when these people here have got any money, they fall in love on a full stomach. And when they've got no money they fall in love with a full pocket. I never was in a more disgusting place. They take their love like some people take after-dinner pills.'

She would watch with her arching, full, strong grey eyes, sitting there erect and silent in her well-bought American clothes. And then she would deliver some such charge of grape-shot. Rico always writhed.

Mrs Witt hated Paris: 'this sordid, unlucky city', she called it. 'Something unlucky is bound to happen to me in this sinister, unclean town,' she said. 'I feel *contagion* in the air of this place. For heaven's sake, Louise, let us go to Morocco or somewhere.'

'No, mother dear, I can't now. Rico has proposed to me, and I have accepted him. Let us think about a wedding, shall we?'

'There!' said Mrs Witt. 'I said it was an unlucky city!'

The marriage is not a success – as Mrs Witt, 'watching as it were from outside the fence, like a potent well-dressed demon, full of uncanny energy and a shattering sort of sense', realizes almost immediately. And we note with what easy economy the different values of the main actors in the drama are established: Rico, representative of modern civilized 'life'; the formidable Mrs Witt, the American female, insatiably dominating,[1] who hardly disguises her contempt for him; and Lou, who can't happily accept either what Rico *is* or her mother's satisfaction in mere destructive negativity. Lou's sense of the nature of the failure of her marriage is brought to full consciousness by the stallion, St Mawr, and we may note how we are sensitized beforehand

1. A type Lawrence pays much attention to, a notable instance being Ethel in the tale *None of That*.

to take his significance as soon as he makes his entrance. An instance occurred in the opening passage quoted above: 'You had only to see the uneasy backward glance at her, from his big blue eyes: just like a horse that is edging away from its master: to know how completely he was mastered.' And here is the consequence of Mrs Witt's will to ride in the Park, where Lou, 'for very decency's sake' ('Mrs Witt was *so* like a smooth, levelled, gun-metal pistol, Lou had to be a sort of sheath'), must ride with her:

'Rico dear, you must get a horse.'
The tone was soft and southern and drawling, but the overtone had a decisive finality. In vain Rico squirmed – he had a way of writhing and squirming which perhaps he had caught at Oxford. In vain he protested that he couldn't ride, and that he didn't care for riding. He got quite angry, and his handsome arched nose tilted and his upper lip lifted from his teeth, like a dog that is going to bite. Yet daren't quite bite.
And that was Rico. He daren't quite bite. Not that he was really afraid of the others. He was afraid of himself, once he let himself go. He might rip up in an eruption of life-long anger all this pretty-pretty picture of a charming young wife and a delightful little home and a fascinating success as a painter of fashionable, and at the same time 'great' portraits: with colour, wonderful colour, and at the same time form, marvellous form. He had composed this little *tableau vivant* with great effort. He didn't want to erupt like some suddenly wicked horse – Rico was really more like a horse than a dog, a horse that might go nasty any moment. For the time, he was good, very good, dangerously good.

Rico is the antithesis of St Mawr; he represents the irremediable defeat of all that St Mawr stands for. Nevertheless, as the passage just quoted conveys, the frustrated drives of life are still there, down below, always threatening trouble in Rico and making security and satisfaction impossible. He's always in danger of 'making a break' of the kind for which St Mawr becomes notorious.

And, we are told, Rico 'was being an artist'.[1] As that way of putting it conveys, he's *not*, in Lawrence's sense, an artist: his 'being' an artist is simply a manifestation of his inability to be anything but superficial; to see anything except out of his superficially and deceptively 'con-

1. See note, 'Being an Artist', p. 310 below.

scious' 'personality'. Introduced to the stallion that has had so profound
an effect on Lou, he can only say:

'Yes, dear, he certainly *is* beautiful! such a marvellous colour! Almost
orange! But rather large, I should say, to ride in the Park.'

'No, for you he's perfect. You are so tall.'

'He'd be marvellous in a composition. That colour!' And all Rico could do
was to gaze with the artist's eye at the horse, with a glance at the groom.

This comes just after the rendering of the first impact of St Mawr on
Lou. She had found herself slipping away at every opportunity from
the charming little house in Westminster to the mews where her sorrel
mare Poppy is kept:

Whatever it was, her life with Rico in the elegant little house, and all her
social engagements, seemed like a dream, the substantial reality of which was
those mews in Westminster, her sorrel mare, the owner of the mews, Mr Saints-
bury, and the grooms he employed.

Then she is shown St Mawr:

The wild, brilliant, alert head of St Mawr seemed to look at her out of
another world. It was as if she had had a vision, as if the walls of her own
world had suddenly melted away, leaving her in a great darkness, in the midst
of which the large, brilliant eyes of that horse looked at her with demonish
question, while his naked ears stood up like daggers from the naked lines of his
inhuman head, and his great body glowed red with power.

What was it? Almost like a god looking at her terribly out of the everlasting
dark, she had felt the eyes of that horse; great, glowing, fearsome eyes, arched
with a question, and containing a white blade of light like a thread. What was
his non-human question, and his uncanny threat? She didn't know.

By now it is plain that we have to do with much more than sardonic
comedy. To call St Mawr a poetic symbol doesn't help much. To call
him a sexual symbol is positively misleading. In fact, this 'story about a
stallion' refutes in the most irrefutable of ways, for those who take
what it offers, the common notion that Lawrence is obsessed with sex,
or preaches some religion of sex, or is more preoccupied with sex than
the T. S. Eliot of *The Waste Land*. The marriage between Lou and Rico,
this attachment of the will and the nerves, does indeed, the datum is

given us, fail at the level of sex, in becoming 'more like a friendship, Platonic'; but the failure there is the index of a failure far transcending that.

St Mawr seemed to look at Lou 'out of another world': this kind of suggestion in Lawrence, irresistibly (one would have thought) as his art conveys it, is often dismissed as 'romantic' – that is, as an indulgence of imagination or fancy that cannot, by the mature, be credited with any real significance or taken seriously. The reader who is inclined to 'place' so the rendering, quoted from above, of the first effect of St Mawr on Lou should pay heed to what follows – to the account of the immediate consequence for Lou's relations with Rico. 'No matter where she was, what she was doing, at the back of her consciousness loomed a great, over-aweing figure out of a dark background,' and Rico senses something unusual:

'You are thinking about something, Lou dear!' Rico said to her that evening. He was so quick and sensitive to detect her moods – so exciting in this respect. And his big, slightly prominent blue eyes, with the whites a little blood-shot, glanced at her quickly, with searching, and anxiety, and a touch of fear, as if his conscience were always uneasy. He, too, was rather like a horse – but forever quivering with a sort of cold, dangerous mistrust, which he covered with anxious love.

At the middle of his eyes was a central powerlessness, that left him anxious. It used to touch her to pity, that central look of powerlessness in him. But now, since she had seen the full, dark, passionate blaze of power and of different life in the eyes of the thwarted horse, the anxious powerlessness of the man drove her mad. Rico was so handsome, and he was so self-controlled, he had a gallant sort of kindness and a real worldly shrewdness. One had to admire him: at least *she* had to.

But after all, and after all, it was bluff, an attitude. He kept it all working in himself, deliberately. It was an attitude. She read psychologists who said that everything was an attitude. Even the best of everything. But now she realized that, with men and women, everything is an attitude only when something else is lacking. Something is lacking and they are thrown back on their own devices. That black fiery flow in the eyes of the horse was not 'attitude'. It was something much more terrifying, and real, the only thing that was real. Gushing from the darkness in menace and question, and blazing out in the splendid body of the horse.

There we have it, the preoccupation that, in Lou Carrington (and in Lawrence), so far transcends sex; 'real' – the something other than attitude; the *real* that, surely, we should be able to oppose to the attitudes, to distinguish *them* for what they are. 'Attitudes' belong to the 'personality', the life of 'ideas' and will and nerves. What else is there? Lawrence believes – knows – that there is, or should be, something else – he believes that 'sincerity' can have a meaning; and if this conviction, which carries with it a belief that irreverence, and an incapacity for awed wonder in the face of life, are deathly, is 'romantic', then Lawrence deserves to be called that.

The passage in *À Propos of Lady Chatterley's Lover* from which I quoted in discussing *The Daughters of the Vicar* comes in aptly here; it might have been written by way of helping us to give an adequate account of the stallion and of the significance that he focusses:

The body's life is the life of sensations and emotions. The body feels real hunger, real thirst, real joy in the sun or the snow, real pleasure in the smell of roses or the look of a lilac bush; real anger, real sorrow, real love, real tenderness, real warmth, real passion, real hate, real grief. All the emotions belong to the body, and are only recognized by the mind. We may hear the most sorrowful piece of news, and only feel a mental excitement. Then, hours after, perhaps in sleep, the awareness may reach the bodily centres, and true grief wrings the heart.

How different they are, mental feelings and real feelings. Today, many people live and die without having had any real feelings – though they have had a 'rich emotional life' apparently, having showed strong mental feeling. But it is all counterfeit. In magic, one of the so-called 'occult' pictures represents a man standing, apparently, before a flat table mirror, which reflects him from the waist to the head, so that you have the man from head to waist, then his reflection downwards from waist to head again. And whatever it may mean in magic, it means what we are today, creatures whose active emotional self has no real existence, but is all reflected downwards from the mind. Our education from the start has *taught* us a certain range of emotions, what to feel and what not to feel, and how to feel the feelings we allow ourselves to feel. All the rest is just non-existent. ... The higher emotions are strictly dead. They have to be faked.

And by higher emotions we mean love in all its manifestations, from genuine desire to tender love, love of our fellowmen, and love of God: we mean love, joy, delight, hope, true indignant anger, passionate sense of justice and injustice, truth and untruth, honour and dishonour, and real belief in *anything*: for belief is a profound emotion that has the mind's connivance.

By 'body', then, Lawrence means all that deep spontaneous life which is not at the beck and call of the conscious and willing mind, and so in that sense cannot be controlled by it, though it can be thwarted and defeated. St Mawr, the stallion, *is* that life. And in presenting the drama in which the stallion figures so centrally Lawrence leaves us unable to doubt that his essential – and triumphant – concern is to vindicate 'love, joy, delight, hope, true indignant anger, passionate sense of justice and injustice, truth and untruth, honour and dishonour', and the capacity for real belief. It is an astonishing triumph of the highest creative art.

As we have seen, the significance of St Mawr is first imparted to us through Lou's sense of it. It is developed and enforced by a wealth of poetic and dramatic means. We may take for illustration the way in which Rico is played off against Lewis, the Welsh groom.

He peered straight at her from under his overhanging black hair. He had pale grey eyes, that looked phosphorescent, and suggested the eyes of a wild cat peering intent from under the darkness of some bush where it lies unseen. Lou, with her brown, unmatched, oddly perplexed eyes, felt herself found out. 'He's a common little fellow,' she thought to herself. 'But he knows a woman and a horse, at sight.' Aloud she said, in her southern drawl:

'How do you think he'd be with Sir Henry?'

Lewis turned his remote, coldly watchful eyes on the young baronet. Rico was tall and handsome, and balanced on his hips. His face was long and well-defined, and with the hair taken straight back from the brow. It seemed as well-made as his clothing, and as perpetually presentable. You could not imagine his face dirty, or scrubby, and unshaven or bearded, or even moustached. It was perfectly prepared for social purposes. If his head had been cut off, like John the Baptist's, it would have been a thing complete in itself, would not have missed the body in the least. The body was perfectly tailored. The head was one of the famous 'talking heads' of modern youth, with eyebrows a trifle Mephistophelian, large blue eyes a trifle bold, and curved mouth thrilling to death to kiss.

The force of this needs no explaining. 'If his head had been cut off ... it would have been a thing complete in itself, it would not have missed the body in the least' – all the same, Rico has a strong desire to own and to ride St Mawr, till he finds him too dangerous: he cannot be happy in his deficiency. Lewis, of course, 'the little aboriginal Lewis', gets on perfectly well with St Mawr – 'he goes with the horse'. ('When I speak to him,' says Mrs Witt, 'I never know whether I'm speaking to a man or a horse.') He has what Rico lacks – or *is* what Rico is not. He explains the ease of his own relations with the stallion, whom the gentlemen have found too much for them, by saying that, like Phoenix the other groom, he is 'different'.

Mrs Witt, with her conscious mind, sees the difference as simple inferiority. After the sardonic comedy of the episode in which she cuts his hair, we have this (a passage that, coming where it does, illustrates the delicacy and range of Lawrence's poetic method):

'It is extraordinary what hair that man has!' said Mrs Witt. 'Did I tell you when I was in Paris, I saw a woman's face in the hotel that I thought I knew? I couldn't place her, till she was coming towards me. *Aren't you Rachel Fannière?* she said. *Aren't you Jannette Leroy?* We hadn't seen each other since we were girls of twelve and thirteen at school in New Orleans. *Oh!* she said to me. *Is every illusion doomed to perish? You had such wonderful golden curls! All my life I've said, Oh, if only I had such lovely hair as Rachel Fannière! I've seen those beautiful golden curls of yours all my life. And now I meet you, you're grey!* Wasn't that terrible, Louise? Well, that man's hair made me think of it – so thick and curious. It's strange, what a difference there is in hair; I suppose it's because he's just an animal – no mind! There's nothing I admire in a man like a good *mind*. Your father was a very clever man, and all the men I've admired have been clever. But isn't it curious now, I've never cared much to touch their hair. How strange life is! If it gives one thing, it takes away another.'

As this passage shows, she has actually been affected, in the depths of herself, by something other than 'mind' in Lewis. The discussion that follows between her and her daughter offers a good example of a method that, as part of the complex process of establishing his values and significances, Lawrence can use with great delicacy. They discuss what may be called his central theme, and while doing so in a wholly dramatic way, bring to the point of explicitness the essential work of implicit definition that has been done by image, action and symbolic presentation. By the end of the exchange certain possibilities of misunderstanding have been eliminated.

'Why, mother!' said Lou impatiently. 'I think one gets so tired of your men with mind, as you call it. There are so many of that sort of clever men. And there are lots of men who aren't very clever, but are rather nice: and lots are stupid. It seems to me there's something else besides mind and cleverness, or niceness or cleanness. Perhaps it is the animal. Just think of St Mawr! I've thought so much about him. We call him an animal, but we never know what it means. He seems a far greater mystery to me than a clever man. He's a horse. Why can't one say in the same way, of a man: *He's a man?* There seems no mystery in being a man. But there's a terrible mystery in St Mawr.'

Mrs Witt watched her daughter quizzically.

'Louise,' she said, 'you won't tell me that the mere animal is all that counts in a man. I will never believe it. Man is wonderful because he is able to *think*.'

'But is he?' cried Lou, with sudden exasperation. 'Their thinking seems to me all so childish: like stringing the same beads over and over again. Ah, men! They and their thinking are all so *paltry*. How can you be impressed?'

Mrs Witt raised her eyebrows sardonically.

'Perhaps I'm not – any more,' she said with a grim smile.

As the conversation proceeds, Lou makes it plain that neither St Mawr nor Lewis represents all that she would wish to find in a man. She doesn't dispute that Lewis 'is a servant', and though she says he has 'far more real mind than … any of the clever men', 'he has a good intuitive mind, he knows things without thinking them', she is far from suggesting that the ideal man wouldn't be able to think. She repudiates any backing of 'blood' and 'instinct' against intelligence, and she repudiates any primitivistic leaning.

'Don't be silly, mother. That's much more your subconscious line, you admirer of Mind. – I don't consider the cave man is a real human animal at all. He's a brute, a degenerate.'

What she wants, in fact, is the real intelligence, the power of really thinking, that the clever men seem to her not to have ('Tameness, like alcohol,' says Lawrence, 'destroys its own creator')[1]:

'I don't know one single man who is a proud living animal. I know they've left off really thinking. But then men always do leave off really thinking, when the last bit of wild animal dies in them.'

1. See 'The Novel and the Feelings' in *Phoenix*.

'Because we have minds.'

'We have no minds once we are tame, mother. Men are all women, knitting and crocheting words together.'

'He stands where one can't get at him. And he burns with life. And where does his life come from, to him? That's the mystery. That great burning life in him, that never is dead. Most men have a deadness in them, that frightens me so because of my own deadness. Why can't men get their life straight, like St Mawr, and then think? Why can't they think quick, mother: quick as a woman: only farther than we do? Why isn't men's thinking quick like fire, mother? Why is it so slow, so dead, so deadly dull?'

The kind of intelligence, 'burning like a flame fed straight from underneath', that Lou postulates – the intelligence of a full thinking man who, more than merely intuitive, can sit the stallion as Lewis does – doesn't prove its possibility by being presented in any character: Lou, at the close, has little hope of meeting the man she would care to mate with. But it *is*, nevertheless, irresistibly present in *St Mawr* the dramatic poem; it is no mere abstract postulate. It is present as the marvellous creative intelligence of the author.

For this is a moment at which one has to point again to the truth that should be plain and unquestionable: creative genius in Lawrence manifests itself as supreme intelligence. What is it but intelligence that we have in that deep insight into human nature; that clairvoyant understanding of so wide a range of types and of social milieux; that generalizing power which never leaves the concrete – the power we have seen exemplified of exposing the movement of civilization in the malady of the individual psyche? It is the same intelligence as that which functions, unmistakably as *that*, one would have thought (but is Lawrence known as a great critic?) in *Phoenix*, the volume of literary criticism, and in *Studies in Classic American Literature*.

Formidably critical though it may be, it is the expression of triumphant creativity, and the associate of reverence and wonder. In the conversation with her mother quoted from above, Lou exclaims:

'Ah no, mother, I want the wonder back again, or I shall die. I don't want to be like you, just criticizing and annihilating these dreary people and enjoying it.'

Lawrence can make 'wonder', as an answer to the potent actuality of Mrs Witt, seem so much more than a vaguely recoiling romanticism because for him it is so much more. He can affirm with a power not given to poor Lou, who is not a genius, and there is nothing of the merely postulated about the positives that he affirms.

The power of the affirmation lies, not in any insistence or assertion or argument, but in the creative fact, his art; it is that which bears irrefutable witness. What his art *does* is beyond argument or doubt. It is not a question of metaphysics or theology – though no doubt there are questions presented for the metaphysician and the theologian. Great art, something created and *there*, is what Lawrence gives us. And there we undeniably *have* a world of wonder and reverence, where life wells up from mysterious springs. It is no merely imagined world; what creative imagination of the artist makes us contemplate bears an unanswerable testimony.

The witness, the affirmation, is there in the very presentment of this 'cardboard world', so desolating to Lou Carrington, of 'personality' and petty will and 'lots of fun', the world of mechanical repetition: the disgust, the exposure, and the rejection are utterly different from what one finds in Aldous Huxley: one can never be unaware of the affirmation, the positive, that gives them their force. The sardonic comedy of Mrs Witt, for instance, turns into something poignant. As the destructive negation, the spirit of rejection and disgust, she 'places' herself.

After the scene, the fiasco, with St Mawr in Rotten Row – provoked by Mrs Witt, he misbehaves (and it should be noted that it is only when he is unreasonably and insufferably thwarted that St Mawr ever 'makes a break') – they all go down to spend the summer on the Welsh border:

So down went Lou and Rico, Lewis, Poppy and St Mawr, to Shrewsbury, then out into the country. Mrs Witt's 'cottage' was a tall red-brick Georgian house looking straight on to the churchyard, and the dark, looming big Church.

'I never knew what a comfort it would be,' said Mrs Witt, 'to have gravestones under my drawing-room, and funerals for lunch.'

She really did take a strange pleasure in sitting in her panelled room, that was painted grey, and watching the Dean or one of the curates officiating at the graveside, among a group of black country mourners, with black-bordered handkerchiefs luxuriantly in use.

'Mother!' said Lou, 'I think it's gruesome!'

Mrs Witt's note is not so merely light as it sounds. The church-yard, with its funerals, becomes an insistent theme. It isn't, for Mrs Witt, an obsession with death as the terrifying and inescapable reality, but a fear that death will prove unreal. Reported in this way, the case may not seem to promise much in the way of convincing poignancy. But this is what we are actually given; the thing is *done*, in its inevitability an astonishing triumph of genius; and since the success – the convincing transmutation, in Mrs Witt, of hard-boiled ironic de-structiveness into agonized despair – is crucial to the success of the whole, a long quotation will be in place:

In the morning she found her mother sitting at a window watching a funeral. It was raining heavily, so that some of the mourners even wore mackintosh coats. The funeral was in the poorer corner of the churchyard, where another new grave was covered with wreaths of sodden, shrivelling flowers. The yellowish coffin stood on the wet earth, in the rain; the curate held his hat, in a sort of permanent salute, above his head, like a little umbrella, as he hastened on with the service. The people seemed too wet to weep more wet.

It was a long coffin.

'Mother, do you really *like* watching?' asked Lou irritably, as Mrs Witt sat in complete absorption.

'I do, Louise, I really enjoy it.'

'Enjoy, mother!' Lou was almost disgusted.

'I'll tell you why. I imagine I'm the one in the coffin – this is a girl of eighteen, who died of consumption – and those are my relatives, and I'm watching them put me away. And you know, Louise, I've come to the conclusion that hardly anybody in the world really lives, and so hardly anybody really dies. They may well say *Oh Death, where is thy sting-a-ling-a-ling?* Even Death can't sting those that have never really lived. I always used to want that – to die without death stinging me. And I'm sure the girl in the coffin is saying to herself: *Fancy Aunt Emma putting on a drab slicker, and wearing it while they bury me. Doesn't show much respect. But then my mother's family always were common!* I feel there should be a solemn burial of a roll of newspapers containing the account of the death and funeral, next week. It would be just as serious: the grave of all the world's remarks –'

'I don't want to think about it, mother. One ought to be able to laugh at it. I want to laugh at it.'

'Well, Louise, I think it's just as great a mistake to laugh at everything as to cry at everything. Laughter's not the one panacea, either. I should *really* like, before I do come to be buried in a box, to know where I am. That young girl in that coffin never was anywhere – any more than the newspaper remarks on her death and burial. And I begin to wonder if I've ever been anywhere. I seem to have been a daily sequence of newspaper remarks, myself. I'm sure I never really conceived you and gave you birth. It all happened in newspaper notices. It's a newspaper fact that you are my child, and that's about all there is to it.'

Lou smiled as she listened.

'I always knew you were philosophic, mother. But I never dreamed it would come to elegies in a country churchyard, written to your motherhood.'

'*Exactly*, Louise! Here I sit and sing the elegy to my own motherhood. I never had any motherhood, except in newspaper fact. I never was a wife, except in newspaper notices. I never was a young girl, except in newspaper remarks. Bury everything I ever said or that was said about me, and you've buried *me*. But since Kind Words Can Never Die, I can't be buried, and death has no sting-a-ling-a-ling for me! Now listen to me, Louise: I want death to be real to me – not as it was to that young girl. I *want* it to hurt me, Louise. If it hurts me enough, I shall know I was alive.'

These exchanges, intimately *tête-à-tête*, between Lou and her mother are marvellous in their range and suppleness, their harmonic richness, and the sureness of their inflexion, which, since the surface, belonging to the conversational everyday world, is always kept in touch with the depths, can blend in one utterance the hard-boiled sardonic with the poignant. It is astonishing what Lawrence can do, in dialogue, with complete convincingness; dialogue that starts from, and, when it likes, lapses back into, slangy colloquialism, yet, invoking the essential resources of poetic expression, can hazard the most intense emotional and imaginative heightening. One would have said that the kind of thing hadn't been done, and couldn't be done, outside Shakespearian dramatic poetry – which has the advantage of the formal, and explicitly poetic, verse mode.

The node of comedy – sardonic comedy – is always within call. It prevails, magnificently, in the scene that immediately precedes the *tête-à-tête* just quoted from; the scene presenting the consequences of the stallion's crowning misbehaviour. During a riding-party over the moors, St Mawr 'makes a break'; he rears, and is pulled over backwards by Rico, whom he lames. He also kicks another young man in the face, and spoils his beauty. Local society – County – represented by

Dean and Mrs Vyner, and the Manbys of Corrabach Hall, are determined now, quite resolutely, that this vicious and dangerous horse
shall be 'put away'.

Well, St Mawr *is* a dangerous horse: he had killed two men, 'accidentally', before Lou bought him for Rico. What we have to note is the
way in which he is made for us something more than, something
decidedly other than, a vicious horse. It's largely the way in which we
see him through Lou's eyes, so that he is invested for us with the significance he has for her. We are really made to feel – and it is an extraordinary creative triumph of the poet – that he represents deep impulsions of life that are thwarted in the modern world; to feel, on the
plane of the outward drama, that he has been mishandled and outraged
by his human master, so that his 'break' isn't mere viciousness, but a
compelled protest of life.

It has already been noted that when he 'makes a break' it is always
because, in some way peculiarly intolerable to vital instinct, he has been
thwarted. Phoenix, the half-Indian Mexican, testifies:

> 'I'm not afraid of no horses', said Phoenix.
> Lou went on quietly. At the gate, she asked him:
> 'Don't you like St Mawr, Phoenix?'
> 'I like him. He's a very good horse.'
> 'Even after what he's done to Sir Henry?'
> 'That don't make no difference to him being a good horse.'
> 'But suppose he'd done it to you?'
> 'I don't care. I say it my own fault.'
> 'Don't you think he is wicked?'
> 'I don't think so. He don't kick anybody. He don't bite anybody. He don't
> pitch, he don't buck, he don't do nothing.'
> 'He rears', said Lou.
> 'Well, what is rearing!' said the man, with a slow, contemptuous smile.
> 'A good deal, when a horse falls back on you.'
> 'That horse don't want to fall back on you, if you don't make him. If you
> know how to ride him. That horse want his own way sometime. If you don't
> let him, you got to fight him. Then look out!'

Lou has already discovered what it was that St Mawr was shying
away from, and refusing to pass, when Rico pulled him over: it was an

adder – a dead one, recently dead, but still an adder. On the discovery
ensues a 'vision of evil'; it possesses her as she rides on to the farm. It
brings to explicitness significances that the action, the symbolism, and
the poetic means in general of the tale have intimated. In doing so it
makes very plain how far from merely sexual the significance of the
stallion is – how much more, indeed, has to be said than that he stands
for forces of life that the modern world frustrates. Standing, we see,
for the deep springs of life – for the life-impulsion, he stands for the
sure intuition, the warning perception, of the vitally dangerous, the
wrong path; he stands for the warning intuition of evil and disaster. He
rightly balks at the adder; but his rider – assertively developed, in-
sulated head and 'speaking face' – blindly and brutally ignores the living
sentience beneath him (we remember Gerald and the Arab mare) and
tries to force St Mawr by sheer dominance of will against that which
his whole being recoils from. Compelled and violated, St Mawr himself plays his part in the manifestation of evil:

It was something horrifying, something you could not escape from. It had come
to her as in a vision, when she saw the pale gold belly of the stallion upturned,
the hoofs working wildly, the wicked curved hams of the horse, and then the
evil straining of that arched, fishlike neck, with the dilated eyes of the head.
Thrown backwards, and working its hoofs in the air. Reversed, and purely evil.
    She saw the same in people. They were thrown backwards, and writhing
with evil. And the rider, crushed, was still reining them down.

Lou's vision is of a flood of evil enveloping the world. Rico, 'being
an artist', and bent on kudos and 'fun', might seem to be too much a
figure of comedy to play the major part assigned to him in so portentous a vision. It is a mark of the wonderful success of the tale in its
larger intention that, irresistible as it is in its comedy, we are not
moved to anything like that criticism: the significance represented by
the visionary role inheres potently in the Rico we have been made to
realize. He is in the first place, we may say, Bloomsbury – the Bloomsbury Lawrence knew and had recoiled from. Lou

thought with horror of St Mawr, and of the look on his face. But she thought
with horror, a colder horror, of Rico's face as he snarled *Fool!* His fear, his
impotence as a master, a rider, his presumption. And she thought with horror
of those other people, so glib, so glibly evil!

We remember Lawrence's now famous outbursts against Bloomsbury and Cambridge – outbursts that Keynes, in his Memoir,[1] explains as the tribute of conscious provincial inferiority to a perceived and daunting superlativeness of 'civilization'. The following is again from Lou's vision, and those who have registered the ethos of the modish literary world will recognize something that is all-too-familiar:

Believe in nothing, care about nothing: but keep the surface easy, and have a good time. *Let us undermine one another. There is nothing to believe in, so let us undermine everything. But look out! No scenes, no spoiling the game. Stick to the rules of the game. Be sporting, and don't do anything that would cause a commotion.*

It was the Bloomsbury hey-day when Lawrence wrote this – that phase of the literary world which erected Logan Pearsall Smith and Desmond MacCarthy into eminences. It saw too in Lytton Strachey a congenial and representative distinguished spirit, of course; yet it was comparatively specious – more plausible in its speciousness than anything that has succeeded it. And as the reference to Keynes and Cambridge reminds us (there is Russell's name[2] to bring in too), it had its intimate connexions with centres of extra-literary power, influence, and intellectual prestige. To recall these things is to recall the conditions in which Lawrence saw Rico as the focus of his vision of evil; it is not to suggest that one *need* recall them in order to feel the inevitable rightness of that intuition of a Rico's significance. Apart from the vision, the sinister potentialities of his kind of nullity are powerfully evoked: 'triviality is the root of evil' – Lawrence's grasp of the truth that Myers points to is very much profounder and fuller than Myers's. And, seeing Rico as so essentially 'one of mankind's myriad conspirators', we can see him as Lou sees him, when her vision of evil possesses her, as a dominant actor in recent human history:

Try fascism. Fascism would keep the surface of life intact, and carry on the undermining business all the better. All the better sport. Never draw blood. Keep the haemorrhage internal, invisible.

1. A relevantly very revealing work which I discuss in 'Keynes, Lawrence, and Cambridge' in *The Common Pursuit*.

2. See the references to him in the *Letters*. And there were recently Russell's revealing broadcasted utterances about Lawrence – revealing not about Lawrence.

And as soon as fascism makes a break – which it is bound to, because all evil works up to a break – then turn it down. With gusto, turn it down.

Mankind, like a horse, ridden by a stranger, smooth-faced, evil rider. Evil himself, smooth-faced and pseudo-handsome, riding mankind past the dead snake, to the last break.

Mankind no longer its own master. Ridden by this pseudo-handsome ghoul of outward loyalty, inward treachery, in a game of betrayal, betrayal, betrayal, betrayal. The last of the gods of our era, Judas supreme!

People performing outward acts of loyalty, piety, self-sacrifice. But inwardly bent on undermining, betraying. Directing all their subtle evil will against any positive living thing. Masquerading as the ideal, in order to poison the real.

Creation destroys as it goes, throws down one tree for the rise of another. But ideal mankind would abolish death, multiply itself million upon million, rear up city upon city, save every parasite alive, until the accumulation of mere existence is swollen to a horror. But go on saving life, the ghastly salvation army of ideal mankind. At the same time secretly, viciously, potently undermine the natural creation, betray it with kiss after kiss, destroy it from the inside, till you have the swollen rottenness of our teeming existences. But keep the game going. Nobody's going to make another bad break, such as Germany and Russia made.

Lawrence wrote this (it will be agreed, I think, that there is point in the reminder) in the middle nineteen-twenties.

We feel St Mawr's 'break', I said, as not mere viciousness, but a compelled and necessary protest or rebellion of life. This effect, by which we are made to take our stand with the horse, is largely got by the way in which the insistence on his being destroyed (it turns into a plot to have him gelded) is brought home to us as both spiteful and mean – as a spiteful, mean, and deadly hatred of the really (as opposed to the mechanically and repetitively) living; or, what amounts to the same thing, a determination to eliminate every element of danger and wildness from life. And *this* effect is got by what might seem to fall within the ordinary conception of the novelist's art. It is got in a subtle and vivid rendering of personality, dramatically evoked in a lively comedy of battle between Mrs Witt and the Vyners – there is observation and insight of a kind (though of a quality rarely found) answering to the reviewer's expectation of a novelist.

It gives Mrs Witt sardonic satisfaction to frustrate the plotters, and save St Mawr from gelding by spiriting him away. Lewis rides him and she accompanies; alone with Lewis, and very much in character, she directs the long cross-country ride across England (where, she remarks, the air is never quite free from coal-smoke). It is during this journey that Mrs Witt makes a proposal of marriage to Lewis. The journey forms a kind of enchanted interlude; but the convincingness of the episode is not a matter of mere enchantment. We are made to realize at the setting-out that Mrs Witt has with her another travelling-companion, a terrible despair, the graveyard mood become extreme: the odd circumstances leave her, but for Lewis, alone with this, in the prolonged lull after her latest triumph of 'annihilating dreary people'. The interlude is one for inescapable meditation:

Almost she was tempted in her heart to cry: 'Conquer me, oh God, before I die!' – But then she had a terrible contempt for the God that was supposed to rule this universe. She felt she could make *Him* kiss her hand. Here she was a woman of fifty-one, past the change of life. And her great dread was to die an empty, barren death. Oh, if only Death might open dark wings of mystery and consolation. To die an easy, barren death. To pass out as she had passed in, without mystery or the rustling of darkness! That was her last, final, ashy dread.

'Old,' she said to herself. 'I am not *old*! I have lived many years, that is all. But I am as timeless as an hour-glass that turns morning and night, and spills the hours of sleep one way, the hours of consciousness the other way, without itself being affected. Nothing in all my life has ever truly affected me. – I believe Cleopatra only tried the asp, as she tried her pearls in wine, to see if it would really, really have any effect on her. Nothing had ever really had any effect on her, neither Caesar nor Antony nor any of them. Never once had she really been lost, lost to herself. Then try death, see if that trick would work. If she would lose herself to herself that way. – Ah, death!'

But Mrs Witt mistrusted death, too. She felt she might pass out as a bed of asters passes out in autumn, to mere nothingness. – And something in her longed to die, at least, *positively*.

Out of this distress she contemplates Lewis, who may have 'no mind', and be 'strictly a nonentity', but who yet ('what made him perhaps the only real entity to her') seems 'to inhabit another world from hers'. It emphasizes the irony of the situation that the groom, in a moment of confidential unselfconsciousness, breaks out into a long fantasia of folk-beliefs ('A man's mind has to be full of something, so I keep to what we used to think as lads'). It is immediately on this that the admirer of 'mind' and of 'clever men' makes her proposal – to be coldly rejected.

The novelist who can bring off this strange country interlude with complete success can then give us (Mrs Witt having arrived at her destination) the comedy of Lou's letters from Shropshire, which describes with a perfectly got feminine edge and vivacity the convalescent Rico's flirtations with Flora Manby, his devoted nurse.

The 'drama' in the ordinary sense is now virtually over. For if *St Mawr* deserves to be called a dramatic poem, it is not because it comes to what would ordinarily be called a dramatic close. The burden that represents its essential inspiration demands something quite other. And the actual close seems to me as clear a proof of genius as anything else about the work (the minor qualification I have to make about it I make in discussing *Mother and Daughter*).[1]

Taking a kind of indefinite leave of Rico, Lou decides to go back with her mother to America: Mrs Witt can't stand England, and Lou can't stand the bright young people. I have remarked already on the way in which the little drama of three main actors, a horse, and two grooms, is given an inclusive effect and a representative significance. We seem to have presented to us the case of modern civilization in general. The journey back to Texas and then up into the mountains illustrates some of the workings of this generalizing process.

They are at sea:

By mid-afternoon it was blue summer, on the blue, running waters of the Channel. And soon, the ship steering for Santander, there was the coast of France, the rocks twinkling like some magic world.

The magic world! And back of it, that post-war Paris, which Lou knew only too well, and which depressed her so thoroughly. Or that post-war Monte Carlo, the Riviera still more depressing even than Paris. No, no one must land, even on magic coasts. Else you found yourself in a railway station and a 'centre of civilization' in five minutes.

They arrive at Havana, and find 'the green leaf of American prosperity shedding itself recklessly, from every roaming sprig of tourist,

1. See p. 287 below.

over this city of sunshine and alcohol' (it is the Prohibition era). As for Texas:

It left Lou blank with wonder. And in the face of this strange cheerful living in the mirror – a rather cheap mirror at that – England began to seem real to her again.

Then she had to remember herself back in England. And no, oh God, England was not real either, except poisonously.

What was real? What under heaven was real?

Out of this they flee north to Santa Fé, and then into the mountain country, the scale and beauty of which are marvellously evoked. The wild, overwhelming, inhuman beauty has its place in the total significance. There's an obvious contrast with the squalor, meanness, and pettiness of human life. But that's not all; it's not so simple as that. There's no defeatism in Lawrence, and no resting in any opposition of loathsome man to beautiful nature. He is very unlike Mrs Witt in his radical attitudes: all his negatives and his critical valuations have their significance in relation to a positive – and that is not of the order of 'Back to Nature'. The total effect of *St Mawr* (as of any characteristic work of Lawrence's) is an affirmation – if that is not a misleading word; for it is the 'tale' we think of as affirming, not the 'artist'. ('Never trust the artist; trust the tale.') There is nothing willed about it.

It's partly a matter of the way in which the nullities and the negative in the drama – Rico and his friends on the one hand, and Mrs Witt on the other – are placed: the positive is powerfully present by implication. And it's there in the extraordinary vitality everywhere of Lawrence's art. The intensity is not an intensity of repulsion and rejection; it is patently and essentially creative, a marvellous and triumphant expression of the creative force of life, in its very nature an affirmation.

And take the concluding pages of *St Mawr*, superficially so inconsequent and tailing-off, essentially so germane, so *belonging* to the significance. The stallion himself and Lewis have been left behind in Texas, and we hear no more of them. Lou buys a ranch, high up in the mountains, in a miraculously beautiful place with a vast outlook over the desert below. The ranch has a history, which is given us in vivid epitome – a history of defeat. But 'defeat' is not the word on which the emphasis rests – the emphasis as conveyed by Lawrence's art. The series of pioneering efforts are evoked with poignant sympathy. You're not at all inclined to any smile of superiority when the little New England wife of the pioneer finally has the mountain water flowing through the bright taps in her kitchen in the log-built farmhouse. You feel it as a real triumph; the triumph of civilization is a triumph of the spirit, though upon exhausting effort and ultimate fatigue defeat ensues, and then decay. On this, Lou supervenes, to make a fresh start. And here is the comment:

> Every new stroke of civilization has cost the lives of countless brave men, who have fallen defeated by the 'dragon', in their effort to win the apples of the Hesperides, or the fleece of gold. Fallen in their efforts to overcome the old, half-sordid savagery of the lower stages of creation, and win to the next stage.
>
> For all savagery is half-sordid. And man is only himself when he is fighting on and on, to overcome the sordidness.
>
> And every civilization, when it loses its inward vision and its cleaner energy, falls into a new sort of sordidness, more vast and more stupendous than the old savage sort. An Augean stables of metallic filth.
>
> And all the time, man has to rouse himself afresh, to cleanse the new accumulation of refuse. To win from the crude wild nature the victory and the power to make another start, and to cleanse behind him the century-deep deposits of layer upon layer of refuse: even of tin cans.

Lawrence can allow himself this because the affirmation merely brings to explicitness what his art has affirmed pervasively and cumulatively. And, with his easy sureness of poise, he can allow the ironical Mrs Witt the closing note. It is a deflating comment on what may be called Lou's personal affirmation. In reply to her mother's interrogatory she has said that, here on the ranch, in the landscape, there is a 'spirit' that 'loves her and wants her' and 'saves her from cheapness'. – 'It's a mission, if you like.' That is, the life she proposes on the ranch, with its history and its symbolic value, in the 'wild America' is the antithesis of that represented by the Bloomsbury world she lived in with Rico. And we still feel that she truly apprehends, in this antithesis, something positive, a possibility of creative life, in spite of the closing sardonic comment.

7

T H E range of the tales, sure in touch and achievement as they are in all their various kinds – so convincingly right with so few exceptions, is immense. They constitute a body of creative work of such an order as would of itself put Lawrence among the great writers – not merely among the memorable, but among the great. Since this truth has certainly not had the recognition it calls for, I think there may be some point in following up the detailed examination I have given to chosen tales with a widely ranging glance over the varieties.

It is surprising how large a proportion of that first volume, published (to Lawrence's annoyance) as *The Prussian Officer*, is good. The title-story and *The Thorn in the Flesh* are in an early Lawrence vein that he soon outgrew; sultrily overcharged, sensuously and emotionally, they seem to associate with *The Trespassers*, and, with all their unpleasant kind of power, they share essentially the same kind of immaturity as the negligible and more obviously immature *A Fragment of Stained Glass*. But in that first volume too – the longest thing in it – is *The Daughters of the Vicar*. The volume contains nothing else of the order of that masterpiece, but a great deal that goes very fittingly with it. *A Sick Collier*, *The Christening*, and *Odour of Chrysanthemums* show Lawrence as the portrayer of the life he knew earliest, that of the miner's home. The presentment has the quality that I discussed in examining *The Daughters of the Vicar*: this is working-class life – to render it in its distinctiveness (as he so incomparably does) is certainly Lawrence's pre-occupation; but it is for him all the same just human life, and his attitude towards it differs in no way from his attitude towards human life anywhere, at any social level or in any conditions.

I have in discussing *The Daughters of the Vicar* described that attitude as one of essential reverence, wholly unsentimental and unidealizing. The point of that description is enforced if we consider *The White*

Stockings and think of Maupassant[1] – consider it, say, along with two tales from *England, My England,* the next collection: *Samson and Delilah* and *The Horse Dealer's Daughter.* The characters in *The White Stockings* are Elsie Whiston, a pretty, feather-brained incorrigible little work-girl flirt, her ordinary good-natured husband, and Sam Adams, his grossly bounderish employer, once hers too, who continues to send her presents which she accepts behind her husband's back because she can't resist them. It might seem that such matter was susceptible only of the lightest treatment, playing only for a lightly engaged response – the reader's interest to be one of superior, if not cynical, amusement. In Lawrence's actual treatment there is lightness right enough; but it is the lightness that registers a fulness of engagement in the writer. This for him is without qualification human life. It evokes, beyond any question, the free flow of his sympathetic consciousness; the lightness of the touch is the index, and is more remarkable than at first sight, perhaps, it is recognized to be. The success of the tale depends on our being made, as we are, to take the precisely right attitude towards the pretty, childish little coquette of a wife; one, that is, enabling us to sympathize with her husband's attitude towards her – to sympathize with it enough to see how a man we respect can be, and is, deeply attached to her. (And in our being made so positively to respect the steady, ordinary, good-natured Whiston we have a very significant power of Lawrence's art.) The play in Elsie Whiston of vanity, flirtatiousness, fear, defiance, and basic affection for her husband, on the one hand; and on the other, the uneasiness of the even-tempered, wisely tolerant Whiston, rising to the ultimate eruption of anger, the blow on the mouth, and the decisive assertion of authority – there is no condescension in our interest in the drama. Whiston strikes his wife a blow on the mouth, but it is not a brutal view of life that we are given, but a positively and essentially humanizing one.

1. I say Maupassant, prompted by *The Times Literary Supplement* critic to whom I refer in Chapter I. But in reading these tales of Lawrence it is still more to the point to think, by way of contrast, of Mauriac, Eliot, and Evelyn Waugh, who have reputations as religious and specifically Christian writers. Unlike them, Lawrence (as I have noted) has a reverence for life, sensitive human feeling, and what seems to me a religious (as distinct from humanitarian – an adjective that so plainly doesn't apply to the other three) sense of human dignity.

We cannot imagine George Eliot making such a subject of an Elsie Whiston, but she would have approved the spirit of Lawrence's art as exemplified here. Free from any sentimentalizing or idealizing bent, with its irresistible truth it gives dignity to human life. For the extraordinarily sensitive response of (in Lawrence's phrase) the sympathetic consciousness that effects this is not, as a great deal of Lawrence criticism has virtually contended, the less essentially human and humane for being so extraordinarily – so supra-normally – sensitive.

What, to take the next instance, can any summary of *Samson and Delilah* suggest of the nature of that little tale? A summary here can tell nothing at all – it can only suggest falsely. A Cornish pub, a buxom middle-aged landlady, a party of billeted soldiers, a stranger who at closing time says he is the landlady's husband and is going to stay, and whom, at the landlady's prompting, the soldiers, when he resists, tie up with her help and put outside, and who, a little later, comes in again through the unfastened door and is tacitly accepted as the husband, back after years of truancy – no elaboration can suggest what the tale actually is, and what interest it has for us. For its effect depends upon the working of vibrations, depths, and potencies – of psychic fields of force – that it takes a Lawrence to register. The actors have a deeper interest for Lawrence than, in such an affair, had we been the direct observers, they would have had for us, and the deeper interest is a richer human interest. This higher value, communicated to us, seems nevertheless to inhere implicitly and inevitably in the presented persons and facts, which, as we respond to them, we feel to belong to the ordinary life we know. The restored marital relations, part sensual attraction, part conflict and part something else, between the returned tin-miner and the landlady of the village pub – we don't ask, at the end of the tale, why we should have been interested in them in this full, wholly uncondescending way. Nor, on the other hand, do we at all feel that the writer's art has brought off a *tour de force*.

When we come to *The Horse Dealer's Daughter* it is not so difficult to suggest, in description, the kind of thing it offers. And yet, the classical perfection of the tale in its simple human centrality is bound up with its remoteness from anything in the nature of cliché. There, at the opening of the tale, is the girl, isolated among her brutally egoistic brothers:

'Well, Mabel, and what are you going to do with yourself?' asked Joe, with foolish flippancy. He felt quite safe himself. Without listening for an answer, he turned aside, worked a grain of tobacco to the tip of his tongue, and spat it out. He did not care about anything, since he felt safe himself.

The three brothers and the sister sat round the desolate breakfast table, attempting some sort of desultory consultation. The morning's post had given the final tap to the family fortunes, and all was over. The dreary dining-room itself, with its heavy mahogany furniture, looked as if it were waiting to be done away with.

But the consultation amounted to nothing. There was a strange air of in-effectuality about the three men, as they sprawled at table, smoking and reflecting vaguely on their own condition. The girl was alone, a rather short, sullen-looking young woman of twenty-seven. She did not share the same life as her brothers. She would have been good-looking, save for the impassive fixity of her face, 'bull-dog' as her brothers called it.

There was a confused trampling of horses' feet outside. The three men all sprawled round in their chairs to watch. Beyond the dark holly-bushes that separated the strip of lawn from the highroad, they could see a cavalcade of shire horses swinging out of their own yard, being taken for exercise. This was the last time. These were the last horses that would go through their hands. The young men watched with critical, callous look. They were all frightened at the collapse of their lives, and the sense of disaster in which they were involved left them no inner freedom.

If we reflect how far from the spirit of Maupassant is this evocation of male brutality, we note too that there is no pathos of feminine charm or feminine helplessness about the girl. She is sullen, impassive, and, one would judge, well able to take care of herself.

The men might be foul-mouthed, the women in the kitchen might have bad reputations, her brothers might have illegitimate children. But so long as there was money, the girl felt herself established, and brutally proud, reserved.

This absence of any obvious element of pathos conditions the in-tensity with which the fact of utter loneliness, the stark unendurable fact, is evoked. It *is* that fact, which with the extreme of economy, has been made present to us when the brief recall of family history has brought us here:

Now, for Mabel the end had come. Still she would not cast about her. She would follow her own way just the same. She would always hold the keys of her own situation.

It is remarkable how utterly without any touch of conventional pathos we are given her visit to the churchyard to tend her mother's grave. To the young doctor who by chance sees her there she 'seemed so intent and remote, it was like looking into another world'. The specific intentness and remoteness are conveyed with wonderful immediacy. The action in which they express their meaning, though it comes with a complete inevitability, comes still with its shock of surprise. The surprise is registered by the young doctor, when, again by chance, he sees her in the 'thick, ugly falling dusk', across the sodden wintry field, enter the pond and walk slowly and deliberately, deeper and deeper, into the motionless water.

The doctor has his further surprise, one that makes us reflect how radically unlike (the unlikeness being his greatness) not only Maupassant but Eliot, Wyndham Lewis, Pound, and Joyce this writer is. The surprise is a complex one, and the complexity is conveyed with a compelling inevitability of truth that, in such a matter, one must recognize to be beyond the power of any but a very great writer. The unerring rightness of touch is, on reflection, hardly credible. There is the young woman lying, with newly recovered consciousness, in the ugly house to which the doctor has carried her back:

Suddenly she sat up. Then she became aware of her own immediate condition. She felt the blankets about her, she knew her own limbs. For a moment it seemed as if her reason were going. She looked round, with wild eye, as if seeking something. He stood still with fear. She saw her clothing lying scattered.

'Who undressed me?' she asked, her eyes resting full and inevitable on his face.

'I did,' he replied, 'to bring you round.' For some moments she sat and gazed at him awfully, her lips parted.

'Do you love me then?' she asked.

He only stood and stared at her, fascinated. His soul seemed to melt.

She shuffled forward on her knees, and put her arms round his legs, she stood there, pressing her breasts against his knees and thighs, clutching him with strange, convulsive certainty, pressing his thighs against her, drawing him to her face, her throat, as she looked up at him with flaring humble eyes of trans-figuration, triumphant in first possession.

'You love me,' she murmured, in strange transport, yearning and triumphant and confident. 'You love me. I know you love me. I know.'

The horror of the young doctor – this, if it were all, would give us a situation that a number of writers might have imagined. But of course it is not all; *The Horse Dealer's Daughter* is a love-story – a story of the triumph of love and of life. For there is no irony (and, it must be added, no more sentimentality than irony): when the doctor finally answers 'Yes' we have no doubt at all about his complete sincerity:

'Yes.' The word cost him a painful effort. Not because it wasn't true. But because it was too newly true, the *saying* seemed to tear open again his newly-torn heart. And he hardly wanted it to be true, even now.

This part of the whole surprise, the surprise that he gives himself, has not been without its preparation. Few words as have been spent on telling us, we know a good deal about him. He is a 'mere hired assistant', worn and depressed by the endless round of drudgery in the ugly little industrial town. Not that we are to take any suggestion of his negatively collapsing into 'love'. After he had seen her at her mother's grave there remained, we are told,

distinct in his consciousness, like a vision, the memory of her face, lifted from the tombstone in the churchyard, and looking at him with slow, large, porten-tous eyes. It *was* portentous, her face. There was a heavy power in her eyes which laid hold of his whole being, as if he had drunk some powerful drug. He had been feeling weak and done before. Now the life came back into him, he felt delivered from his own fretted, daily self.

– His unwilling response to her challenge is something profound and positive; it was prefigured in the impression made on him when he saw her at her mother's grave. The 'portentous' eyes were intent on death, and death plays a major part in this story of the triumph of life (the young doctor himself has his narrow escape).

But the nature of the closing love-scene is plain enough. I am not suggesting that there is any need for detailed analysis, but merely in-sisting that it is what it is – which, when I think of the implications of '*quand ses personnages font l'amour*'[1] and of Lawrence's reputation in general, there seems some point in doing.

The Horse Dealer's Daughter is profoundly characteristic of Lawrence; it is at the centre of his treatment of the relations between men and women. For to speak of Lawrence as being preoccupied with 'sex' is a wholly misleading emphasis. Maupassant deals in sex; T. S. Eliot in *The Waste Land* is preoccupied with sex; but Lawrence, for whom sex is a matter neither for disgust nor for cynical knowingness, and who hates 'emancipation' (tough or sentimental) and reductive functionalism, is concerned always with the relations between individual human beings – the relations in all their delicate complexity. The actual variety of cases that he presents should surely be found very striking; he is an incomparable master of the field that has been supposed to be peculiarly the business of the novelist.

Against *The Horse Dealer's Daughter* may be set for contrast another tale in the same volume: *You Touched Me*. One might be inclined to suggest the nature of the contrast by saying that the latter would hardly be called a love-story. Yet the question arises, getting its force when we think of the clear relation between this tale and *The Fox*: if love is not the theme of *You Touched Me*, where does the boundary come between what *is* love and what is not? An attempted summary of the tale might suggest that Matilda Rockley was the victim of a callous league between the ruggedly perverse wilfulness of the Midlands 'character', her father, and the calculating materialism of Hadrian, his adopted charity-boy son. But the way in which the actual tale differs essentially from anything that we could associate with Arnold Bennett is pointed to, of course, in the title. The touch of Matilda's hand in the dark, she having forgotten that her father no longer occupies *this* room, is what starts his interest in her:

the soft straying tenderness of her hand on his face startled something out of his soul. He was a charity-boy, aloof and more or less at bay. The fragile exquisiteness of her caress startled him most, revealed unknown things to him.

In the morning she could feel the consciousness in his eyes, when she came downstairs. She tried to bear herself as if nothing at all had happened, and she succeeded. ...

1. See footnote to p. 23 above.

But she could not control him as she thought she could. He had a keen memory stinging his mind, a set of new sensations working in his consciousness.

We are made to feel at one and the same time the profound attraction (which is certainly not crudely and simply sexual) felt by him, and the incredibility to Matilda and her sister of any such thing in the small cocky charity-boy 'mannie'. It is the attraction that, felt by a man towards a woman, inspires him with the specific and deliberate conviction that he must marry her – that the fulfilment of his life depends upon his marrying her:

He looked at her curiously. She was not beautiful, her nose was too large, her chin was too small, her neck was too thin. But her skin was clear and fine, she had a high-bred sensitiveness. This queer, brave, high-bred quality she shared with her father. The charity boy could see it in her tapering fingers, which were white and ringed. The same glamour that he saw in the elderly man he now saw in the woman. And he wanted to possess himself of it, he wanted to make himself master of it. As he went about through the old pottery-yard, his secretive mind schemed and worked. To be master of that strange soft delicacy such as he had felt in her hand upon his face – this was what he set himself towards. He was secretly plotting.

When he proposes, Matilda and Emmie inevitably believe that what he wants is their father's money. Emmie puts it to him forcibly.

He turned his back on her to think. It had not occurred to him that they would think he was after the money. He *did* want the money – badly. He badly wanted to be an employer himself, not one of the employed. But he knew, in his subtle, calculating way, that it was not for money he wanted Matilda. He wanted both the money and Matilda. But he told himself the two desires were separate, not one. He could not do with Matilda *without* the money, but he did not want her *for* the money.

The surprise in the tale is the way in which Matilda does finally agree to marry him. It is true that the father, who is on his deathbed, tells her that if she doesn't, he will make a will leaving all his property to Hadrian:

'If you won't,' he said, 'you're a fool, and I'll make you pay for your foolishness, do you see?' Suddenly a cold fear gripped her. She could not believe her senses. She was terrified and bewildered. She stared at her father, believing him to be delirious or mad or drunk. What could she do?

'I tell you,' he said, 'I'll send for Whittle tomorrow if you don't. You shall neither of you have anything of mine.'

Whittle was the solicitor. She understood her father well enough. ...

But, bad as is the shock produced by her father's threat, and unpleasant as is her situation, we are not allowed to suppose her simply forced into acceptance by material fears for herself or Emmie (Emmie vehemently urges defiance – 'we can look after ourselves'). In however equivocal a way, there is something more subtle about the surrender:

'You put your hand on me, though,' he said. 'You shouldn't have done that, and then I should never have thought of it. You shouldn't have touched me.'

'If you were anything decent, you'd know that it was a mistake, and forget it,' she said.

'I know it was a mistake – but I shan't forget it. If you wake a man up, he can't go to sleep again because he is told to.'

*

'What do you persecute me for, if it isn't for the money? I'm old enough to be your mother. In a way I've been your mother.'

'Doesn't matter,' he said. 'You've been no mother to me. Let us marry and go out to Canada – you might as well – you've touched me.'

She was white and trembling. Suddenly she flushed with anger.

'It's so *indecent*,' she said.

'How?' he retorted. 'You touched me.'

But she walked away from him. She felt as if he had trapped her. He was angry and depressed. He felt again despised.

That same evening she went into her father's room.

'Yes,' she said suddenly. 'I'll marry him.'

It is made plain that, in some way of which we cannot suppose her able to give a full account, Hadrian's argument and attitude – not his mere persistence, but the spirit and meaning of it – have told. The situation of the sisters, imprisoned in old-maidhood by class – 'In a thorough industrial district, it is not easy for the girls who have expectations to find husbands'[1] – has affinities with that of the girls in *The*

1. The whole passage deserves quoting as an example of that 'sociological' observation in which Lawrence's work is so rich:

'Matilda and Emmie were already old maids. In a thorough industrial district, it is not easy for the girls who have expectations to find husbands. The ugly industrial town was

Daughters of the Vicar. In fact, Matilda and Emmie themselves, Matilda tall and graceful and 'naturally refined and sensible', with the shorter and plumper Emmie looking up to her, have their clear recall of Mary and Louisa Lindley. But if Matilda's marrying Hadrian is most decidedly not the triumph of life figured in Louisa's resolute adhesion to her collier, neither is it the equivalent of Mary's marrying, for 'safety', the little abortion. In the father's confident sense of things, Hadrian stands for life, and the marriage is the assurance of a living future; we know, without needing to be told in so many words, that essentially the dying man sees the dead-end of old-maidhood in the Pottery House as a defeat of life. And we have been given too strong a sense of the symbolic value of the 'square, ugly brick house girt in by the wall that enclosed the whole grounds of the pottery itself' to feel that old Rockley's interposition, his brutal assertion of will, is just the caprice of rugged masculine 'character':

The Pottery itself was now closed, the great doors of the yard permanently shut. No more the great crates with yellow straw showing through stood in stacks by the packing shed. No more the drays drawn by great horses rolled down the hill with a high load. No more the pottery-lasses in their clay-coloured overalls, their faces and hair splashed with grey fine mud, shrieked and larked with the men. All that was over.

'We like it so much better – oh, much better – quieter,' said Matilda Rockley.

'Oh yes,' assented Emmie Rockley, her sister.

'I'm sure you do,' agreed the visitor.

But whether the Rockley girls really liked it better, or whether they only imagined they did, is a question. Certainly their lives were much more grey and dreary now that the grey clay had ceased to spatter its mud and silt, its dust over the premises. They did not quite realize how they missed the shrieking, shouting lasses, whom they had known all their lives and disliked so much.

Matilda and Emmie were already old maids.

full of men, young men who were ready to marry. But they were all colliers or pottery-hands, mere workmen. The Rockley girls would have about ten thousand pounds each when their father died: ten thousand pounds' worth of profitable house-property. It was not to be sneezed at: they felt so themselves, and refrained from sneezing away such a fortune on any mere member of the proletariat. Consequently, bank-clerks or nonconformist clergymen or even school-teachers having failed to come forward, Matilda had begun to give up all ideas of ever leaving the Pottery House.'

We remember the different, but related, position of Alvina Houghton in *The Lost Girl.*

The delicate poise of the tone, especially in the close, where an essential complexity of tone has to be conveyed with extreme economy, is wonderfully sure; this is indeed a different art from Arnold Bennett's:

Emmie raved and wept, the secret flew abroad. But Matilda was silent and unmoved, Hadrian quiet and satisfied, and nipped with fear also. But he held out against his fear. Mr Rockley was very ill, but unchanged.

On the third day the marriage took place. Matilda and Hadrian drove straight home from the registrar, and went straight into the room of the dying man. His face lit up with a clear twinkling smile.

'Hadrian – you've got her,' he said, a little hoarsely.

'Yes,' said Hadrian, who was pale round the gills.

'Ay, my lad, I'm glad you're mine,' replied the dying man. Then he turned his eyes closely on Matilda.

'Let's look at you, Matilda,' he said. Then his voice went strange and unrecognizable. 'Kiss me,' he said.

She stooped and kissed him. She had never kissed him before, not since she was a tiny child. But she was quiet, very still.

'Kiss him,' the dying man said.

Obediently, Matilda put forward her mouth and kissed the young husband.

'That's right! That's right!' murmured the dying man.

If the concluding 'That's right! That's right!' is not, for the reader, the note of a happy ending, neither is it a pure irony. No simple judgement, no simple determination of the sympathies, is in place. Nor do we feel ourselves incited by the close to work out a sum of for or against by way of deciding whether Matilda chose on the whole rightly and her father did well, or whether the major truth is that she was cruelly compelled. What we do feel is the challenge to realize the full complexity presented, and the tale leaves us with a sharp sense of how much, to what rare effect, this is an art calculated to promote one's imaginative perception in the face of ordinary human life.

So, for that matter, does *The Fox*, which offers something different from that particular kind of complexity. It is a much longer tale, a good deal more than twice as long as *You Touched Me*, and goes in for other kinds of effect than those which depend on brevity of presentment and a wealth of undeveloped implication. Its strength lies – and it is one of the supreme things among the major tales – in the fulness, depth, and unambiguous clarity with which it presents its theme, the theme that bears so obvious a relation to that of *You Touched Me*.

Instead of the two sisters marooned in the Pottery House, we have two landgirls, March and Banford, committed, at nearly thirty, to making a life together on their isolated little farm. The nature of the miscalculation, the strain involved, and the impossibility (unrecognized by them) of success in any sense are fully conveyed to us before the supervention of the young man. Nothing goes right, and we see that nothing *can* go right: the misfortunes with heifers and fowls are only outward manifestations. In spite of March's protective devotion to Banford and Banford's affection for March, no vital flow goes into the joint enterprise; the farming cannot succeed, and no life they may make together can be really a life.

Both Banford and March disbelieved in living for work alone. They wanted to read or take a cycle-ride in the evening, or perhaps March wished to paint curvilinear swans on porcelain, or else make a marvellous fire-screen by processes of elaborate cabinet-work. For she was a creature of odd whims and unsatisfied tendencies. But from all these things she was prevented by the stupid fowls.

Though March is the man of the two, she is nevertheless wholly a woman; 'her eyes were big and wide and dark, when she looked up again, strange, startled, shy, and sardonic at once', and in the 'something odd and unexplained about her' we recognize 'unsatisfied tendencies' that no amount of time for hobbies or cycle-rides can satisfy. The most striking thing about the tale is the way the fox is used to focus her characteristic 'absent' state and reveal the significance of her oddities. She is actually out after the fox at sunset with her gun when it surprises her.

The fowls were round about – the ducks were still swimming on the pond under the pine-trees. March looked at it all, saw it all and did not see it. She heard Banford speaking to the fowls in the distance – and she did not hear. What was she thinking about? Heaven knows. Her consciousness was, as it were, held back.

She lowered her eyes, and suddenly saw the fox. His chin was pressed down, and his eyes were looking up. They met her eyes. And he knew her. She was spell-bound – she knew he knew her.

The idea of shooting doesn't occur to her till it is obviously too late. And when she follows, determined 'in her heart' to find him, it is not because she means to kill him. The significance of his possessing the 'blank half of her musing' for weeks and months afterwards defines itself when Henry makes his appearance. Banford, when he has explained his arrival and been admitted, is 'no more afraid of him than if he were her own younger brother', and gossips happily with him. But to March (who seized her gun when he made his entrance) he is the fox:

Whether it was the thrusting forward of his head, or the glisten of fine whitish hairs on the ruddy cheek-bones, or the bright keen eyes, that can never be said: but the boy was to her the fox, and she could not see him otherwise.

Lawrence's genius appears strikingly in the power with which her state is defined and communicated. There is something in it that is not exactly fear, but that makes her shrink back into the shadow and desire intensely to escape his notice. At the same time, as long as she remains unnoticed by him, his presence brings her a kind of spell-bound relaxation:

He was identified with the fox – and he was here in full presence. She need not go after him any more. ... She was only at peace while he forgot her, talking to Banford. Hidden in the shadow of the corner, she need not any more be divided in herself, trying to keep up two planes of consciousness. She could at last lapse into the odour of the fox.

The strain involved in her life with Banford on the farm is symbolized for her by the search after the fox. It is also, without her distinguishing, at the same time the strain of keeping her mind sufficiently on the everyday business of the farm against the continual pull exercised by the fox in her profound 'musing'. The fox, of course, merely provided a focus for her 'musing', and the significance of his doing so with such effect is not obscure. He is a male creature, of a fascinating strangeness and vitality; a marauder out of the unknown, a kind of incalculable enemy, to be guarded against (and we see how subtly vigilance becomes positive seeking). Towards Henry himself the significant ambiguity of her attitude is powerfully communicated: his presence brings her this relaxed peace, but, recognized as a man, he disturbs her; she is desperately shy of him, and he brings her peace only while she can think of him as the fox.

The whole fox-motive in all its development is remarkable for its inevitability of truth and the economy and precision of its art. There are March's dreams. That which she has on the night of Henry's arrival (he is fair, we note, with whitish glistening down on his ruddy cheeks) comes before he has made any advances:

> That night March dreamed vividly. She dreamed she heard a singing outside which she could not understand, a singing that roamed round the house, in the fields, and in the darkness. It moved her so that she felt she must weep. She went out, and suddenly she knew it was the fox singing. He was very yellow and bright, like corn. She went nearer to him, but he ran away and ceased singing. He seemed near, and she wanted to touch him. She stretched out her hand, but suddenly he bit her wrist, and at the same instant, as she drew back, the fox, turning round to bound away, whisked his brush across her face, and it seemed his brush was on fire, for it seared and burned her mouth with a great pain. She awoke with the pain of it, and lay trembling as if she were really seared.
>
> In the morning, however, she only remembered it as a distant memory.

The tension that underlies her peace when he has with mastering insistence proposed to her in the dark of the wood-shed is betrayed by her sudden ejaculation afterwards as, in the half-lit room, she suddenly sees him watching her intently 'from under the edge of the lamplight': '"There he is!" she cried involuntarily, as if terribly startled.' It is the fox she sees. The second dream, coming just after Henry has shot the fox, conveys with astonishing vividness and subtlety the emotional dilemma, the complication of her feelings, caused by her solicitude and fears for Banford, towards whom she has been the 'man'. The death of the fox has made a great impression, but in the dream the idea of death attaches, not to Henry, but to Banford; and, knowing 'that it wasn't right, that this was not what she should have', it is in a fox-skin that she wraps her friend's dead body:

> That night March had another dream. She dreamed that Banford was dead, and that she, March, was sobbing her heart out. Then she had to put Banford into her coffin. And the coffin was the rough wood-box in which the bits of chopped wood were kept in the kitchen, by the fire. This was the coffin, and there was no other, and March was in agony and dazed bewilderment, looking

for something to line the box with, something to make it soft with, something
to cover up the poor, dead darling. Because she couldn't lay her in there just
in her white, thin nightdress, in the horrible wood-box. So she hunted and
hunted, and picked up thing after thing, and threw it aside in the agony of
dream-frustration. And in her dream-despair all she could find that would do
was a fox-skin. She knew it was all she could find. And so she folded the brush
of the fox, and laid her darling Jill's head on this, and she brought round the
skin of the fox and laid it on top of the body, so that it seemed to make a whole
ruddy, fiery coverlet, and she cried and cried, and woke to find the tears streaming down her face.

It is such things that partly explain how the drama gets its emotional
depth and dignity. These are very remarkable, seeing how unpromising
the characters might seem to be. Banford, March, and Henry are all
lower-middle class and ordinary, with extremely limited powers of
expression. Their speech hasn't the advantages of the vernacular that
serves Lawrence so well in his working-class characters. That of the
girls is just suburban – flat and uneducated in an elementary-school
kind of way. It is perfectly got, and never transcended, for even March's
'witless humour' that so puzzles Henry is merely silly and pointless.
And yet there is nothing amused or ironical in the presentment of the
characters. They are human beings – just human beings and fully
human beings; and their emotional problems are seen as having a
dignity and interest not lower than the highest we feel to inhere in our
own. The tone of *The Fox* all the way through may be described as
simply and overtly serious; there is in the tale no sardonic element and
no irony. It illustrates Lawrence's range that not only *The Ladybird*,
with its exalted incantatory mode, but also one of his best things, *The
Captain's Doll*, the characters of which are upper-middle class and
aristocratic, and the tone of which has a flexibility corresponding to the
range and resource of their speech, should have appeared in the same
volume.

I have said that the use of the fox-motive helps to explain how the
drama comes to have its emotional depth and dignity. But it is surprising what sensitiveness and expressive power the dialogue itself
actually has. The apparently flat and incompetent idiom as Lawrence
uses it (with full dramatic convincingness) seems to be informed with

the speaker's own sense of the importance and poignancy of the drama.

Henry's part in this has yet to be considered. His relation to Hadrian of *You Touched Me* is plain. Henry, too, is ten years younger than the woman whom, with the same kind of conviction, he makes up his mind to marry (and he even, like Hadrian, has come back from Canada – and Banford, it may be added, regards him as socially inferior, or low). But in *The Fox* the conviction is more fully explored and presented, and what we have is much more fully and unequivocally a study of love. For that is what *The Fox* is, even if it doesn't answer to the ordinary notion of a love-story. It is a study of human mating; of the attraction between a man and a woman that expresses the profound needs of each and has its meaning in a permanent union.

The particular uneducated quality of the actors has its obvious point. Henry, who is very young, has been a farmer's boy, then on the land in Canada, and then in the army: he has no literary ideas about love that he can relate to his own life. In his shrewd, confident way he is both experienced (compared with March) and naïve. He doesn't think of falling in love, and when the idea of marrying March occurs to him, it doesn't present itself as a matter of 'love' at all:

> The dusk was falling as he came home, and with the dusk, a fine, late November rain. He saw the fire-light leaping in the windows of the sitting-room, a leaping light in the little cluster of the dark buildings. And he thought to himself it would be a good thing to have this place for his own. And then the thought entered him shrewdly: why not marry March? He stood still in the middle of the field for some moments, the dead rabbit hanging still in his hand, arrested by this thought.

But actually there is nothing mercenary about his attitude; his feeling for March is more unquestionably disinterested than Hadrian's for Matilda. The fact, soon established, that Banford's hostility leaves him no hope of 'having this place for his own' has no effect on him except that he now knows that, if he has his way, he will take March with him to Canada.

And already before that thought of marriage comes to him the peculiar personal attraction that draws him to March (but remains unassociated with any idea of 'love') has been evoked for us. His attention, secretly, has been continually on her:

Particularly he watched March. She was a strange character to him. Her figure, like a graceful young man's, piqued him. Her dark eyes made something rise in his soul, with a curious elated excitement, when he looked into them, an excitement he was afraid to let be seen, it was so keen and secret. And then her odd, shrewd speech made him laugh outright. He felt he must go further, he was inevitably impelled.

The form in which the idea of marriage comes to him reveals, not any mercenary bent. but the profound seriousness with which, implicitly, he thinks of March as a *mate*. The naïve natural wisdom that, for all his youth, he represents in comparison with the girls, has come out in his first evening's talk with them.

He was very curious about the girls, to find out exactly what they were doing. His questions were those of a farm youth, acute, practical, a little mocking. He was very much amused by their attitude to their losses: for they were amusing on the score of heifers and fowls.

'Oh well,' broke in March, 'we don't believe in living for nothing but work.'

'Don't you?' he answered. And again the quick young laugh came over his face. He kept his eyes steadily on the obscure woman in the corner.

The conversation, like all the dialogue, is marvellous in its delicacy of tone and its truth. Henry's politely amused attitude conveys his radical criticism of the whole enterprise. When he says, 'There wants a man about the place,' he is not, as Banford supposes, thinking merely of efficiency. And when he says, 'Yes, that's it; you aren't willing to put yourselves into it,' he knows that, in the nature of things, they *cannot* put themselves into it.

The way in which the idea of marrying March presents itself to him issues out of this conversation and gives us the positive correlative of his scepticism. It is an idea of *marriage* that presents itself; marriage as the whole fulfilling life of which, in his unanalytical and unintrospective manner, he has so strong a sense. But if there is this naïve wisdom of his youthfulness which contracts him so with March, there is also the touching inexperience of his reaction to her as a woman who attracts him. It is a study of youthful *love*, done, in its firsthandness, its unconventional truth, with an exquisite delicacy that is wholly Lawrence. Very characteristic is the account of his first seeing her in a dress instead of landgirl's uniform; an account which ends:

and strangely, suddenly, he felt a man, no longer a youth. He felt a man, with all a man's grave weight of responsibility. A curious quietness and gravity came over his soul.

The youth, while remaining a youth, is movingly and in a profound sense a man in the second proposal scene. His expression is naïve, but it achieves a perfect, a classical rightness.

'You'd easily find somebody else who'd suit you better,' she said.

'Yes, I might easily find another girl. I know I could. But not one I really wanted. I've never met one I really wanted, for good. You see, I'm thinking of all my life. If I marry, I want to feel it's for all my life. Other girls: well, they're just girls, nice enough to go for a walk with now and then. Nice enough for a bit of play. But when I think of all my life, then I should be very sorry to have to marry one of them, I should indeed.'

'You mean they wouldn't make you a good wife.'

'Yes, I mean that. But I don't mean they wouldn't do their duty by me. I mean – I don't know what I mean. Only when I think of my life, and of you, then the two things go together.'

That, I say, seems to me a classical statement of something for which it is not the less necessary to use the word 'love' because, though he 'held her hands in his', he 'did not make love to her', and 'did not want to make love'. His criticism of her life-committal with Banford has the same quality:

'Do you wish you were with Miss Banford? Do you wish you'd gone to bed with her?' he asked, as a challenge.

She waited a long time before she answered:

'No,' she said at last. 'I don't wish that.'

'And do you think you would spend all your life with her – when your hair goes white, and you are old?' he said.

'No,' she said, without much hesitation. 'I don't see Jill and me two old women together.'

'And don't you think, when I'm an old man and you're an old woman, we might be together still, as we are now?' he said.

'Well, not as we are now,' she replied. 'But I could imagine – no I can't, I can't imagine you an old man. Besides it's dreadful!'

'What, to be an old man?'

'Yes, of course.'

'Not when the time comes,' he said. 'But it hasn't come. Only it will. And when it does, I should like to think you'd be there as well.'

The wooing as a whole has that quality; it is so humanly central, so strongly delicate, so direct and untouched by convention in the imagining and so inevitably right. Now, thirty years after it was written, the reflection that today a Henry's *naïveté* – or humanity – could hardly so have escaped the culture of the films doesn't injure the inevitability; it only adds a poignancy.

All Henry's conviction and grasp of his purpose are needed to rescue March – for that is what it amounts to: she is incapable of decision. She assents under his compulsion when she is with him and relapses when she is with Banford, and yet, when she is with him, she wishes 'she had married him and it was all over': 'she wanted the boy to save her'. The drama of resolution on his side and irresolution on hers has the dignity given it by her loyalty to Banford; as her dream recognizes, the end that her deepest need demands must be a death for her friend. Henry cannot but *will* Banford's death. In the force with which we are made to realize this we have one of the many manifestations of the Laurentian genius in this tale. The accident by which he kills her *is* willed, and it comes as a wholly significant denouement. On the point of striking the final blow with the axe, he tells her that she had better stand further away, but tells her in such a tone that, the relations of hostility between them being what they are, she will certainly defy him: 'the tone of his voice seemed to her to imply that he was being falsely solicitous, and trying to make her move because it was his will to move her'. The tree spins round, and the end of the bough kills her.

The willed accident is the external event that completes the significance of the essential Laurentian drama – Henry *had* to will Banford's death; and March, who wept in her dream over the dead Banford – the dream that betrayed her own profound desire to marry Henry, can, now that Banford *is* dead, say to herself that it is better so:[1]

1. There has been a significant association in March's mind of the tree, which died in the summer, with Banford. March has long been trying to cut it down for firing. The identification is betrayed in March's dream, when the only coffin she can find for Banford is the box where firewood is kept.

She was glad Jill was dead. For she had realized that she could never make her happy. Jill would always be fretting herself thinner and thinner, weaker and weaker. Her pains grew worse instead of less. It would be so for ever. She was glad she was dead.

And if Jill had married a man it would have been just the same. The woman striving, striving to make the man happy, striving within her own limits for the well-being of her world. And always achieving failure.

It is a characteristic burden of Lawrence's, but it comes in the close of *The Fox* from March with perfect dramatic rightness. She herself is in the state in which the tale leaves her:

Poor March, she had set off wonderfully towards the blue goal. And the further and further she had gone, the more fearful had become the realization of emptiness. An agony, an insanity at last.

She was glad it was over. She was glad to sit on the shore and look westwards over the sea, and know the great strain had ended. She would never strain for love and happiness any more. And Jill was safely dead. Poor Jill, poor Jill. It must be sweet to be dead.

For her own part, death was not her destiny. She would have to leave her destiny to the boy. But then, the boy. He wanted more than that. He wanted her to give herself without defences, to sink and become submerged in him. ...

And she was so tired, so tired, like a child that wants to go to sleep, but which fights against sleep, as if sleep were death. She seemed to stretch her eyes wider in the obstinate effort and tension of keeping awake. She *would* keep awake.

The statement, of course, is Lawrence, but what it states, the strain from which March suffers, has been strongly enough evoked. It has been an essential part of Henry's attraction for her that he so firmly takes the 'responsibility'. And now there is 'nothing to do, and no direction in which to strain'. The difficulty of adjustment is what the tale ends on: 'she still felt she ought to *do* something, to strain herself in some direction'. But Henry insists that all the responsibility must be relinquished to him: 'she had to be passive, to acquiesce, and to be submerged under the surface of life'.

We may think of normative conclusions that preoccupy Lawrence elsewhere, but the psychological truth of *The Fox* is so compelling, and the close belongs so much to the concrete specificity of the situation presented, that the tale can hardly seem involved in any questionable generality of intention.

England, My England, the tale that gives its title to the volume preceding that which contains *The Fox*, has for theme a man who refuses responsibility. That is not the only respect in which it differs from *The Fox*: the social level is that of the cultivated middle class (the volume closes, it may be noted by way of illustrating Lawrence's range, with *Fanny and Annie*; it contains also, among other things, *You Touched Me*, *Samson and Delilah*, and *The Horse Dealer's Daughter*). Egbert *refuses* responsibility. He is not a nullity, and his dilettantism has nothing contemptible about it – it has for us something of the effect of a positive vocation, in his adherence to which he shows marked character. The glamour of the early married life of passionate love with Winifred at Crockham Cottage, 'buried deep among the commons and the marshes', is evoked with great power. The retired place, through which the 'spear of modern invention had not passed', is like a corner of the 'old England of hamlets and yeomen', and Egbert and Winifred are happily caught there:

> For Egbert had no intention of coming to grips with life. He had no ambition whatever. He came from a decent family, from a pleasant country home, from delightful surroundings. He should, of course, have had a profession. He should have studied law or entered business in some way. But no – that fatal three pounds a week would keep him from starving as long as he lived, and he did not want to give himself into bondage. It was not that he was idle. He was always doing something in his amateurish way. But he had no desire to give himself to the world, and still less had he any desire to fight his way in the world. No, no, the world wasn't worth it. He wanted to go his own way apart, like a casual pilgrim down the forsaken side-tracks. He loved his wife, his cottage and garden. He would make his life there, as a sort of epicurean hermit. He loved the past, the old music and dances and customs of old England. He would try and live in the spirit of these, not in the spirit of the world of business.

The theme of the tale is the impossibility of making a *life* with no more than this. The impossibility is manifested in Egbert's failure with Winifred. It is not merely that devotion to the 'old music and dances and customs of old England' at Crockham Cottage depends upon the 'world of business', and Winifred feels secure materially in raising a family because there is always her father to meet the expenses. That is not the most essential way in which she is dependent on her father:

she loved Egbert with passion. But behind her was the power of her father. It was the power of her father she referred to, whenever she needed to refer. It never occurred to her to refer to Egbert, if she were in difficulty or doubt.

Had Egbert been a real creative artist, the financial dependence on old Godfrey Marshall might have been another thing and needn't have mattered. But, with a characteristic touch, astringent but without animus, Lawrence puts him unambiguously where he belongs: 'In town Egbert had plenty of friends, of the same ineffectual sort as himself, tampering with the arts, literature, painting, sculpture, music.' Winifred couldn't have said this; but the essential truth she knows profoundly: there is nothing in or behind Egbert corresponding to the 'power' of her father.

What had been taken for granted, and had seemed not to matter, begins to show its consequences when the first child is born: 'it was never quite the same again between him and Winifred'. Winifred has 'what the modern mother so often has in the place of spontaneous love: a profound sense of duty towards her child', and, 'strangely' (but the insight is compelling), it goes deeper than love for her husband. Moreover, her child 'seems to link her up again in a circuit with her family'. Egbert finds himself shut out, 'Without anything happening, he was gradually, unconsciously excluded from the circle.'

The process that we see inexorably working is the consequence of the inadequacy in Egbert; but the tale is so painful because he commands so large a measure of our sympathy. Essentially a dilettante, he is nevertheless not weak, and it is a remarkable triumph of the tale to make him so decidedly not contemptible. Indeed, the quiet endurance with which he continues without deflection to be what he is, when his world has turned against him, has an effect of resistant strength of character and gives his dilettantism a kind of stoic dignity. In the matter of the scythe and Joyce's cut knee, which raises the painfulness of the tale to its highest pitch, he is put so terribly in the wrong, that he commands something of the sympathy that goes out to a victim. Between the suffering of the child, the maternal intensity of Winifred, and the effective managing solicitude of Winifred's father, he is in a position that affects us as hardly endurable. He is shut out with a new emphasis and finality, yet agonizingly involved.

But of the complete failure of his life we are left in no doubt (and we are left in no doubt of the essential moral). There is no issue, and nothing to be called a life, remaining for him. His death in action in the war of 1914 brings us to the 'sociological' intention of the tale – the intention intimated in the ironical title (from Henley:

> What have I done for you,
> England, my England?).

Egbert stands for the old cultured leisure days; or, if that is too inclusive a generalization, for that element in the old English culture which Forster, in *Howards End*, represents by the Schlegels. He stood, says Lawrence, 'for nothing'. He is irresponsible, ineffective, and, in his 'independent' way, parasitic, and there is obviously an intentional and apt symbolism in his relations with his father-in-law, the businessman. His death in the war in regard to which he has no sense of responsibility, and in which (in a very different way from his father-in-law – who is very different from Forster's Mr Wilcox, and incomparably more real) he doesn't believe, is not tragic, but, in its inevitability and depressing 'rightness', painful: with him dies what he stands for. The tale as a whole is perfect in touch, and adds its particular originality to the immensely varied demonstration of the author's genius.

The variety is strikingly manifested in the variety of tone, of which there are more shades among the tales than there are apt terms ready to hand for describing them. That of *England, My England* is grave, without any inflexion of irony. That of *The Princess*, or at any rate of the earlier part, has an astringent liveliness, a dryness, about it:

> Mrs Urquhart lived three years in the mist and glamour of her husband's presence. And then it broke her. It was like living with a fascinating spectre. About most things he was completely, even ghostly, oblivious. He was always charming, courteous, perfectly gracious in that hushed, musical voice of his. But absent. When all came to all, he just wasn't there. 'Not all there,' as the vulgar say.

The effect is to establish a certain distance – the remoteness in relation to the reader's sympathies that belongs to the theme itself at its introduction. It is of the essence of Colin Urquhart to defeat the engagement of the sympathies. 'He treated the Prescotts as if they were not of his world, not realities to him,' we are told: 'just casual phenomena, or gramophones and talking-machines that had to be answered.' What may lie behind his charm and glamour – 'His voice came direct out of the hushed Ossianic past' – neither his American relatives nor his wife can say (and she dies, having 'no great desire to live'). And when we are allowed to go behind the impression made by him on the world it is to hear him telling his 'little Princess' that people don't matter:

'But don't take any notice, my little Princess. Because it is all nothing. Inside everybody there is another creature, a demon which doesn't care at all. You peel away all the things they say and do and feel, as the cook peels away the outside of the onions. And in the middle of everybody there is a green demon which you can't peel away. And this green demon never changes, and it doesn't care at all about all the things that happen to the outside leaves of the person, all the chatter-chatter, all the husbands and wives and children, and troubles and fusses. You peel everything away from people, and there is a green, upright demon in every man and woman; and this demon is a man's real self, and a woman's real self. It doesn't really care about anybody, it belongs to the demons and primitive fairies, who never care. But even so, there are big demons and mean demons and splendid demonish fairies and vulgar ones. But there are no royal fairy women left. Only you, my little Princess. You are the last of the royal race of the old people; the last, my Princess. There are no others. You and I are the last. When I am dead there will be only you. And that is why you will never care for any of the people in the world very much. Because their demons are all dwindled and vulgar.'

We are reminded of *The Man Who Loved Islands*, that tale so notable for its success in a mode suggestive of the *märchen* (it begins: 'There was a man who loved islands') – or, rather, it resembles closely Hawthorne's kind of fable, which is psychological, moral, and philosophical. In this tale, instead of the glamour of the private world in which Colin Urquhart encloses himself with his little Princess ('we are the last of the royal race of the old people') we have the wonderfully evoked enchantment of isolation on the successive islands. The islander's withdrawal from human relations, his fastidious desire for self-sufficiency in a world that is wholly his own, pursues its logic through to the end he doesn't foresee – doesn't foresee (there is an effect of his both willing and not willing what he is inevitably moving towards) because of illusion about the nature of the individual life he is asserting. Even the first comparatively populated island (he has servants) brings him the apprehension of another order of challenge to his serenity than that represented by such human relations as remain to him:

But once isolate yourself on a little island in the sea of space, and the moment begins to heave and expand in great circles, the solid earth is gone, and your slippery, naked dark soul finds herself out in the timeless world. ...

Mysterious 'feelings' come upon the islander that he isn't used to:

To escape any more of this sort of awareness, our islander daily concentrated upon his material island. Why should it not be the Happy Isle at last? Why not the last small isle of the Hesperides, the perfect place, all filled with his own gracious, blossom-like spirit? A minute world of pure perfection made by man himself.

But the perversity of things and his servants and himself defeat him. He moves to a smaller island, with the minimum of staff to look after him. This time he finds himself involved with the daughter of the widow who does his housekeeping. In disgust, he moves again, to a mere rock far out in the Atlantic, this time alone.

The fable is perfectly done. The successive phases of island life have an astonishing enchanted actuality, and the significance of the islander's developing 'self-sufficiency' makes itself plain in the most natural way. On the second island the islander begins to find a kind of serenity coming upon him.

The islander said to himself: 'Is this happiness?' He said to himself 'I am turned into a dream. I feel nothing, or I don't know what I feel. Yet it seems to me I am happy.' Only he had to have something upon which his mental activity could work.

He goes on writing his book about the flowers mentioned in the Greek and Latin authors (for it is in the case that he too is a would-be artist, a conceited *poseur* incapable of real creative work), but he no longer cares whether it is published or not. On the third island all positive interests lapse. He loathes the thought of any human contact, and has a shock of horror when, for a moment, he mistakes the black heads of seals swimming in for the heads of men. He leaves unopened the last letters brought him before the storms of winter shut him off, and hides them away, hating to read his name on an envelope. He keeps no track of time, and no longer thinks of opening a book: 'The print, the printed letters, so like the depravity of speech, looked obscene.' He derives his 'single satisfaction from being alone, absolutely alone, with the space soaking into him'. The tale ends in a succession of heavy snow-storms, at the moment when the 'mutter of unsatisfied thunder' rolling over the sea announced yet another. Life is about to lapse out into a world of white emptiness.

Lawrence's insistence on the 'disquality' of the individual is in-separable from his clairvoyant preoccupation with the complementary truth: the truth that, without his relations with other lives, the indi-vidual is nothing. Thus, in *The Princess* Colin Urquhart proposes to 'peel away' all the things people 'say and do and feel' – 'all the chatter-chatter, and all the husbands and wives and children, and troubles and fusses', and leave the 'man's real self' and the 'woman's real self'. But he has his daughter, and his daughter has him (the tale might have been called *Father and Daughter* to pair with *Mother and Daughter*); they have their life together, keeping the world at a distance, and his queer-ness doesn't become positively madness till the two or three years be-fore his death.

We see them vividly, in their strange distinguished remoteness, as the world sees them: he big and handsome, 'like some old Celtic hero', with 'a wide-open blue eye that seemed sometimes to be looking at nothing'; she 'always strangely wise and always childish', still when grown-up 'almost tiny', her complexion 'pure apple-blossom' – she was something like a changeling, 'not quite human'. But of course it is not the point of the tale to let us forget that she *is* human. We take the full human force of the question asked her when, young and childish as she still looks, she is no longer very young:

'Don't you ever think what you will do when your father is no longer with you?'

She looked at her interlocutor with that cold, elfin detachment of hers:
'No, I never think of it.'

When her father does die, she being thirty-eight and looking ten years younger, it is 'as if everything had evaporated around her'; she is faced with nothingness.

She had lived in a sort of hot-house, in the aura of her father's madness.
Suddenly the hot-house had been removed from around her, and she was in the raw, vast, vulgar open air.

Her plight is presented with great subtlety, illustrating Lawrence's extraordinary command of the *nuance*. A creature so limited in sympathy (she is still the Princess, 'looking out sardonically on a princeless world'), there can be nothing approaching the sentimental in the sympathy she exacts from us. But, though she may not be fully human, we are made to realize fully that she is a human case. The irony with which she is presented – feeling, for the first time in her life, that she must *do* something ('since she could not evaporate into nothingness like alcohol from an unstoppered bottle'); 'looking at men with a shrewder eye: an eye to marriage' ('Not that she felt any sudden interest in men, or attraction towards them') – the irony is perfect, exemplifying that delicacy of rightness in this matter of tone which is so much a mark of Lawrence's genius, and evidences his profound humanity.

The development of the tale has the unpredictableness of life, yet it is perfectly imagined. Romero, the guide with whom, finally, she has her odd – her inevitably odd – affair, is the one man, we feel (once we have been faced with the actual situation), with whom she could have had such a contact. A Mexican, last of the dispossessed Spanish family, aloof and reserved, his black eyes betraying a spark of pride at the centre of their hopelessness, he is in the right way different from the mass of men. She perceives that he is a gentleman; that 'his "demon", as her father would have said, was a fine demon', and 'instantly her manner towards him changed'. As he attends on her trout-fishing, she feels him 'helping her across the distance'; she feels an 'insidious male *kindliness* she had never known before waiting upon her'. But pleasant as she finds the unspoken intimacy that grows up between them, she 'doesn't see' how it can lead to marriage. 'Almost she could more easily marry one of the nice boys from Harvard or Yale.'

The peculiar complications of her state are suggested with great power. They are expressed in the obstinate resolution to push on with the expedition into the mountains alone with Romero after Miss Cummins turns back. The characteristically vivid evocation of the mountains plays its part in the development of the theme. If we reflect critically we observe that the ironical note has dropped out of the tale: it dropped out when the Princess began to press for the expedition, and it doesn't come back. The experience of the climb comes to us as something very immediate and, involved in the immediacy, we have the reactions of the Princess to the disturbing strangeness and the beauty (the expedition *is*, of its nature, a testing departure from the normal day-to-day world of human convention, a kind of ordeal):

And again the chill entered the Princess's heart as she realized what a tangle of decay and despair lay in the virgin forests. ...

In the same silence, save for the clinking of the horses and the splashing as the trail crossed streams, they worked their way upwards in the tight, tangled shadow of the canyon. Sometimes, crossing streams, the Princess would face upwards, and then always her heart caught in her breast. For high up, away in heaven, the mountain-heights shone yellow, dappled with dark spruce firs, clear almost as speckled daffodils against the pale turquoise blue lying high and serene above the dark-blue shadow where the Princess was. And she would snatch at the blood-red leaves of the oak as her horse crossed a more open slope, not knowing what she felt.

Her normal state of 'not knowing what she feels' is heightened by the conditions and circumstances of the mountain excursion and brought to a crisis. Of course, in her willing with such determination that the adventure shall be arranged we see a significance unrecognized by herself. And the inner compulsion, the profound will that no conscious intention acknowledges, makes itself felt in the stubbornness with which she insists on carrying the adventure through, alone with Romero. Or if we are to talk of will in a being so incapable of resolving her inner contradictions, then what happens in the hut is willed by her against her will. The reaction follows, with its consequence in Romero's death.

In this violence of frustration we have the meaning that underlay, so to speak, the Princess's virginal remoteness: there is no issue for her from the defeat of life, the *impasse*, that her father's crazy egoism entailed. For what the last brief sentence of the story records is something approaching the order of her father's lapse from a hardly sane self-sufficiency into actual madness.

The only reason for mentioning *The Woman Who Rode Away* next is that in it too we have evoked with immense power the strangeness, beauty, and inhuman remoteness of the mountains. It is pure Lawrence, but it stands alone; there is nothing else like it among the tales. By a marvellous triumph of incantation – incantation that proceeds supremely in something that *The Plumed Serpent* fails in. It imagines the old pagan Mexican religion as something real and living; living enough for its devotees to entertain the confident hope of reconquering Mexico.

It is remarkable how the fascinated curiosity of the woman about the Indians seems to take on the significance given it by the Indians into whose hands she falls. The talk of a visitor starts the obsession:

And this peculiar vague enthusiasm for unknown Indians found a full echo in the woman's heart. She was overcome by a foolish romanticism more unreal than a girl's. She felt it was her destiny to wander into the secret haunts of these timeless, mysterious, marvellous Indians of the mountains.

The strength of the obsession has some explanation in the circumstances of the woman's life. A Californian blonde, who had thought that 'this marriage of all marriages would be an adventure', there she is, kept 'guarded among these mountains of Chihuahua', in the adobe house below the deserted silver-mine. The little 'sheikh', her husband, twenty years older than herself, is an energetic idealist who 'really hates the physical side of life', and loves 'work, work, work and making things'. It is a tiny, forlorn outpost of Western civilization, with all the essential inner emptiness and none of the excitements and distractions. We realize easily enough the desperation of the American woman of thirty-three:

Gradually her nerves began to go wrong: she must get out. She must get out.

Her husband takes her for three months across the border into the United States; but, the three months ended, she is back again, 'just the same, in her adobe house among those eternal green or pinky-brown hills, void as only the undiscovered is void'.

It is now that the romantic obsession takes hold of her – the belief that, if she could slip away and penetrate to the secret strongholds of Indian life that she has heard of, she would find something mysterious and wonderful. Her actual planned setting-out during one of her husband's absences is a neurotic escapade, an answer to the unending daily monotony. By the time she is afraid and thinks of turning back, it is too late. Her first intimation that this escapade is not going to be a romance is the unchivalrous behaviour of the wild Indians who take her in charge. A further great shock of the kind is finding that the Indian chiefs are immune to American feminine charm and despise what she represents. It is only slowly that we come to realize what effect her answers have on the Indians conducting her:

The black eyes watched her shrewdly. She, for all her weariness, smiled faintly in the pride of her own adventure and the assurance of her own womanhood, and the spell of the madness that was on her.

'And what do *you* want to do?' the Indian asked her.

'I want to visit the Chilchui Indians – to see their houses and to know their gods,' she replied.

The young man turned and translated quickly, and there was a silence almost of consternation. The grave elder men were glancing at her sideways, with strange looks from under their decorated hats.

Taken up and up, and over the final rock-face into the Indian village or town in the high valley beyond, lodged apart and closely guarded, she slowly recognizes the truth. It is almost as if she acquiesces in the fate that to the Indians she seems to have willed, or at any rate to have been unmistakably destined to:

Her kind of womanhood, intensely personal and individual, was to be obliterated, and the great primeval symbols were to tower once more over the fallen individual independence of woman. The sharpness and the quivering nervous consciousness of the highly-bred white woman was to be cast once more into the great stream of sex and impersonal passion. Strangely, as if clairvoyant, she saw the immense sacrifice prepared. ...

More and more her ordinary personal consciousness had left her, she had gone into that other state of passional cosmic consciousness, like one who is drugged. The Indians, with their heavily religious natures, had made her succumb to their vision.

Her succumbing seems to us an inevitable process, so strong is the spell worked by the tale. The rites, the ceremonies, the colours, all the strangeness of the Indian world, are evoked with irresistible actuality, and with them the quiet certitude of the Indians, and the hypnotic effect produced upon the woman. It is for her a vivid dream actuality; she knows what is going to happen to her, feels a kind of unrealizing agony of despair, but no impulse of resistance. The winter days shorten towards the shortest day, when the ceremonial procession of dancers escorts the litter up through the high frozen world to the cave in the rock-face. The tense barbaric tableau within the cave, all eyes fixed on the fang of ice hanging at the entrance (the last red beam of the sun will in a moment strike it and strike through), makes a perfect close.

The whole thing is an astonishing feat of imagination. If we do not, in reading it, think of it as a feat, that is because it all seems so real. And this reality derives from the intensity and profound seriousness of Lawrence's interest in human life. We haven't to ask here as, by general agreement, we have of *The Ancient Mariner*: what is the relation of this poetic world to the world of full waking judgement, and what is the nature of the significance. The poetic power of the tale is, in its creative way, an earnestness and profundity of response to the problems of modern civilization.

The point might be made by saying that *The Woman Who Rode Away* comes radically and essentially from the same kind of preoccupation with humanity as *Mother and Daughter*. However striking the contrast between them, they have their centre in the same place and draw their life from the same depth; it is not a matter of sardonic comedy, focussed sharply upon the real world, as against the wonder-indulging romantic dream. I go on to *Mother and Daughter* next, of course, because of the contrast, which illustrates once more the extraordinary range of Lawrence's art. And *Mother and Daughter is* sardonic comedy; but how much and how little that description says may be brought out by comparing the tale with *St Mawr*, to which it bears so interesting a relation.

It is a very close relation – closer than that between *You Touched Me*
and *The Fox*. Mrs Bodoin and Virginia *are* Mrs Witt and her daughter,
Lou Carrington. They are unmistakably the same persons, though Mrs
Bodoin (with more point) is Irish, a Fitzpatrick, instead of an American,
and Virginia (who, like Lou, has a very slight and piquant cast in one
of her brown eyes) earns her own living in the Civil Service as head of
a department. The great difference between the two tales is the absence
from *Mother and Daughter* of the stallion and what goes with him. It is
a great difference of course. It means that *Mother and Daughter* is without the range, and without the marvellous flexibility of tone, for which
St Mawr is so notable. The sardonic comedy is there in *St Mawr*, with
so much else.

But the point can be made at once that, if in *Mother and Daughter*
sardonic comedy hasn't those accompaniments, it is of a kind with
which they have been demonstrated to be wholly reconcilable. And
here we have one of the profits of comparing the two tales: it helps to
explain the difference between Lawrence's ironic note everywhere and
that of other writers who might seem to be practising the same kind of
thing. What is so remarkable about Lawrence's irony is that, astringent
as it may be, it never has a touch of animus; never a touch of that
egoistic superiority which makes the ostensibly comparable work of
other writers seem cheap – so often cheap and nasty. The difference,
one feels, is one of depth. What we notice is Lawrence's incomparable
sensitiveness of touch and tone, and this, the juxtaposition of *St Mawr*
with *Mother and Daughter* suggests, is the index of the profound humanity that is implicitly present in the surface lightness. It brings home to
us, this juxtaposition, how embracing and exquisitely sensitive is the
organization engaged in the sardonic comedy of the latter.

The distinction of *Mother and Daughter* is that it exhibits its particular
mode so perfectly: it keeps to its given limits and achieves perfection
with them. Its range, of course, is less than that of *St Mawr*, but not so
much less as may appear at first sight, and the advantage it gains is the
unquestionable, the immediately convincing, perfection. No doubt
arises like that which puts itself when one has finished *St Mawr*: would
Lou Carrington really have maintained for long her heroic self-dedica-
tion to loneliness and the 'wild spirit' of the region, 'keeping to herself'

on the 'little wild ranch, hung right against the savage Rockies, above the desert'? The question throws no doubt on what goes before in the tale; it merely leads to reflections about the difficulty of bringing to a convincing close a work so boldly symphonic that, within so limited a compass, hazards so daring a scope.

Virginia is not fascinated by any St Mawr; and she doesn't find herself reflecting on the nullity of men. Her Henry doesn't play anything like the major part that Rico plays in the other tale; he is merely a 'rather spoilt young man who is musical', and he backs out of the relation with Virginia, 'lets her down', simply because he 'can't stand her mother' and her mother 'can't stand him'. The tale, in fact, as the title announces, concentrates on the relation between mother and daughter. Mrs Bodoin's amazing energy is, in its sardonic way, destructive, and Virginia resists its power over her – 'a strange *female* power, nothing to do with parental authority' – less than Lou does that of Mrs Witt.

And she never realized the funny little grin that came over her own elvish face when her mother, even in a letter, spread her skirts and calmly sat on Henry. She never realized that in spirit she promptly and mischievously sat on him too: she could no more have helped it than the tide could have helped turning to the moon.

Neither Virginia nor her mother counts on losing Henry, but he 'saves his life', to Virginia's grief and her mother's exasperation. In spite of their mutual recoil, the women remain 'ceaselessly aware of one another', and finally, Virginia being now over thirty, set up their 'married life together, mother and daughter', in the Bloomsbury flat that Mrs Bodoin furnishes with her distinguished and very positive taste. It is now that the sardonic comedy of the tale reveals its quality of depth – the depth that goes with the dryness.

A dry irony certainly fits the presentation of the inevitable consequences of their attempt to live together. In one sense they get on too well with one another, as appears in their entertaining – their dinners and 'well-arranged evenings' ('They had, of course, mostly men'). Each rather dazzled young man who *begins* to fall in love with Virginia finds it after all impossible – he can't get on: 'All the flow was between mother and daughter.' He is in some way shut out and annihilated:

The spontaneity was killed in his bosom. While the two women sat, brilliant and rather wonderful, in magnetic connexion at opposite ends of the table, like two witches, a double Circe turning the men not into swine – the men would have liked that well enough – but into lumps.

But it is of the irony of the situation that the women should get on so well together only to defeat their essential purpose and that these perverse victories should increase the tension between them. Mrs Bodoin, with her annihilating contempt for men, desperately wants her daughter to get married, and it is plain that her wanting avails less than nothing, and that her very existence makes the impossibility. For all the dry and sardonic presentment, this last fact is conveyed with disturbing power. There is something rather terrible in the way in which forces of life ignored in Mrs Bodoin's calm self-sufficiency assert themselves in the 'married' relations between mother and daughter and make it impossible for them to live together. The impossibility presents itself to us as the most formidable of facts; a field of force seems to be generated between them in spite of themselves that leaves no relation possible except antagonism.

Virginia has no illusions of being calmly self-sufficient, and the moods in which, under a kind of hypnotic spell, she plays the 'young witch' to her mother's 'old witch' are destructive to herself. She knows that she cannot exist emotionally on the significance for her life represented by her work in the Civil Service department, any more than she can exist on her relation with her mother. She doesn't *say* things like those which Lou Carrington says to Mrs Witt, but the extremity of despair to which she is reduced affects us as an immediate fact. It is a fact that troubles even Mrs Bodoin's calm, but what, with all her energy, can she do? Virginia, coming home from work nervously exhausted, ignores and defeats all the social distractions arranged for her. The sense of a situation hopeless and insufferably charged, but without exit – of life at a terrible dead-end – is communicated with painful intensity.

It is now that Virginia brings home her Armenian patriarch, her 'Turkish Delight'. And in her marriage to him the peculiar sardonic comedy of the tale has its sharp focus. The confrontation of Mrs Bodoin ('Monsieur le Marquis') with Arnault, so inconceivable as a son-in-law, is certainly very funny: the remarkable thing is that such an effect should be part of a whole that is so little merely or mainly funny. We never forget the full human significance of the stress that has brought Virginia here: our sharp sense of that stress, and of the whole issueless plight, is what makes this outcome so credible.

Virginia of course did not know why she liked being with Arnault. Her cleverness was amazingly stupid when it came to life, to living.

We, however, know – as Arnault does ('he was the tribal father; father through all the ages'). The worn Virginia is a long way from the proud gesture with which Lou Carrington invites her mother's closing irony. Virginia, in her relaxed, luxurious surrender to the sense of destiny ('Oh, so nice, not to have to struggle'), gives a 'fleeting, half-poignant, half-vindictive thought to her mother'. Actually, the surrender is not without its revulsion, occasioned by a characteristic movement of sympathy with her mother that *is*, also, a kind of pride. Arnault, in his interview with Mrs Bodoin, has established that the beautifully furnished 'apartment' is to go with Virginia:

He looked at Virginia. She too was white and haggard now. And she flung away from him, as if in resentment. She resented the defeat of her mother. She was still capable of dismissing him for ever, and going back to her mother.

'Your mother is a wonderful lady,' he said, going to Virginia and taking her hand. 'But she has no husband to shelter her, she is unfortunate. I am sorry she will be alone. I should be happy if she would like to stay with us.'

The sly old fox knew what he was about.

'I'm afraid there's no hope of that,' said Virginia, with a return to her old irony.

She sat on the couch, and he caressed her softly and paternally, and the very incongruity of it, there in her mother's drawing-room, amused her. And because he saw that the things in the drawing-room were handsome and valuable, and now they were his, his blood flushed and he caressed the thin girl at his side with passion, because she represented these valuable surroundings, and brought them to his possession. And he said: 'And with me you will be very comfortable, very content, oh, I shall make you content, not like madame your mother. And you will get fatter and bloom like the rose. And shall we say next week, hein? Shall it be next week, next Wednesday that we marry? Wednesday is a good day. Shall it be then?'

'Very well!' said Virginia, caressed again into a luxurious sense of destiny, reposing on fate, having to make no effort, no more effort, all her life.

Mrs Bodoin moved into a hotel next day. ...

In *Mother and Daughter* it is the daughter who has the last word. Virginia having delivered her home-thrust, a non-disclaimer ('All the harem was left out of you, so perhaps it all had to be put back into me'), by way of retorting to her mother's 'You're just the harem type, after all':

> Mrs Bodoin flashed a look at her.
> 'You have *all my pity*!' she said.
> 'Thank you, dear. You have just a bit of mine.'

If, by way of illustrating Lawrence's range in distinctively ironic modes, we pass from *Mother and Daughter* to *Two Blue Birds*, the latter, perhaps, in comparison, seems slight. And it does, indeed, in addition to being one of the shorter tales, maintain perfectly the light tone of its irony. But to suppose that the lightness means any lack of seriousness or depth would be a mistake – it would be a mistake I think to suppose that *The Cocktail Party*, in which sin and sanctity figure with the gin, is more serious and goes deeper (the contrary seems to me true). I mention Eliot's play because *Two Blue Birds* deals, it may fairly be said, with what is very much the world, the civilization, the ethos of *The Cocktail Party*, with the same kind of failure in marriage. The handsome, perfectly groomed 'young' author of forty, whose charm serves him so well, lives, it is true, in what might have been a family house (which in fact serves to emphasize the non-existence of the very idea of family) but it is to the civilization of the luxury-flat that he really belongs. As for his wife:

> at the back of his mind, with a certain grim fidelity, he was aware of his wife, her strange yearning to be loyal and faithful, having her gallant affairs away in the sun, in the south. And she, as she drank her cocktail on the terrace over the sea, and turned her grey sardonic eyes on the heavy dark face of her admirer, whom she really liked quite a lot, she was actually preoccupied with the clear-cut features of her handsome young husband, thinking of how he would be asking his secretary to do something for him, asking in that good-natured, confident voice of a man who knows that the request will be only too gladly fulfilled.

The comedy of the wife's arrival to blight, to puncture, the blameless felicity of the husband, so wonderfully served and cared-for, and the little adoring secretary, is done with a perfect light precision of touch; the dialogue – wife, husband, and secretary – has a living delicacy of rightness. Of course, it *is* comedy; no more portentous note is struck than that represented by the two bluetits – the 'blue-birds of happiness' – whose pugnacious flutterings round the devoted secretary's feet distract the handsome author, dictating from the garden-hammock, at the moment when the ironically observing wife chooses to make her presence felt. But in the way in which the particular poise of comedy is maintained we have the precision of insight and judgement with which Lawrence has seen and diagnosed the given case and established the whole context. When the wife hears from beyond the hedge the 'steady, rather theatrical voice' dictating, it is an article about the Future of the Novel that the little secretary is taking down:

'What the modern novel lacks is architecture.' Good God! Architecture! He might just as well say: What the modern novel lacks is whalebone, or a tea-spoon, or a tooth stopped.

Yet the secretary took it down, took it down! No, this could not go on! It was more than flesh and blood could bear.

She went quietly along the hedge, somewhat wolf-like in her prowl, a broad, strong woman in an expensive mustard-coloured silk jersey and cream-coloured pleated skirt. Her legs were long and shapely, and her shoes were expensive.

With a curious wolf-like stealth she turned the hedge and looked across at the small, shaded lawn where the daisies grew impertinently. 'He' was reclining in a coloured hammock under the pink-flowering horse chestnut tree, dressed in white serge with a fine yellow-coloured linen shirt. His elegant hand dropped over the side of the hammock and beat a sort of vague rhythm to his words. At a little wicker table the little secretary, in a green knitted frock, bent her dark head over her notebook, and diligently made those awful shorthand marks. He was not difficult to take down, as he dictated slowly, and kept a sort of rhythm, beating time with his dangling hand.

'In every novel there must be one outstanding character with which we always sympathize – with *whom* we always sympathize – even though we recognize – even when we are most aware of the human frailties –'

Every man his own hero, thought the wife grimly, forgetting that every woman is intensely her own heroine.

It will be noted how truly dramatic this is (like the whole tale); the setting, including a colour-scheme, plays its part in the total effect, the positions of every person and object in the scene being realized with precision and given us. The economy of the quoted passage, again representative, is unsurpassable. We need to be told no more about the kind of author the husband is – or why the literary world has always instinctively hated Lawrence. He has more than once, with an irony the more final for being unmalicious, presented and placed the type: the successful modish writer who is wholly uncreative, and has essentially nothing to say, but who *has* his 'personality', his assurance of his place in the social-personal world that determines success in contemporary letters, and his uncreativeness, which enables him to be easily and acceptably in the mode.[1] The characteristic egoism of the type, registered in the wife's apt comment on her dictating husband, is beautifully defined in the whole situation: the wife is capable of criticizing him, and has a strong impulse to it (she has her own egoism) – they cannot conceivably live together. The repetition of the adjectives 'histrionic' and 'theatrical' to characterize him makes the point that he is dependent on a responsive audience. If he is to function, and live swimmingly in his role, he must have the assurance of being uncritically accepted; the adoring little secretary, who is beyond question an admiring inferior, represents what he needs.

Lawrence has diagnosed a whole social setting, a representative mode of modern life. And that is always so, in his tales as in his novels: in Lawrence modern civilization has a student and analyst of incomparable range as well as insight. The personal problems and situations he presents are the problems and situations of persons with specific social contexts, and his presentations of individual lives have such force and reality because they are at the same time, and inseparably, studies of the society to which the individuals belong.

We may go on, for instance (and gain by way of contrast), to *Sun*, another of the shorter tales, and one that also deals with a failure in marital relations. The failure is of a different kind from that of *Two Blue Birds*, and Lawrence deals with it in a different way: there is no

1. We have the same type in Rico (of *St Mawr*) who was 'being an artist'. See note on p. 310.

irony in the tale, and no comedy. It is one of Lawrence's most notable successes. And a point that can be made is that the ability to achieve *that* kind of success is implicit in the poised ironic comedy of *Two Blue Birds*.

But what I have in view now is the difference of case that called for the difference of treatment. The New York businessman whose neurotic wife is ordered Mediterranean sun-bathing is a conscientious husband, full of consideration for her:

He was thinking of her in the New York flat, pale, silent, oppressing him terribly, in his human relations, and her silent, awful hostility after the baby was born had frightened him deeply. Because he realized she couldn't help it. Women were like that. Their feelings took a reverse direction, even against their own selves, and it was awful – awful! Awful, awful to live in the house with a woman like that, whose feelings were reversed even against herself! He had felt himself ground down under the millstone of her helpless enmity. She had ground even herself down to the quick, and the child as well. No, anything rather than that.

We are given the effect he himself makes when he appears in the sunny Mediterranean place among the lemon-groves:

He was a man of forty, clean-shaven, grey-faced, very quiet, and really shy. ... The old woman of Magna Graecia saw him at a glance: he is good, she said to herself, but not a man, poor thing.

And then we have the effect on *him*, when, looking for his wife, he suddenly comes on her sun-bathing:

He was dazed with admiration, but also at a deadly loss. What should he do with himself? He was utterly out of the picture, in his dark grey suit and pale grey hat, and his grey monastic face of a shy businessman.

There is no touch of comedy about the scene, which affects us painfully, so acute is the embarrassment communicated. He tries hard to adjust himself, but no amount of goodwill can do that: his disability is too deepseated. The incongruity is poignant, for much more than embarrassment is involved:

He took his coat off and laid it carefully aside, then again took his son in his arms. The naked woman looked down at the naked infant in the arms of the man in his shirt-sleeves. The boy had pulled off the father's hat, and Juliet looked at the sleek, black-and-grey hair of her husband, not a hair out of place. And utterly, utterly indoors. She was silent for a long time, while the father talked to the child, who was fond of his Daddy.

'What are you going to do about it, Maurice?' she said, suddenly.

He looked at her swiftly, sideways.

'Er – about what, Julie?'

'Oh, everything! About this! I can't go back into East Forty-Seventh.'

'Er –' he hesitated, 'no, I suppose not – not just now, at least.'

'Never,' she said, and there was a silence.

The impossibility of her 'going back into East Forty-Seventh' is something we feel with great force, and can't (she and the child are glowing figures of health) think of in the least as neurotic. We share and wholly adopt her sense of it. For the point of *Sun* is not to recommend to us some mystical, pseudo-mystical, or even merely hygienic sun-worship. The tale presents a terrible criticism of an aspect of industrial megalopolitan civilization. It is done with great subtlety, perhaps the most remarkable manifestation of the Laurentian genius in it being the wholly successful delicacy of the peasant's role – the peasant who introduces the theme of desire. What the grey-faced New York businessman represents is the loss of the life of the body, and for a commentary on the truth conveyed by the tale we can once again invoke the passage on the body in *À Propos of Lady Chatterley's Lover*.

In *Things* it is from the 'Sodom and Gomorrah of industrial materialism' that the two New England idealists flee. But they are subjects for Lawrence's most astringent irony. The consummate little history is an ironical 'idealist's progress'. We follow Valerie and Erasmus from their virgin faith in a 'full and satisfying life to be lived in Europe' through the stages of their disillusionment, back, ultimately, to America – specifically to Cleveland, Ohio, where, at forty, Erasmus has at last to let himself be trapped in a university post:

But when he looked at the furnaces of Cleveland, vast and like the greatest of black forests, with red and white-hot cascades of gushing metal, and tiny gnomes of men, and terrific noises, gigantic, he said to Valerie:

'Say what you like, Valerie, this is the biggest thing the modern world has to show.'

The tale is high-spirited in its astringency, a wonderful ironic exhibition of the given kind of American idealism and the given kind of
American 'culture'. The ethos is established with swift precision in the
opening:

Ah! Freedom! To be free to live one's own life! To be twenty-five and
twenty-seven, a pair of true idealists with a mutual love of beauty, and an
inclination towards 'Indian thought' – meaning, alas, Mrs Besant – and an income a little under three thousand dollars a year! But what is money? All one
wishes to do is to live a full and beautiful life. In Europe, of course, right at the
fountain-head of tradition. It might possibly be done in America: in New
England, for example. But at the forfeiture of a certain amount of 'beauty'.
True beauty takes a long time to mature. The baroque is only half-beautiful,
half-matured. No, the real silver bloom, the real golden-sweet bouquet of
beauty had its roots in the Renaissance, not in any later or shallower period.

That the particular ethos is out of date doesn't make its bearing on
the present of American intellectual culture – and the present of
American cultural relations with Europe – the less significant. And the
tale has its salutary significance for admirers of *The Golden Bowl*:

And when they were in their up-to-date little house on the college lot of
Cleveland University, and that woe-begone débris of Europe, Bologna cup-
board, Venice book-shelves, Ravenna bishop's chair, Louis Quinze side-tables,
'Chartres' curtains, Siena bronze lamps, all were arrayed, and all looked perfectly out of keeping, and therefore very impressive; and when the idealists had
had a bunch of gaping people in and Erasmus had showed off in his best European manner, but still quite cordial and American; and Valerie had been most
lady-like, but for all that, 'we prefer America'; then Erasmus said, looking at
her with queer sharp eyes of a rat:

'Europe's the mayonnaise all right, but America supplies the good old
lobster – what?'

'Every time!' she said with satisfaction.

That is from the close, when the idealists have given in – have lost
their 'freedom'. But the whole tale is a commentary on that representative artistic 'culture', that ethos of 'beautiful things' which has its
odd quivocal document in *The Golden Bowl*.

At the same time, in examining the notions of 'freedom' and a 'full
and beautiful life', the tale communicates some profound and character-

istic Laurentian wisdom about human nature, and the conditions of human life, in general. The Melvilles, both of them, husband and wife, cherish their 'freedom' as Egbert of *England, My England* does, and, for all the differences between the New England idealists and the English dilettante, the relations with art are essentially the same:

They both painted, but not desperately. Art did not take them by the throat. They painted; that's all. They knew people – nice people, if possible, though one had to take them mixed. And they were happy.

The irony of their happiness is that it always leaves them with a sense of something lacking, so that after a bit they have to move on:

Yet it seems as if human beings must set their claws in *something*. To be 'free', to be 'living a full and beautiful life', you must, alas, be attached to something. A 'full and beautiful life' means a right attachment to *something* – at least, it is so for all idealists – or else a certain boredom supervenes; there is a certain waving of loose ends upon the air, like the waving, yearning tendrils of the vine, that spread and rotate, seeking something to clutch, something up which to climb towards the necessary sun. Finding nothing, the vine can only trail, half-fulfilled, upon the ground. Such is freedom! a clutching of the right pole. And human beings are all vines. But especially the idealist.

At first, Paris is enough. With fervent application they become almost Parisians:

Still, you know, you never talk French with your *soul*. It can't be done. And though it's very thrilling, talking French to clever Frenchmen – they seem so much cleverer than oneself – still, in the long run, it is not satisfying. The endless clever *materialism* of the French leaves you cold, in the end, gives a sense of barrenness and incompatibility with true New England depth. So our two idealists felt.

They move on to Italy:

It seemed much nearer to the New England conception of beauty; something pure and full of sympathy, without the materialism and the *cynicism* of the French. The two idealists seemed to breathe their own true air in Italy.

And in Italy, much more than in Paris, they felt they could thrill to the teachings of the Buddha. They entered the swelling stream of modern Buddhistic emotion, and they read the books, and they practised meditation, and they deliberately set themselves to eliminate from their own souls greed, pain, and sorrow. They did not realize – yet – that Buddha's very eagerness to free himself from pain and sorrow is itself a sort of greed. No, they dreamed of a perfect world, from which all greed, and nearly all pain, and a great deal of sorrow, were eliminated.

But 'Indian thought' lets them down; it doesn't 'emerge very triumphant from the long crisis' of the war:

They simply hadn't enough *sitzfleisch* to squat under a bho-tree and get to Nirvana by contemplating anything, least of all their own navel. If the whole world was not going to be saved, they, personally, were not very keen on being saved just by themselves. No, it would be so lonesome. They were New Englanders, so it must be all or nothing. Greed, pain, and sorrow must either be eliminated from *all the world*, or else, what was the good of eliminating them from oneself? No use at all! One was just a victim.

And even Italy lets them down. Europe as a whole lets them down:

Europe was lovely, but it was dead. Living in Europe, you were living on the past. And Europeans, with all their superficial charm, were not *really* charming. They were materialistic, they had no *real* soul. They just did not understand the inner urge of the spirit, because the inner urge was dead in them, they were all survivals. There, that was the truth about Europeans; they were survivals, with no more getting ahead in them.

The irony centres where the title suggests: in the 'things' they collect, the beautiful things with which they furnish their second floor of the old Palazzo on the Arno. To these 'things' the idealists remain faithful, even when the

halo died from around the furniture, and the things became things, lumps of matter that just stood there or hung there, *ad infinitum*, and said nothing; and Valerie and Erasmus almost hated them.

For the 'things' themselves turn out to be not permanently satisfying:

The glow of beauty, like every other glow, dies down unless it is fed. The idealists still dearly loved their things. But they had got them. And the sad fact is, things that glow vividly while you are getting them, go almost quite cold after a year or two. Unless, of course, people envy them very much, or the museums are pining for them. And the Melvilles' 'things', though very good, were not quite so good as that.

So the glow gradually went out of everything, out of Europe, out of Italy – 'the Italians are *dears*' – even out of that marvellous apartment on the Arno. 'Why, if I had this apartment, I'd never, never even want to go out of doors! It's too lovely and perfect.' That was something, of course – to hear that.

And yet Valerie and Erasmus went out of doors: they even went out to get away from its ancient, cold-floored, stone-heavy silence and dead dignity.

Yet to the 'things' they remain faithful. When they decide that they are 'through' with Europe, and, 'for the boy's sake', must, so reluctantly, get back to America, they ship the 'things' (like the Ververs):

They left Europe behind, but they took as much of it along with them as possible. Several van-loads, as a matter of fact. All those adorable and irreplaceable 'things'. And all arrived in New York, idealists, child, and the huge bulk of Europe they had lugged along.

The 'things' are put in store, while the idealists, by way of further unsatisfying experiences, bring themselves to accept the necessity of settling in America. One of the experiences is going West and 'living the simple life' in the mountains:

But doing their own chores became almost a nightmare. 'Things' are all very well to look at, but it's awful handling them, even when they're beautiful. To be the slave of hideous things, to keep a stove going, cook meals, wash dishes, carry water, and clean floors: pure horror of sordid anti-life.

The irony has an added force when we recall Rawdon Lilley in the flat in Covent Garden, a true picture, we know, of Lawrence, going with gay efficiency about the 'chores'. The idealists finally settle down in their 'up-to-date little house in the college lot'; Erasmus is at last trapped:

He was in the cage: but it was safe inside. And she, evidently, was her real self at last. She had got the goods. Yet round his nose was a queer, evil, scholastic look, of pure scepticism. But he liked lobster.

The last tale I shall discuss is one of the longest, *The Virgin and the Gipsy*. It is long enough to have been published first in a separate volume as a novel. And it will certainly bear that kind of emphasis, for it is one of Lawrence's finest things and is itself enough to establish the author's genius as major and as distinctively that of a novelist. The genius must be apparent to any reader in the ease and economy with which the rectory household is established; established in all its personal and physical actuality and its ethos. There it is for us, as it is for the two girls, returned from their finishing year at Lausanne. The rectory seems 'almost sordid, with the dank air of that middle-class, degenerated comfort which has ceased to be comfortable and has turned stuffy, unclean'. The family itself is life gone stagnant. As an ostensible social fact it is a decent, solid, self-respecting family, stronghold of soundness and moral stability, fronting the world with a natural and proper cohesion. What we see it to be in essential fact is a system of stagnation, maintained by fear of life, furtive self-love, and love of power.

There is nothing satiric about the exposure of the rector and of the pieties and loyalties of the rectory; one can read the tale without a thought of Samuel Butler (though the comparison would make a good elementary critical exercise – it would be a good way of exposing Butler's complacent cheapness). The intensity and depth of Lawrence's positive preoccupation determine the tone. His art is directed to making it possible to write such a passage as this, knowing that it will do its work:

Only dimly, after the row, Yvette began to realize the other sanctity of her sensitive, clean flesh and blood, which the Saywells with their so-called morality succeeded in defiling. They always wanted to defile it. They were the life unbelievers. Whereas, perhaps She-who-was-Cynthia had only been a moral unbeliever.

Yvette 'only dimly begins to realize' – we don't *tell* ourselves that we are not necessarily to think of her as having these actual phrases in her mind; the convention is immediately understood. And the phrases get their force not only from the dramatic situation that seems to give us the state of mind they point to, but from what, more generally, has gone before in the tale. The phrase, 'life unbeliever', for instance, resumes or focusses a complex work of definition that has been done by creative means. 'Life unbeliever' is for us above all the rector; what the rector is we know very well, and it is something that charges the descriptive phrase with a potent and very specific force of meaning.

In the negative, of course, the positive is invoked. And in the presentment of the rector his relations with the wife who has left him play a crucial part (we note that the tale is significantly inscribed to Frieda). As her daughters remember her, 'she had made a great glow, a flow of life, like a swift and dangerous sun in the home, forever coming and going'. But now

the glamour was gone. ... The danger of instability, the peculiarly *dangerous* sort of selfishness, like lions and tigers, was also gone. There was now a complete stability, in which one could perish safely.

However flagrant may have been Cynthia's wrong-doing (and we know that, in her 'glamorous' and 'dangerous' way she was selfish – her significance, the value she represents, is plain enough), the view we are given of the rector's connivance in the attitude established for him by his mother, the 'Mater', and of the way he lets her exploit it, defines his inferiority with highly specific effect: the self-love, the fear of life, the unbelief. For the essential duplicity of the attitude is gross (and unpleasantly convincing); and the kind of safety the rector gains by it goes with the end attained by the Mater; the perpetuation of her 'female power'. She has ensured that he will not marry again: he is nobly and tragically faithful to the pure white 'snow-flower that still blooms in his heart'; and the cunning old woman – the centre of the family loyalty – will continue to reign as she goes forward through her seventies, and on into her eighties.

For in the family there was a tradition of 'loyalty', loyalty to one another, and especially to the Mater. The Mater, of course, was the pivot of the family. The family was her extended ego. Naturally she covered it with her power. And her sons and daughters, being weak and disintegrated, naturally were loyal. Outside the family, what was there for them but danger and insult and ignominy? Had not the rector experienced it in his marriage? So now, caution! Caution and loyalty, fronting the world! Let there be as much hate and friction *inside* the family as you like. To the outer world, a stubborn face of unison.

Hate and friction there are. Above all there is poor Aunt Cissie, whose life 'had been sacrificed to the Mater, and Aunt Cissie knew it, and the Mater knew she knew it'. Aunt Cissie hates Yvette, because she is young and spoilt, and has some of the 'vague, careless blitheness of She-who-was-Cynthia':

The rector adored Yvette, and spoiled her with a doting fondness; as much as to say: am I not a soft-hearted, indulgent old boy! He liked to have this opinion of himself, and the Mater knew his weaknesses to a hair's breadth. She knew them, and she traded on them by turning them into decorations for him, for his character. He wanted, in his own eyes, to have a fascinating character, as women want to have fascinating dresses. And the Mater cunningly put beauty-spots over his defects and deficiencies. Her mother-love gave her the clue to his weaknesses, and she hid them for him with decorations. Whereas She-who-was-Cynthia –! But don't mention *her*, in this connexion. In her eyes, the rector was almost hump-backed and an idiot.

The self-love is there in the indulgence. And the rector's 'life un-belief' gets a sharper definition in the two affairs in which he turns on Yvette, and his rage and panic betray him into his venomous references to her mother, She-who-was-Cynthia. These affairs leave us knowing perfectly what is meant by saying that 'he was born cowed', that he is 'powerless against the basest insinuations of his own mind', and that he still 'curls up before She-who-was-Cynthia because of his slave's fear of her contempt, the contempt of the born-free nature for a base-born nature'. The 'base-born' quality of the man and the ethos of the family centred in the Mater are brought together in a sharp focus in his ad-monition to Yvette against the 'Eastwoods' (they aren't married yet – the woman hasn't got her divorce):

The rector backed into the curtains, as if the girl menaced him with something fearful.

'Don't say any more,' he snarled, abject. 'Don't say any more. You've said too much, to implicate you. I don't want to learn any more horrors.'

'But what horrors?' she persisted.

The very *naïveté* of her unscrupulous innocence repelled him, cowed him still further.

'Say no more!' he said in a low, hissing voice. 'But I will kill you before you go the way of your mother.'

She looked at him, as he stood there backed against the velvet curtains of his study, his face yellow, his eyes distraught like a rat's with fear and rage and hate, and a numb frozen loneliness came over her. For her too, the meaning had gone out of everything.

It was hard to break the frozen, sterile silence that ensued. At last, however, she looked at him. And in spite of herself, beyond her own knowledge, the contempt for him was in her young, clear, baffled eyes. It fell like a slave's collar over his neck, finally.

'Do you mean I mustn't know the Eastwoods?' she said.

'You can know them if you wish,' he sneered. 'But you must not expect to associate with your Granny, and your Aunt Cissie, and Lucille, if you do. I cannot have *them* contaminated. Your Granny was a faithful wife and a faithful mother, if ever one existed. She has already had one shock of shame and abomination to endure. She shall never be exposed to another.'

The effect on us is horrifying, because we feel so immediately the dazed, tender inexperience of Yvette. She doesn't know what he means, and is shaken by the suggestion of undefined horrors and depravities. But underneath she makes, all the same, her judgement on her father. Yet he *is* her father, her indulgent old boy of a father, gallant and handsome, and she is his affectionate daughter: the complexity – her inevitable dazed vagueness and confusion – is perfectly conveyed.

The tale is a tenderly reverent study of virginal young life. As such it seems to me unsurpassable, and it has certainly never been surpassed. The freshness, the inexperience, the painfully conscious ignorance, the confidence and the need to believe in life are touchingly evoked. We have, beautifully done, the wisdom of the sisters' discussion of love and marriage; a wisdom that they have to assume in order to persuade themselves that they are not, as they are, wholly without bearings. There is no sentimentalizing of their very ordinary case; they are not represented as, in any obvious sense, anything but indulgently treated by their elders:

Their parents let them do almost entirely as they liked. There wasn't really a fetter to break, nor a prison-bar to file through, nor a bolt to shatter. The keys of their lives were in their own hands. And there they dangled inert.

It is very much easier to shatter prison bars than to open undiscovered doors to life. As the younger generation finds out somewhat to its chagrin.

The most difficult achievement of the tale is yet to be mentioned. It is the most difficult to talk about. We have yet to consider Yvette's relation to the gipsy. The difficulty is not a matter of anything strange or abnormal about the relation. It is that the indispensable unambiguous precision is so hard to achieve: the terms to hand (a significant fact, bearing pregnantly on the essential difficulty of the achievement and its importance) are of so little use; the necessary definition required Lawrence's genius and the resources of his art. One can say that, for Yvette, the gipsy represents the antithesis of the rectory, with its base self-love, its fear of life, its stagnation, and its nullity. That, so far as it goes, is true:

Only she lay there and wished she were a gipsy. ... She hated the rectory, and everything it implied. The whole, stagnant, sewerage sort of life, where sewerage is never mentioned, but where it seems to smell from the centre to every two-legged inmate, from Granny to the servants, was foul. If gipsies had no bathrooms, at least they had no sewerage. There was fresh air. In the Rectory there was *never* fresh air. And in the souls of the people, the air was stale till it stank.

But the essential theme of the tale has nothing to do with Wraggle-taggle-gipsyism. It focusses in the look Yvette catches in the eyes of the gipsy, and the effect it has on her. The word one has to use is 'desire'. It is a necessary word, and Lawrence himself uses it, but it leaves, of course, a delicate work of definition to his art. The tale is concerned with defining and presenting desire as something pre-eminently real – 'real', here, having its force in relation to the nullity of life at the rectory. There is the direct explicitness of the conversation about love at the Eastwoods' cottage:

'Is there never any man that makes you feel quite, quite different?' said the Jewess, with another big-eyed look at Eastwood. He smoked, utterly unimplicated.

'I don't think there is,' said Yvette. 'Unless – yes! – unless it is that gipsy –'

'Which gipsy?' bawled the little Jewess. ...

'You're not in love with that *gipsy*!'   she said.

'Well!' said Yvette. 'I don't know. He is the only man that made me feel – different! He really is!'

'But how? How? Has he ever *said* anything to you?'

'No! No!'

'Then how? What has he done?'

'Oh, just looked at me!'

'How?'

'Well, you see, I don't know. But different! Yes, different! Different, quite different from the way any man ever looked at me.'

'But *how* did he look at you?' insisted the Jewess.

'Why – as if he really, but *really, desired* me,' said Yvette, her meditative face looking like the bud of a flower.

'What a vile fellow! What *right* had he to look at you like that?' cried the indignant Jewess.

'A cat may look at a king,' calmly interposed the Major, and now his face had the smiles of a cat's face. ...

'I wondered!' said Yvette. 'Because it *was* rather wonderful really. And it was something quite different in my life.'

'I think,' said the Major, taking his pipe from his mouth, 'that desire is the most wonderful thing in life. Anybody who can really feel it is a king, and I envy nobody else!' He put back his pipe.

The Jewess looked at him stupefied.

'But Charles!' she cried. 'Every common low man in Halifax feels nothing else!'

He again took his pipe from his mouth.

'That's merely appetite,' he said.

That, by itself (though it reminds us of Ursula and the bargeman in *The Rainbow*[1]), doesn't take us very far. There would be little point in trying to summarize the means by which *The Virgin and the Gipsy* takes us so much further; but seeing the difficulties put in the way by the civilization out of which Lawrence writes, there may be some point in emphasizing the remarkable nature of the success. And there is some point too, I think, in emphasizing the value of the achievement. It is an achievement about which one can feel more unreservedly happy than about *Lady Chatterley's Lover*. The point of the comparison is perhaps plain enough. The latter is notorious, of course, for its hygienic undertaking in relation to the obscene vocabulary and the corresponding physical facts; but its essential aim commits it, for success, to the achievement of *The Virgin and the Gipsy*; that of disengaging unambiguously the fact, and the crucial significance, of desire – of vindicating desire in the sense of compelling a clear and clean and reverent recognition. It may be that the offences against taste entailed in the hygienic enterprise can be justified on the plea of good achieved; but they remain – and must, I think, always remain –

1. See p. 143 above.

offences against taste. No such objection holds against *The Virgin and the Gipsy*.

The thing is done there with a perfection of sensitiveness and tact. While there is not the faintest touch of sentimentality, a tender, reverent sense of the virginal quality of Yvette determines the tone. At the close there is the cool recognition that the affair (if it can be called an 'affair') with the gipsy is no more than what it is – or, rather, has been (or *could* have been):

> And Yvette, lying in bed, moaned in her heart: 'Oh, I love him! I love him! I love him!' The grief over him kept her prostrate. Yet practically she was acquiescent in the fact of his disappearance. Her young soul knew the wisdom of it.

It completes, this passage, the subtle touch of definition given in the conversation earlier between Yvette and Lucille:

> 'That's just it!' said Yvette. 'Perhaps neither of us has. Perhaps we really haven't *got* any sex, to connect us with men.'
>
> 'How horrible it sounds: *connect us with men*!' cried Lucille, with revulsion. 'Wouldn't you hate to be connected with men in that way? Oh I think it's an awful pity there has to *be* sex! It would be so much better if we could still be men and women, without that sort of thing.'
>
> Yvette pondered. Far in the background was the image of the gipsy as he had looked round at her, when she had said: 'The weather is so treacherous.' She felt rather like Peter when the cock crew, as she denied him. Or rather, she didn't deny the gipsy; she didn't care about his part in the show, anyhow. It was some hidden part of herself which she denied: that part which mysteriously and unconfessedly responded to him. And it was a strange, lustrous black cock which crew in mockery of her.

The climax and resolution brought by the bursting of the dam seem to have the arbitrariness of life; but they come, nevertheless, as right and unquestionable in the tale. The physical catastrophe – the terrifying assault of the water, the collapse of the house, the cold and the horror – is done with a power that registers, we can see, the impact on Lawrence's imagination of some actual event he knew of. The symbolic effect, suggesting the contained force of life that implicitly menaces (there was once Cynthia) the stagnation of the rectory and the catastrophic event needed to break it up and sweep it away, needs no exposition. There is the further symbolism of the gipsy, who not only saves her from the flood-water, but warms her into life when she would otherwise have perished of cold. The significance of his role is set off by the comedy of the policeman, no pariah but an accredited agent of society, who is terrified at being alone with Yvette in her bedroom – he an unmarried man.

There are well over eleven hundred large pages in the one-volume collection of the tales. Of this great body of work all but a very small fraction is transcendently good – the successful work of a rare original genius. Of the nearly fifty tales there are only five or six that one would mark as certainly to be excluded from a volume that should represent Lawrence's strength; to the two or three against which I have already urged critical grounds there are to be added a couple of minor things: *The Rocking Horse Winner*, which it is exasperating to find so widely regarded (especially in America, it would seem) as representative of the Laurentian short story, and *The Last Laugh*. The thousand large pages of strong work not only contain their immense range of life and variety of art; the range and the variety give us a profound unity of creative purpose. Taken together, the tales represent one of the major creative achievements of literature.[1]

How, one asks, can they have failed to become, by now, known as such? How can recognition have been so almost wholly denied them? – a question that puts itself with the sharper irony, when one considers how the tiny talent of Katherine Mansfield was acclaimed: how promptly, and to what an inflationary tune. They present none of the difficulties of *The Rainbow* and *Women in Love*; and it should, one would have thought, have been immediately plain to any educated reader that they are the wonderfully sure work of a great original genius. Unspoken preconceptions and expectations, of course, hinder the recognition of all really new art: the firsthandness of Lawrence's insight into human experience, even when the insight, as conveyed, might seem to be irresistible, meets with blankness for a response, and the case of the tales enforces still more strikingly the truth exemplified

1. 'Only comparatively few of his short stories are of the highest standard. ...' (*British Council Guide*).

in the reception of the novels.[1] There are, however, absurd as they should seem to any educated reader, undoubtedly special preconceptions and expectations in the way of the tales. We had them in the critical formula used by a well-known 'intellectual', broadcasting in a 'Critics' conversation-piece: we heard that certain things hadn't that 'twist at the end' which the short story ought to have. There is an 'art of the short story', and it is represented in what one has to call educated taste – or in taste at the level of the Third Programme – by Maupassant, Kipling, O. Henry, and Maugham.

It will be plain, I hope, that I do not end on the suggestion that the failure to recognize the nature and quality of Lawrence's tales may be, perhaps, a little excused as in some sense a decent aberration, critically respectable. What chance, we must rather ask, can there be of the recognition of Lawrence, or any genuine new talent, in an age that can take Maugham's kind of success (that of a magazine-writer with a formula) as entitling him to the critical homage of the *élite* that controls fashion – the homage due to the creative and significant?

Lawrence's art, then, has no relations with the journalistic short story. As a writer of tales he belongs with Hawthorne, Henry James, and T. F. Powys (who has never had the recognition he deserves – but neither has Hawthorne, and even James's achievement has been neglected or misrepresented). I do not, of course, offer these four writers, the great masters of the shorter forms of significant prose fiction, as representing some common alternative conception of the 'short story' or the 'tale': their work exhibits an immense variety in kind and mode. What associates them, and distinguishes them from the journalist practitioners, is their being major creative powers, developing in their art serious and intensely first-hand approaches to life, and their having all used shorter forms, with classical success, to explore and define a profound interest in human experience.

1. And of Henry James's; the Author of Beltraffio tells his disciple: 'If you're going into this kind of thing there's a fact you should know beforehand; it may save you some disappointment. There's a hatred of art, there's a hatred of literature – I mean of the genuine kinds. Oh the shams – *those* they'll swallow by the bucket!'

BEING AN ARTIST

LAWRENCE'S attitude towards the Ricos, the Cameron Gees, and the Sir Clifford Chatterleys is that of every real creative artist. That it so often gets expression in his work is to be explained by the way in which, in the nineteen-twenties, the present state of affairs was coming on: the triumph in the literary world of those social-personal values which, human nature being what it is, must always play a great part there – or (we may put it) the growing emancipation of the literary world from critical standards as the educated public disintegrated. (The very beginning of this process is noted and analysed by Gissing in *New Grub Street*.) Both Lawrence's attitude and the attitude towards Lawrence are illuminated by an episode in *Anna Karenina* (it ought to be a *locus classicus* – though completely a part of the organized whole, it can be read as a short story). Tolstoy, of course, as Henry James did, uses the painter to represent the artist in general, painting being easier to handle briefly than the more complicated set-up of literature. Dickens did the same in *Little Dorrit* with the very relevant case of Henry Gowan.

Gowan and Vronsky are both men of family who have taken to 'being an artist' *faute de mieux*. Vronsky feels that he must, as a gentleman and an educated man and a connoisseur of art, be as good an artist if he chooses as anyone. Gowan represents a more sophisticated variant of this position – being, he also, a gentleman and a dilettante, and finding he cannot pass as having genius, and with the instinctive animus of his type against the truly creative, he insinuates that because his own work doesn't amount to anything serious then neither does anyone else's, and that all artists are merely humbugs like himself, and greater charlatans than he for refusing to admit the fact. Dickens's indignant sense that the Gowans of the literary world undermined his status and took the meaning out of his achievement produced this strikingly original addition to the panorama of social falseness that is

Little Dorrit. The intention, the judgement, that lies behind the creation of Henry Gowan is to be seen in the disapproval with which Dickens regarded Thackeray; it is given in the sentence he felt bound to insert even in the obituary appreciation of Thackeray he wrote for the *Cornhill*:

I felt that he too much feigned a want of earnestness, and that he made a pretence of undervaluing his art, which was not good for the art that he held in trust.

Vronsky, in Italy with Anna, having thrown up his career for her sake and so lost his function in life, takes to painting by way of escaping from his 'freedom':

As in his youth he had shown aptitude for art and not knowing how to spend his money had begun to collect engravings, he now settled down to painting and began to work at it, putting into it the surplus stock of desire which demanded satisfaction.

He had a talent for understanding art and for imitating it with accuracy and good taste, and he imagined that he possessed the real power an artist needs. After wavering for some time between various kinds of art – religious, historical, genre, or realistic – he began to paint. He understood all the different kinds and was able to draw inspiration from all, but he could not imagine that it is possible to be quite ignorant of the different kinds of art and to be inspired directly by what is in one's soul, regardless of whether what one paints belongs to any particular school. As he did not know this, and was not inspired directly by life but indirectly by life already embodied in art, he found inspiration very readily and easily, and equally readily and easily produced paintings very similar to the school of art he wished to imitate.

Established in the old palazzo in the little Italian town, Vronsky is 'being an artist':

The role Vronsky had chosen, with their removal to the palazzo, was quite successful ... and he even began to wear his hat and throw his cloak across his shoulder in a medieval manner which was very becoming to him.

Vronsky is encouraged in his conviction of his talent by Golenishchev, an old school-friend and now a critic, who 'never misses an opportunity to instil into Mikhaylov a true understanding of art'. Mikhaylov is the poor, 'uneducated', but recognized artist whom Vronsky commissions to paint Anna's portrait by way of patronizing him – the attitude he instinctively adopts towards the lower-class professional who does not even wear the right clothes.

After the fifth sitting the portrait struck everyone not only by its likeness but by its beauty. It was strange that Mikhaylov had been able to discover that special beauty. 'One needed to know and love her as I love her, to find just that sweetest spiritual expression of hers,' thought Vronsky, though he himself had only learnt to know that 'sweetest spiritual expression' through the portrait. But the expression was so true that it seemed both to him and to others that they had always known it.

'How long have I been struggling without accomplishing anything,' he said, referring to the portrait he was painting; 'and he just looked, and – painted this! That is where technique comes in.'

'That will come in good time,' said Golenishchev, consolingly. In his opinion Vronsky had talent, and especially the education that gives a lofty outlook on art. Golenishchev's conviction that Vronsky possessed talent was supported by the fact that he required Vronsky's sympathy and praise for his articles and ideas, and felt that praise and encouragement should be mutual.

The relation between the real artist, the uncreative 'social' pseudo-artist, and the critic whose vocation it is to back the latter against the former, is beautifully epitomized here. All the originality is the real artist's; but its very effectiveness ensures that he gets little credit for it: 'the expression was so true that it seemed both to [Vronsky] and to others that they had always known it'. What Vronsky concedes is that Mikhaylov has the professional's advantage, 'technique' – something, Golenishchev points out, that a talented and educated man like Vronsky can acquire. And Vronsky, in having been at the Russian Eton and being a gentleman, has the advantage over the 'uneducated' Mikhaylov. Golenishchev's conviction that this is so owes something to the fact that he needs Vronsky's 'sympathy and praise for his articles and ideas', and feels that 'praise and encouragement should be mutual': here we have a very familiar 'social' principle, the working of which does so much to make the literary world safe for the uncreative.

Both Vronsky and Golenishchev show themselves utterly unable to recognize the nature of Mikhaylov's distinction – to realize the difference between him and them made by his originality, his creativeness.

In the scenes in which the three figure together, their essential relations are piquantly enacted:

> Golenishchev never missed an opportunity to instil into Mikhaylov a true understanding of art. But the latter remained equally cold toward them all. Anna felt by his look that he liked looking at her, but he avoided conversation with her. When Vronsky talked about his art Mikhaylov remained stubbornly silent, and as stubbornly silent when they showed him Vronsky's picture; and he was evidently oppressed by Golenishchev's discourses, to which he made no rejoinder.
>
> Altogether, his reserved, disagreeable, and apparently hostile attitude when they came to know him better much displeased them, and they were glad when the sittings were over, the beautiful portrait was theirs, and his visits ceased.

Now comes the passage that has so close a bearing on the continually reiterated assertion that Lawrence suffered from a sense of inferiority. Keynes and David Garnett[1] took it as a fact that Lawrence was jealous of that famous Cambridge 'civilization'. How could he *not* be, seeing its supreme social-intellectual advantages and his own background in the working class? If he was unimpressed and unresponsive it must be that he was *too much* impressed, and if he was critical it must be out of inferiority and envy. The same attitude is seen in the reiterated charges of snobbery. And the recent British Council monograph informs the world, authoritatively, that Lawrence was 'dogmatic' because of 'a deep-seated feeling that he had missed the fruits of the normal public school and university education, which gave his literary contemporaries a breadth of knowledge and an assurance that he always lacked'.[2]

1. See 'Keynes, Lawrence, and Cambridge' in *The Common Pursuit*.

Lawrence's reaction to Garnett's 'art' is significant: 'That lady into fox stuff is pretty piffle – just playboy stuff'(*Letters*). It is significant too that the 'playboy stuff' was what that literary-academic world backed which could say with confidence: 'In ten years' time Lawrence will be completely forgotten.' (And see Eliot's pronouncement on Garnett in the footnote to p. 23 above.)

2. It also informs the world, with the authority of a piece of quintessential critical scholarship commissioned and endorsed by the British Council: 'He was a snob, and part at least of his satisfaction with Frieda, his wife, was due to the fact that she was a German aristocrat. On his notepaper he had stamped a coronet.' For the gross impertinence (offered as a fact) about his relations with Frieda there is no better ground than the Golenish-chevian conviction that, since Lawrence *must* have felt inferior, he *must* have been a snob (another authoritatively offered 'fact'). As for the assertion about the coronet, so far as I

These assertions and charges are utterly without foundation. The evidence of everything in his work, everything in his letters, and everything that is known about him makes them ludicrous. But they are significant, and their significance is what Tolstoy diagnoses. Tolstoy was himself an aristocrat, with all the advantages of class and 'civilization', and he understands perfectly what Vronsky felt. But he was also a great creative writer, and, as such, he leaves us in no doubt that he endorses the 'uneducated' artist against Vronsky and the academic critic. The last passage quoted continues:

Golenishchev was the first to express the thought that was in all their minds, namely, that Mikhaylov was simply jealous of Vronsky.

'We won't say "jealous" because he has talent, but he is vexed that a man of the Court, a rich man, and a Count into the bargain (men like him hate all that), should, without any particular difficulty, do as well or even better than he, who has devoted his whole life to the work. Especially, there is the education which he lacks.'

Vronsky took Mikhaylov's part, but in the depths of his heart he believed

know it has nothing better in the way of fact behind it than Lawrence's having written some letters on his wife's notepaper. This authorizes the British Council to present him to the world in the posture of a Baron Corvo! The whole journalistic performance, irresponsible and critically null as it is (it contradicts itself, being by someone who brings to Lawrence the usual prejudices and preconceptions, but no sign of intelligent interest) would be negligible if it were not an authoritative British Council guide. And it is at the expense of the greatest English writer of recent times. It is an illustration of the disgraceful way in which the influence, prestige, and resources (derived from public funds) of the British Council are employed to the injury of the real interests of English literature.

That whole enterprise of the British Council which is represented by the series of critical monographs (they are more than 'bibliographical') is obviously of very questionable propriety. Of the pamphlet on Lawrence it must be said that it should certainly be withdrawn.

It is significant, one may add, relevantly to the charge of snobbery, that the British Council publication on Virginia Woolf does not find it necessary to state that she (on the testimony of her great friend, E. M. Forster, in his obituary address) was a snob. Nor does the one on Mr T. S. Eliot find it necessary to point out the implicit snobbery of *The Family Reunion* and *The Cocktail Party*. Snobbery, in fact, seems to be the natural trait of the consciously privileged whose social advantage gives them their assurance – the Vronskys and the Golenishchevs (see, for instance, Lord David Cecil's wholly unjustified strictures on Hardy quoted in the footnote below); it is absent from the genuine major writer.

what Golenishchev said, for he considered that a man of that other and lower world must envy him.[1]

Anna's portrait, the same subject painted from nature by both of them, should have shown him the difference between Mikhaylov and himself; but Vronsky did not see it. He merely left off painting Anna, deciding that it would be superfluous now. He went on, however, with his medieval picture. And he, as well as Golenishchev, and especially Anna, thought it very good because it resembled famous pictures much more than Mikhaylov's did.[2]

Meanwhile Mikhaylov, though Anna's portrait had much engrossed him, was even better pleased than they when the sittings were over and he was no longer obliged to listen to Golenishchev's disquisitions on art, and was able to forget Vronsky's paintings. He knew it was not possible to forbid Vronsky to trifle with art, knew that he and all the dilettanti had a perfect right to paint what they liked – but to him it was unpleasant. One cannot forbid a man's making a big wax doll and kissing it. But if the man came and sat down with his doll in front of a lover, and began to caress it as the lover caresses his beloved, it would displease the lover. It was this kind of unpleasantness that Mikhaylov experienced when he saw Vronsky's pictures: he was amused, vexed, sorry, and hurt.

Vronsky 'trifles with art'; Egbert's friends, in *England, My England*, 'tamper with the arts'. Lawrence's 'tamper' conveys his own essential attitude towards the Ricos and the Sir Clifford Chatterleys. But the Ricos and the Sir Cliffords command the literary world today, and are

---

1. Golenishchev had originally disposed of the undeniable achievement of the artist by telling Vronsky: 'He is the son of a head footman, I think, and has had no education.' Compare Lord David Cecil on Hardy (and he has taken a similar line about George Eliot and Lawrence, and should logically take it about Shakespeare, 'the clown of Stratford' – but there the *reductio ad absurdum* would be apparent): 'Indeed, it is the inevitable defect of a spontaneous genius like Hardy's that it is impervious to education. No amount of painstaking study got him within sight of achieving that intuitive good taste, that instinctive grasp of the laws of literature, which is the native heritage of one bred from childhood in the atmosphere of a high culture.' This is remarkably like Mr T. S. Eliot's strictures on Lawrence, when he writes, in *After Strange Gods*, of Lawrence's 'lack of intellectual and social training' and says, 'Lawrence, even had he acquired a great deal more knowledge and information than he ever came to possess, would always have remained uneducated.'

2. What Lawrence wrote to J. B. Pinker (*Letters*, p. 295) has its relevance here: 'Tell Arnold Bennett that all rules of construction hold good only for novels which are copies of other novels. A book which is not a copy of other books has its own construction, and what he calls faults, he being an old imitator, I call characteristics.'

publicized by the British Council. So are the successful professionals who have the same uncreative relation to literature (Cameron Gee, the 'photogenic' author of *Two Blue Birds*, is a professional), and depend for their position on a social-personal system. The evidence is conveniently presented in those illustrated 'surveys' which are commissioned and sponsored by the British Council. The Golenishchevs in alliance with the playboys (there are professionals as well as amateurs), through the British Council, the Third Programme, the organs of literary opinion, and the universities, form a comprehensive system which has successfully brought the function of criticism – to distinguish the real artist and secure backing for him, to place the uncreative and to maintain critical standards – into abeyance. There is no need to ask why English literature for so long has had so little new life to show.

MR ELIOT AND
LAWRENCE[1]

I LIVE in hopes that Lawrence's recognition is at last to come – to come after all in my lifetime; I mean, his recognition for what I am convinced he is: the great creative genius of our age, and one of the greatest figures in English literature. By 'our age' I mean the climatic phase (so to speak) in which we still live at present – for, though Lawrence died twenty years ago, he may properly be said, I think, to belong to that. My immediate excuse for this sanguine note is the Foreword contributed by Mr T. S. Eliot to Fr William Tiverton's book. Fr Tiverton recommends Lawrence as a positively improving author for Christians and Mr Eliot says that his reason for contributing a preface is that he thinks the book 'a serious piece of criticism of Lawrence of a kind for which the time is now due'. (He adds that 'we need books about him by critics who know him only through his works'.)

If Mr Eliot finds that the time for giving serious critical attention to Lawrence's writings is more due now than it was, say, twenty years ago (or even earlier), the only reason I can think of is that there has been a change in Mr Eliot. For those of us who, all these years, have steadily contended that the time was due, and overdue, have always known Mr Eliot as, in various ways, the reverse of an ally. He has lent all his weight and subtlety to the enemy – the enemy that has maligned and slighted and dismissed. In fact, we have had reason for seeing in him the essential opposition in person. So that when so significant and influential a voice suddenly becomes encouraging we may feel there has been a change worth attending to.

The history the more deserves pondering in that our time, in literature, may fairly be called the age of D. H. Lawrence and T. S. Eliot:

1. This appeared as a review in *Scrutiny* (vol. XVIII, no. 1) of *D. H. Lawrence and Human Existence* by Fr William Tiverton (Foreword by T. S. Eliot).

the two, in creative pre-eminence, I think, though Lawrence appears to me so immensely the greater genius, will be seen in retrospect to dominate the age together. True respect for genius is to take it seriously and appraise it critically, and it seems to me that Mr Eliot's attitude towards Lawrence has a significance in respect of himself that, pondered, entails limiting and qualifying criticism of a kind for which the time is now very decidedly due. My business at the moment, of course, is rather with appraising the genius of Lawrence, but to that business, it should be plain, what I have said is immediately relevant. Moreover, history is history, and it is important that this particular history should not go unrecorded.

And indeed it is not yet the history of an outgrown past. For, though the Foreword to which I have referred recommends Lawrence for serious study, it perpetuates the misconceptions, misrepresentations, and misdirections that have already, over so long a period, worked so much mischief. Not only does Mr Eliot make no recantation; he shows himself to be still unemancipated from his disabling prejudices (for no one, I am convinced, who had been able to *read* what Lawrence wrote could have pronounced as Mr Eliot does). If they are expressed now less offensively, they are the more insidious – and the more insidious because associated with a recommendatory approach. And to tackle them seems to me to be, at the present moment, very much the way to set about one's work, when faced with contending, as effectively as one can, for a just appreciation of Lawrence's genius.

Here then, is Mr Eliot in his preface to Fr Tiverton's *D. H. Lawrence and Human Existence*:

He was an impatient and impulsive man (or so I imagine him to have been; for, like the author of this book, I never knew him). He was a man of fitful and profound insights, rather than of ratiocinative powers; and therefore he was an impatient man; he expressed some of his insights in the form least likely to make them acceptable to most of his contemporaries, and sometimes in a form which almost wilfully encouraged misunderstanding.... Wrong he often was (I think) from ignorance, prejudice, or drawing the wrong conclusions in his conscious mind from the insights which came to him from below consciousness: it will take time to dissociate the superficial error from the fundamental truth. To me, also, he seems often to write very badly; but to be a writer who had to write often badly in order to write sometimes well. As for his religious attitude ... we can now begin to see how much was ignorance, rather than hostility; for Lawrence was an ignorant man in the sense that he was unaware of how much he did not know.

These observations in themselves are ill-calculated to remove the preconceptions and obtusenesses that have prevented Lawrence's work from being seen for what it is and have made the shameful history of misrepresentation and abuse possible; and it seems to me very much in place to relate them to those past judgements that Mr Eliot has never shown regret for and in part now repeats.

Take, for example, that charge of ignorance. It is made twice in the passage quoted. The second time the formulation might seem to give it a special limited, almost esoteric, force that makes it, however grave as addressed to Mr Eliot's and Fr Tiverton's special religious connexion, not obviously, perhaps, exceptionable as itself an expression of prejudice and ignorance. But already in this Foreword, in the same paragraph in fact, the charge has been made in a general form: 'Wrong he often was (I think) from ignorance, prejudice.' The attendant suggestions – 'a man of fitful and profound insights, rather than of ratiocinative powers', 'drawing the wrong conclusions in his conscious mind from the insights that came to him from below consciousness', 'a writer who had to write often badly in order to write sometimes well' – these attendant suggestions plainly give the charge of 'ignorance' an ordinarily unsophisticated and pejorative intention. What Mr Eliot meant by such criticism in the past was fully explicit; and what has never been withdrawn, and is far from being unsaid now, must be recalled to be refuted. There is no way of getting Lawrence's genius recognized except by dealing with these fallacies and prejudices and misrepresentations.

In the *Cambridge Journal* for February (1951) a writer – and one not at all inclined to the corrective severity that seems to me called for – testifies: 'With one or two exceptions' – he mentions only myself – 'critics since Lawrence's death have tended to follow the lead of Mr Eliot in *After Strange Gods*.' Let me recall then some of the things that Mr Eliot says in that book. I pick on some judgements and assertions that are immediately relevant to the charge of ignorance. 'The point is', we are told, 'that Lawrence started life wholly free from any restriction of tradition or institution. ....' He suffered 'from a lack, not so much of information, as of the critical faculties which education should give, and an incapacity for what is ordinarily called thinking'. Again Mr Eliot speaks of Lawrence's 'lack of intellectual and social training'. A reference to Lawrence's mother tells us, I'm afraid, what Mr Eliot means by this 'lack of social training': he speaks of her 'vague hymn-singing pietism ... which does not seem to have provided her with any firm principles by which to scrutinize the conduct of her sons' – Lawrence was working class, in fact a miner's son; and therefore brought up in the midst of ignorance and uncouthness and spiritual barbarity and moral squalor, disinherited of all the humaner achievements of civilized living. We are to see him as an extrĕme case of the 'crippling effect upon men of letters of not having been brought up in the environment of a living and central tradition'.

It is when I come to these things in Mr Eliot that I find myself saying: '*I* am a fellow-countryman of D. H. Lawrence.' Mr Eliot is not – the fact that is in any case sufficiently obvious insists here upon recognition. For no educated Englishman of Mr Eliot's generation and Mr Eliot's intelligence, I am convinced, could so confidently have expressed such ignorance. And yet there is something familiar about the tone and manner: it is as if, not to the manner born, Mr Eliot were showing himself to have been impressed by the aplomb with which Lord David Cecil intimates *his* sense of the disadvantages suffered by low-born writers such as Hardy and George Eliot – and D. H. Lawrence. (I well remember the *Spectator* article in which Lord David Cecil put *Mr* Lawrence, recently dead, impeccably in his place.)

To be born, with that genius, a miner's son at Eastwood in the eighteen-eighties – it is as if Destiny, having given him the genius, had arranged also that he should be enabled to develop it to the utmost and qualified to use it for the purpose for which it was meant. If he had not been born into the working class he could not have known working-class life from the inside. As it was he enjoyed advantages that a writer middle-class born could not have had: the positive experience and a freedom both from illusions and from the debilitating sense of ignorance. On the other hand, gifted as he was, there was nothing to prevent his getting to know life at other social levels.

And the disadvantages, what were they? In education? It seems to me that he had a better education, one better calculated to develop his genius for its most fruitful use, than any other he could have got. That is what strikes one as one reads the admirable Memoir of D. H. Lawrence by E. T. I some years ago, in an article (*Scrutiny*, VI, 3)[1] referred to by Fr Tiverton, discussed the extraordinarily active intellectual life enjoyed by that group of young people of which Lawrence was the centre, and pointed to the obvious fact that, though in all this the initiative and drive of Lawrence's genius must have counted enormously, the initiative and drive could neither have been what they were, nor could they have worked to such effect, if there hadn't been conditions other than personal genius, or 'the individual talent', favouring. To examine these conditions adequately would be to go into a large part of English social and cultural history.

It must be enough here to say that the religion of Lawrence's mother does not deserve the contempt with which Mr Eliot dismisses it. The Chapel, in the Lawrence circle, was the centre of a strong social life, and the focus of a still persistent cultural tradition that had as its main drive the religious tradition of which Mr Eliot is so contemptuous. To turn, as Lawrence did, the earnestness and moral seriousness of that tradition to the powering of a strenuous intellectual inquiringness was all in the tradition. That the Lawrences were Congregationalists is a relevant point – their Nonconformity was very far from being the debased tin-chapel salvationism that Mr Eliot appears to think it. Congregationalism had a peculiarly strong intellectual tradition – in what ways does Mr Eliot think Unitarianism superior? As for the part played by Nonconformity in English civilization, I suggest that he reads Halévy, though books alone will not cure that kind of ignorance.

And for those young people in the eighteen-nineties their intellectual education was intimately bound up with a social training, which, even if it didn't give them Wykehamist or Etonian or even Harvard manners, I see no reason for supposing inferior to that enjoyed by Mr Eliot. Moreover, they met and talked and read in a setting of family life such as, to judge from *The Cocktail Party*, Mr Eliot cannot imagine to have existed – a family life beset by poverty and the day-to-day

1. 'The Wild Untutored Phoenix', reprinted in *The Common Pursuit*.

exigencies of breadwinning, yet quite finely civilized. And further, with what advantageous consequences for English literature I have pointed out in some detail, Lawrence knew every day of his life in intimate experience the confrontation, the interpenetration, of the old agricultural England with the industrial; the contrast of the organic forms and rhythms and the old beauty of humane adaptation with what had supervened.

As for the intellectual training, *that* Lawrence, I have insisted, did not lack (and Fr Tiverton says that he has to agree with me here as against Mr Eliot). Lawrence, we know, was not denied acquaintance with formal academic standards. He says some severe things about Nottingham University College, but he was qualified to make incomparable use of his opportunities, and that he made good use, in formal study, and in informal intercourse intellectual and social, with his friends, we know. In short, I cannot see on what grounds Mr Eliot could assume it to be obvious (if he does – and I don't know what else his tone means) that he himself at twenty-one was better trained intellectually than Lawrence at the same age. He was certainly more sophisticated, and his ability, years older, to proclaim himself, ceremonially, Anglo-Catholic, Royalist, and Classicist, suggests to me that he was certainly less mature.

I have already made my comment on Mr Eliot's ignorance of the English cultural history, of the English civilization, that is illuminated in E. T.'s Memoir of D. H. Lawrence. It will not be found surprising if I sum up on this head of Lawrence's 'ignorance' by saying that to take him as an example of 'the crippling effect upon men of letters of not having been brought up in the environment of a living and central tradition' seems to me nothing more respectable than an astonishing feat of prejudice – and ignorance.

That Lawrence *was* brought up in a living and central tradition – there, it seems to me, is where to lay the stress. And it seems to me the right answer to the less bluntly repellable form in which Mr Eliot brings his charge in this recent Foreword: 'for Lawrence was an ignorant man in the sense that he was unaware of how much he did not know.' Mr Eliot imputes in particular some defects of knowledge about religion and theology, and I cannot forbear concluding this matter of ignorance with a direct retort. I am not, then, impressed by any superiority of religious and theological knowledge in a writer capable of exposing what is to me the shocking essential ignorance that characterizes *The Cocktail Party* – ignorance of the possibilities of life; ignorance of the effect the play must have on a kind of reader or spectator of whose existence the author appears to be unaware: the reader who has, himself, found serious work to do in the world and is able to be unaffectedly serious about it, who knows what family life is and has helped to bring up children and who, though capable of being interested in Mr Eliot's poetry, cannot afford cocktail civilization and would reject it, with contempt and boredom, if he *could* afford it.

I come out with these things in order to bring home the force of my insistence that Lawrence *was* brought up in the environment of a living and central tradition. Anything in the nature of *The Cocktail Party* from him is inconceivable, and he, in his good-humoured way (the charge of impatience is very ill-founded), with that light and unstrained but complete seriousness of his, would have made the unanswerable diagnostic comment. (There are two reviews of *The Cocktail Party* I should like to see – one by Lawrence and one by Albert Schweitzer.)

Another damaging suggestion about Lawrence that is propagated by Mr Eliot is that which is conveyed with the word 'insights': 'He was a man of profound insights, rather than of ratiocinative powers.' In the nineteen-twenties they used commonly to grant that Lawrence had *genius*; but intelligence, which really mattered – for that you must go to Aldous Huxley. I myself have always felt bound to insist – though it should, I can't help thinking, be obvious – that genius in Lawrence was, among other things, supreme intelligence. It is on intelligence, and not on 'insight' or 'intuition', that I choose to lay the stress; and Mr Eliot's formulation explains well enough why. 'He was a man of fitful and profound insights, rather than of ratiocinative powers' – which amounts to the earlier judgement: 'a lack of the critical faculties which education should give, and an incapacity for what is ordinarily called thinking'.

This account seems to me completely mistaken. Lawrence's 'insights' were a matter of being able to see what was there, as only genius can, and they went with an extraordinary power of relating insights, and not only of understanding situations comprising elements difficult to get at and recognize, but of understanding whole comprehensive and complete fields of experience. His thinking, in fact, is so much superior to what is ordinarily called thinking that it tends not to be recognized for thinking at all. If 'ratiocinative powers' means anything worth having, then Lawrence's seem to me superlative; in logical stamina, the power to pursue an organizing process of thought through a wide and difficult tract, with a sustained consistency that is at the same time a delicate fidelity to the complexities of the full concrete experience, Lawrence seems to me to be superior to Mr Eliot (yes, to the author of *Four Quartets*).

If I wanted to win recognition most readily for the justice of this claim (presuming it not granted), I should turn first to *Psychoanalysis and the Unconscious*. This is the sober prose exposition corresponding to the *Fantasia of the Unconscious*, the work that Mr Eliot commends in *After Strange Gods*. In *Psychoanalysis and the Unconscious* Lawrence explains his conception of the nature and the function of intelligence, in doing which he exemplifies intelligence, so conceived, in operation.

What he undertakes to do in the book (and I think that he does it with wonderful lucidity and complete convincingness) is to set forth the conditions of health and wholeness in the psyche. I have recently quoted key passages in discussing *Women in Love* in these pages. The relevant stress at this moment is this: Lawrence makes plain that without proper use of intelligence there can be no solution of the problems of mental, emotional, and spiritual health. We are committed, he insists, to consciousness and self-responsibility. The mind – mental consciousness – has its essential part in the prosperous functioning of the psyche; but it cannot, with its will-enforced ideas or ideals, command the sources of life, though it can thwart them. The power of recognizing justly the relation of idea and will to spontaneous life, of using the conscious mind for the attainment of 'spontaneous-creative fulness of being', is intelligence. It is intelligence we see at work in the exposition of Lawrence's theme in *Psychoanalysis and the Unconscious* – the intelligence that was necessary for the undertaking just as it is necessary for the attaining and preserving of wholeness in the psyche.

Lawrence's intelligence, in its superlative fineness and vitality, always seems to me – and in the closely argued prose treatise and in the criticism as much as anywhere else – essentially the intelligence of the creative artist. It is significant that Mr Eliot, who in effect denies the distinction of intelligence, denies the artist too. At least he once – and has never recanted – made a point of the denial, seizing on a statement (quoted in Huxley's introduction to the *Letters*) of what I take to be the truth as a challenge to a counter-demonstration. There is nothing in this recent Foreword to suggest that he has changed his mind,[1] and, whatever Fr Tiverton's position in the abstract may be, the book itself might have been written by someone quite incapable of perceiving for himself that Lawrence is a great creative writer. And I very much fear that the books about him that Mr Eliot says we need are not to be any more books of literary criticism than Fr Tiverton's is. In particular I view with the gravest distrust the prospect of Lawrence's being adopted for expository appreciation as almost a Christian by writers whose religious complexion is congenial to Mr Eliot.

What, on such challenges, one has to say in general about Lawrence's genius is this: it manifests itself in an infallible centrality of judgement – that which makes him an incomparable literary critic. I repeat with, if possible, even greater conviction what I have said before: he has an unfailingly sure sense of the difference between that which makes for life and that which makes against it; of the difference between health and that which tends away from health. It is this that makes him a so much better critic than Eliot, whose major value-judgements, when he risks them (especially in the contemporary field), have nearly always been bad – often disastrously bad. But I ought at this point to add that I speak as one who, when years ago Mr Eliot wrote in *The Criterion* of the frightful consequences that might have ensued if Lawrence 'had been a don at Cambridge, "rotten and rotting others"', was widely supposed – at Cambridge, anyway, where it mattered – to share the honour of the intention with Lawrence.

1. As for Lawrence's writing 'often badly', I have allowed that he *sometimes* does. But badness in him is never of the order of the badness of Mr Eliot's writing (e.g. in *The Use of Poetry and the Use of Criticism*), where it betrays thwarting of intelligence by unrecognized emotional bias, and unwillingness or fear in the author to criticize his self-suspect intentions.

Penguinews, which appears every month, contains details of all the new books issued by Penguins as they are published. From time to time it is supplemented by *Penguins in Print*, which is a complete list of all books published by Penguins which are in print. (There are well over three thousand of these.)

A specimen copy of *Penguinews* will be sent to you free on request and you can become a subscriber for the price of the postage – 4s. for a year's issues (including the complete lists) if you live in the United Kingdom, or 8s. if you live elsewhere. Just write to Dept EP, Penguin Books Ltd, Harmondsworth, Middlesex, enclosing a cheque or postal order, and your name will be added to the mailing list.

Some other books published by Penguins are described on the following pages.

Note: *Penguinews* and *Penguins in Print* are not available in the U.S.A. or Canada

F. R. Leavis

REVALUATION

Revaluation is a study of tradition and development in English poetry from the early seventeenth to the early nineteenth century. Dr Leavis discusses first the 'line of wit' that sprang from Jonson and Donne, and then devotes a chapter each to Milton's verse, Pope, the Augustan tradition, Wordsworth, Shelley and Keats. These revaluations, which are marked by that profound sense of the creative force of great literature that informs all Dr Leavis's work, have taken their place among the classics of modern literary criticism.

'This book seems to me of the utmost importance as well as of endless fascination. Dr Leavis has done so much in this volume, and done it so brilliantly, that there is nothing left for a serious student of poetry but to read him' – Edwin Muir

NEW BEARINGS IN ENGLISH POETRY

It seems remarkable now that the *Cambridge Review* had to go outside Cambridge to find a reviewer for *New Bearings in English Poetry* when it was first published in 1932. For Dr Leavis's estimate of Eliot, Pound, and Hopkins – which seemed so controversial at the time – has since been widely accepted in its general outlines. Many people, therefore, will want to possess one of the major works of modern criticism, a pioneer appreciation of poems like *The Waste Land* and *Hugh Selwyn Mauberley* when they were still being widely denounced as obscure, unpoetic nonsense. And for younger people, who may be approaching Hopkins, Eliot, and Pound for the first time, *New Bearings* provides a helpful introduction to these major poets and an appraisal of their originality and vitality in comparison with the late Victorians and Georgians.

This edition contains Dr Leavis's 'Retrospect 1950', in which he explains why he had no wish to re-write the book twenty years later.

F. R. Leavis

THE COMMON PURSUIT

' "The common pursuit of true judgement": that is how the critic should see his business and what it should be for him. His perceptions and judgements are his, or they are nothing; but, whether or not he has consciously addressed himself to cooperative labour, they are inevitably collaborative. Collaboration may take the form of disagreement, and one is grateful to the critic whom one has found worth disagreeing with.'

The tone, categorical, uncompromising, and deeply committed to the critic's task, is wholly and unmistakably Dr Leavis's, the most controversial critic of our time. In this series of essays he ranges from Shakespeare to Auden, from Bunyan to E. M. Forster. The essays on Shakespeare, Milton, Johnson, Swift, and Pope are particularly important and what he has to say about E. M. Forster, T. S. Eliot, and D. H. Lawrence displays a challenging concern with modern letters.

'There is some of Dr Leavis's most mature criticism in this volume' – Edwin Muir in the *Observer*

'What stamps his work as being by a critic of the first rank is the quality of his perception' – Noel Annan in the *Guardian*

Also available in Peregrines: *The Great Tradition*